When the Magisterium Intervenes

When the Magisterium Intervenes

The Magisterium and Theologians in Today's Church

Includes a Case Study on the Doctrinal Investigation
of Elizabeth Johnson

Edited by
Richard R. Gaillardetz

A Michael Glazier Book

LITURGICAL PRESS
Collegeville, Minnesota

www.litpress.org

A Michael Glazier Book published by Liturgical Press

Cover design by David Manahan, OSB.

Excerpts from documents of the Second Vatican Council are from *Vatican Council II: The Basic Sixteen Documents*, by Austin Flannery, OP © 1996 (Costello Publishing Company, Inc.). Used with permission.

In her pieces that appear in "The Elizabeth Johnson Dossier," Elizabeth Johnson, CSJ, uses excerpts from *Documents of Vatican II*, ed. Walter M. Abbott, SJ, © 1966.

Scripture texts in this work are taken from the *New Revised Standard Version Bible* © 1989, Division of Christian Education of the National Council of the Churches of Christ in the United States of America. Used by permission. All rights reserved.

1   2   3   4   5   6   7   8   9

Library of Congress Cataloging-in-Publication Data

When the magisterium intervenes : the magisterium and theologians in today's church : includes a case study on the doctrinal investigation of Elizabeth Johnson / edited by Richard R. Gaillardetz.
    p. cm.
  Includes bibliographical references and index.
   ISBN 978-0-8146-8054-4 — ISBN 978-0-8146-8055-1 (e-book)
  1. Church—Authority.   2. Authority—Religious aspects—Catholic Church. 3. Catholic Church. United States Conference of Catholic Bishops. Committee on Doctrine.   4. Catholic Church—Doctrines.   5. Johnson, Elizabeth A., 1941– Quest for the living God.   I. Gaillardetz, Richard R., 1958–
  BX1746.W485   2012
  262'.8088282—dc23   2012004684

Contents

Introduction

Richard R. Gaillardetz

Boston College

This volume has its origin in a three-year research project associated with the Catholic Theological Society of America (CTSA). In 2008, a number of Catholic theologians submitted a proposal to the CTSA board of directors to create a special interest group titled, "When the Magisterium Intervenes. . . ." At three consecutive CTSA conventions (Halifax in 2009, Cleveland in 2010, and San Jose in 2011), papers were given at sessions that were remarkably well attended and in which there was a lively discussion by the CTSA membership. The first seven essays in this volume were all offered, in a more provisional form, at one of those three sessions. But why had we chosen to address ourselves to this topic? Our interest was not, strictly speaking, in continued development of a theology of the magisterium *per se*. What drew our attention was a pronounced magisterial activism, beginning for the most part with the pontificate of John Paul II and continuing under Pope Benedict XVI. As Catholic theologians, all of us accept, in principle, the authority of the pope and bishops to pronounce on church doctrine as a means of preserving the integrity of the apostolic faith. However, we found ourselves considering the recent history of magisterial interventions and asking ourselves about, first, the theological assumptions at play in this record of magisterial activism, and, second, the interplay between the exercise of magisterial authority and key features of the emerging cultural context often designated by that admittedly slippery term, postmodernity. We hoped that our study would build on, without rehearsing in any great detail, the important historical and theological contributions to the study of the magisterium that had been made throughout the second half of the twentieth century by such important figures as Roger Aubert, John P. Boyle, Yves Congar, Christian Duquoc, Avery Dulles, John Ford,

Josef Fuchs, Patrick Granfield, Hubert Jedin, Joseph Komonchak, Richard McCormick, Harry McSorley, André Naud, Francis Oakley, John O'Malley, Ladislas Örsy, Hermann Pottmeyer, Karl Rahner, Max Seckler, Bernard Sesboüé, Francis Sullivan, Gustave Thils, Brian Tierney, Jean-Marie Tillard, and so many others. Because of their contributions, we are able to place the role of the magisterium today in a richer and more nuanced historical context. A few features of that historical context are worth our recalling at the outset.

Magisterium in Retrospect

At the risk of great simplification, what that enormous body of scholarship produced in the twentieth century has taught us is that the "magisterium," as we understand it today, emerged largely as a part of an ecclesiological framework that was first constructed in the nineteenth century.

In the Middle Ages, the primary arbiter of theological disputes was the theology faculty of the great universities like those in Paris and Bologna. The term *magister* was used to refer to various modes of teaching authority in the church. Thomas Aquinas famously distinguished between a *magisterium cathedrae pastoralis* (a pastoral teaching office generally exercised by the bishops) and a *magisterium cathedrae magistralis* (a teaching authority exercised by a master of theology, a scholar).[1] For centuries the pope and bishops played a relatively peripheral role in the authoritative resolution of doctrinal disputes, and when they did intervene, their mode of intervention was striking. Consider, if you will, the sixteenth- and seventeenth-century *de auxiliis* ["regarding the divine helps"] controversy between the Jesuits and the Dominicans regarding the relationship between divine grace and human freedom. The papacy inserted itself into the controversy only after the two religious orders had begun accusing each other of heresy. Papal investigations were begun under Pope Clement VIII but came to their conclusion two papacies later, under Pope Paul V. The papal investigation included the conduct of seventeen debates between representatives of the principal theological

---

[1] *Quodl.* 3, q. 4, a. 1 (9). Yves Congar contributed two classic studies of the history of the term *magisterium*: "A Semantic History of the Term 'Magisterium'" and "A Brief History of the Forms of the Magisterium and Its Relations with Scholars," in *The Magisterium and Morality: Readings in Moral Theology No. 3*, ed. Charles E. Curran and Richard A. McCormick (New York: Paulist Press, 1982), 297–313; 314–31.

positions. Finally Paul V resolved the matter by way of a decree that prohibited either side from condemning the views of the other, with the pope reminding each side of the need for humility when delving into the holy mystery of God. Such a circumscribed doctrinal teaching role for the papacy would soon be snuffed out by the threatening winds of modernity and supplanted by a far more expansive one.

In the eighteenth century, the Catholic Church soon felt itself under threat in the face of an Enlightenment rationality that appeared to marginalize external religious authorities as a source of religious truth. It saw the French Revolution for what it was: the death knell to Christendom and any hope of a stable partnership between Church and monarch. As T. Howland Sanks observed, "if the Age of Reason had threatened the authority of the church in various intellectual spheres, the Age of Revolution threatened its very existence."[2] What was fast emerging was the birth of modern liberalism, characterized in simplest terms by the exaltation of the individual and a predominantly negative understanding of freedom as freedom from external constraint. From the perspective of Catholic leadership at the time, liberalism funded a cultural perspective rooted in "the Lutheran revolt against the church's authority and on behalf of free examination, in the naturalism of the Renaissance, in the Enlightenment's repudiation of tradition, authority and community, in the secularization of the political sphere, in the possessive individualism of capitalist economics, and in the cultural anarchy produced by an unrestrained freedom of opinion, speech, and the press."[3] What was required, in the eyes of Catholic leadership, was an aggressive, comprehensive response: the creation of "Roman Catholicism" as a "counter-society" offering the only godly alternative to modern liberalism.[4] The Catholic Church's stance toward the world moved from a confident, if often combative, engagement with society to a defensive siege mentality. Soon, ecclesiastical pronouncements on "worldly affairs," condemnations of unwarranted state interference in church matters, denunciations of anti-clericalism,

---

[2] T. Howland Sanks, *Salt, Leaven and Light: The Community Called Church* (New York: Crossroad, 1992), 99.

[3] Joseph Komonchak, "Vatican II and the Encounter between Catholicism and Liberalism," in *Catholicism and Liberalism: Contributions to American Public Philosophy*, ed. Bruce Douglass and David Hollenbach (Cambridge: Cambridge University Press, 1994), 76–99, at 76.

[4] Joseph Komonchak, "Modernity and the Construction of Roman Catholicism," *Cristianesimo nella storia* 18 (1997): 335–85, at 356.

and a repeated assertion of the state's obligation to preserve the right
of Catholics to practice their faith would reflect the Church's negative
judgment on the demise of Christendom and the rise of liberalism. Pope
Gregory XVI produced a series of condemnations of various aspects of
modern liberalism. Pope Pius IX, initially open to the liberal impulse,
was shocked by the wave of nationalist revolution that swept Western
Europe in 1848. He would henceforward further Gregory's program,
most famously in the *Syllabus of Errors* with its repudiations of religious
freedom and the autonomy of conscience.

With the pontificate of Leo XIII in the late nineteenth century, the
Church embarked on a more positive, if still cautious, engagement with
the issues of the larger world. Yet, this stance was short-lived. The vio-
lent reaction to modernism early in the pontificate of Pope Pius X, reflected in *Pascendi* and *Lamentabili*, reinforced key elements of the siege
mentality preponderant since the French Revolution. A largely critical
stance toward society continued in the first half of the twentieth century,
with the papacy issuing sharp rebukes of significant elements of modern
capitalism, socialism, industrialism, and a continued program of state
encroachment in church matters.

At the heart of this construction of Roman Catholicism as a "counter-
society" was the creation of a vast institutional apparatus with the papacy at its head. It is no coincidence that it was during this same period,
beginning in the early nineteenth century, that the term "magisterium"
acquired its modern meaning as a reference to, first, the authority of
the pope and bishops and then to the Church hierarchy itself. Although
from this period on the term would be used in reference to the teaching
authority of pope and bishops, the rise of Ultramontanism guaranteed
that it was the teaching authority of the pope that constituted its essential
core. Over the course of little more than a century, from Pope Gregory
XVI to Pope Pius XII, the papacy would be transformed from the doctrinal court of final appeal to the supreme doctrinal watchdog vigilant
to snuff out any sign of theological innovation.

It is worth recalling that the principal instrument of the exercise of
papal teaching authority in the Church today, the papal encyclical, is a
relatively recent development that was first employed in the eighteenth
century by Pope Benedict XIV. However, his encyclicals were all very
brief and largely either disciplinary or exhortatory in character. In the
nineteenth century, Popes Gregory XVI and Pius IX made use of the encyclical, often addressing doctrinal matters, but these too were generally
short in length. When they condemned erroneous views, there was no

intention of stimulating new theological insight.[5] With such noteworthy encyclicals as *Aeterni Patris, Providentissimus Deus, Satis Cognitum* and *Rerum Novarum,* Pope Leo XIII instigated a significant shift in the teaching role of the pope. While popes had always claimed doctrinal authority on matters of faith and morals, at least going back to the fifth century, the actual exercise of that authority had been relatively infrequent, and when employed, was usually limited to fairly terse doctrinal pronouncements. The pontificate of Leo XIII marks the beginning of a modern development in the papacy, in which popes begin to offer, as part of their teaching ministry, extended theological treatments issued in formal magisterial documents on important topics. Pius X would follow Leo's precedent with *Pascendi,* and both Pius XI and Pius XII would issue lengthy encyclicals during their successive pontificates.

Pope Pius XII, in his 1950 encyclical *Humani Generis,* limited the task of the theologian to that of faithfully explicating that which was proclaimed by the pope and bishops. Theologians were teachers of the faith only by virtue of a delegation of authority from the bishops. They were expected to submit their work to authoritative scrutiny and potential censorship of the magisterium. "Dissent," understood as the rejection or even questioning of any authoritative teaching of the magisterium, was viewed with suspicion as an attack on the authority of the magisterium itself.

Of course, this restriction was not absolute. The dogmatic manuals acknowledged the legitimacy of limited speculative discussion that was critical of certain doctrinal formulations. Moreover, the manual tradition also incorporated a sophisticated taxonomy of church teaching known as the "theological notes." Theological notes were formal judgments by theologians or the magisterium on the precise relationship of a doctrinal formulation to divine revelation. Their purpose was to safeguard the faith and prevent confusion between binding doctrines and theological opinions. Within this neoscholastic framework, the assumption was that if theologians discovered a significant difficulty with a doctrinal formulation that had not been proposed infallibly, they were to bring the difficulty to the attention of the hierarchy in private and to refrain from any public speech or writing that was contrary to received church teaching.

The Second Vatican Council offered a potentially new framework for understanding the relationship between the pope and bishops on the one hand and between pope/bishops and theologians on the other. The

---

[5] Klaus Schatz, *Papal Primacy: From Its Origins to the Present* (Collegeville, MN: Liturgical Press, 1996), 167–68.

"trickle-down" theory of divine revelation, conceived as a collection of propositional truths transmitted exclusively to the bishops, was largely replaced by a theology of revelation that began with the Trinitarian self-communication of God in the person of Jesus Christ by the power of the Holy Spirit. According to the council's Dogmatic Constitution on Divine Revelation (DV 10), this revelation was given to the whole Church and not just the bishops. Although the bishops would remain the authoritative guardians of that revelation by virtue of their apostolic office, the Word of God resided in the whole Church, as each of the baptized was given a supernatural instinct for the faith (*sensus fidei*) that allowed them to recognize God's Word, penetrate its meaning more deeply, and apply it more profoundly in their lives (LG 12; DV 8).

The council did not reflect on the role of the theologian in any depth. However, several passages are worth considering. The council insisted that the work of biblical exegesis and theology must be done under the guidance of the magisterium: "Catholic exegetes and other workers in the field of sacred theology should work diligently together and under the watchful eye of the sacred magisterium" (DV 23). They reiterated that it was the responsibility of theologians to interpret and explicate church teaching faithfully. However, these tasks did not exhaust the work of theologians. "With the help of the holy Spirit, it is the task of the whole people of God, particularly of its pastors and theologians, to listen to and distinguish the many voices of our times and to interpret them in the light of God's word, in order that the revealed truth may be more deeply penetrated, better understood, and more suitably presented" (GS 44). Theologians must also consider new questions: "recent research and discoveries in the sciences, in history and philosophy bring up new problems which have an important bearing on life itself and demand new scrutiny by theologians. Furthermore, theologians are now being asked, within the methods and limits of theological science, to develop more efficient ways of communicating doctrine to the people of today" (GS 62). Elsewhere, the council encouraged theologians to explore unresolved doctrinal questions (LG 54). The council's very decrees gave evidence of a legitimate development of doctrine in such areas as religious freedom, ecumenism, authority of conscience, and the sacramental foundations of the episcopate.

Perhaps more illuminating for our topic than the documents of the council was the conduct of the council itself. Jared Wicks suggests that the council "constituted a unique case of cooperation between the theologians, who serve by research and explanation, and the Church's episcopal and papal magisterium."[6] Theologians and bishops collaborated at numerous points in the process of moving from preliminary drafts to final promulgation of the sixteen documents. Both individual bishops and regional episcopal groupings would often seek out theological experts like Congar, Rahner, Ratzinger, Daniélou, Philips, Smulders, and others, asking for theological background, position papers, and often even unofficial draft texts. Wicks writes elsewhere that "one can see here a well-functioning epistemological duality between (1) the consultative thought of the theologian-experts, that is, their perceptions and concepts drawn from the doctrinal sources, with their provisional judgments, and (2) the decisive judgments by the Council members, who discerned, evaluated, adopted, or rejected the experts' proposals, and so became the responsible authors of Vatican II's teaching and decrees."[7] This kind of substantive bishop-theologian cooperation, so vital to the success of the council, raised hopes for a new framework for considering the theologian-magisterium relationship.

The first decades immediately after the council held promise for just such a new framework. A few years removed from the council, Pope Paul VI would create the International Theological Commission as a way of formalizing a positive and constructive relationship between the magisterium and the theological community. In 1975, that commission published an important document, "Theses on the Relationship between the Ecclesiastical Magisterium and Theology,"[8] that offered a helpful framework for considering the magisterium-theologian relationship. Unfortunately, this commission was placed under the presidency of the prefect for the Congregation for the Doctrine of the Faith (CDF) and over the course of the first decades of its existence curial pressure gradually led to the exclusion from its membership of voices that were at times critical of certain church pronouncements. Any hopes for the establishment of a new magisterium-theologian relationship were dashed by the widespread theological criticism that greeted Pope Paul VI's final encyclical, *Humanae Vitae*.

Although much in the ambitious pontificate of John Paul II can be seen as a legitimate development of the vision of Vatican II, when it concerns

---

[6] Jared Wicks, "Vatican II on Revelation—From Behind the Scenes," *Theological Studies* 71 (2010): 637–50, at 650.

[7] Jared Wicks, *Doing Theology* (New York: Paulist Press, 2009), 222–23.

[8] The document can be found in *The Magisterium and Morality: Readings in Moral Theology No. 3*, ed. Curran and McCormick, 151–70.

the exercise of formal magisterial authority, it is difficult not to see that long pontificate as an attempt to recover the trajectory evident from Pius IX to Pius XII, in which the pope was being fashioned as chief theologian of the Church. In terms of total pages of text, no pope has written more in the genre of the encyclical than John Paul II. Indeed, the comparison becomes more dramatic if one were to include his often weighty post-synodal exhortations and shorter documents. By my informal tabulation, at least five of his encyclicals exceed the length of the longest encyclical of any of his predecessors. In spite of some of his rhetoric, the policies of his pontificate appeared to sustain Pius XII's suspicion of any legitimate theological autonomy. As will be demonstrated in several essays in this volume, the pontificate of John Paul II offers us the "Profession of Faith and Oath of Fidelity" (1989), the "Vatican Instruction On the Ecclesial Vocation of the Theologian" (1990), and the papal letter *Ad Tuendam Fidem* (1998), all of which were oriented toward limiting the theologian's freedom to critically assess even church teachings that had not been proposed infallibly. The early years of the current pontificate have given no sign of a departure from these policies.

Sadly, what has emerged in the five decades since the opening of the council is not a consensus regarding a systematic theology of magisterial authority but a series of unresolved issues regarding (1) the subject of magisterial authority (e.g., the authority of the Roman Curia, the synod of bishops, and episcopal conferences); (2) the object of magisterial teaching (e.g., the disputed status of "definitive doctrine"); (3) the exercise of magisterial authority (e.g., the exercise of the ordinary papal magisterium to "confirm" teachings of the ordinary universal magisterium); and (4) the reception of magisterial teaching (e.g., the permissibility of legitimate dissent from authoritative but nondefinitive teaching).

A half century removed from the close of Vatican II, we still await not simply the resolution of these *quaestiones disputatae* but a new framework to emerge for conceiving the relationship between the magisterium and theologians, one that attends to both the promising theological trajectories introduced at the council and the peculiar demands of our time. This project stands as a modest contribution toward the construction of such a framework.

The Structure of This Volume

Part 1 of this volume, "Magisterial Interventions," includes three essays that attend to the recent history of magisterial interventions of various kinds. Bradford Hinze offers a sweeping review of magisterial interventions that have transpired globally over the past decade by the CDF, doctrinal committees of episcopal conferences, and individual bishops. His study considers shifts in the kinds of doctrinal topics about which current ecclesiastical authorities have seemed particularly concerned, and it delineates the various cases of ecclesiastical investigation and discipline by geography, process, and outcome. Hinze also explores the evolution of the procedures developed for investigating theologians. Yet his work is no mere catalog; throughout the essay he offers incisive theological analysis and concludes with a list of theological "laments" regarding our current situation and concrete proposals for moving us forward.

The second essay serves as a companion to Hinze's essay. James Coriden offers a canonical analysis of the recent history of interventions summarized by Hinze. While acknowledging the canonical basis of the bishops' exercise of teaching authority, he raises concerns regarding the manner in which that authority has been exercised, complaining, in particular, about the failure to make use of the *Doctrinal Responsibilities* document. Coriden considers whether its relative neglect was due to procedures that might be viewed as too formal and complex to work effectively. Of particular relevance today, in the wake of the Elizabeth Johnson case, is Coriden's analysis of the role of the doctrinal committees of episcopal conferences. He concludes with a series of reflections on basic canonical principles that ought to govern the investigation of theologians.

Colleen Mallon contributes the final essay in part 1. Her essay is occasioned by both the recent Vatican visitation of American women religious communities and the Vatican investigation of the Leadership Conference of Women Religious. Mallon places these interventions in the context of five decades of the renewal of religious life inspired by Vatican II and dares to ask whether these interventions are, in some sense, the consequence of the failure of the pope and bishops to undergo an analogous renewal of their own office and ministry.

In part 2, "Theological and Contextual Reflections," we turn to broader considerations of our current situation. Ormond Rush offers a carefully nuanced essay that elucidates the much-neglected pneumatological dimension of the Church's teaching office, exploring the relationship between the *sensus fidelium*, theologians, and the magisterium. Rush takes as his starting point *Lumen Gentium*'s teaching regarding the participation of the whole people of God in the threefold offices of Christ (as priest, prophet and king). His focus, however, is on the "prophetic office," as he considers the tensions present in Vatican II's teaching. Of particular concern is the tension between chapter 2 of *Lumen Gentium*, which affirmed the way in which the whole people of God participate in the prophetic office of the Church, and chapter 3 on the hierarchy, which considered the prophetic office exclusively in relation to the bishops. Rush concludes with proposals for a more synthetic understanding of the Church's prophetic office, one that resists the tendency to reduce the prophetic office to the work of the magisterium.

In the second essay of part 2, Gerard Mannion employs the notion of a "social imaginary," developed especially in the work of Charles Taylor, as an interpretive instrument that can help us understand the impasse so many are experiencing regarding the exercise of authority in the Roman Catholic Church today. The value of this concept is that it acknowledges that contemporary church leadership is influenced by more than a mere theology or ideology; it is shaped by a pervasive imaginative framework that encourages contemporary church leaders to exercise their authority in a particular fashion. According to Mannion, this social imaginary is hampered by a lack of historical consciousness, an ecclesiastical fundamentalism, a propositional view of revelation, and a paranoia regarding pluralism which renders it incapable of acknowledging pluralism as a graced manifestation of the catholicity of the Church today.

Anthony Godzieba's essay calls contemporary theologians and church commentators to go beyond debates regarding the authoritative status of this or that church teaching in order to consider a distinctive feature of our world today, the impact of "digital reproduction." Godzieba draws on the work of Walter Benjamin, who held that a work of art loses its essential "authenticity" in the process of widespread reproduction. Godzieba applies this theory to challenges we face today properly receiving church teaching. Using the example of the late Pope John Paul II's allocution on assisted nutrition and hydration, Godzieba explores the way in which the authority of this allocution was artificially absolutized through the process of "digital immediacy." Instant access to this document through the Vatican web site and various other web sites, blogs, list-serves, etc., allowed it to be detached from any "thick" process of communal interpretation and reception. In a digitally immediate culture, immediacy equals authenticity equals authority. For Godzieba, this has two consequences: (1) structures of church authority take on the characteristics of contemporary managerial culture, while authentic *communio* is diminished; and (2) traditional criteria for discerning the authority of magisterial statements are exposed as inadequate to cope with the flood of ecclesial representations in a "digital storm," leaving the Church desperately in need of new hermeneutically "thicker" criteria.

Part 2 concludes with Vincent Miller's essay, "When Mediating Structures Change: The Magisterium, the Media, and the Culture Wars." Miller continues and expands on the cultural analysis offered by Godzieba. He argues that the commodifying tendencies of our digital culture work to undermine the authentic exercise of authority. When believers encounter magisterial teaching in commercial and popular media, they are likely to engage it with the interpretive habits of those contexts. Miller considers the impact of two processes associated with globalization, heterogenization and deterritorialization, and notes how these twin dynamisms reduce community and orthodoxy to the politics of identity. Finally, Miller considers how both bishops and theologians are in danger of being assimilated to the model of "special purpose organizations"—advocacy groups defined by a carefully circumscribed agenda of issues and concerns. These various cultural processes, Miller claims, have had the effect of marginalizing the exercise of authority in the Church.

This volume concludes with part 3: "Recent Developments." Several months before the final session of our research project at the CTSA convention in June of 2011, the USCCB Committee on Doctrine issued a statement harshly critical of a recent book by Elizabeth Johnson, *Quest for the Living God: Mapping Frontiers in the Theology of God.* Johnson's sterling reputation in the theological community (she is both a past president of the CTSA and a recipient of the society's John Courtney Murray Award for excellence in theology), the unusually harsh language employed by the committee in their condemnation of her work, and the refusal of the committee to attempt to communicate with her privately to resolve difficulties in advance of their public statement all led to a much publicized controversy. The extensive documentation associated with the investigation of Prof. Johnson's work provides, we believe, an instructive case study for the consideration of our volume's topic. With that in mind, we are including in this final section a documentary dossier in the Johnson case, which includes an introductory narrative of the case and six documents: (1) the original statement by the Committee on Doctrine; (2) "Bishops as Teachers," a document produced by Donald Cardinal Wuerl in response to questions that had been raised regarding the legitimacy of the committee's action; (3) Prof. Johnson's extended response, "To Speak Rightly of the Living God: Observations by Dr. Elizabeth A. Johnson, CSJ, on the Statement of the Committee on Doctrine"; (4) an additional appendix to her original observations that Johnson sent to Cardinal Wuerl in July 2011; (5) the Committee on Doctrine's final statement, "Response to Observations by Sr. Elizabeth A. Johnson, CSJ, Regarding the Committee on Doctrine's Statement About the Book *Quest for the Living God*"; and (6) Johnson's concluding public statement. This final section concludes with a commentary on the case by Richard Gaillardetz that focuses on the distinctive forms of teaching authority proper to theologians and bishops and then considers how the exercise of those two expressions of the Church's teaching authority were enacted in the Johnson case.

Although this project is not formally endorsed by the Catholic Theological Society of America, the participants are nonetheless grateful for the opportunity afforded by the CTSA to meet at three successive conventions. We are grateful as well for the widespread participation by CTSA members at each of our sessions. The lively discussion offered by our many esteemed colleagues helped us advance and refine our respective viewpoints. The editor of this volume would like to thank his research assistant, Megan Anechiarico, for her work on this project. Finally, we would like to thank Liturgical Press, and especially Peter Dwyer and Hans Christoffersen, for recognizing the value of our work and agreeing to publish these papers.

Part 1

Magisterial Interventions

Chapter 1

A Decade of
Disciplining Theologians[1]

Bradford E. Hinze

Fordham University

This is a report on actions taken by the Congregation for the Doctrine of the Faith, doctrinal committees of national episcopal conferences, and individual bishops to investigate and discipline theologians and to restrict open discussion of certain theological issues over the last decade. It offers basic information about the processes involved and currently available data about actions undertaken. The arbitrary time frame of ten years provides a reasonable sample to initiate a broader inquiry into the range of issues involved in this topic and these will be set against the backdrop of disciplinary actions taken since the Second Vatican Council. This report will inevitably be impressionistic because some of the theologians consulted have asked to have their names withheld and in some cases information is incomplete. Sources have been contacted on all the continents working through the channels of national and regional societies for Catholic theology. This paper is not intended to offer an in-depth analysis of particular theological issues raised by investigations of theologians. Rather, it aims to establish a framework and to offer basic information about the processes involved in order to identify recurring patterns, surface vexing concerns, and provide a data base for subsequent discussion of the larger ecclesiological and criteriological issues involved.

---

[1] An earlier version of this chapter appeared in *Horizons* 37, no. 1 (Spring 2010): 92–126; that material appears here with the permission of the journal's editor. It has been revised and expanded for this volume.

Contexts and the Cases Pursued by the CDF

Without rehearsing its long history, it is helpful to remember that the origins of the Congregation for the Doctrine of the Faith can be traced back to the establishment of the Holy Office of the Inquisition by Pope Pius III in 1542 during the Renaissance and Reformation. The Holy Office was instituted to challenge, thwart, and discipline those involved in certain reforming efforts in the Church and those working at the frontiers of human learning in the sciences, both of which were questioning and challenging official teachings and the exercise of authority structures in the Church. This mandate of the Holy Office was bolstered by the teaching of the First Vatican Council's Dogmatic Constitution, *Pastor Aeternus* (1870), and its assertion that the authority of papal primacy entails immediate, implying direct, authority over every Catholic around the world (DS 3060). The Office's reputation for strong action was matched by repeated calls for its reform. Paul VI, on the last day of the Second Vatican Council, December 7, 1965, issued *Integrae Servandae* that set forth a reform of the Holy Office under its mandate "to investigate new teachings and new opinions . . . and to promote studies of these matters and congresses of scholars." These reforms included a new name, the Congregation for the Doctrine of the Faith, and also called for relinquishing the practice of secrecy and consulting regional bishops about individual cases if they were interested in them. Theologians under investigation were allowed to defend themselves, in writing if desired, and there were instituted rights of appeal and juridical representation. It furthermore called for the use of university professors as consultors and ended the *Index of Forbidden Books*.[2] Any consideration of the actions of the CDF since Vatican II will consequently entail an evaluation of the effectiveness of these reforms.

Cases during the last ten years need to be placed in the context of other investigations and disciplinary actions taken during the forty-five years since Vatican II and situated in relation to the longer history of theologians, among them some of the most distinguished thinkers of the twentieth century, who were investigated and disciplined both during the modernist crisis and in the wake of Pius XII's encyclical *Humani generis* through the administration of this office. This list includes such notable figures as Alfred Loisy, George Tyrrell, Marie-Dominique Chenu, Yves Congar, Henri de Lubac, Karl Rahner, and John Courtney Murray.

---

[2] *Acta Apostolicae Sedis* (AAS) 57 (1965), 952–55; for English translation, see *Council Daybook, Session 4* (Washington, DC: National Catholic Welfare Conference, 1966), 354–55.

In short, the pattern of behavior we are witnessing in the post-Vatican II period has a history that stretches back throughout the twentieth century and further. We need to distinguish and assess this current set of practices in relation to analogous patterns in previous generations.

The Congregation for the Doctrine of the Faith: Its Current Composition

Before reviewing the criteria, procedures, and cases involved, it may help to know something about the current composition of the CDF. The group is comprised of 19 members—cardinals, archbishops, and bishops: at present there are sixteen cardinals and three bishops, two of whom are ordinaries in local churches. One is currently in his fifties, eight are in their sixties, and ten are in their seventies. They are predominantly from Europe (four from Italy, two from France, two from Spain, two from Germany, two from Poland, one from the Czech Republic), with two from the United States, two from Africa (Nigeria and Tanzania), one from Asia (India), and one from Latin America (Argentina). All of the cardinal members serve as prefects or members of other Congregations, Pontifical Councils, and Commissions. Since 2005 the CDF has been led by the prefect, William Cardinal Levada, a post previously held by Joseph Cardinal Ratzinger between 1981 and 2005. The secretary, Archbishop Luis Francisco Ladaria Ferrer, SJ, was appointed in July 2008 to replace Archbishop Angelo Amato, SDB, and in June 2009 Msgr. Damiano Marzotto replaced Joseph Augustine Di Noia, OP, as under-secretary; Msgr. Charles J. Scicluna serves as promoter of justice. In addition, there are three office supervisors and an additional staff of 33 people. This congregation meets in plenary assembly annually.

In addition, the congregation has twenty-nine regular consultors who are chosen by the prefect and approved by the pope, five of whom are titular bishops; the others are priests of whom 18 are from religious orders (six Jesuits, three Salesians, two Franciscans, two Conventual Franciscans, two Augustinians, two Dominicans, one Missionary of St. Charles, one Legionnaire of Christ, and one Redemptorist). The majority of the consultors teach at pontifical universities in Rome (Gregorian [Jesuit], Biblical Institute, Angelicum [Dominican], Alphonsianum [Redemptorist], Lateran, Santa Croce [Opus Dei] and Salesian). There are no lay consultors, and, of course, no women.[3]

---

[3] See *Annuario Pontificio* (Rome: Liberia Editrice Vaticana, 2009), 1189–91. Thanks to Eric Meyer for background research on the members and consultants. The information provided on the Vatican web site (http://www.vatican.va) concerning the

Norms and Criteria

Cases over the last ten years were judged according to the standards established by the new formula of the "Profession of Faith and the Oath of Fidelity," issued in 1989 by the CDF and further delimited by the 1998 apostolic letter of John Paul II, issued *motu proprio*, *Ad Tuendam Fidem*, the commentary by the CDF in the same year (which required that theologians accept not only doctrine definitively declared by the magisterium, but also non-definitively intended official pronouncements), and the CDF's "Instruction on the Ecclesial Vocation of the Theologian" (1990).[4] Other relevant documents include the statement by the Conference of German Bishops on "The Procedure for Settling Grievances in Matters of Doctrine" (1972);[5] the 1989 statement of the United States Catholic Conference of Bishops, "Doctrinal Responsibilities: Approaches to Promoting Cooperation and Resolving Misunderstandings between Bishops and Theologians";[6] the 1999 statement of the Australian Catholic Conference of Bishops, "The Examination of Theological Orthodoxy";[7] and the 1977 statement by the International Theological Commission, "Theses on the Relationship between the Ecclesiastical Magisterium and Theology."[8]

---

officers and total number of members of the CDF and counselors does not always correspond with the latest information provided in the *Annuario Pontificio* and is available through other channels.

[4] For further background, see Gerard Mannion, "'Defending the Faith': The Changing Landscape of Church Teaching Authority and Catholic Theology," in *The Vision of John Paul II: Assessing His Thought and Influence*, ed. Gerard Mannion (Collegeville, MN: Liturgical Press, 2008), 78–106.

[5] "Beschluss der Deutschen Bischofskonferenz von 21 September 1972 zur Regelung eines Lehrbeanstandungs-verfahrens," *Archiv für katholisches Kirchenrecht* 141 (1972): 524–30.

[6] National Catholic Conference of Bishops, *Doctrinal Responsibilities: Approaches to Promoting Cooperation and Resolving Misunderstandings between Bishops and Theologians* (Washington, DC: National Catholic Conference of Bishops, 1989); based on *Cooperation between Theologians and the Ecclesiastical Magisterium*, prepared by the Joint Committee of the Canon Law Society of America and the Catholic Theological Society of America, ed. Leo J. O'Donovan (Washington, DC: Canon Law Society of America, Catholic University of America, 1982).

[7] Australian Catholic Bishops' Conference, "The Examination of Theological Orthodoxy," http://www.acbc.catholic.org.au/bishops/confpres/199912100.htm (accessed May 2, 2009).

[8] "Theses on the Relationship between the Ecclesiastical Magisterium and Theology" with commentary by Otto Semmelroth and Karl Lehmann, *International Theological Commission: Texts and Documents 1969–1985*, vol. 1 (San Francisco: Ignatius Press, 1989), 133–48.

What Doctrines Currently Preoccupy the CDF?

Three issues have received the most attention by the CDF over the last decade: women's ordination, homosexuality, and religious pluralism. Other doctrinal issues in Christology, ecclesiology, and a range of moral issues have also resulted in actions taken by the CDF.

In order to put these topics in a fuller context, let us examine the information provided on the Vatican web site which offers an official record that includes many materials available in the monthly record *Acta Apostolicae Sedis*.[9] I will follow the Vatican web site protocol of proceeding from the more recent texts to earlier ones. Certain documents by the CDF—declarations, instructions, and letters to bishops—as well as papal encyclicals and apostolic letters, help to demarcate and contextualize shifts in the attention of the CDF to particular issues in the work of theologians. In doctrinal theology as distinct from moral theology, the CDF 2000 "Declaration on the Unicity and Salvific Universality of Jesus Christ and the Church" (*Dominus Iesus*) is the most important document defining the concerns raised over the last ten years (in the areas of Christology and ecclesiology) about religious pluralism and relativism. It provides the frame of reference for understanding the 2007 documents "Responses to Some Questions Regarding Certain Aspects of the Doctrine of the Church" and "Doctrinal Note on Some Aspects of Evangelization."[10] The earlier 1989 "Letter on Certain Aspects of Christian Meditation" was a precursor of these documents.

During the previous period, roughly from the 1980s to the mid-1990s, special attention was devoted to Christological, soteriological, and ecclesiological issues surrounding liberation theology. This is reflected in the "Instruction on Certain Aspects of the 'Theology of Liberation,'" (1984)

---

[9] http://www.vatican.va/roman_curia/congregations/cfaith/index.htm (accessed May 12, 2009).

[10] This transition is marked by Cardinal Joseph Ratzinger's essay, "Current Situation of Faith and Theology," delivered in May 1996 to the Doctrinal Committee of the Bishops' Conference of Latin America held in Guadalajara; also published as "Relativism: The Central Problem for Faith Today," *Origins* 26 (1996): 309, 311–17. A similar report was delivered in Bogotá 1984; Kinshasa 1987; Vienna 1989; Hong Kong 1993; and Menlo Park, California, 1999. Also in 1996, the secretary of the CDF, Archbishop Tarcisio Bertone, SDB, published "Magisterial Documents and Public Dissent," in *L'Osservatore Romano* (December 20, 1996) 1, col. 5–6, 5, col. 4–6; English edition, (January 29, 1997): 6–7; on the latter, see Francis A. Sullivan, "Recent Theological Observations on Magisterial Documents and Public Dissent," *Theological Studies* 58 (1997): 509–15.

and the "Instruction on Christian Freedom and Liberation" (1986). During this same period of time, a range of ecclesiological issues received heightened attention by the CDF. These included topics surrounding the exercise of power and authority in the Church and the mission of the Church in the world as treated by liberation theologians and other Catholic theologians around the world. In these investigations ecclesiological writings were evaluated in light of the "Final Report from the Extraordinary Synod of Bishops" in 1985, which identified communion as the central motif in the ecclesiology of Vatican II. Significantly, communion was the defining theological rubric for the new *Code of Canon Law* in 1983 and also an organizing doctrine for the *Universal Catechism of the Catholic Church* in 1992. This provides the broader context for the 1992 "Letter on Some Aspects of the Church Understood as Communion." This official communion ecclesiology provided the theological frame of reference for the documents treated in the previous section on norms and criteria in the "Profession of Faith and Oath of Fidelity" (1989), "The Vocation of the Theologian" (1990), and *Ad Tuendam Fidem* (1998). John Paul II's Apostolic Letter, *Ordinatio Sacerdotalis* (1994), on the inadmissibility of the ordination of women, should be situated in this context as well, along with the CDF *Responsum ad dubium circa doctrinam in Epist. Ap."Ordinatio Sacerdotalis" traditam* (1995). These sought to bring closure to the debate raised by the CDF 1976 declaration, *Inter Insigniores,* to dubious effect.

Completing this consideration in reverse order of official statements during the decade following Vatican II, issues concerning ecclesiology (infallibility in particular), and Christology and the hermeneutics of doctrinal formulas were addressed in the statements *Mysterium Ecclesiae* (1973) and *Mysterium Filii Dei* (1972). The formula to be used for the profession of faith was issued in 1967 and an instruction on the necessity of establishing the doctrinal commissions in the episcopal conferences was issued that same year.

A range of statements by the pope and by the CDF on moral teachings have emerged since Vatican II. There does not seem to be a clear differentiation of periods in this area. Prescinding from social encyclicals, we can concentrate on those topics that have been central in cases that have come before the CDF. The most significant were the encyclicals by John Paul II, *Veritatis splendor* (1993) and *Evangelium vitae* (1995). Among the most noteworthy statements by the CDF on moral issues have been the "Declaration on Certain Questions Concerning Sexual Ethics" (1975), "Responses to Questions concerning Sterilization in Catholic Hospitals" (1975), "Declaration on Euthanasia" (1980), "Pastoral Care of Homosexual Persons" (1986), "Respect for Human Life in its Origin and on the Dignity of Procreation" (1987), "Doctrinal Note on Some Questions Regarding the Participation of Catholics in Political Life" (2003), and the "Instruction *Dignitas Personae*: On Certain Bioethical Questions" (2008).

The Procedure for Investigating Theologians

The cases investigated by the CDF considered in this report were conducted following the procedure established by the revised "Regulations for Doctrinal Examination" (*Ratio Agendi*) issued in 1997, which superseded the 1971 edition.[11] I will briefly describe the procedure followed by the CDF in its investigation of works by theologians as set forth in the "Regulations" in accordance with the general mandate of John Paul II's Apostolic Constitution, *Pastor Bonus*, issued in 1988.[12]

First, certain writings or teachings come to the attention of the CDF. The person is said to be delated; that is, the work of a theologian has been accused of having doctrinal errors or dangerous opinions. Delations frequently come from a local bishop, but there have been cases where vigilante groups (e.g., Catholics United for the Faith) and individuals have complained about a theologian's writings or lectures. Delations are received and initially considered by the *Congresso*, which consists of the "Superiors and Officials of the Congregation"—the prefect, secretary, sub-secretary, the promoter of justice, and three office supervisors who meet weekly (reportedly on Wednesdays) and who decide whether the materials should undergo a preliminary Office Study.

Second, if the *Congresso* judges that the materials may contain erroneous or dangerous doctrine they authorize an Office Study whereby one or

---

[11] The 1971 version of the *Ratio Agendi* can be found in AAS 63 (1971): 234–36; English translations can be found in *Canon Law Digest* 7 (1968–72): 181–84; and *Origins* 1 (1972): 648. This text is not available on the internet. Patrick Granfield, OSB, describes and comments upon the 1971 procedure in "Theological Evaluation of Current Procedures," *Cooperation between Theologians and the Ecclesiastical Magisterium*, 117–43, at 125–32.

[12] The Apostolic Constitution *Pastor Bonus* and the CDF's "Regulations for Doctrinal Examination" are available on the Vatican web site. For a description and commentary on the 1997 "Regulations," see Ladislas Örsy, "Are Church Investigation Procedures Really Just?" *Doctrine and Life* 48 (1998): 453–66, previously published in *Stimmen der Zeit* 216 (1998): 363–74; and Paul Collins in *The Modern Inquisition: Seven Prominent Catholics and Their Struggles with the Vatican* (Woodstock and New York: The Overlook Press, 2002), originally *From Inquisition to Freedom* (East Roseville, New South Wales: Simon & Schuster, 2001), 32–45.

more consultors, and possibly other experts, study the works in question and present their findings to the *Congresso*. The *Congresso* considers the observations on the work(s) produced by designated consultor(s) and expert(s) when appointed and chooses one of three options: not to pursue the matter further, to ask for the bishop or religious superior to take appropriate action, or to initiate a formal process, either following the ordinary form or employing an urgent form. "The criteria for this decision are the potential errors which have been noted, taking into consideration their prominence, seriousness, dissemination, influence and the danger of harm to the faithful" (art. 6). It is possible that a theologian will be asked for a written response to these initial observations before any formal process begins.

Third, the ordinary form of investigation has two phases. The first internal phase takes place in complete secrecy. The *Congresso* selects a council of two or more experts who examine the writings and determine if they comply with Church teachings, and a *relator pro auctore*, who is chosen to make sure that an accurate and comprehensive interpretation of the author's writings is the basis for judgment in the process and who is charged with "expressing a judgment regarding the influence of the author's opinions" (art. 10). Once these tasks have been completed, all of the relevant materials—the Office Study report from the preliminary study and any relevant antecedent materials, the observations of the experts, and the presentation of the *relator pro auctore*—are given to the members of the *Consulta*, which is convened when the case has been prepared. The *Consulta* includes the 29 consultors, the *relator pro auctore*, and the author's ordinary (if he wishes to be present). A comprehensive presentation is made by the *relator pro auctore*, followed by reports by the experts. The consultors and the bishop can then offer their opinions orally or in writing, which can result in clarification made by either the *relator pro auctore* or the experts. "When the discussion is finished, the consultors alone remain in the room for the general vote on the outcome of the examination, aimed at determining whether doctrinal errors or dangerous opinions have been found in the text, and specifically identifying these in light of the different categories of truth-propositions found in the *Professio fidei*" (art. 13). The vote of the consultors and all of the written materials are presented to the Ordinary Session of the Congregation, which also takes place on Wednesdays and includes the prefect, secretary, sub-secretary, and the cardinals and local bishops who are members. The decisions of the Ordinary Session on the case are then taken by the prefect to the pope on Friday.

If the previous phase concludes that the objections about the writings of an author should be pursued, a second phase follows in this ordinary form. The theologian's ordinary or religious superior is informed of this decision, as are other relevant dicasteries in the Curia. A list of "erroneous or dangerous propositions at issue" and argumentation including questions are given to the ordinary or religious superior to be passed on to the author. The author is permitted to choose an advisor who can assist him or her in preparing a response. The author is given three months to respond in writing. This written response is reviewed by the *Congresso*. It may then be judged that the matter has been positively resolved and no further action is needed. When matters have not been satisfactorily addressed, it is decided at the Ordinary Session what additional actions need to be taken: (a) additional written observations and questions might be prepared and sent to the theologian with a request for a further written response (sometimes the theologian is told to prepare an essay expressing adherence to the official position as specified by the CDF, which is to be vetted and approved by the *Congresso*; and in some cases the theologian is required to publish the essay without indicating that the CDF is making this request, and at other times a brief clarification of one's position in writing is required); (b) an invitation might be submitted to the theologian to appear before a colloquium with delegates of the CDF, at which time the author may be accompanied by his or her theological advisor and bishop (or religious superior), both of whom could be active in the discussion; or (c) some other course of action might be taken by the CDF (arts. 20-21); all of which are submitted to the pope for approval. These decisions, once approved by the pope, are communicated to the ordinary, the episcopal conference of the theologian, concerned dicasteries, and the theologian (art. 22).

Fourth, if a particular case is judged by the *Congresso* to merit urgent attention, a special Commission is established to determine the erroneous or dangerous propositions. This process does not include the experts evaluating the texts in question, nor the appointment of a *relator pro auctore*, nor voting by the group of consultors after hearing from these investigators. Instead, the report from the *Congresso* (in light of what the special Commission gleans) is submitted to the Ordinary Session for deliberation. If a decision is made for immediate action, the matter is brought to the pope for approval and communicated to the author through the ordinary or religious superior for correction. Once a response is received from the author a decision is made in the Ordinary Session whether further action needs to be taken.

Are there any noteworthy changes in the 1997 version of the procedure? The Explanatory Note that accompanied the new norms stated that the old norms "were unquestionably sufficient. However, in consideration of the heightened sensitivity in this area characteristic of contemporary thinking, they have been significantly expanded." There are two main areas where changes have taken place since the 1971 version. First, the theologian's local ordinary has a heightened role in the process, which has been added to protect the rights of the theologian being investigated. The bishop acts as the intermediary in any communication that takes place between the theologian and the CDF. Moreover, the bishop is invited now to participate in the internal phase, under the conditions of strict secrecy. In the ordinary procedure the bishop may participate in the discussion that takes place in Rome with the *Consulta*—the consultors, experts, *relator pro auctore*, and in the external phase, he is invited to participate in any face-to-face colloquium that takes place with the theologian and delegates from the CDF, including the theologian's advisor.

The second major change in the new norms, also added to safeguard the rights of the theologian, is that during the second external phase the theologian is now able to select a theological advisor. This person helps the theologian being investigated to prepare any written defense, and, if a colloquium is requested, the advisor may accompany the theologian and participate in the discussion with the representatives of the CDF.

Beyond these two changes, the steps in the various phases of the process have been delineated in greater detail in the 1997 "Regulations."

The Public Record of Cases

The following cases pertain to written articles or books by theologians that have been investigated since Vatican II, listed in the order in which they appear on the Vatican web site, beginning with the more recent. Cases pertaining to priests and women religious involved in pastoral ministry are not listed here, but will be mentioned later.

- Jon Sobrino, SJ, *Jesus the Liberator: A Historical-Theological Reading of Jesus of Nazareth* (Spanish edition, 1991) and *Christ the Liberator: The View from the Victims* (Spanish edition, 1999). Notification in 2006.[13]

---

[13] International Theological Commission of the Ecumenical Association of Third World Theologians, *Getting the Poor Down from the Cross: Christology of Liberation*, http://servicioskoinonia.org/LibrosDigitales/LDK/EATWOTGettingThePoorDown.

- Roger Haight, SJ, *Jesus Symbol of God* (1999). Notification in 2004. Haight was banned from teaching at a non-Catholic institution in January 2009.

- Marciano Vidal, CSsR, numerous writings in moral theology. Notification in 2001.

- Jacques Dupuis, SJ, *Toward a Christian Theology of Religious Pluralism* (1997). Notification in 2001.[14]

- Reinhard Messner, Innsbruck University liturgical historian, for various writings. Notification in 2000.

- Anthony De Mello, SJ, spiritual writings. Notification in 1998.

- Tissa Balasuriya, OMI, *Mary and Human Liberation* (1990). Notification in 1997.

- André Guindon, OMI, *The Sexual Creators: An Ethical Proposal for Concerned Christians* (1986). Notification in 1992.

- Edward Schillebeeckx, OP. His books on the theology of ministry were investigated in 1984 and 1986 and his work on Christology in 1979 and 1980.

- Charles E. Curran, for various writings. Curran was suspended from the Catholic University of America faculty in 1986.

- Leonardo Boff, OSF, *Church: Charism and Power, Essay on Militant Ecclesiology* (Portuguese edition, 1981). Notification in 1985.[15]

- Anthony Kosnik, editor of CTSA book on *Human Sexuality* (1977). Observations in 1979.

- Jacques Pohier, OP, *Quand je dis Dieu* (1977). Declaration in 1979.

- Hans Küng, *Die Kirche* (1967) and *Unfehlbar? Eine Anfrage* (1970). Declaration in 1974.

Of these cases, three from the post-Vatican II period have had a significant number of their CDF procedural documents published: Hans

---

pdf (accessed May 10, 2009); Stephen J. Pope, ed., *Hope and Solidarity: Jon Sobrino's Challenge to Christian Theology* (Maryknoll, NY: Orbis Books, 2008).

[14] See Gerald O'Collins, "Jacques Dupuis: His Person and His Work," in *In Many and Diverse Ways*, ed. Daniel Kendall and Gerald O'Collins (Maryknoll, NY: Orbis Books, 2003), 18–29; *Jacques Dupuis Faces the Inquisition*, intro. and ed. William R. Burrows (Eugene, OR: Pickwick Books, 2011).

[15] Harvey Cox, *The Silencing of Leonardo Boff* (Oak Park, IL: Meyer Stone Books, 1988).

Küng, Charles Curran, and Edward Schillebeeckx.[16] These cases provide illustrative prototypes for the process we have witnessed over the last twenty years.

From Known Cases to Those Not Widely Known

Besides this public list of cases since Vatican II, there are many other theologians who have been investigated. Some have been "cleared" of any doctrinal errors or ambiguities; others have complied with orders to write clarifications, retractions, or essays indicating that they subscribe to particular teachings. There are still others who have been disciplined that are not included on the above list. Liberation theologians Leonardo Boff and Jon Sobrino are on the list. But it is important to note that Sobrino came under investigation earlier for his 1976 work, *Cristología desde América Latina* (*Christology at the Crossroads*, 1978). When his later two books came out in the early 1990s, the CDF *Congreso* decided in this case to proceed using the urgent form. Although he has never received a notification, Gustavo Gutiérrez's writings have repeatedly been questioned and criticized by the CDF. The Peruvian bishops received ten complaints about Gutiérrez's writings as early as 1983 and they refused to condemn his work. In 1988 a new investigation into Gutierrez's works began, which again was inconclusive.

Works by African theologians have also been investigated for their treatment of post-colonial approaches to inculturation and religious pluralism and to moral issues, but these cases are not widely known. The Cameroon Jesuit theologian Meinrad Hebga's 1976 book *Emancipation d'Eglise sous tutelle: Essai sur l'ère post-missionnaire* raised numerous challenges to traditional missionary practices, and his 1977 book *Depassements* offered an approach that was more in keeping with the official position.[17] Jean Marc Ela was investigated for his advocacy of inculturation.

---

[16] Hans Küng and Leonard J. Swidler, *Küng in Conflict* (Garden City, NY: Doubleday, 1981); U.S. Catholic Conference, *The Küng Dialogue* (documentation from the CDF and German bishops' conference) (Washington, DC: USCC, 1980); Peter Hebblethwaite, *The New Inquisition: Schillebeeckx and Küng* (London: Collins, 1980); Ted Schoof, ed., *The Schillebeeckx Case: Official Exchange of Letters and Documents in the Investigation of Fr. Edward Schillebeeckx by the Sacred Congregation for the Doctrine of the Faith, 1976–1980*, trans. Matthew J. O'Connell (New York: Paulist, 1894 [Dutch orig., 1980]); Charles E. Curran, *Faithful Dissent* (Kansas City, MO: Sheed & Ward, 1986).

[17] See Paulin Poucouta, "Meinrad Pierre Hebga: Theologian and Healer," *African Theology in the 21st Century: The Contribution of the Pioneers*, ed. Bénézet Bujo, Juvénal Elunga Muya (Pauline Publications Africa, 2005), 70–92.

There are African women religious theologians who have been and are currently being investigated, but their names and locations will not be mentioned. Likewise other African theologians working in the area of religious pluralism and ecclesiology are currently under investigation.

There have been a number of moral theologians who have been disciplined beyond those mentioned on the Vatican web site. Charles Curran's original investigation began in 1979 for his position on the possibility of dissent from ordinary, non-infallible teachings of the magisterium, most prominently concerning issues involved in sexual ethics, and resulted in his expulsion from the pontifical faculty of theology at the Catholic University of America in 1986.[18] The book *Human Sexuality: New Directions in American Catholic Thought*, published in 1977 under the editorship of Anthony Kosnik as a study of the Catholic Theological Society of America, was publicly denounced by the CDF in 1979. André Guindon, OMI, was investigated for his 1986 book, *The Sexual Creators*; a notification on the book was released in 1992. Marciano Vidal, CSsR, was investigated for a number of his books on moral theology, *Diccionario de Ètica Teológica* (1991), *La Propuesta moral de Juan Pablo II: Comentario Teológico-Moral de la Encíclica "Vertitatis Splendor"* (1994), and the three-volume work *Moral de Actitudes* (first edition begun in 1975; 1981–85). As in the previous cases, questions were raised about his methodology and his positions on birth control, homosexualilty, masturbation, in vitro fertilization, sterilization, and artificial insemination. A notification was approved for his book and changes were required for future publications. Some comments about the past few decades in moral theology accompanied the notification on Vidal. This period is described as one of tension, and the note compared the situation with the relation of theologians and the magisterium in the 1950s: "These tensions later revealed their fruitfulness in becoming a point of departure for the Second Vatican Council, as the Magisterium recognizes" (no. 4). Tensions are one thing, an attitude of opposition is another, the statement argues. Moral theologians must recognize that their vocation is "essentially a service which should promote the growth in goodness of the People of God and collaboration with the

---

[18] Curran lists the questions raised about his views on "fundamental option, theory of compromise, charge of physicalism against Aquinas and Catholic moral theology, understanding of the indissolubility of marriage in Scripture as an ideal, . . . abortion, and issues of sexual morality, including masturbation, homosexuality, premarital sexuality, contraception, and sterilization." Charles E. Curran, *Loyal Dissent: Memoir of a Catholic Theologian* (Georgetown University Press, 2006), 107.

Magisterium in exercising its task as final arbiter of truth in the Church" (no. 3). Bernard Häring, CSsR, who was the mentor of Charles Curran, was investigated for his book *Medical Ethics*, which originally appeared in German in 1972; the second edition was published in English in 1974 and was investigated by the CDF from 1975 to 1979.[19] Another Häring student, a Claretian priest, Benjamin Forcano, was investigated and disciplined for his 1981 work, *Nueva ética sexual*. The book *Does Morality Change?* (1997) by Seán Fagan, SM, a priest of Dublin, Ireland, was also investigated for six years by the CDF before being criticized by the Irish Episcopal Conference in 2004.[20] This pattern of investigations initiated by the CDF and actions subsequently taken by episcopal conferences will be treated in more detail below.

The issue of homosexuality has been a recurring reason for CDF interventions. The 1976 book by Jesuit theologian John McNeill, *The Church and the Homosexual*, was investigated; the CDF required in 1977 that the Jesuit General Superior, Pedro Arrupe, remove "the right to publish" (*imprimi potest*) from the book and forbade McNeill to lecture on homosexuality or minister to gays and lesbians. McNeill refused to comply and consequently was expelled by the Jesuits in 1987. Father Jack Bonsor was investigated by the CDF for his article, "Homosexual Orientation and Anthropology: Reflections on the Category 'Objective Disorder'" published in 1998 in *Theological Studies*. More widely known is the notification regarding the ministry to homosexuals conducted by Sister Jeannine Gramick, SSND, and Father Robert Nugent, SDS, in 1999. Three other cases in the United States should also be noted. On September 8, 2003, there was a news announcement in the journal *America*: "the Jesuit Conference on Aug. 26 announced that as a result of questions raised by the Congregation for the Doctrine of the Faith about certain writings of John R. Sachs, SJ, and at the request of the congregation, Father Sachs has formally declared his assent to the church's teaching concerning homosexuality as taught in the *Catechism of the Catholic Church* (*editio typica*, no. 2357, 2390) and the church's teaching concerning the ordination of women as taught in *Ordinatio Sacerdotalis*." (I will return to the issue of

---

[19] For personal testimony and documentation, see Bernard Häring, *My Witness for the Church*, trans. Leonard Swidler (New York and Mahwah, NJ: Paulist Press, 1992), 90–188.

[20] In honor of Seán Fagan, see *Quench Not the Spirit: Theology and Prophecy for the Church in the Modern World*, ed. Angela Hanley and David Smith, MSC (Dublin: Columba Press, 2005).

the ordination of women below.) Two essays on homosexuality were published in the September issue of *Theological Studies* in 2004, one by Paul G. Crowley, SJ, "Homosexuality and the Counsel of the Cross," the other by Stephen J. Pope, "The Magisterium's Arguments Against 'Same-Sex Marriage': An Ethical Analysis and Critique." In 2008 Crowley offered "A Clarification" on his previous essay at the insistence of the CDF after several years of exchanges. It is interesting that Crowley's essay did not even call into question the Church's official position on homosexuality and yet he was investigated, while lay theologian Stephen Pope's essay raised a series of critical issues and he was not investigated. Finally, mention should be made of the case of Edward Vacek, SJ, who offered a "Clarification" of his views in the July 30, 2007, edition of *America,* on intrinsically evil acts, homosexuality, unions between homosexual persons, and admission to the seminaries of candidates with homosexual tendencies.

Writings by other moral theologians that have been and currently are being investigated by the CDF concern fundamental moral theology, including Seán Fagan's questions concerning whether morality changes, and the implications of the primacy of conscience and role of dissent from non-infallible teachings. Other investigations are underway for positions taken on sexual ethics in particular. In addition, priest and women religious theologians who have called for a more open discussion of public policy issues surrounding abortion, especially during election cycles, have been investigated, something we will discuss below in terms of academic appointments.[21]

The CDF has been particularly vigilant in taking actions against those who support the ordination of women or who wish to have this topic discussed and discerned openly in the Church.[22] We have already noted the case of John R. Sachs, SJ. There have been a series of actions taken by the CDF against individuals, although not many are theologians. The

---

[21] "A Catholic Statement on Pluralism and Abortion" appeared as an ad in the *New York Times* on October 7, 1984, with ninety-seven signers, twenty-four of whom were women religious, including a small number of theologians. On November 30, 1984, Cardinal Jerome Hamer of the Congregation for Religious and Secular Institutes called for a public retraction by the women religious, otherwise they would be dismissed from membership in their religious communities. Barbara Ferraro, SNDdeN, and Patricia Hussey, SNDdeN, refused and left their order in 1988.

[22] Francine Cardman, "Sisters of Thecla: Knowledge, Power, and Change," in *Prophetic Witness: Catholic Women's Strategies for Reform,* ed. Colleen Griffith (New York: Crossroad, 2009), 46–54.

most recent case surrounds the investigation of the Leadership Conference of Women Religious. Cardinal Levada, in his February 20, 2009, letter to the LCWR, indicates that at the 2001 meeting between the LCWR and the CDF the issue of compliance with the Church's teaching on women's ordination was one of three raised (including religious pluralism and homosexuality) and that there now is need for a doctrinal assessment of the religious organization. In 2001, the Women's Ordination Conference held its first international assembly in Dublin, Ireland. American Benedictine sister Joan Chittister was to address the conference, but the prioress of her community, the Benedictine Sisters of Erie, Pennsylvania, Christine Vladimiroff, was instructed by Vatican Officials from the Congregation for Institutes of the Consecrated Life and Societies of Apostolic Life (CICL-SAL) to prohibit Chittister's participation in the event.[23] The prioress discerned this command in light of the Benedictine understanding of obedience and chose to support Chittister's trip. On June 29, 2002, there were "illicit" ordinations of seven women on the Danube River between Austria and Germany by Bishop Romulo A. Braschi of Argentina. On July 10, "Cardinal Ratzinger as the head of the Congregation for the Doctrine of the Faith, issued a *monitum* (canonical warning) that the women would be excommunicated unless they say their ordinations were invalid and repent by July 22, the Feast of Mary Magdalene. All seven women ordained on the Danube were formally excommunicated by January 2003."[24] This was followed by a series of ordinations of women, six to deaconate in June 2004, again on the Danube, four to priesthood and five to deaconate in July 2005, and in the United States eight women in July 2006, and twenty-one in 2007. Maryknoll priest Roy Bourgeois concelebrated and was the homilist on August 9, 2008, at the ordination ceremony of Janice Sevre-Duszynska, the sixth woman ordained in 2008 with the Roman Catholic Womenpriests movement. At the direction of the CDF the leadership of the Maryknoll Order entered into protracted discussion with Bourgeois concerning a repudiation of his course of action. The CDF issued the first formal warning in September 2008 threatening to excommunicate him unless he recanted his beliefs and public statements in support of women's ordination. After protracted discussions with the head of his order he was removed from the order and excommunicated in August 2011.

---

[23] See Judith K. Schaefer, OP, *The Evolution of a Vow: Obedience as Decision Making in Communion* (Graz, Austria: Lit Verlag, 2008), 122–25.

[24] Women's Ordination Conference, "Our Story," http://www.womensordination.org/content/view/8/59/ (accessed April 26, 2009).

Finally, attention should be devoted to those investigated for their views on religious pluralism.[25] Paul Knitter, whose book *No Other Name? A Critical Survey of Christian Attitudes toward the World Religions* was published in 1985, was explicitly mentioned in the 1996 lecture by Cardinal Ratzinger, "Relativism: The Central Problem of Faith Today." Knitter was initially contacted by the CDF in 1988.[26] Tissa Balasuriya's book *Mary and Human Liberation* was published in 1990; he was contacted in 1994 by the CDF, received a notification in 1997 and was excommunicated, but this was rescinded after negotiations. Certain writings by the Indian Jesuit spiritual writer Anthony de Mello received a posthumous notification in 1998. Jacques Dupuis's *Toward A Christian Theology of Religious Pluralism* appeared in 1997 and the notification appeared in 2001. Roger Haight's *Jesus Symbol of God* appeared in 1999 and the external phase began in February 2000. Peter Phan's *Being Religious Interreligiously: Asian Perspectives on Interfaith Dialogue*, was published in 2004 and the internal (secret) phase of this investigation began that same year. He was notified in July 2005, thus initiating the external phase of the investigation.

Polish theologian Wacław Hryniewicz, now retired from the Catholic University of Lublin, who had a distinguished career as an ecumenical theologian, was investigated because of an article he published in an online journal, in which he was critical of the CDF's 2007 statement "Responses to Some Questions Regarding Certain Aspects of the Doctrine of the Church." In January of 2008, he was contacted by Archbishop Angelo Amato, then secretary of the CDF. Suffering from cancer he responded: "I am close to death and do not see how I can now go against my conscience by writing an article with clarifications and rectifications, even though I've been told to expect disciplinary sanctions. What worries me most of all is that this judgment may now be expanded to cover all my previous work as well, in which I expressed similar views and convictions."[27]

Are there other people who have been investigated on other topic areas? In particular, I have wondered whether there are any investigations that

---

[25] Cardinal Jozef Tomko, Prefect of the Congregation for the Evangelization of Peoples, offered a critique of writings of Paul Knitter, Michael Amaladoss, SJ, and Jacob Kavunkal, SVD, for undermining evangelization in his 1988 lecture, "Christian Mission Today," in *Christian Mission and Interreligious Dialogue*, ed. Paul Mojzes and Leonard Swidler (Lewiston, NY: Edwin Mellen Press, 1990), 236–62.

[26] See above, n. 10.

[27] "Top Polish Theologian Rejects Vatican Demand to Retract Article," http://www.catholicnews.com/data/stories/cns/0804732.htm (accessed June 17, 2009).

have been undertaken concerning the debate about the interpretation of Vatican II, in terms of the hermeneutics of discontinuity or "rupture," as it has been called, in contrast to the official emphasis on continuity.[28] I raise this as a question because as I have reflected on the last decade in light of the last fifty years of interventions, it strikes me that the interpretation of history and ecclesial identity has surfaced repeatedly, going all the way back to the debates surrounding the modernists, and continuing in the investigations of Marie-Dominique Chenu's 1937 book *Le Saulchoir: Une école de théologie;* Yves Congar's works on ecumenism (1937), reform in the Church (1959), and the laity (1951);[29] and Henri de Lubac's masterwork *Surnaturel* (1945-6). Much attention in the Schillebeeckx case concentrated on the interpretation of history, Scripture, and dogmas as these bear upon Christological and ecclesiological issues. The investigation of Paul Collins's *Papal Power: A Proposal for Change in Catholicism's Third Millennium* (1997), was launched in the same year as its publication and dealt with these kinds of questions. Beyond this particular topic area, the question remains as to what other cases have not appeared in the public realm.

It has been noted that numerous Jesuits have been investigated during this period of time, the public cases since 1995 involving notifications about Jon Sobrino, Roger Haight, Jacques Dupuis, and Anthony De Mello.[30] Mindful of the cases of influential Dominican theologians Chenu, Congar, and Schillebeeckx before and after the council, I have learned that during the same period of time, since 1995, eighteen Dominicans have been investigated by the CDF.

---

[28] See John W. O'Malley's discussion of the problematic in his "Vatican II: Did Anything Happen?" which originally appeared in *Theological Studies* and was reissued in the book with the same title, ed. David G. Schultenover (New York: Continuum, 2007), 52–91; and the recent essay by Joseph A. Komonchak, "Novelty in Continuity: Pope Benedict's Interpretation of Vatican II," *America* (February 2, 2009), http://www.americamagazine.org/content/article.cfm?article_id=11375&comments=1 (accessed May 15, 2009).

[29] *Chrétien désunis: Principe d'un 'œcuménisme'*, 1937; *Vraie et fausse réforme dans l'Église*, 1950 (in English translation as *True and False Reform in the Church*, trans. and intro. Paul Philibert, OP [Collegeville, MN: Liturgical Press, 2011]); *Jalons pour un théologie du laïcat*, 1951.

[30] Hans Waldenfels, "Theologen unter römischem Verdacht: Anthony De Mello SJ—Jacques Dupuis SJ—Roger Haight SJ—Jon Sobrino SJ," *Stimmen der Zeit* 4 (2008): 219–31.

Actions Taken by Doctrinal Committees of Episcopal Conferences

Over the past ten years there has been increased activity by doctrinal committees of episcopal conferences in investigating and censuring the works of theologians. The CDF issued "The Instruction on the Necessity to Establish the Doctrinal Commissions in the Episcopal Conferences" on February 23, 1967. A letter was sent by the CDF to the presidents of episcopal conferences further encouraging the establishment of doctrinal committees on July 10, 1968. A second letter was sent to presidents of episcopal conferences on November 23, 1990, not only recommending again the formation of these doctrinal committees, but also urging that they take on greater responsibility. From the mid-1980s to the end of the 1990s, representatives of the CDF held meetings with representatives of doctrinal committees of episcopal conferences to clarify their responsibilities (with Latin Americans in Bogotá in 1984, Africans in Kinshasa in 1987, Europeans in Vienna in 1989, Asian conferences in Hong Kong in 1993, and English-speaking conferences [Australia, Canada, Papua New Guinea and Solomon Islands, New Zealand, United States, and CEPAC—Episcopal Conferences of the Pacific] in Menlo Park, California, February 9–12, 1999).[31] The areas of responsibility of doctrinal committees include exercising vigilance over scholarly writings, as well as other modes of communication, non-scholarly publications, and public lectures. It was recommended that a yearly letter be prepared by the president of the doctrinal committee to be sent to the CDF "on the work of the Commission and on the doctrinal questions of greatest importance in that particular country; suggestions could be included regarding the best way for the Holy See to address such questions."[32]

Known cases of actions taken by doctrinal committees of episcopal conferences include:

---

[31] The papers from the gathering held in California have been published by the CDF and the Doctrinal Commissions from North America and Oceania, *Proclaiming the Truth of Jesus Christ: Papers from the Vallombrosa Meeting* (Washington, DC: USCC, 2000).

[32] Adriano Garuti, OFM, who worked at the CDF from 1975–2003, offered the directives on "Collaboration between the Congregation for the Doctrine of the Faith and Doctrinal Commissions of Episcopal Conferences" at the Menlo Park gathering (ibid., 49–59). These included "serving as a supervisory body for Catholic publishers in particular dioceses" which is in accordance with the 1992 document of the CDF on "Some Aspects of the Use of Instruments of Social Communication in Promoting the Doctrine of the Faith."

- Hubertus Halbfas, *Fundamentalkatechetik: Sprache und Erfahrung in Religionsunterricht* (1968). The Episcopal Conference of Germany censured this book in the year of its publication.

- Anthony Kosnik, et al., *Human Sexuality: New Directions in American Catholic Thought* (New York: Paulist Press, 1977); "Statement of the U.S. Bishops' Committee on Doctrine," November 1977, (and Statement of the CDF, August 8, 1979).

- Richard McBrien, *Catholicism* (1st edition, 1980; 2nd study edition, 1981; 3rd completely revised edition, 1994); "Statement on Father Richard McBrien's 'Catholicism'" issued on July 5, 1985; "Review of Third Edition of Father McBrien's 'Catholicism'" issued on April 9, 1996.

- Dominique Cerbelaud, OP, *Marie, Un parcourse dogmatique* (2003). The doctrinal committee of the Episcopal Conference of France in 2004 wrote a notification concerning certain aspects of this work as well as a text on Mary written by a Catholic journalist Jacques Duquesne.

- Seán Fagan, *Does Morality Change?* was censured by the Irish Bishops' Conference in their "Notification on Recent Developments in Moral Theology and Their Implications for the Church and Society," July 2004.

- Daniel Maguire, "Statement Concerning Two Pamphlets Published by Professor Daniel Maguire, 'The Modern Roman Catholic Position on Contraception and Abortion' and 'A Catholic Defense of Same-Sex Marriage'" was issued in March 2007.

- Peter Phan, "Clarifications Required by the Book *Being Religious Interreligiously: Asian Perspectives on Interfaith Dialogue* by Reverend Peter C. Phan" was issued on December 17, 2007.

- José María Vigil, CMF, originally from Zaragoza, Spain, has worked in Latin America since Vatican II. The Episcopal Conference of Spain issued in 2008 "Nota sobre del libro del Rvdo. P. José María Vigil, CMF, *Teología del pluralismo religioso. Curso sistemático de Teología Popular*, 2005."

- Jose Antonio Pagola, "Note of Clarification about José Antonio Pagola's Book, *Jesús. Aproximación histórica*" was issued in June 2008 by the Spanish Episcopal Conference.

- Todd A. Salzman and Michael G. Lawler, "Inadequacies in the Theological Methodology and Conclusions of *The Sexual Person: Toward a Renewed Catholic Anthropology* by Todd A. Salzman and Michael G. Lawler," issued September 15, 2010.

• Elizabeth Johnson, "Statement on *Quest for the Living God: Mapping Frontiers in the Theology of God*, by Sister Elizabeth A. Johnson," issued March 24, 2011; "Response to Observations by Sr. Elizabeth Johnson, C.S.J., Regarding the Committee on Doctrine's Statement about the Book *Quest for the Living God*," issued October 11, 2011.

There are numerous questions about the roles being exercised by these doctrinal committees. Are we witnessing the outsourcing of investigations and disciplinary measures by the CDF in the interest of increased efficiency or out of a certain frustration at not achieving closure on certain cases? Is this an instance of the Curia implementing the principle of subsidiarity?[33] What is the nature of the coordination taking place between these groups? With the exception of the cases of Daniel Maguire and Elizabeth Johnson, the involvement of the CDF in each of the above-mentioned cases has been documented. The CDF was consulted in the preparation of the initial review of the 1980 edition of McBrien's book in 1985, and in 1995 the CDF contacted the doctrinal committee of the U.S. Bishops' Conference concerning the 1994 edition. Moreover, the "Regulations for Doctrinal Examinations" (no. 22) states that once a decision has been made by the Ordinary Session of the CDF and signed by the pope this decision is to be communicated to the theologian's ordinary, episcopal conference, and pertinent dicasteries in the Vatican. In other words, certain specifics of individual cases have been conveyed to the episcopal conference. For members of a doctrinal committee to suggest that they are working independently of the CDF seems contrary to the information conveyed by the "Regulations," which indicates that judgments and decisions reached by the CDF are passed on to the leadership of episcopal conferences and that the presidents of doctrine committees have been asked to submit annual reports to the CDF delineating theological questions being raised in the particular nation (and possibly naming theologians) and suggestions about how best to address them.

Interventions in the Academic Careers of Theologians

John Alesandro and John P. Boyle have offered helpful treatments of the history of the Church's involvement in the teaching of theology in academic settings from a canonical perspective. There are three stages in

---

[33] Patrick Granfield draws attention to the mention of the principle of subsidiarity in the private CDF letter of July 10, 1968, to presidents of episcopal conferences, "Theological Evaluation of Current Procedures," 122, 141–43.

this history: in the medieval period, an official teaching license, a *licentia docendi*, was granted to people teaching in the newly established universities; a *missio canonica* was devised during the post-Reformation period, especially after the French Revolution and the Napoleonic wars; and the new Code of Canon Law (1983) introduced the category of a *mandatum* (Canon 812) as a requirement to teach theology, which advances a model of a positive deputizing of teachers rather than simply a negative vigilance as was operative in the 1917 Code. It is important to appreciate that Church officials in the nineteenth century had an escalating concern that the Church was losing its authority to safeguard the teaching of the faith in the face of the increased power of the secular state. Boyle describes the turning point: "The bishops met in Würzburg in October, 1848 with their theological and canonical advisors. What emerged was the first formal demand to the modern state that those who taught Catholic theology (or religion in lower schools) must have from the bishop not the historic *licentia docendi* but what the bishops called a *missio canonica*."[34] This *missio canonica* became a requirement of professors of theology teaching in universities covered by various concordats, as in Germany, where professors were required to receive a *nihil obstat* from the local ordinary to be cleared to receive a call, but also of those teaching theology in institutions around the world that had papal constitutions and pontifical faculties that awarded ecclesiastical degrees (STB, STL, STD, and JCL and JCD). The implementation of the provision of the *mandatum* in Canon 812, as established by the U.S. Bishops in 2001, represents a distinctive practice.[35]

With this history in mind we can identify four specific situations presently operative: (1) institutions adhering to older concordats that require a *nihil obstat* associated with the *missio canonica* to fulfill the requirements for a *mandatum* as found in the new Code; (2) pontifical faculties around the world that operate with similar requirements; (3) Catholic colleges and universities where theologians may request, but are not by civil law required to request or be in possession of, a *mandatum* to teach; and (4)

---

[34] John P. Boyle, "Church Teaching Authority in the 1983 Code," *Dissent in the Church: Readings in Moral Theology No. 6*, ed. Charles E. Curran and Richard McCormack (Mahwah, NJ: Paulist Press, 1988), 191–230, esp. 218–24, at 220; John A. Alesandro, "The Rights and Responsibilities of Theologians: A Canonical Perspective," *Cooperation between Theologians and the Ecclesiastical Magisterium*, 76–116, esp. 106–9.

[35] For background, see Catholic Theological Society of America, *Report of the Ad Hoc Committee on the Mandatum*, September 2000.

faculties teaching in seminaries, who are treated under a different section of the Code devoted to "The Formation of Clerics," which specifies that teachers can be removed who are gravely deficient in their function (Canons 253–54).

The CDF has been involved in cases in the first category during the past decade. In Germany there have been instances where three ranked candidates for a chair in theology have been submitted to the local ordinary for a *nihil obstat* indicating that nothing stands in the way of any of these persons being appointed to this position. Local bishops have regularly consulted with the CDF concerning these cases and there have been a number of cases where the highest ranked candidates have been passed over, possibly because of their research agendas (e.g., religious pluralism or feminist issues), lay status, or gender. In 1969, Hubertus Halbfas was not approved to accept a new position in a *Hochschule* in Bonn and his canonical mission was revoked. Hans Küng's canonical mission to teach Catholic theology at the University of Tübingen was revoked in 1979 by the German bishops' conference, but he remained on the faculty in the new chair of ecumenical theology. Uta Ranke-Heinemann was the first woman to hold a chair of Catholic theology at the University of Essen, but was removed in 1987 because of her published theological views on the historicity of the virgin birth. More recently, Johannes Brosseder (Cologne) and August Jilek (Regensburg) also had their canonical missions revoked. A widely known case is that of political theologian Johann Baptist Metz who was ranked first by the faculty in 1979 for a chair at the University of Munich, but was passed over by Joseph Ratzinger, who was at the time the local ordinary. Regina Ammicht-Quinn (moral theology) and Wolfgang Pauly (systematic theology), both from the diocese of Trier, were denied a *nihil obstat*, as was Perry Schmidt-Leukel in Munich for his views on religious pluralism. Several other cases involved significant delays in granting the *nihil obstat*. There are some theologians who have never heard back about the request for a *nihil obstat*; and although it is not formally a denial, it functions as such.

In the second category, there is the case at Catholic University of America (CUA), the only pontifical university (though not the only pontifical faculty) in the United States, where Charles E. Curran was removed from his position in 1986. During the same period of time, a number of cases for tenure at CUA received close scrutiny by the U.S. bishops on the CUA board with Archbishop James Hickey as chancellor. Notably Elizabeth Johnson, CSJ, underwent a protracted period of investigation, which included preparing a written response to a set of concerns and a formal colloquium conducted with all the cardinals of the United States as a precondition for the *nihil obstat* to be granted in order for her tenure to be awarded. Roger Haight, SJ, was prohibited from teaching at Weston School of Theology, a pontifical faculty, when the notification on his book *Jesus the Symbol of God* was issued in 2005. He subsequently accepted a position teaching at Union Theological Seminary in New York, where distinguished Protestant and Catholic scholars have taught, including Catholic scholars Raymond Brown, SS, Mary Boys, SNJM, Janet Walton, SNJM, and Paul Knitter. However, in the summer of 2008, Jesuit superiors informed Haight that he would not be allowed to teach courses at Union beginning in the fall term of 2009.

In the fourth category of seminary professors, Carmel McEnroy, Sister of Mercy, was fired from her position at St. Meinrad School of Theology, Indiana, in May 1995 for her "public dissent" on the issue of women's ordination. In light of a recent Vatican report, undoubtedly other seminary professors, especially in the field of moral theology, will be added to this list. On December 15, 2008, the final report concerning the apostolic visitations of American seminaries that took place between September 2005 and May 2006 to address concerns about seminary formation raised by the clergy sex abuse scandal was issued by the prefect of the Congregation for Catholic Education, Cardinal Zenon Grocholewski and secretary Arcbishop Jean-Louis Bruguès, OP. The document describes a "remarkable amount of unity and harmony" among the faculties of most diocesan and religious order seminaries, which is attributed to sound leadership. However, "a lack of harmony . . . is almost always due to one or more educators being less than faithful to the Magisterium of the Church. These people, therefore, are out of kilter with the rest of the faculty and with the seminarians themselves. In centers of priestly formation with an atmosphere of more widespread dissent—which is the case particularly in centers run by religious—there can be no possibility of a unity of direction." Homosexuality was a particular area of concern in the document. In addition, the report spoke of some faculty members who "show reservations about [certain] areas of magisterial teaching. This is particularly true in the field of moral theology. Other points of Church teaching, such as ordination being restricted to men alone, are also questioned. Such lack of *sentire cum Ecclesia* is often not overt, but the students receive the message clearly nonetheless. In a few seminaries, and particularly in some schools of theology run by religious, dissent is widespread. Without doubt, the most contested area of theology today is moral theology." The report indicated that actions must be taken "to resolve the remaining long-standing difficulties in their respective institutions (including the long-standing presence of some problematic faculty members)." The implication would seem to be that certain moral theologians need to be removed. Whether this has taken place or is planned is not yet in evidence.

Ivone Gebara, a Brazilian Sister of Our Lady (Canoness of St. Augustine), was investigated in 1993. In 1995 she was banned from teaching at the Theological Institute of Recife for two years because of calling for more tolerance in dealing with women who chose to have an abortion. The situation that has recently unfolded with Catholic feminist theologian Rosemary Radford Ruether presents a rare case. She was appointed to an honorary endowed chair in Catholic theology at the University of San Diego for 2009–10, but it was rescinded, reportedly because of her call for wider latitude concerning the moral choice of abortion.[36]

The remaining question pertains to category 3: what has happened to the controversial policy adopted in June 2001 by the U.S. bishops that requires theologians to obtain a *mandatum*? United States faculty members in theology at Catholic colleges and universities were instructed to request a *mandatum* from their local ordinary, who in turn may grant or withhold it; and once given it may be withdrawn. Little information is available about the implementation of this policy of the U.S. bishops. Some dioceses have yet to implement it. Others have done so quietly. Most administrations of Catholic colleges and universities have insisted that they want nothing to do with this requirement because it violates academic freedom. What is not known is whether there are people who have requested a *mandatum* but been refused. Most important, it is not known whether there are any cases where a *mandatum* has been given to a faculty member and then rescinded. And if so, have there been repercussions for his or her position at that Catholic college or university? The *mandatum* is one of the criteria for inclusion used by the *Newman Guide to Choosing a Catholic College*, developed by the Cardinal Newman Society, which includes in its 2010–11 edition twenty U.S. Catholic Colleges and Universities.[37]

---

[36] See the recent book by Rosemary Radford Ruether, *Catholic Does Not Equal the Vatican: A Vision for Progressive Catholicism* (New York: The New Press, 2008); the work of Ivone Gebara is treated by Ruether, 128–38.

[37] On the Newman Guide, see http://www.catholichighered.org/TheNewman Guide/tabid/356/Default.aspx (accessed August 19, 2011). The Newman List as of 2010–11 includes Aquinas College (Nashville, TN); Ave Maria University (Naples,

Interventions in Publishing

In the area of publications, the CDF has intervened in a variety of cases since Vatican II, some over the last ten to fifteen years. The most widely discussed in the United States is that of Thomas Reese, SJ, who resigned as editor-in-chief of the magazine *America* after the CDF voiced concerns about the diversity of Catholic positions presented in the journal on the subjects of *"Dominus Iesus* . . . , same-sex marriage, stem-cell research, and the reception of Communion by Catholic politicians who support legal abortion." As John Thavis reported in Catholic News Service, the situation with Reese is not the only one. Pressure was also brought to bear by the CDF on the editors of *Famiglia Cristiana*, operated by the Pauline Fathers in Italy, for running articles "advocating Communion for divorced-remarried Catholics and arguing against censuring teenagers for masturbation. The papal action came shortly after the order's superior general reportedly refused demands by Cardinal Ratzinger to rein in the magazine's editorial independence and to submit all articles to advance review by a panel of theologians appointed by the cardinal. The controversy ended with the removal of the magazine's director and, shortly after, his departure as a columnist."[38] Another case in 2002 concerned the magazine *U.S. Catholic*, published by the Claretians, which had published a story reporting on an interview with five women who felt called to Catholic priesthood. It has likewise been reported that the Jesuit magazine, *Stimmen der Zeit*, had been under close scrutiny by the CDF for articles published that raised questions about certain official documents.

FL); Belmont Abbey College (Belmont, NC); Benedictine College (Atchison, KS); The Catholic University of America (Pontifical Faculty; Washington, DC); Christendom College (Front Royal, VA); The College of Saint Thomas More (Fort Worth, TX); DeSales University (Center Valley, PA); Franciscan University of Steubenville (Steubenville, OH); Holy Apostles College and Seminary (Cromwell, CT); Institute for the Psychological Sciences (Arlington, VA); John Paul the Great Catholic University (San Diego, CA); The College of Saint Mary Magdalen (Warner, NH); Mount St. Mary's University (Emmitsburg, MA); Providence College (Providence, RI); St. Gregory's University (Shawnee, OK); Thomas Aquinas College (Santa Paula, CA); The Thomas More College of Liberal Arts (Merrimack, NH); University of Dallas (Irving, TX); University of St. Thomas (Houston, TX); Wyoming Catholic College (Lander, WY). Although Thomas Aquinas College (Santa Paula, CA) is on the Newman list, the diocesan bishop does not require a *mandatum* because no theologians are on the faculty.

[38] John Thavis, "Jesuit Officials Say *America* Editor Resigned after Vatican Complaint," *Catholic News Service* (May 9, 2005) http://www.catholicnews.com/data/stories/cns/0502817.htm (accessed May 7, 2009).

The extent of CDF interventions in the publication of Catholic theological journals is unclear. There is evidence that the CDF has intervened with the Jesuit journals *Theological Studies* in the United States, *Vidyajyoti Journal of Theological Reflection* published in Delhi, India, and the *Gregorianum* published in Rome concerning *quaestiones disputatae* in the fields of moral theology, Christology, and ecclesiology. In light of these three cases, it is reasonable to hypothesize that journals run by other religious orders have been contacted by the CDF protesting the publication of certain essays and requesting either a stricter policy of not publishing essays critical of or at odds with official positions, or insisting that defenses of official positions be published when critical essays have appeared in print, or the imposition of vetting policies using CDF-approved theologians.

There have also been cases where books that have been censured by the CDF have no longer been published by Catholic presses. There are two well known cases. The volume *Human Sexuality*, edited by Anthony Kosnik, published by Paulist Press, was taken off of their list after the notification appeared. The 1994 book by Lavinia Byrne, IBVM, *Woman at the Altar: The Ordination of Women in the Roman Catholic Church*, was published by the Benedictine owned and operated Liturgical Press, which destroyed the remaining 1,300 copies of her book. Questions have been raised with superiors of Maryknoll and with editorial staff about certain books and series published by Orbis.

Actions Taken by Local Bishops

Local bishops have chosen to intervene in the work of theologians in certain instances by refusing to grant individuals permission to receive public awards or to speak in official Catholic settings. Two instances will illustrate this. One concerns the distinguished French Dominican Claude Geffré, who has retired from the Institut Catholique in Paris. In 2007 he was to receive an honorary degree at Kinshasa School of Theology in the Democratic Republic of the Congo, but the Vatican Congregation for Education, in consultation with the CDF, vetoed this action and, in their customary way, gave no rationale. There are other instances where the local ordinary or his representative has intervened to prohibit speakers who have been commissioned to give public lectures at diocesan gatherings and universities from making addresses, sometimes with the hosting Catholic institution protesting and proceeding nevertheless. Documented instances come from the Los Angeles Religious Education Congress.

Individuals who were invited and agreed to be public speakers were subsequently informed that they were not on the approved speakers' list for the Archdiocese of Los Angeles. In the cases of Geffré and in two instances in Los Angeles, the individuals were never informed why they were not able to give their lectures. In one case, repeated formal requests for information about why this person was being blacklisted were met with no response. There have been reported cases where theologians invited to speak were asked whether they had a *mandatum*. There have been numerous instances when well-known theologians have been told by organizers of an event that certain officials in the diocese had indicated that the invited theologian is not allowed to speak at Catholic institutions in that diocese. The question is whether these cases are isolated, episodic incidents, initiated by a local bishop or chancery official, or whether there is a larger pattern emerging whereby diocesan bishops have been encouraged during *ad limina* meetings or through the episcopal conferences to be vigilant in not allowing certain theologians to speak at approved diocesan venues.

A Litany of Theologians' Laments

What further avenues need to be explored to come to a fuller assessment of the interventions of the magisterium over the last ten to forty-five years? There are some logical options. One would be to consider the criteriological issues as these are being articulated by the CDF and employed in the aftermath of *Ad Tuendam Fidem* to close off inquiry and debate about major issues in the Church and theology today: the ordination of women, homosexuality and a variety of issues in moral theology, religious pluralism, and the exercise of authority in the Church.[39] Second, it might be valuable to consider how the current practices of the CDF as they are being increasingly coordinated with doctrinal committees of episcopal conferences compare and contrast with the forms of report-

---

[39] Here, of course, we will be guided by the work of Francis Sullivan, *Creative Fidelity: Weighing and Interpreting Documents of the Magisterium* (Mahwah, NJ: Paulist, 1996), and his numerous commentaries on subsequent statements by John Paul II and the CDF, and the work of Richard R. Gaillardetz, including *By What Authority? A Primer on Scripture, the Magisterium, and the Sense of the Faithful* (Collegeville, MN: Liturgical Press, 2003). Also noteworthy is the dissertation by Anthony J. Figueiredo, *The Magisterium-Theology Relationship: Contemporary Theological Conceptions in the Light of Universal Church Teaching since 1835 and the Pronouncements of the Bishops of the United States* (Rome: Editrice Pontificia Università Gregoriana, 2001).

ing and disciplining that developed during the modernist crisis and the controversy surrounding *nouvelle théologie* in order to offer a sharper historical evaluation of what is transpiring today. Third, it would be important to consider substantive theological issues that are at stake during this period of time. Fourth, there is the larger problematic concerning the understanding of the nature and mission of the Church as this relates to collaborative roles of bishops, theologians, and representatives of the people of God as a whole, especially including lay people and in particular women religious and lay ecclesial ministers.

Before we explore any of these specific issues, I think we need to gather together the lamentations of the theologians who have undergone investigations and been disciplined. The notifications and the occasional official commentaries on the cases of disciplined theologians offer "official narratives" of what has transpired. The testimonies of laments by theologians who have been investigated offer contrasting narratives that merit attention and from which there are important lessons to learn. I am proposing that in the field of pastoral practice, ecclesiology, and spirituality we need to cultivate a personal and collective awareness of lamentations, develop a hermeneutics of lamentations, and devise a method for discerning their significance for the *ongoing formation* of the Church's identity and mission.[40]

For some time now, I have made the case for what is widely acknowledged: that the Church's identity and mission are recognized and realized through communicative practices whereby the aspirations, desires, and intentions of ecclesial collectivities are discerned by means of a range of practices, notably conciliar and synodal practices. It is abundantly clear to those who have been involved in these practices of collective discernment that the desires and intentions associated with being Church and acting as Church are frequently not met. Reflecting on this phenomenon and an ecclesial dynamic of frustrated desires and failure, I have come to advance a theology and hermeneutics of lamentations as a resource for designating and discerning experiences of thwarted ecclesial desires and intentions. When the underlying problems that give

---

[40] On the role of lamentation in ecclesiology and pastoral practice, see Bradford E. Hinze, "Ecclesial Impasse: What Can We Learn From Our Laments?" *Theological Studies* 72 (2011): 470–95; and for related suggestions, see Hinze, "The Reception of Vatican II in Participatory Structures of the Church: Facts and Friction," *Proceedings of the Seventieth Annual Convention of the Canon Law Society of America* (Washington, DC: Canon Law Society, 2009), 28–52.

rise to these laments are particularly entrenched, I believe we should follow the lead of Constance Fitzgerald and speak of them as instances of ecclesial impasse.[41] These laments and impasses merit special attention; they should neither be ignored as if they are insignificant, belittled as irreverent, denied, nor repressed.

When considering those individual theologians investigated by the magisterium, we cannot simply pursue a hermeneutics of intentionality of authoritative texts and traditions and ecclesial bodies as is customarily recommended. We also need to interpret and discern the laments of the theologians involved in these cases. Their laments give voice to the frictions, frustrations, and failures involved in these procedures, but also articulate something that is occurring in local church communities and in certain cases in the wider Church. The phenomenology and hermeneutics of intentionality that have come to define the theological and specifically ecclesiological enterprise in the aftermath of the work of Karl Rahner, Bernard Lonergan, and Hans Urs von Balthasar must be augmented with a hermeneutics of lamentation, one that offers a further theological and philosophical development of Edward Schillebeeckx's hermeneutics of negative contrast experiences and of what countless other theologians express in other terms.[42]

Lamentations offer a source of wisdom, renewal, and reform in the Church. They are a privileged site for hearing the Spirit of God who groans in the human heart and the suffering world when something new is struggling into existence and when the Spirit is being stifled. We need to gather testimonies of the laments of theologians from interviews and memoirs as resources for discerning a way forward.[43] My investigation

---

[41] Constance Fitzgerald, OCD, "Impasse and Dark Night," in *Living with Apocalypse, Spiritual Resources for Social Compassion*, ed. Tilden Edwards (San Francisco: Harper & Row, 1984), 93–116; also http://www.baltimorecarmel.org/ (accessed June 30, 2009).

[42] Bryan Massingale has treated groans and grieving in the Church in "See, I Am Doing Something New!" (December 16, 2004) http://www.jknirp.com/massin.htm (accessed May 15, 2009).

[43] I have personally interviewed over ten people who have been investigated by the CDF including Charles Curran, Roger Haight, Paul Knitter, and others who have asked not to have their names cited. I have also consulted Paul Collins's interviews with Tissa Balasuriya, Jeannine Gramick, Robert Nugent, Lavinia Byrne, and Hans Küng, and Küng's own testimony in *The Modern Inquisition*. Published testimonies by Charles E. Curran, Hans Küng, and Edward Schillebeeckx have been previously cited. Also noteworthy are Bernard Häring, *My Witness for the Church*, trans. and intro. Leonard Swidler (New York: Paulist, 1992); Jon Sobrino, "Conflict within the Church," *The Way* 26 (January 1986): 33–43; and Sobrino's "Epilogue" to *Getting the*

disclosed particular laments voiced in interviews, in memoirs, and essays. Here are ten.

1. *Anonymous Accusers and Critics.* Theologians being investigated frequently complain that they were never informed who brought the original accusation to the attention of the CDF, whether it was a bishop, a theologian, a member of some religious organization, or a group like Catholics United for the Faith. The accused are left to wonder why and how their work is receiving this attention. What are the motives? What expertise does this person have to make an accusation? Is there a vendetta or an ulterior motive? Moreover, those whose works are being scrutinized have no knowledge about the consultor who is examining the work in the role of official critic. What is his (always his) area of expertise and training? What particular competency does this person have?

2. *The Scourge of Secrecy, Torturous Isolation.* The issue of secrecy arises in the earliest phases of an investigation. Instead of a theologian being informed that they have been delated, the earliest phase of investigation is done in secret in the CDF office. Even in cases where observations made by a consultor for the Office Study are sent to the theologian (through the bishop or religious superior), the theologian being investigated is often urged to maintain secrecy about the proceedings. Since the revised "Regulations" of 1997, the theologian is permitted to talk matters over with his or her local bishop or superior and can chose a

---

Poor Down from the Cross, 305–14; an important source currently not available by Jacques Dupuis, *Do Not Stifle the Spirit: In Conversation with Gerry O'Connell* (unpublished); Roger Haight, "The Social Edge Interview: Jesuit Roger Haight," (2007), http://webzinc.thesocialedge.com/; and *idem*, "Religion Dispatches Column: No Zombie Jesus; The Vatican and Roger Haight," interviewed by Jason VonWachenfeldt, http://www.religiondispatches.org/archive/religionandtheology/1318/ (accessed June 30, 2009). Also see Karl Rahner, *Sämtliche Werke*, vol. 25, *Erneuerung des Ordenslebens: Zeugnis für Kirche und Welt*, ed. Andreas R. Batlogg (Freiburg im Breisgau: Herder, 2008), 65–69, 75–77, 115–18; Yves M.-J. Congar in *Journal d'un théologien* (1946–56), ed. Étienne Fouilloux (Paris: Cerf, 2001); and Henri de Lubac, *At the Service of the Church: Henri de Lubac Reflects on the Circumstances That Occasioned His Writings*, trans. A. E. Englund (San Francisco: Communio Books/Ignatius Press, 1993). In Elizabeth Johnson's written response to the particular criticisms made by the Statement by the Committee on Doctrine of the USCCB, she includes numerous grievances about the lack of due process used in her case and how her work has been misrepresented; see "To Speak Rightly of the Living God," in *Origins* 41, no. 9 (2011): 129–47 (reproduced below, 213–58). Besides these comments by Johnson and the interview with Jeannine Gramick, testimonies by other women theologians who have been investigated by the CDF need to be incorporated into this dossier.

theologian to assist him or her in preparing a response. While the new "Regulations" do not mandate secrecy during subsequent phases in the deliberation, silence is often recommended by bishops or religious superiors and is customary. This is said to be in the interest of the theologian—safeguarding his or her reputation and curtailing false accusations. However, there is no transparency surrounding the actions of the CDF and as a result there are no public procedures whereby its actions can be evaluated and the CDF can be held accountable for those actions by wider circles in the Church. Moreover, the assumption, if not imposition, of secrecy in these matters can be painfully onerous and in effect become a means of isolating an individual and thereby depriving him or her of support in time of need. Although this manner of proceeding may not be intended as a form of persecution, it is experienced by many as torturous isolation.

3. *Unfair Interpretations*. It is a common lament among theologians investigated that their works have not been fairly and accurately interpreted. Sentences have been taken out of context. Inferences are made that are nowhere suggested in the text. In fact, their work is not contextualized at all. There is a genuine conflict of interpretations operative in these investigations, but the officials function as the sole arbiters of correct interpretation.

4. *Contested Doctrines Frozen in Time*. Theologians who are working in the Church at the frontiers of theology are being held to doctrinal definitions and standards that are treated as frozen in time by means of ahistorical appeals to doctrinal positions. In areas where dramatic doctrinal developments are occurring, the CDF is judging people using a strict and often narrow propositional approach to doctrinal formulations. Dogmatic propositions are treated as rigid rules, rather than as a living tradition. There is too little acknowledgement of the fact of doctrinal development and of the hierarchy of truths. There is no acknowledgment that certain doctrines are widely contested among bishops, clergy, lay faithful, and theologians. Often there is an attempt to elevate non-infallible teachings to infallible norms by papal or curial edicts. From this concern results the widespread charge of creeping infallibilism.

5. *The Same People are Investigators, Prosecutors, and Judges*. The CDF chooses its own members to serve in all roles in the process of investigation and disciplining. Moreover, the accused often get the impression they are presumed guilty rather than innocent.

6. *A Failure to Communicate*. Many theologians have complained that when they reply by mail to inquiries, they either never hear word that

their letter was received or must wait a long time, up to a year or longer in some instances, for a response. This failure to communicate in a timely fashion is often perceived as a delaying tactic, and it cannot be concluded that "no news is good news." Whether intended or not, this serves as another cause of anguish that weighs on the minds, psyches, and bodies of those being investigated.

7. *Interrogation Masked as Dialogue.* In those cases when a theologian is called to Rome for a colloquium with representatives of the CDF, there is a hope that some light can be shed on what many theologians believe are misunderstandings of their work—passages taken out of context, slanted interpretations, and unfair implications attributed to the author. In fact, what transpires is an interrogation in which the theologian is placed in the position of defending his or her position before a group of people who have already reached certain conclusions about what is required of the theologian, what positions must be repudiated, what innovations are deemed unacceptable. There is no possibility for mutual listening and learning to take place in this environment. There is no genuine dialogue. Even in those cases when certain concessions are granted to theologians under these conditions, it cannot be inferred that this is an open, non-hostile space for mutual discovery.

8. *Defamation of Character.* The "Regulations" make clear and many notifications repeat that when a negative judgment has been rendered, it is a judgment about a written work of a theologian, not of the theologian-author's intention or character. However, in the end this course of action results in a defamation of character. Often there are serious consequences for one's life and work; in some cases a theologian loses his or her academic position and means of livelihood.

9. *Failure to Trust the Community of Theologians and the Faithful People of God as Whole.* The members of the CDF proceed as if they (as representatives of the pope and bishops) are the primary or sole guardians of the truth of the faith, while theologians and the faithful at large have no authoritative role in the defense, protection, and advancement of the faith of the Church. The CDF provides the only court of judgment. There is no dynamic role for the faithful and specifically for theologians in the ecclesial process of recognition, reception, and discernment of the truth of Catholic faith and morals. Bishops are rarely, if ever, instructed or pastorally encouraged to foster communicative relationships with theologians and with wider circles of the faithful about doctrinal matters of substance. They frequently act as if they are the teaching Church, the guarding Church, and everyone else is the learning Church and in need

of their paternalistic protection.[44] One can have the further impression that not only are bishops not trusting theologians and the faithful about the most important treasures of faith and the Church's mission, but that they do not have a robust trust that God is at work in the everyday lives and vocations of theologians and the priestly, religious, and lay faithful. They trust God to work through the bishops, but significantly less so through these other channels of grace and truth.

10. *Larger Repercussions: Creating a Culture of Surveillance, Policing, Control, and Intimidation.* One of the most ominous laments is that the CDF has relentlessly and effectively fostered the formation of the Church not as a disciplined Church of witness in a weary world, but as a disciplinary community that is stifling the critical and creative agency of the Spirit. How many times since Vatican II have we heard theologians cry out: "Do not extinguish the Spirit!"? This articulates a fear shared by theologians of every generation and every continent, and it is voiced by many other members of the Church as well, lay people, women religious, and clergy. But there is a special concern for and among younger theologians, especially lay theologians, who may not have had regular opportunities to establish relationships, close ties, and friendships with bishops—an unfortunate situation. Priest theologians have always had a wider range of opportunities to do this, made possible by clerical culture. Instead of creating cultures of mutual listening and mutual learning, of friendship and communion, of mutual sharing of pastoral concerns between theologians and bishops and among them with the wider faithful people of God, we have witnessed the creation of a culture of paranoia, fear, and

---

[44] Many Catholic theologians have urged the development of synodal modes of discernment and decision making on doctrinal and pastoral matters where bishops, theologians, and the people of God participate. See, for example, Bradford Hinze, "On Fostering Ecclesial Dialogue: Engaging Contrasting Ecclesiologies," *Ecclesiological Investigations* 4, no. 2 (2008): 166–82; Bernd Jochen Hilberath, "Die Wahrheit des Glaubens: Anmerkungen zum Prozeß der Glaubenskommunikation," in *Dimensionen der Wahrheit: Hans Küng im Disput*, ed. B. J. Hilberath (Tübingen: Francke Verlag, 1999), 51–59; Ormond Rush, *The Eyes of Faith: The Sense of the Faithful and the Church's Reception of Revelation* (Washington, DC: Catholic University of America Press, 2009), 251–74; Michael Fahey, "Magisterium," *The Routledge Companion to the Christian Church*, ed. Gerard Mannion and Lewis S. Mudge (New York and London: Routledge, 2008), 525–35; and John J. Burkhard, "The Sensus Fidelium," *The Routledge Companion to the Christian Church*, 560–75. Also see Peter Hünermann, "Die Kongregation für die Glaubenslehre und ihre strukturellen Problem mit der Theologie. Eine nicht-kanonistische, auf Erfahrung basierende Reflexion," *Theologische-praktische Quartalschrift* 157 (2009): 55–65.

intimidation that is squelching the desire of younger theologians and their passion for the theological pursuit, driving wedges between theologians and bishops when we should be fostering communion. Such intimidation often results in self-censoring; as a result the Church as a whole, the Church of the future, suffers.

Ecclesial Impasse and Eschatological Fragments of a Reforming Church

The gathering of this data reveals not isolated instances, but a pattern of ecclesial impasse. There seems to be no way out and no way forward, just more of the same. In many ways, and despite its intention, the CDF has contributed to undermining the authority and credibility of the Church in the world and among its own constituents. Many conclude that it has stifled the Spirit in the Church and impeded the Church's dynamic development in communities. The procedures and outcomes of these investigations have wounded communion in the Church and have been a source of scandal among ecumenical and interfaith communities. The lamentations we have examined express the wounded Church, the groaning of the body of Christ, given utterance by the wailing Spirit of God.

Lamentations, however, are not only expressions of brokenness, but also disclose aspirations for ecclesial reform and doctrinal development. They reflect the eschatological nature of the Church as a pilgrim people, striving to bring to light and to witness to the living faith among us. This means these laments can serve as a catalyst and a dynamic force for promoting new life in the Church. We need to be admonished to heed the laments in the Church and learn their lessons. But equally important, we need to develop a theological and practical process for interpreting and discerning these laments as they bear upon the Church's identity and mission at the local diocesan level, in episcopal conferences, and at the universal level.

With their current way of proceeding, the CDF and doctrinal committees of episcopal conferences are impeding the cultivation of closer, more collaborative relationships of mutual learning among bishops, theologians, and representatives of the people of God as a whole. To address this situation of brokenness and impasse, I wish to conclude by suggesting that closer relationships among bishops, theologians, and the faithful should be developed at three levels:

- *At the diocesan level*, every diocesan bishop, especially metropolitans, should establish a council of theologians (like presbyteral councils and diocesan pastoral councils) that would meet regularly to cultivate closer relationships between theologians who are representative of different theological orientations and disciplines (not just those reflecting the bishop's theological proclivities) and the various Catholic universities, colleges, seminaries, and pastoral centers in the diocese. The bishop would meet with this council of theologians to discuss the pressing pastoral and theological issues in the diocese, in the nation, and in the global Church as identified by the bishop and the theologians.

- *At the level of episcopal conferences*, there must be renewed experimentation with models of collaboration between bishops and theologians. For example, every episcopal conference should follow the lead of the Indian Episcopal Conference and hold an annual weekend meeting with a workable-sized group of representatives of the episcopal conference (between ten and fifteen members) and representatives of the societies for Catholic theologies (a similar number) to discuss a topic chosen jointly by a representative of the bishops and a representative of the theologians. Moreover, we need to reestablish the synodal style of collective discernment employed by the U.S. episcopal conference in the development of the pastoral letters on peace and on the economy, which was so effective in generating a Church-wide process of discernment and deliberation on matters of common concern, but which has been virtually abandoned or dramatically curtailed after repeated criticisms of this method by the CDF.

- *At the level of the universal Church*, moving forward requires far more than heeding the often-heard call for the greater internationalization of the CDF with more cardinals from Africa, Asia, and Latin America. This is a woefully inadequate solution. The mimetic power of the culture of the CDF reproduces and entrenches destructive patterns in the exercise of authority that cannot be broken or reformed. The results of the reforms of the CDF after Vatican II can only lead us to this conclusion. The more fundamental, and in fact, more tradition-based question is this: Why can't we leave doctrinal issues to councils and synods? As so many theologians have argued in other contexts, let us return to the practices of communion developed in the first millennium, but now more fully conceived and expanded in light of the theology of the baptismal charisms and the *sensus fidelium* bestowed on all the faithful, and the collaboration of theologians and bishops advanced at Vatican II. Before the formation of the Holy Office, doctrinal disputes were addressed at councils and synods. Following this venerable practice, if there are grave doctrinal problems or concerns, invoke councils or extraordinary synods to address them. But even when this is done, we need to make sure that theologians are allowed to fulfill their vocation by participating as theological advisors and trusted collaborators as happened in an exemplary fashion at Vatican II, and we must continue to find new ways for representatives of the entire people of God to be consulted in matters of faith in preparation for these assemblies. Isn't more harm than good being done by these investigations by the CDF? Has any long-term good been served by these clarifications and notifications?

Chapter 2

Canonical Perspectives on the Ecclesiastical Processes for Investigating Theologians

James A. Coriden

Washington Theological Union

Introduction

We begin with an account of what actually happens when the magisterium takes notice of the work of theologians. Our point of departure is Bradford Hinze's survey included in this volume, "A Decade of Disciplining Theologians." Hinze chronicled a range of "magisterial interventions," the actions taken as a result, and some of the procedures associated with them. They can be summarized in eight categories:

a) Congregation for the Doctrine of the Faith investigations, followed by notifications, observations, declarations, and sometimes severe disciplinary actions; the procedures are those stated in CDF "Regulations for Doctrinal Examination" (June 29, 1997).[1]

b) The doctrinal commissions of episcopal conferences conduct investigations, sometimes pursuant to requests from the CDF and sometimes in response to requests from individual bishops; these

---

[1] Available on the Vatican web site; also published in *Doctrine and Life* 47, no. 8 (1997): 499–506; also in *Origins* 27, no. 13 (1997): 221–24; and in *CLGBI Newsletter* 112 (December 1997): 7–17; hereafter CDF Regs. These regulations are an update of the CDF *ratio agendi* of 1971. Hinze outlines the procedures in "A Decade of Disciplining," above, 9–12.

result in public statements or notifications that point out errors or inadequacies; their procedures are not known.[2]

c) Congregation for Catholic Education or the chancellor of a pontifical university withholds or withdraws the *nihil obstat* or *missio canonica* for faculty appointments in countries with concordats with the Holy See or in pontifical faculties; the procedures are governed by the apostolic constitution *Sapientia Christiana* (April 15, 1979).[3]

d) The diocesan bishop (or the bishops responsible for a regional seminary) or the religious ordinary (when the seminary belongs to a religious community or communities) removes seminary faculty members,[4] e.g., after a pontifical visitation of seminaries; the procedures are not known.

e) The diocesan bishop ("ecclesiastical authority") denies or withdraws the *mandatum docendi* for those teaching theological disciplines in institutions of higher learning;[5] the procedures are in NCCB "Guidelines Concerning the Academic *Mandatum* in Catholic Universities (Canon 812)" (June 15, 2001).[6] These guidelines include the recommended use of NCCB, *Doctrinal Responsibilities* (June 17, 1989).[7]

f) Congregation for the Doctrine of the Faith, directly or through superiors of religious institutes, brings pressure on journals or maga-

---

[2] USCCB published *Procedures for Resolving Conflict* in 2002. It was a republication of the NCCB booklet *On Due Process* issued in 1972 and the procedures of the NCCB *Committee on Conciliation and Arbitration* approved in 1979. The 2002 version is a ninety-one-page booklet; the *On Due Process* section includes the Canon Law Society of America's Report, which contains positive suggestions for resolving conflicts in the "doctrinal area" (16–18).

[3] Published in AAS 71 (1979): 469–521, and in *Origins* 9 (1979): 33ff. The *nihil obstat* is given or denied by the Congregation for Catholic Education; the *mission canonica* is given or withdrawn by the chancellor of the university, unless other provisions have been made. For a CTSA committee report on *Sapientia Christiana* see "Report of the CTSA Committee on Ecclesiastical Academic Legislation," *The Jurist* 40, no. 2 (1980): 435–44.

[4] Canon 253§3, 1983 *Code of Canon Law*.

[5] Canon 812, *CIC*.

[6] *Origins* 31, no. 7 (2001): 128–31. The *mandatum* is given, denied, or withdrawn by the diocesan bishop or someone delegated by him.

[7] NCCB, *Doctrinal Responsibilities: Approaches to Promoting Cooperation and Resolving Misunderstandings between Bishops and Theologians*; hereafter *DR* (Washington, DC: NCCB, 1989); also in *Origins* 19, no. 7 (1989): 99–110, and in *Canon Law Digest* 12, 480–505.

zines, e.g., requires corrective responses to published articles, causes the journal to give advance notice of an article that does not conform to current authoritative Church teaching, and has editors removed; the procedures are not known.

g) Congregation for the Doctrine of the Faith, diocesan bishops, or religious superiors prevent re-publication or sale of books or the destruction of remaining copies; the procedures are not known.

h) Individual diocesan bishops deny the award of an honorary degree or withdraw a speaking invitation in the diocese; the procedures are not known.

Hinze named scores of theologians investigated and censured by the CDF over the span of thirty-five years, and at least ten who were the objects of actions taken by doctrinal commissions of bishops' conferences. He wrote of a few specific actions taken by local bishops, but also noted that it is not unusual for theologians to be disinvited as public speakers in some dioceses.

A Reminder of Our Common Context: Ecclesial Communion

We might begin our reflections by recalling that we are all in this together: theologians, bishops, and all baptized believers. This is a theological conviction (LG 12, 31), but it also reflects a canonical perspective. The Church's canons remind us that we are all members of the Christian faithful, sharers in Christ's own prophetic function, and we are called to exercise the Church's mission in the world (c. 204).[8] We are linked to Christ by the ties of profession of faith, the sacraments, and governance, and thus fully in communion with one another in the Church (c. 205). In other words, we are all on the same team, engaged in a common enterprise, not on opposing sides.

More specifically, in regard to the Church's teaching function, the canons insist that Christ has entrusted the deposit of faith to all of us in the Church, so that, with the assistance of the Holy Spirit, we might protect revealed truth reverently, examine it closely, proclaim it faithfully, and preach the gospel to all peoples (c. 747). Each one of us is bound to seek the truth in matters related to God and the Church, and each one has

---

[8] Canons are paraphrased, not quoted, from the 1983 *Code of Canon Law*, Latin-English Edition (Washington, DC: Canon Law Society of America, 1999).

the duty and right to embrace and observe the truth discovered (c. 748). We are all witnesses of the Gospel message by word and the example of a Christian life, in virtue of our baptism and confirmation (c. 759). We are not strangers or adversaries, but members of the same body, closely related, of common faith and common cause, obliged to show love for one another.[9]

What Is Going on Canonically When the Magisterium Intervenes?

Are the interventions of the CDF, episcopal committees on doctrine, or individual diocesan bishops exercises of their teaching authority (*munus docendi*) or of their governing power (*potestas regiminis*)? Or are these actions simply exercises of the pastoral role (*pastores in ecclesia*) of the pope and bishops (cc. 331 and 375, respectively), which obliges them to nourish and protect the faithful entrusted to them?

DR answers these questions in reference to bishops in its section on "The Rights and Responsibilities of Bishops," in terms of their "pastoral task of authoritative teaching" within a single pastoral office. Bishops are charged to preserve and protect the truths of faith, that is, to transmit the authentic gospel of Christ. In the particular church where he serves, the bishop "is to make the pastoral judgment as to how the faith of the community will be publicly expressed at a given time and place. For that reason, the bishop is called upon to judge whether some opinions endanger or are contrary to faith and the Christian life."[10]

The canons of the *Code* give ample support for the bishop's teaching authority, for example:

- c. 375, all bishops are "teachers of doctrine" and receive the "function of teaching";
- c. 386, the diocesan bishop has the duty to propose and explain the truths of faith, to protect the integrity and unity of the faith;
- c. 754, all bishops are authentic teachers and instructors of the faith for the faithful entrusted to them;
- c. 756, the diocesan bishop is the moderator of the entire ministry of the word in the church entrusted to him;

[9] *DR* opens with a well-balanced statement of what bishops and theologians have in common: "Context and Principles," 3–4.

[10] *DR* 6.

> • c. 823, bishops have the duty and right to be watchful so that no harm is done to the faith or morals of the Christian faithful through writings or other instruments of communication.

I do not disagree with the statements from *DR* quoted above, but I would respond to the above questions about the kind of authority being exercised in these "magisterial interventions" by describing the actions as disciplinary (*potestas regiminis*) while presuming magisterial authority (*munus docendi*). In other words, the actual interventions are directive actions, functions of governing authority, but they are based on the duty "to protect the integrity and unity of the faith that must be believed (*fides credenda*)," c. 386.2. The *fides credenda* here refers to that narrow range of dogmas that are considered necessary for salvation. At the same time, all are exercised within a unitary pastoral office. (After all, the pastoral office is one, and we only *distinguish* it into three *munera* for the purposes of analysis.) So the interventions are exercises of disciplinary oversight of the teaching of others, teaching that affects, actually or potentially, the Christian faithful entrusted to the bishop for pastoral care. The same is true, *mutatis mutandis*, of the papal authority exercised by the CDF.

But of more practical importance than the nature of the authority being exercised is the issue of the *way* that the authority is asserted, and, when there are conflicts or misunderstandings, by what *process* are those differences reconciled. This procedural question brings us to a historical attempt to fashion a fair process for the United States.

The Development of *Doctrinal Responsibilities*

The document approved and issued by the National Conference of Catholic Bishops in 1989 derived from an initiative taken by the CTSA (Catholic Theological Society of America) in 1980, a collaborative effort of the CTSA and the Canon Law Society of America (CLSA) in 1982, and further collaboration between the two societies, individual bishops, and the doctrinal committee of the NCCB.

Widespread concern among theologians in 1979 regarding the recent interventions related to the writings of Edward Schillebeeckx and the book *Human Sexuality: New Directions in American Catholic Thought* (a product of a CTSA committee and edited by its chair, Anthony Kosnik) caused the CTSA president, William Hill, to name a committee to search "for more cooperative and constructive relations between theologians and the Church's teaching authority."[11] The committee described the state of the question and proposed a joint committee with the CLSA to develop a "set of norms to guide the resolution of difficulties which may arise in the relationship between theologians and the magisterium in North America."[12]

The joint committee, chaired by Leo O'Donovan, and consisting of three other theologians and three canonists,[13] was appointed in September 1980. The members authored six background papers on the rights and responsibilities of bishops and theologians, and evaluations of the procedures available to settle misunderstandings or conflicts between them. The committee added a consensus statement, "In Service to the Gospel."

This "Report of the Joint Committee," entitled *Cooperation Between Theologians and the Ecclesiastical Magisterium,* was published in 1982.[14] The committee continued its work, entering into further collaboration with bishops, theologians, and canonists, and formulated the procedural document *DR*. This document was presented to and approved unanimously by the national meetings of both societies in 1983.[15] The document was then submitted to the NCCB Committee on Doctrine, where it was revised and amended. It was subject to a consultation at the Holy See,[16] and then approved overwhelmingly (the vote was 214 to 9) by the body of American bishops in June 1989.

DR is divided into three sections. The first, "The Context of Ecclesial Responsibilities," sketches the active participation that all members of the body of Christ have in the proclamation of the Gospel, and then the particular rights and responsibilities of bishops and of theologians. The second section, "Promoting Cooperation and Informal Dialogue,"

---

[11] "CTSA Committee Report on Cooperation between Theologians and the Church's Teaching Authority," *CTSA Proceedings* 35 (1980): 325.

[12] Ibid., 331.

[13] Namely, John Boyle, Patrick Granfield, Jon Nilson; John Alesandro, Robert Carlson, James Provost.

[14] Edited by Leo O'Donovan, it was issued as a 189-page booklet by the CLSA.

[15] The document as presented to the two societies is found in *CLSA Proceedings* 45 (1983): 261–84. The CLSA minutes report the unanimous votes of both societies; ibid., 328–29.

[16] The concerns of the CDF are reflected in a communication from Archbishop Bovone, the secretary of the congregation, "Development of Text Regarding Relationship between Bishops and Theologians" (Nov. 11, 1988), *Canon Law Digest* 12, 476–78; also in *Origins* 18 (1988): 389–91.

recommends various ways in which bishops and theologians can enhance cooperation in their common service to the Gospel. The third
section is entitled, "A Possibility for Formal Doctrinal Dialogue." It sets
out in detail a suggested procedure to deal with doctrinal disputes between bishops and theologians in dioceses. It is intended to be flexible
and adaptable to local situations and needs. The document makes clear
that its suggested procedures are not Church law, but guidelines that
may be followed when needed.

The process set forth in *DR* was recommended for use in the NCCB
"Guidelines Concerning the Academic *Mandatum* in Catholic Universities (Canon 812)," (June 15, 2001).[17]

DR has not been replaced, remanded, or revoked. It is not well known,
but it may yet prove to be of service. The document's official endorsement by the bishops' conference, that is, by the entire body of bishops
and not only by a committee of the conference, gives it an enhanced
status.

Why Were the Procedures of *Doctrinal Responsibilities* Not More Widely Used?

There is hearsay evidence that part three of this remarkable document,
the procedural portion titled "A Possibility for Formal Doctrinal Dialogue," was employed on a few occasions, but we have not discovered
any written records of its use. It was intended to deal with "differences
of opinion, disagreements, or questions concerning doctrinal matters."[18]
Specifically it was "to deal with doctrinal disputes between bishops and
theologians in dioceses."[19] Why wasn't it employed more often? How is
it that a process so carefully crafted, repeatedly refined, long considered,
vetted at all levels, officially approved by the conference of bishops in
1989 and then re-recommended in 2001, was rarely tried? Were there
few opportunities to employ it? Were bishops or theologians unwilling
to enter into the dialogue process? Was it simply forgotten? Or did it
miss the mark?

Perhaps the procedure, "Formal Doctrinal Dialogue," is not entirely
appropriate for use in the actual "disputes." Maybe it is *too* formal. The

---

[17] *Origins* 31, no. 7 (2001): 128–31.
[18] *DR* 14.
[19] *DR* 1.

description of its several stages takes up seven pages.[20] It may appear too refined, too complex for use in small or middle-sized dioceses (although it explicitly invited local adaptation[21]). Perhaps this "structured pattern for doctrinal discussion" looks more like a doctoral dissertation defense than a constructive conversation between two Christian colleagues. Maybe some scaled down and simpler procedures are called for.

The following "contrast experience" with two other quite different structural innovations may provide a parallel example. Among the new organs of consultation introduced by the 1983 *Code of Canon Law* were diocesan pastoral councils (cc. 511–15) and parish pastoral councils (c. 536). Both of these consultative structures were intended to elicit the participation and views of the Christian faithful. Generally speaking, the former are not working, and the latter represent a relative success. There are many exceptions to this sweeping judgment, but the one (parish pastoral councils) seems to "fit," and the other (diocesan pastoral councils) does not. Perhaps the "procedures for formal doctrinal dialogue" are something like diocesan pastoral councils: they are not quite suited to their purposes. Perhaps we need to look for another process.

What Is the Role of the Doctrinal Committee of the Bishops' Conference?

Bradford Hinze's survey described and critiqued the procedures of the CDF.[22] As a complement to that, it might serve our purposes here briefly to reflect on the role and authority of the doctrinal committees of episcopal conferences.[23]

These committees, or "commissions" as the CDF refers to them, represent a big step down from the CDF in terms of their authority and a sort of an intermediary agency between the CDF and the individual diocesan bishop. But just as the CDF must always be seen within the scope of papal authority, the doctrinal committee must always be envisioned within

---

[20] *DR* 16–24.

[21] *DR* 15.

[22] Hinze, "A Decade of Disciplining"; see above, 4–20, 23–25, 28–29, 33–37.

[23] The bishop members of the USCCB committee on doctrine (who normally serve for a term of three years), the consultants, and staff are listed in *The Official Catholic Directory* published annually by P. J. Kenedy & Sons, New Providence, NJ. Updated information may be found on the USCCB's website at http://www.usccb.org/doctrine/.

the authority of the bishops' conference. After all, it is no more and no less than a committee of the conference. "Doctrinal commissions are responsible to and act by the mandate of the Episcopal conferences."[24]

First, then, one must be aware of the authority of episcopal conferences, and how that authority was narrowly circumscribed in the canonical revision process. Conferences derived directly and quite explicitly from the Vatican II "Decree on the Pastoral Office of Bishops in the Church."[25] They were a structure already familiar to the bishops of Europe and America, having arisen more or less spontaneously over the preceding hundred years. But what little authority the conferences exercised was resented both "from above and below," that is, both by the Roman Curia which saw them as a threat to papal power (and possibly to the unity of the Church), and by individual bishops who viewed them as limiting their authority in their dioceses. Hence, the rule-making power of conferences, that is, their legislative authority, was severely limited (see c. 455 for the detailed restrictions).[26]

Second, the teaching authority of conferences, clearly acknowledged in the *Code* (c. 753: "bishops . . . joined together in conferences . . . are authentic teachers and instructors of the faith for the Christian faithful entrusted to their care"), was greatly restricted by the 1998 apostolic letter of John Paul II on the "Theological and Juridical Nature of Episcopal Conferences."[27] Individual bishops are teachers of the faith only to the faithful of their own diocese, the letter stated, unless they are acting in concert with the entire college of bishops worldwide. Doctrinal declara-

[24] Letter from the CDF (signed by Joseph Cardinal Ratzinger) to the presidents of Episcopal Conferences on the constitution and functioning of doctrinal commissions (Nov. 25, 1990; Prot. N. 3317/69), n. 3.

[25] *Christus Dominus* (Oct. 28, 1965), chapter 3, "The Cooperation of Bishops for the Common Good of a Number of Churches."

[26] For the canons on episcopal conferences and excellent references, see John Johnson, "Conferences of Bishops," *New Commentary on the Code of Canon Law*, ed. John Beal et al. (New York: Paulist Press, 2000), 588–602. The CTSA drew attention to the diminished authority of episcopal conferences in its statement on the twenty-fifth anniversary of the closing of the Second Vatican Council, "Do Not Extinguish the Spirit" (Dec. 13, 1990), *Origins* 20, no. 29 (1990): 463–67, n. 16.

[27] *Apostolos Suos* (May 21, 1998); AAS 90 (1998): 641–58; *Origins* 28, no. 9 (1998): 152–58. On the extent of these restrictions, cf. Thomas Green, "The Authority of Episcopal Conferences: Some Normative and Doctrinal Considerations," with its extensive bibliography, *CLSA Proceedings* 51 (1989): 123–36. For the background to this apostolic letter see *Episcopal Conferences: Historical, Canonical, and Theological Studies*, ed. Thomas Reese (Washington, DC: Georgetown University Press, 1989).

tions of the conference constitute "authentic magisterium" only if they are approved unanimously or receive the subsequent approval of the Apostolic See.[28] These two conditions are fulfilled very rarely.

To sum up, episcopal conferences are valuable structures for communications, coordination, planning, and policy making among the bishops of a nation,[29] but in the present canonical discipline of the Church, they are accorded very slight juridical or doctrinal authority. It is within this context that their doctrinal committees must be viewed.

The CDF issued an instruction in 1967 that urged episcopal conferences to establish doctrinal commissions as soon as possible "to keep an eye on published writings, encourage religious knowledge worthy of the name, and render assistance to the bishops in the evaluation of books."[30] The congregation expressed its desire that the bishops inform it of "those things which they believe have notable importance regarding the teaching of faith and morals," and to suggest remedies to eradicate errors.[31] The doctrinal commissions are to work to achieve such communications. The congregation also requested that bishops in whose territories publishing houses exist send it "publications which are foreseen to have a broad notable influence, for good or bad."[32]

In 1968 the CDF sent a letter, over the signature of Cardinal Seper, its prefect, to the presidents of episcopal conferences explaining its 1967 instruction in greater detail and suggesting ways in which doctrinal commissions could function better.[33] Among those suggestions, the first was that the commissions act positively to set forth current doctrine. The letter also stated that it is

> necessary that the scientific labor itself of theologians be spent on the proclamation, the illumination, the deeper understanding, and, finally, the safeguarding of revealed truth. Certainly these endeavors will achieve the desired effect if both the individual bishops and the doctrinal commission cultivate mutual relationships in a spirit

[28] Ibid., Complementary Norms, art. 1.

[29] It is important to remember that conferences represent a coming together of *bishops*, not a council of the *churches* of a country (cc. 447 and 439.1).

[30] "Instruction Regarding Establishment of Doctrinal Commissions" (Feb. 27, 1967); *Canon Law Digest* 6, 816.

[31] Ibid.

[32] Ibid., 817.

[33] "Greater Activity by Doctrinal Commissions" (July 19, 1968), *Canon Law Digest* 10, 207.

of collaboration with theologians, professors in universities and seminaries, and other learned men [*sic*] and, at appropriate times, come together.[34]

Another suggestion was that the commissions were to assist bishops in their task of vigilance, lest harm to correct doctrine find its way into publications, and they might perform the task of prior censorship of books for bishops. The letter reminded the conferences that the principle of subsidiarity requires that matters that do not go outside the territorial limits of the conference should be handled by the conference itself and not sent to the congregation. However, the congregation asked that the presidents of the commissions send the CDF a report of its activities at least once a year, and include matters that should be treated by the Holy See. The letter also suggested that it would be useful for the commissions to prepare private notes (*notas reservatas*) for the bishops on questions of importance and current opinions.[35]

The CDF issued another circular letter to the presidents of episcopal conferences in 1990,[36] reflecting the experiences of the congregation and the doctrinal commissions since 1968, and clarifying the structure and functions of the commissions. They are described as consultative bodies instituted to aid the conference itself and individual bishops in their solicitude for the teaching of the faith (n. 3). The commissions are not to make public statements in the name of the conference unless explicitly authorized to do so (n. 4). The commissions are to promote the work of theology, and they should foster good mutual relations with theologians and teachers in universities and seminaries (n. 8). The commissions are to provide assistance to individual bishops in monitoring and evaluating theological works published in their territories, but the task of vigilance must remain properly that of the bishop (n. 9). The letter notes that "the Holy See can always intervene and normally does so when the impact of some published work is felt beyond the area of a particular Episcopal Conference" (n. 10).[37]

---

[34] Ibid.

[35] Ibid., 208.

[36] *Congregatio pro Doctrina Fidei*, November 25, 1990, Prot. No. 3317/69, signed by Joseph Ratzinger, prefect, and Alberto Bovone, secretary.

[37] This jurisdictional principle was stated even more sharply in the 1997 CDF Regs.:

To this end (that the faith and morals of the members of the faithful not suffer harm), they (bishops, individually or gathered in Episcopal Conferences)

The doctrinal commissions are to cooperate with other commissions of the conference, specifically, in the fields of education, catechetics, liturgy, and ecumenism, and those commissions should not publish important documents without first hearing the judgment of the doctrinal commission (n. 11). Communications between the commissions and the congregation should increase, and an annual report to the CDF on doctrinal difficulties would be helpful (n. 14).

This 1990 circular letter and the CDF's own "Regulations" of 1997 come as close as anything to "marching orders" for the doctrinal commissions of episcopal conferences.[38] The USCCB doctrinal committee has no other published procedures. The CDF sometimes asks the committee to conduct or pursue investigations on its behalf, in effect deputizing the American committee to do its work. But most of the committee's work, besides consulting with and advising the conference and its other committees, involves assisting individual bishops who seek its help regarding publications that they find questionable.

What Canonical Prerogatives and Processes Are Available for These Interventions?

A preliminary answer to this question is indicated in the list of interventions and associated procedures above in the Introduction to this

---

can also be served by Doctrinal Commissions, institutionalized consultative bodies which assist Episcopal Conferences and individual Bishops in their solicitude for the doctrine of faith. The principle remains, however, that the Holy See can always intervene and, as a rule, does so when the influence of a publication exceeds the boundaries of an individual Episcopal Conference, or when the danger to faith is particularly grave. (Art. 2, in *Origins* 27, no. 13, 221)

All mention of subsidiarity, explicit in the 1968 letter, has been removed. The Holy See can always intervene.

[38] To these two official documents should be added the published results of a 1999 meeting between representatives of the CDF (including its prefect, Joseph Ratzinger, and its secretary, Tarcisio Bertone) and doctrinal commissions from North America and Oceania. It was published by the USCC as *Proclaiming the Truth of Jesus Christ: Papers from the Vallombrosa Meeting* (Washington, DC: USCC, 2000). Though not authoritative, the booklet contains a set of "concrete proposals" for collaboration between the CDF and doctrinal commissions which are presumably to give guidance to the commissions (7–10). The proposals are said to have "emerged from the meeting," but they bear a remarkable resemblance to the contents of the 1990 circular letter from the CDF.

chapter. For several categories, we do not know what, if any, procedural steps were taken before decisions were made and executed. I strongly suspect that many interventions were made informally, for instance, with a phone call, a private conversation, a personal letter, or a remark in executive session of a committee or board of trustees. For other categories of interventions in the above list, the canonical sources for the designated procedures are indicated.

It might help to consider those "special processes" (like the CDF Regs. and the NCCB Guidelines for the *mandatum*) against the background of the authoritative context of the 1983 *Code of Canon Law*: The *Code* contains the basic set of rules for the Western or Latin-Rite Catholic Church. The *Code* includes statements of rights related to theological activity as well as several different procedural paradigms. The rights are of fundamental importance, and the procedures may provide parallels or at least ideas for application in our theological arena.

Assertions of Rights

The first four on this list are among the "Obligations and Rights of All the Christian Faithful," (cc. 208–23), at the outset of book 2, "The People of God":

1) The Christian faithful have the right and sometimes the duty, in keeping with the knowledge and competence which they possess, to manifest to the bishops their opinions on matters pertaining to the good of the Church, and they have the right to make their opinions known to the rest of the Christian faithful, with due regard for the integrity of faith and morals (c. 212.3).

2) Those engaged in the sacred disciplines have a just freedom of inquiry and of prudent expression of their opinions (c. 218).

3) Everyone has a right to his or her good name (c. 220).

4) The faithful can vindicate and defend their rights in the Church in a competent ecclesiastical forum according to the norms of canon law, and they may not be punished with canonical penalties except according to law (c. 221).

5) Among the duties and rights of diocesan bishops (cc. 381–402) are these, that they are to protect the integrity and unity of the faith (*credenda*, those things which must be believed), while acknowledging a just freedom in further investigating truths of faith (c. 386.2).

Canonical Procedures for Various Kinds of Actions

1) Appointment and removal of seminary teachers by the bishop (c. 253): no specific procedure is suggested in the *Code*, but the general rule when issuing any singular decree (for example, a letter that contains a decision) is that "the authority is to seek out the necessary information and proofs . . . and to hear those whose rights can be injured" (c. 50).

2) Appointment and removal of college and university professors: the procedures defined in the statutes of the institution are to be observed (c. 810).

3) Permission to publish books or their subsequent approval (cc. 822–32): the canons name the bishop's duty and right to be watchful lest harm come to the faithful, and to condemn writings which cause such damage (c. 832.1), the censor's criterion of judgment, namely "to consider only the doctrine of the Church concerning faith and morals as it is proposed by the ecclesiastical magisterium" (c. 830.2), and the duty to communicate reasons to the author in the event of non-approval (c. 830.3).[39]

4) Penal process to impose a penalty for the commission of a canonical crime (cc. 1717–28): the penal process calls for a preliminary investigation (c. 1717), followed by a judicial or administrative procedure with notification of the accused, revelation of the evidence, opportunity for self-defense, assistance of counsel, and right of appeal (cc. 1718–28). Punishable offenders include, for example:

a) Those who obstinately reject doctrines proposed definitively, or even non-definitively, by the magisterium may be punished with a "just penalty," but only if they refuse to retract their position after being admonished by Church authority (cc. 1371, 750.2, 752).

b) Apostates, heretics, and schismatics (defined in c. 751) are guilty of crimes that call for the *latae sententiae*, that is, automatic, excommunication of the offender (c. 1364), but the formal procedures just mentioned are required to *declare* the penalty, i.e., to make it publicly effective, or to add further penalties.

---

[39] See, in addition, USCCB Committee on Doctrine, *The Permission to Publish: A Resource for Diocesan and Eparchal Bishops on the Approvals Needed to Publish Various Kinds of Written Works* (Washington, DC: USCCB, 2004).

5) Judicial procedure for the pursuit or vindication of rights or the imposition or declaration of penalties (cc. 1400–1670): this is the formal tribunal process involving canonical judges that, in practice, is used almost exclusively for determining the validity or nullity of marriages. This is a written procedure, but there is also an "oral contentious process" (cc. 1656–70; cannot be used in marriage cases, c. 1690) that should not be overlooked when considering various paradigms.

6) Administrative recourse against decrees that aggrieve a person (cc. 1732–39): this process offers the possibility of reconsideration and revocation of a harmful decision, for instance, termination of employment; it also offers the possibility of conciliation or mediation,[40] or, finally, recourse to the hierarchical superior of the one who issued the decree.

7) Procedures for the removal or transfer of pastors (cc. 1740–52): these two processes were introduced with the 1983 *Code* and offer relatively simple and balanced steps to be taken when a pastor of a parish is not willing to resign or transfer to another parish when the bishop asks him to. The procedures provide a model for peer involvement in the decision-making that could be used by analogy in theological disputes.[41]

8) Procedures for the denial or withdrawal of the *mandatum* to teach theological disciplines in a college or university (c. 812): these recommended procedures, called "guidelines," were approved (by voice vote) by the conference of American bishops on June 15, 2001.[42] While they are suggested rather than obligatory, they are part of the canonical apparatus related to the *mandatum* from "competent ecclesiastical authority" to teach theology stipulated in canon 812 of the *Code* and by the 1990 apostolic constitution on Catholic higher education, *Ex Corde Ecclesiae*.[43]

---

[40] Alternative dispute resolution procedures such as mediation, conciliation, and arbitration are also recommended elsewhere in the *Code*: cf. cc. 1446 and 1713.

[41] For an evaluation of these canonical procedures and their possible accommodation to theological investigations, see James Provost, "Canonical Evaluation of Current Procedures," *Cooperation between Theologians and the Ecclesiastical Magisterium*, 144–74.

[42] *Origins* 31, no. 7 (2001): 128–31.

[43] *Origins* 20, no. 17 (1990): 265–76.

When a bishop contemplates denying or withdrawing the *mandatum* the procedures call for an initial informal discussion between the bishop and theologian, giving reasons and sources, and allowing all appropriate responses. If the decision is made to withhold or withdraw the *mandatum*, reasons must be stated in writing, and opportunity given for recourse. Both parties should have competent theological and canonical counsel. *DR* should be followed for the resolution of disputes, but the formal canonical process of "Recourse Against Administrative Decrees" (cc. 1732–39) is also to be available.[44]

What Should We Want by Way of Fair Processes?

Patrick Granfield concluded his study on "Theological Evaluation of Current Procedures" (in the 1982 CLSA/CTSA Committee Report *Cooperation between Theologians and the Ecclesiastical Magisterium*) with an insistence on procedural rights. The examination of a theologian's writings and public utterances is a serious matter, and at every level of formal investigation certain rights should be guaranteed. He listed these procedural rights that "seem reasonable if a procedure is to be fair and not arbitrary or overly secretive":

- the right to know the charges;
- the right to know one's accusers;
- the right of confidentiality;
- the right to be informed of any proposed action which may prejudicially affect one's rights;
- the right to respond to the charges in writing and in person;
- the right to a counsel of one's choosing;
- the right to call witnesses;

---

[44] These provisions are in "Guidelines," nos. 4–6, pages 129–30. They provide, at least by analogy, an appropriate framework for investigations of theologians for other reasons than the denial or withdrawal of the *mandatum*.

It must be noted that these guidelines were crafted and modified in dialogue with the CTSA: see Daniel Finn, "Theologian Addresses the Draft Guidelines for the *Mandatum*," *Origins* 30, no. 27 (2000): 129–30, a talk delivered to the body of bishops on November 15, 2000. Finn was the chair of the CTSA committee on the *mandatum* and a consultant to Archbishop Daniel Pilarczyk's NCCB committee on the *mandatum*.

- the right to have access to all pertinent documentation;
- the right to a speedy resolution of the case; and
- the right to appeal.[45]

The rights are based on the dignity of the human person, Granfield wrote. They set forth some goals or parameters of fair play from the perspective of Anglo-American law. Granfield also stressed the value of subsidiarity: doctrinal conflicts should, if possible, be resolved at the local level and only if necessary referred to a higher body.[46]

James Provost, in his "Canonical Evaluation of Current Procedures" (as part of the same *Cooperation* Report), after reviewing eleven different kinds of procedures, drew up a grid of "basic elements of procedure" against which to measure the appropriateness and adequacy of processes:

- the nature of the procedure, for instance, is it to determine the fitness of a person for office, to seek the truth or orthodoxy of a writing, or to resolve a dispute?
- who can initiate the case? Who has standing? For example, may only office-holders bring claims, only aggrieved parties, or also interested parties?
- is there probable cause, does an initial investigation reveal adequate grounds and lead to a determination to proceed?
- emergency procedures for urgent cases; scandal, special gravity, public harm, but still retaining protection of rights;
- ordinary procedures, which include three basic elements: identifying the issues, investigating the facts, and resolving the case;
- review or appeal.[47]

Provost added a set of four "safeguards" or elements within procedures to assure fair treatment and respect for the rights of all concerned:

- right to counsel, usually of one's own choosing;
- identity of one's accusers;

---

[45] "Theological Evaluation of Current Procedures," *Cooperation between Theologians and the Ecclesiastical Magisterium*, 141.

[46] Ibid. The CDF embraced the principle of subsidiarity in its 1968 letter on doctrinal commissions. *Canon Law Digest* 10, 207, n. 3.

[47] "Canonical Evaluation of Current Procedures," *Cooperation*, 158–66.

• access to the record, opportunity to review it;

• confidentiality and good name, protection of reputation.[48]

Both the CLSA/CTSA joint study, *Cooperation Between Theologians and the Ecclesiastical Magisterium*, and NCCB's *Doctrinal Responsibilities*, which was based on that study, emphasize the importance of a climate of cooperation, of conversation and collaboration within which misunderstandings or conflicts can be successfully resolved. Also both documents give special attention to bishops' need to "respect the gifts which the Holy Spirit imparts to various members of the Church."[49]

These sets of observations, both theological and canonical, trace some parameters within which to fashion structures beforehand for dialogue and dispute resolution for use if and when a theological disagreement occurs.

Conclusion

Bradford Hinze concluded his survey of hierarchical interventions with a set of "lamentations," that is, frustrations and procedural failures that theologians have voiced in reaction to the interventions. "Lamentations offer a source of wisdom, renewal, and reform in the church. They are a privileged site for hearing the Spirit of God who groans in the human heart and the suffering world when something new is struggling into existence and when the Spirit is being stifled."[50]

Most of these laments were occasioned by the policies and actions of the CDF, but some are reflected in the interventions of the episcopal conference committees on doctrine and of individual diocesan bishops.

As a practical matter, what should the Catholic theological community *do* when confronted with these lamentations? One response might be to restate some of them more formally as procedural shortcomings that

---

[48] Ibid., 167–69.

[49] *DR* 6, and *Cooperation*, 180.

[50] See Hinze, "A Decade of Disciplining," above, 30–37, at 32. We can summarize his laments as follows: (1) anonymous accusers and critics; (2) secrecy of investigations; (3) unfair interpretations; (4) contested doctrines frozen in time; (5) same persons serving as investigators, prosecutors and judges; (6) failure to communicate in a timely fashion; (7) interrogation masked as dialogue; (8) defamation of character; (9) failure to trust the community of theologians and the people of God; and (10) a culture of surveillance, policing, control and intimidation.

should be remedied or at least mitigated.[51] Such a brief could be made in the form of an invitation to the CDF to dialogue about its "function of promoting and safeguarding doctrine on faith and morals throughout the Catholic world."[52] More up-to-date and fairer procedures would enhance the congregation's own function as well as afford greater justice to theologians.

What needs to be done at local or national levels? I think that it is time to initiate another joint committee (this time all three societies: CTSA/CLSA/CTS [College Theology Society]) to do the following:

a) re-examine *DR*, suggest modifications, and promote its use;[53] craft one or two simpler, more streamlined forms of doctrinal dialogue and dispute resolution;

b) study the role of the USCCB in doctrinal matters and suggest appropriate procedures for its investigations and assistance to bishops;[54] models exist in the *Code* procedures mentioned above, in

---

[51] See Ladislas Örsy, "Are Church Investigation Procedures Really Just," *Doctrine and Life* 48 (1998): 453–66. Paul Collins, *The Modern Inquisition: Seven Prominent Catholics and Their Struggles with the Vatican* (Woodstock, NY: Overlook Press, 2002), 43, summarizes Örsy's arguments. The "Canonical Observations on the New Regulations of the Congregation for the Doctrine of the Faith," of Velasio De Paolis, and the "Comment," of Gordon Read [*CLSGBI Newsletter* 112 (December 1997): 26–35, 18–25], should be weighed in such an effort.

[52] John Paul II, apostolic constitution, *Pastor Bonus* (June 28, 1988), art. 48. Published as an appendix to the CLSA, 1999, edition of the *Code of Canon Law*.

[53] This task of reworking procedures for examining and resolving doctrinal issues between bishops and theologians has special urgency in view of the 1997 CDF Regs., article 7, which, at the conclusion of the "Office Study" (the "in house" first phase of an inquiry) asserts that the *Congresso* "can entrust the case directly to the author's ordinary and, through him, bring the doctrinal problem presented in the text to the author's attention. In such a case, the ordinary is invited to deepen the study of the question and to ask the author to provide the needed clarification for submission to the judgment of the Congregation." The bishop or religious superior should have at hand a simple, suitable, and sensible process for complying with such a request.

For precedents, cf. the procedures of the German and Australian bishops' conferences cited in Hinze, "A Decade of Disciplining," above, 6, notes 5 and 7, as well as the NCCB procedures related to the denial of the *mandatum* referenced above.

[54] Some parameters for the work of doctrinal commissions are articulated in the CDF circular letter of November 25, 1990, and repeated in Adriano Garuti, "Collaboration between the Congregation for the Doctrine of the Faith and Doctrinal Commissions of Episcopal Conferences," USCC, *Proclaiming the Truth of Jesus Christ*, 53–59. Also note

the NCCB guidelines related to the *mandatum*, in the processes recommended in *DR*, and in the USCCB *Procedures for Resolving Conflict* of 2002 (see note 2 above);[55]

c) review the CDF "Regulations" and make recommendations for their improvement.

Finally, here are four challenges to the American/Canadian Catholic theological community to take action:

1) Continue to do whatever we can to restore and promote a climate of dialogue and cooperation between bishops and theologians (with full acknowledgement of what the CTSA leadership is already doing).

2) Engage in the following exercise of creative imagination: we recognize that the roles of theologians and bishops within the community of faith are both necessary and distinct—imagine reversing the two roles. How would we go about investigating or intervening in relation to a theologian, if the bishop's responsibility was our own?

3) Explore how to involve effectively the three authorities (the *sensus fidelium*, theologians, bishops)[56] in the exercise of the one teaching office. How can the Church hear all three voices in our conversations, consultations, and procedures?

4) Attend to the Holy Spirit, always and everywhere.

---

the set of "concrete proposals" on pages 7–10. In addition, cf. the USCCB "Committee on Doctrine Protocol" (August 19, 2011), below, 60–62.

[55] A recent book of canonical studies, *Parola di Dio e missione della Chiesa*, ed. Davide Cito and Fernando Puig (Milan: Guiffrè, 2009), offers some further background for this project, especially the chapter on the CDF by Brian Ferme.

[56] Cf. the structure of the teaching office so ably stated by Ormond Rush in his chapter in this volume and in his recent book, *The Eyes of Faith: The Sense of the Faithful and the Church's Reception of Revelation* (Washington, DC: Catholic University of America Press, 2009), 193–207, 241–91.

Appendix

Draft 19 August 2011

Committee on Doctrine Protocol (2011)

The Committee on Doctrine is a consultative body that serves the Bishops of the USCCB, both individually and collectively, in the promotion and defense of the Catholic faith. The Committee collaborates with other USCCB Committees in promoting the universal Magisterium of the Church and, when requested, it assists local Bishops in the exercise of their teaching ministry within the particular churches.

At times the Committee, in keeping with its approved mandate, reviews the published writings of individuals or groups to determine their conformity to the Church's authentic teaching on faith or morals, especially when these writings are widely circulated within Catholic academic and/or catechetical settings. This could be in response to a request for assistance from a bishop or USCCB committee or in response to a proposal for Committee action by one of its members.

The following Protocol was developed by the Committee to assist it in responding both to requests for assistance from outside and to proposals for action from inside the Committee.

I. Preliminary Analysis

A consideration of the totality of facts and circumstances related to a request for assistance or proposal for action is essential for determining whether Committee action is recommended. To aid the Committee in making this determination, following receipt of a request or proposal, the Executive Director will prepare for the Chairman a written preliminary analysis that takes into account the following considerations:

A. The origin of the request for assistance or proposal for action.

B. The nature and gravity of the doctrinal issues in question.

C. The Committee's competence to take action.

D. The intended audience of the writing or statement.

E. The genre of the writing or statement.

F. The dissemination of the writing or statement.

G. The pastoral implications of the writing or statement.

H. Prior attempts by ecclesiastical authority to address the problem.

I. Published scholarly reviews of the writing or statement.

The results of the preliminary analysis are to be reported by the Chairman to the Committee at its next available meeting.

II. Scholarly Review

On the basis of the preliminary analysis, the Committee may determine that a more thorough evaluation of the writing or statement is warranted. Ideally, two or more experts should be assigned to prepare written evaluations of the writing or statement. The assignment of experts is ordinarily made by the Executive Director, in consultation with the Committee Chairman. The written evaluations of the experts should address: 1) the positive aspects of the writing or statement; 2) areas where differences of opinion may legitimately exist; and 3) instances where the writing or statement departs from the Church's teaching on faith and morals, e.g., through error and/or ambiguity. The *Catechism of the Catholic Church* is to provide an important and reliable guide for the written evaluations. Upon their completion, the evaluations are then submitted to the Committee for deliberation.

III. Options for Response

As a result of its review of the written evaluations, the Committee may determine that no further action is needed on the international, national, or local levels. If, however, the Committee determines that some action is warranted, one or more of the following options may form a suitable response:

A. The Committee may offer its own evaluation, or an evaluation prepared by the Secretariat of Doctrine staff, to the proper Diocesan Bishop for the issuance of a statement in the Bishop's own name. The Committee may also refer the Bishop to a theologian particularly expert in the matter who may be contacted directly. The task of monitoring and evaluating theological works belongs properly to the Diocesan Bishop.

B. The Committee may refer the matter to the competence of the Congregation for the Doctrine of the Faith, due to the gravity of the teachings in question, or when the impact of the writing or statement clearly extends beyond the territorial boundaries of the USCCB.

C. The Committee may refer the matter to the competence of another USCCB Committee.

D. The Committee may take action itself in one or more of the following ways:

   1. The Committee may engage the author or representative in a constructive dialogue resulting in the publication of the requisite clarifications and/or corrections.

   2. The Committee may encourage an individual scholar, or group of scholars, to publish a critique of the writing or statement in a journal or magazine, in their own name(s). The Committee may offer to review the critique of the scholar(s) prior to publication.

   3. The Committee may disseminate a published scholarly review of the writing or statement, e.g., by distributing it to the Bishops, providing a bibliography on the Committee's website, etc.

   4. The Committee may authorize for publication a critique of the writing or statement in the name of the Executive Director, with the prior approval of the USCCB General Secretary, or a critique published in the name of one or more consultants to the Committee.

   5. The Committee may designate the Chairman to publish a critique of the writing or statement in a journal or magazine in his own name, with the prior authorization of the USCCB President.

   6. The Committee may issue a statement in its own name. Because the publication of a statement by a USCCB committee is an extraordinary action, authorization by the Administrative Committee is needed for its publication. If circumstances appear to require more immediate action, a committee statement may be published with the authorization of the Executive Committee or the USCCB President.

Prior to the submission of the Committee's statement to the Administrative Committee, the Executive Committee, or USCCB President for authorization, the author or representative of the writing in question may be invited to respond to the Committee's observations in writing. The Committee on Doctrine, however, reserves the right to seek authorization to publish its statements without the prior consultation with the author or representative, if it judges that intervention is needed for the pastoral guidance of the Catholic faithful.

In any event, before authorization is sought for a Committee on Doctrine statement, Secretariat of Doctrine staff is encouraged to collaborate with other appropriate USCCB Committees, and the USCCB Communications Offices, to develop a comprehensive communications strategy for the promotion and distribution of the Committee statement.

Finally, the author's or representative's Ordinary or competent major superior should be duly notified of the actions being undertaken by the Committee. The Committee's actions, moreover, ought always to be conducted with a respect for the natural rights to a good reputation and to the lawful freedom of inquiry (Cf. *Code of Canon Law*, cc. 218, 220).

Sources Consulted

Congregation for the Doctrine of the Faith, Circular Letter on Doctrinal Commissions, November 25, 1990.

———, Instruction on the Ecclesial Vocation of the Theologian, May 24, 1990.

———, Regulations for Doctrinal Examination, June 29, 1997.

Congregation for the Doctrine of the Faith and the Doctrinal Commissions from North America and Oceania, *Proclaiming the Truth of Jesus Christ: Papers from the Vallombrosa Meeting*, 2000.

National Conference of Catholic Bishops, *Doctrinal Responsibilities: Approaches to Promoting Cooperation and Resolving Misunderstandings between Bishops and Theologians*, 1989.

———, *The Teaching Ministry of the Diocesan Bishop*, 1992.

Pope John Paul II, Apostolic Letter *Motu Proprio, Apostolos suos*, May 21, 1998.

United States Conference of Catholic Bishops, Regulations Regarding USCCB Statements and Publications, 2010.

———, Strategic Plan 2008–2011.

Chapter 3

Gracious Resistance
Religious Women Charting an Ecclesial Path

Colleen Mary Mallon, OP

Aquinas Institute of Theology

From the Church's earliest times there were women and men who set out to follow Christ more freely and to imitate him more closely by practicing the evangelical counsels. In their different ways they led lives dedicated to God. Many of them, under the inspiration of the holy Spirit, became hermits or founded religious families, which the church, by virtue of its authority, gladly accepted and approved. Thus, in keeping with the divine purpose, a wonderful variety of religious communities came into existence. This has helped considerably to equip the church for every good work (see 2 Tim 3:17) and for ministry aimed at building up the body of Christ (see Eph 4:12).[1]

With these opening words of *Perfectae Caritatis*, the magisterium set before the Church and the world at Vatican II its desire to realize the renewal "of the life and discipline of religious orders" so that "the church today may derive greater benefit from the outstanding worth of a life consecrated by the profession of the counsels and from the vital function which it performs" (*Perfectae Caritatis* 1). Almost fifty years later, the magisterium, represented by two separate curial offices, the Congregation for Institutes of Consecrated Life and Societies of Apostolic Life (CICLSAL) and the Congregation for the Doctrine of the Faith (CDF), initiated official inquiries into the state of renewal among women religious of the

---

[1] Vatican Council II, "Decree on the Up-to-Date Renewal of Religious Life," *Perfectae Caritatis* (hereafter PC), in *Vatican Council II: The Basic Sixteen Documents*, ed. Austin Flannery, OP (Northport, NY: Costello, 1996), n. 1.

United States and the theological fidelity of the Leadership Conference of Women Religious (LCWR).[2] What directions are women religious in the United States taking that would create such curial concern? Moreover, what new ways are being forged in light of such official scrutiny?

Considering just these questions alone is a challenge. We all recognize a certain grassroots ecclesial wisdom that is often invoked when magisterial feathers are ruffled: ignore it politely and it will go away. (I'm told it is a time-honored Italian, even Continental, strategy.) However, I do not think it is possible to avoid what these events expose about the state of our ecclesial communion, the challenges and opportunities that are being afforded. I use the future perfect form of the verb because I believe it cannot be emphasized enough that we continue to be in the midst of the larger ecclesial work of receiving the Second Vatican Council. *And* we are doing this during a time of profound external challenge while confronting threats to our distinctiveness as a community of faith. The tensions and the concerns that birth these challenges/opportunities are real. The particularity of our tradition, our truth claims about the Living God manifested in the dual missions of Christ and the Spirit, and the mission of the Christian community, face unprecedented risk in a market-driven, commodifying, global world. We can hardly come to consciousness about the seductions working on our sensibilities. Recognizing the divorce between ecclesial meanings and praxes so wisely limned by Vincent Miller is only half the battle.[3] Learning to journey together as a people of faith in a globalized world is our task. We must become that space in the world where the difference Jesus continues to make is experienced and embraced.

This essay is an ecclesiological reflection on the experience of the visitation of U.S. women religious and the investigation of the LCWR. As an ecclesiological reflection, I am most interested in teasing out from the particularity of experience points of challenge and growth for the whole People of God. If we are still receiving the Second Vatican Council, then "the joys and hopes, the grief and anguish" that we experience together as a community of faith must also be a *locus theologicus* so that we might hear the Gospel, together, anew. Following a brief overview of the dual Vatican inquiries, this paper explores three interrelated concerns that I

---

[2] LCWR represents approximately 95% of women's religious institutes in the United States.

[3] Vincent Miller, *Consuming Religion: Christian Faith and Practice in a Consumer Culture* (New York, NY: Continuum, 2005).

contend are significant points of departure for further ecclesiological reflection and development: (1) the ongoing reception of the renewal of religious life within the Church; (2) the implications of this reception of renewal for emerging ecclesial ministries; and (3) the gift and task of *being ecclesial* for a global world.

This is not a defensive lament for perceived or real injustices perpetrated on American women religious by the magisterium. We who have embraced the evangelical counsels for the sake of the reign of God have long understood that we walk "a road less travelled" and that our lifestyles will generate consternation both *ad extra* and *ad intra*. The lives of our founders attest to as much. The question that has been raised is whether our walk is an ecclesial walk, with all the grace and struggle that comes with ecclesial belonging. This is a question worthy of our exploration.

A Tale of Two Inquiries: A Visitation and An Investigation

A Visitation

On December 22, 2008, Cardinal Franc Rodé, Prefect for the Congregation for Institutes of Consecrated Life and Societies of Apostolic Life (CICLSAL), initiated a three-year apostolic visitation of institutes of women religious in the United States, appointing Mother Mary Clare Millea, Superior General of the Apostles of the Sacred Heart of Jesus, as the official Apostolic Visitator.[4] In a subsequent letter to leaders of U.S. congregations and institutes, Cardinal Rodé outlined a three phase visitation process to culminate in the Apostolic Visitator's final confidential report made to the CICLSAL.[5] The three phase visitation, purposed to "look into the quality of the life of apostolic Congregations of women religious" in the U.S., would include dialogue with major superiors, extensive surveys, and on-site visitations.[6] Phase 1 asked major superiors to communicate personally with Mother Mary Clare sharing the "hopes,

[4] *Congregazione per gli istituti di vita consacrata e le società de vita apostolica* (Dec. 22, 2008; Prot. N. 16805/2008), http://www.apostolicvisitation.org/en/materials/decree.pdf (accessed April 8, 2011).

[5] Cardinal Franc Rodé, CM, letter to Superiors General, February 2, 2009, http://www.apostolicvisitation.org/en/materials/cardinal_rode.pdf (accessed April 8, 2011).

[6] http://www.apostolicvisitation.org/en/materials/index.html (accessed April 8, 2011).

joys, concerns and observations" they held for their own sisters.[7] In phase 2, initiated in the fall of 2009, a series of extensive questionnaires were to be completed.[8] Concerns regarding the intrusive nature of some of the questions caused a number of major superiors to seek the counsel of both canon and civil lawyers and eventually resulted in the Apostolic Visitator's decision to rescind the request for information concerning financial audits and properties owned.[9] Even so, a January 2010 letter from Mother Clare to women religious leadership cites her "sadness and disappointment that not all congregations have responded to this phase of dialogue with the Church in a manner fully supportive of the purpose and goals of the Apostolic Visitation."[10]

In April 2010, the first of the on-site visits began.[11] Approximately one quarter of the congregations participating in the visitation were

[7] http://www.apostolicvisitation.org/en/approach/index.html (accessed April 8, 2011).

[8] Divided into three parts, the initial questionnaire (Part A) surveyed membership demographics: numbers, ages, ethnicities, living arrangements, care of elders, and range of ministerial service. Parts B and C asked explicit questions concerning the life and practices of institutes canvassing religious identity, governance, vocation and formation policies, spiritual and liturgical life, mission and ministry, and finally, finances and assets. Responses to parts B and C were to be sent directly to the Apostolic Visitation Office in Hamden, CT.

[9] "The documents *not* to be sent to the Apostolic Visitation Office include: 5. A list of each sister, year of birth, address and type of ministry (full time/part time). 6. A list of properties owned and/or (co)sponsored by your unit. 7. A complete copy of the most recent independent audit of your religious unit or your last internal financial statement if an external audit has not been made. This should include a statement of financial position, statement of activity, statement of changes in net assets and statement of cash flows." S. Mary Clare Millea, ASCJ, letter to Sister Superiors, November 5, 2009, http://www.apostolicvisitation.org/en/materials/MajorSupLtr-11052009.pdf (accessed April 8, 2011).

[10] http://www.apostolicvisitation.org/en/materials/index.html (accessed April 8, 2011).

[11] Previous to this, visitators-to-be, seventy-eight in all, met in St. Louis, Missouri, for a weekend workshop to prepare for their roles and responsibilities. A personal e-mail from one sister visitator recounted the major thrust of the meeting. Emphasizing the difference between a visitation and an investigation, visitators were schooled in the interview process, focus group scenarios, and report writing. Besides learning how to conduct the visitation process, visitators also gave feedback to Mother Clare; some suggested changes were adopted during the meeting. Presenters consistently emphasized that the on-site visits were not designed to search for abuses. Visitators were to allow sisters to speak frankly of the joys and challenges of their religious life. Mary Peter Traviss, OP, "Weekend Workshop for Visitors," personal e-mail to author, March 2, 2011.

selected for on-site visits during the weeks of April 11 to May 30 and September 12 to December 12. According to the Apostolic Visitation web site, representative institutes were chosen "based on congregation size and growth patterns, principle apostolic works, and geographical location."[12] Following the visitations and completion of on-site reports, a final workshop in March 2011 for those who assisted in on-site visitations gathered more than half the visitators. Participants were invited to "share their personal impressions of their on-site visit experience, as well as their observations of the common hopes, challenges, and concerns that women religious presently face. The group also offered suggestions for further promoting respectful dialogue and collaboration among religious congregations and within the Church."[13] Mother Clare's final, confidential reports were due to Cardinal Joseph Tobin, CSsR, recently appointed Secretary of CICLSAL, by the end of 2011.

The Investigation

The Leadership Conference of Women Religious received formal notification of a doctrinal assessment of the organization's activities and initiatives on March 10, 2009. Three areas of concern emerged from the Congregation for the Doctrine of the Faith's letter: women's ordination, issues pertaining to ecumenism/interreligious dialogue, and homosexuality.[14] These three areas of concern, first raised in 2001, had not, from the point of view of the CDF, been adequately addressed. As reported in the *National Catholic Reporter*, Cardinal William Levada, Prefect for the CDF, stated, "Given both the tenor and the doctrinal content of various addresses given at the annual assemblies of the Leadership Conference of Women Religious in the intervening years, this Dicastery can only conclude that the problems which had motivated its request in 2001 continue to be present."[15] Bishop Leonard Blair of Toledo, Ohio, conducted the investigation on behalf of the CDF. In an email communication to LCWR members in May 2011, the conference's national office shared the outcomes of the annual visit to Rome, April 27–May 4, 2011. Meeting

[12] http://www.apostolicvisitation.org/en/materials/av_phase_begins.pdf (accessed April 8, 2011).

[13] http://www.apostolicvisitation.org/en/materials/av_news_releases_03-07-11.pdf (accessed August 28, 2011).

[14] "Vatican Investigates U.S. Women Religious Leadership," *NCRonline.org*, http://ncronline.org/print/12804 (accessed August 28, 2011).

[15] Ibid.

with Monsignor Charles Brown, representative of the CDF, LCWR officers sought explicit information on the state of the doctrinal assessment.

> In our letter we asked: "Is there anything more needed from the LCWR? Are there any other matters that have been raised by U.S. Cardinals and Bishops that are of concern to the Congregation for the Doctrine of Faith regarding the LCWR?" Monsignor Brown indicated that at this time there are no new concerns and that, as Bishop Leonard Blair had previously told us in his July 2011 [sic] letter, the work he was asked to do for the Congregation for the Doctrine of the Faith office is completed.[16]

LCWR officers have consistently articulated the desire to remain in engaged conversation with the USCCB, CICLSAL and the CDF. At this writing, it is unclear whether LCWR can expect future Vatican action in this case.

Ecclesiological Reflections

Having offered a brief overview of the dual inquiries facing U.S. women religious, I will now consider three interrelated ecclesial points for discussion: the ongoing reception of Vatican II's call for the renewal of religious life, the impact of this reception on emerging ecclesial ministries, and the gift and task of becoming ecclesial persons. At the heart of these three distinct points is an evolving ecclesial concern for the faithful and fruitful renewal of consecrated life in the United States.

Ongoing Reception of the Renewal of Religious Life

The ecclesial task of the renewal of religious life following Vatican II is well documented, but the real impact of the renewal is etched in the memories and embodied in the flesh of the women and men who lived through the renewal. The upheaval of a very stable and predictable form of life in the Church caused no small amount of consternation, stress, and disruption. The religious superiors and prioresses who successfully navigated these changes for their congregations and provinces are among the unnamed saints of our Church. This was a daunting task, filled with personal and communal challenges. What does a renewed

---

[16] Gloria Marie Jones, OP, "LCWR Annual Visit to Rome," personal e-mail to author, May 16, 2011.

religious life look like? What are our roots and how do we adapt our founders' visions for our times? How shall we govern and structure our life? How shall we pray? Where and whom shall we serve? Are we who we are supposed to be or have we evolved into something our founding sisters would not recognize? In my own congregation, our wise and truly saintly Mother Mary Dominic Engelhard chose the way of scriptural prayer to root our congregation in a renewed form of Dominican life. Eulogized as a religious woman of singular grace, "Sister Mary Dominic [inaugurated] a vibrant program of spiritual renewal . . . to reawaken the contemplative dimension of Dominican life through prayer rooted in the Word of God. Impelled by the Vatican Council's call for all to open up the treasures of Sacred Scripture, Sister Mary Dominic guided us to move from meditation on spiritual texts to immersion in God's revealed word. How many of us can see her proclaiming and teaching the word, her Jerusalem Bible opened in her hands?"[17] Every sister was invited to make a 30-day retreat that introduced her to contemplative prayer rooted in the Scriptures. Scripture scholars were regular retreat directors and many of our sisters were sent to study Scripture, theology, and liturgy.

This time of exploration and experimentation was a new moment in the lives of women religious. Study of the sacred sciences opened to sisters by women like Sister Madeleva Wolff, CSC, soon extended into the behavioral and political sciences. Awakened in the mid-1960s, it is not possible to ignore or discount the Spirit's timing. The internal upheaval of renewal was happening simultaneously with cultural, social, and political upheaval. An examination of the photo record of the march on Selma and other civil rights demonstrations reveals the presence of habited Catholic sisters.[18] Questions and critique abound, and women religious found themselves in even more complex territory than they could have initially imagined. How does a congregation of women religious discern the signs of the times and not disturb the status quo in society and the Church?[19]

---

[17] Dominican Sisters of Mission San Jose, *Necrology, 2005–2010*, 19–22, at 20.

[18] See in particular the PBS documentary *Sisters of Selma: Bearing Witness to Change*, Hartfilms and Alabama Public Television, http://home.earthlink.net/~sistersofselma/sos.htm (accessed May 28, 2011).

[19] "Institutes should see to it that their members have a proper understanding of people, of the contemporary situation and of the needs of the church, this to the end that, evaluating the contemporary world wisely in the light of faith, and fired with apostolic zeal, they may be more helpful to people" (*Perfectae Caritatis* 2).

Clearly the seeds of renewal within consecrated life were planted before the council, as evidenced by the Sisters Formation Conference and the inauguration of the Conference of Major Superiors of Women (CMSW), both organizations that developed from Pope Pius XII's convening of the First General Council of the States of Perfection in 1950.[20] Intimations of new energies and gifts within religious life awaiting ecclesial recognition and nurturance received hierarchical attention and encouragement from Cardinal Leon Suenens and his influential book, *The Nun in the World.*[21] Papal and episcopal initiatives, even previous to the council, introduced thousands of missionary-minded U.S. women religious to the particular needs of the church in Latin America. The call in 1961 to religious superiors to offer ten percent of their personnel to support the Latin American church in its resistance to the incursion of both evangelical Protestantism and Communist socialism no doubt contributed to an awakening and a conversion of these women to the plight of the vast majority in Latin America and the oppressive economic systems that meted out death-dealing poverty despite the rhetoric of development and dependency.[22] The impact of this conscientization on women's religious life in the United States cannot be underestimated. Coupled with the social movement for civil rights in this country, it would not be long before highly educated women religious came to recognize overlapping systems of oppression and, on occasion, the Church's structural complicity in these systems.

These social, cultural, and political insights and awakenings were not happening in a vacuum. Challenged to renew according to "both a constant return to the sources of Christian life in general and the primi-

---

[20] Judith Schaefer, OP, *The Evolution of a Vow: Obedience as Decision-Making in Communion* (Zürich: Lit Verlag GmbH, 2008), 15.

[21] Leon Joseph Cardinal Suenens, *The Nun in the World*, trans. Geoffrey Stevens (Westminster, MD: Newman Press, 1963).

[22] James F. Garneau, "The First Inter-American Episcopal Conference. November 2–4, 1959: Canada and the United States Called to the Rescue of Latin America," *The Catholic Historical Review* 87, no. 4 (2001): 662–87, at 676. Garneau notes that Archbishop Antonio Samorè, Secretary for the Pontifical Commission on Latin America "was scheduled to address a joint meeting of the Conferences of Major Superiors of Men and Women Religious, held at the University of Notre Dame on August 17, 1961. Due to the death of Cardinal Tardini (on July 30, 1961), Monsignor Agostino Casaroli, substituting for Samorè, made the presentation, culminating in a request that "each religious province aim to contribute to Latin America in the next ten years a tithe—ten per cent—of its present membership as of this current year."

tive inspiration of the institutes, and their adaptation to the changed conditions of our time," women religious set about experimenting with new forms of institutional life and mission.[23] In the context of renewing structures and making adaptations in light of both the Gospel and the vision of the founders, women religious charted new paths, even as they were rediscovering the deepest wellsprings of their evangelical commitments. This journey did not happen without significant personal and communal distress. So much of what had been considered integral to religious life was reevaluated in the light of how to form and sustain women in true evangelical commitment. Workshops on holistic human development, communication, justice, Scripture studies, retreats, and theological studies are but a few of the long list of engaged encounters, immediately following Vatican II, that contributed toward renewed self-understandings as vowed ecclesial women. Through these varied encounters, new ways of embodying the evangelical counsels began to emerge. In particular, the vow of obedience (and by implication, communal structures of accountability) was (were) being significantly "repositioned." While all three vows of poverty, chastity, and obedience are dynamically interrelated in their capacity to discipline the heart and being of the religious toward a singular gift of self to God, the practice of the vow of obedience has undergone a particularly significant structural renewal. Judith Schaeffer notes that

> Obedience, the central organizing principle of religious life, has been transformed in the spirit and vision of collegiality, collaboration, and participation. Superiors, once regarded as mediators of the will of God, are now envisioned as animators and leaders who are at the service of the community. Authoritarian methods of decision making have shifted toward the communal participation of all members in congregational legislative sessions such as provincial and general chapters, for the purpose of articulating new goals and visions.[24]

Schaeffer astutely observes that more recent documents on the Church, emphasizing communion ecclesiology and the Trinitarian unity of the divine persons as source of ecclesial *koinonia*,[25] offer an external support for the efforts of women religious creating and sustaining credible and effective dialogical leadership structures within their respective

---

[23] *Perfectae Caritatis* 2.
[24] Schaefer, *The Evolution of a Vow*, 18–19.
[25] Extraordinary Synod of 1985, "The Final Report," *Origins* 15 (1985): 445.

congregations, institutes, and ministries. Initially somewhat foreign and suspect, these structures developed and became formative of the renewed lifestyle of consecrated life. And they continue to develop and deepen as the renewal of an authentic evangelical life lived with spiritual maturity, internal authority, and gracious self-gift finds expression among the various charisms of consecrated life.[26]

In the face of the recent Vatican interventions, all of this raises a difficult question for women religious (and others, no doubt): have episcopal structures and offices undergone *similar* renewal and redesign?[27] The key word here is *similar*. On the dawn of the fiftieth anniversary of the opening of the Second Vatican Council, women religious can look back over the sojourn of renewal and see the places where rupture, discontent, confusion, and acrimonious disagreement over the sacred work of refounding their institutes have left their marks. They can also see grace: reconciliation, full commitment, respectful dialogue, and most certainly, unrelenting hope in the Holy Spirit "whose power . . . can do infinitely more than we can ask or imagine" (Eph 3:20). Real renewal that dialogically impacts all the dimensions of ecclesial life and witness is soul-stretching, messy work. Can this be any less true for those among us "commissioned to perpetuate the work of Christ, the eternal Pastor"?[28] The manner of ecclesiastical investigation into the lives, ministry, and structures of American women religious leads us to question whether an analogous process of renewal is in evidence in the office of our bishops. This, too, is a question worth exploring.

Without doubt Vatican II attempted to reposition the office of the bishops in their relations with one another, with their local churches, and with the Bishop of Rome. We know that the debates surrounding papal primacy and episcopal collegiality were among the longest and "most contentious of the conciliar debates."[29] Denis Hurley, himself an active bishop at the council, has noted that the discussion on the pastoral office of bishops was the longest debate of the Second Vatican Council, lasting

---

[26] In particular see Bradford Hinze, *Practices of Dialogue in the Roman Catholic Church: Aims and Obstacles, Lessons and Laments* (New York: Continuum, 2006).

[27] I owe a debt of gratitude to my colleague, Patricia Walter, OP, who asked a version of this question during an engaging dinner discussion in 2010, and thus planted the seeds of these remarks.

[28] *Christus Dominus* 2.

[29] Denis Hurley, OMI, "Bishops, Presbyterate and the Training of Priests (*Christus Dominus; Presbyterorum Ordinis; Optatam Totius*)" in *Modern Catholicism: Vatican II and After*, ed. Adrian Hastings (New York: Oxford University Press, 1991), 141–50, at 142.

from September 30 to October 31, 1963.[30] When the bishops look over their shoulders 50 years later, how do they see the council's teaching on episcopal collegiality, both in its *local articulation* and its *cohesive apostolic unity*? What effective dialogical structures are in place, sustaining the kind of collegiality that lies at the heart of our apostolic tradition? Truly we speak of a work in progress.

The "Copernican shift" toward the local church as an authentic expression of the whole Church "in this place" invited a repositioning of the bishops in their particular responsibility for the apostolic ministry.[31] The proper relationship between the local and universal church experienced a new tension as diverse understandings and applications of subsidiarity came to the fore. This tension has unfortunately devolved in some ecclesial imaginations into a zero-sum game: more local somehow necessarily implies less universal and vice versa. Even now in the eyes of some, the cohesive unity that must bind the Church universal, for which all bishops share a fiduciary responsibility, is under threat from contemporary political and philosophical emphases on the local and particular. Diversity, thus construed, spawns fear that ecclesial unity will slip down the slippery slope into modern day Febronianism or Gallicanism. However, premature assessments of distinct local church faith expressions undermine subsidiarity, and contribute toward a "creeping infallibilism" that casts suspicion on unfamiliar forms and interpretations that reflexively question the adequacy of traditional understandings in a new situation.

The old struggle between "unity" and "uniformity" remains and will remain as long as the whole Church in its multiple local expressions seeks a living *communio*. The teaching office must assess the fidelity and intelligibility of local theologies. When, however, the local episcopacy is reduced functionally to a "branch office" representing the "home office" we are far from the relational unity of the bishops with one another and the Bishop of Rome that the council called us to and which was envisioned in John Paul II's *Ut Unum Sint*:[32] "When the Catholic Church

---

[30] In his words, this discussion "was one of the key debates of Vatican II, perhaps one should say *the* key debate." Ibid., 142.

[31] "The diocese is a section of God's people entrusted to a bishop to be guided by him with the assistance of his clergy so that, loyal to its pastor and formed by him into one community in the holy Spirit through the Gospel and the Eucharist, it constitutes one particular church in which the one, holy catholic and apostolic church is truly present" (*Christus Dominus* 11).

[32] "It is significant that it was Pope Pius IX, who defined the dogma of papal primacy and infallibility, who also vigorously upheld the public statement of the German

affirms that the office of the Bishop of Rome corresponds to the will of Christ, she does not separate this office from the mission entrusted to the whole body of Bishops, who are also 'vicars and ambassadors of Christ.' The Bishop of Rome is a member of the 'College,' and the Bishops are his brothers in the ministry."[33]

In response to *Ut Unum Sint*, Archbishop John R. Quinn's much cited Oxford lecture captures a critical point in the ongoing reception of Vatican II and the hope for structures of right relationship between the college of bishops and the Bishop of Rome; that being the real, structural reform of the *Curia Romana*. At the heart of Archbishop Quinn's assessment is the conviction that the dynamism that should mark episcopal, collegial solicitude for both the local churches and the universal Church collapses when the curia usurps certain prerogatives that *by doctrine* belong to the college of bishops.[34] Fifteen years after Quinn's lecture, the structural reform of the curia still waits to be undertaken in any substantive way. As the recent Vatican interventions we have been considering suggest, this ecclesial centralization continues unabated.

What, then, can be said about the degree of reception of the council's teaching on collegiality and the office of the bishop? Those contentious October 1963 conversations on the proper relationship between pope and bishops are still being worked out, but they are being worked out in a "new situation," one marked by significant opportunities for communion and solidarity as well as grave challenges to human well-being and flourishing.[35] Archbishop Quinn ends his lecture by indicating that ultimately the real question underlying *Ut Unum Sint's* exploration of

---

Bishops that bishops are not mere legates of the pope. This doctrine was more amply articulated in the Second Vatican Council. Such a doctrine cannot be affirmed in theory and denied in practice. Yet there are practical instances which are tantamount to making bishops managers who only work under instructions rather than true witnesses of faith who teach—in communion with the pope—in the name of Christ." John R Quinn, "The Exercise of the Primacy and the Costly Call to Unity" in *The Exercise of the Primacy: Continuing the Dialogue*, ed. Phyllis Zagano and Terrence W. Tilley (New York: Crossroad, 1998), 1–28, at 15.

[33] John Paul II, Encyclical Letter on Commitment to Ecumenism (*Ut Unum Sint*) 95, http://www.vatican.va/holy_father/john_paul_ii/encyclicals/documents/hf_jp-ii_enc_25051995_ut-unum-sint_en.html (accessed August 30, 2011).

[34] Quinn, "The Exercise," 13.

[35] "The 'new situation' for the primacy is indeed comparable to the situation which confronted the primitive church when it abandoned the requirements of the Mosaic Law and embraced the mission to the gentiles. This action required immense courage, vision and sacrifice. It was an uncharted path, a major change. . . . Similarly today, these are strong divisions within the Church and accompanying pressures pulling in

Christian unity is not the manner in which the Petrine ministry is exercised, but "What is the will of God?"[36] I wonder whether what we are experiencing today is a disparity in the ways in which professed religious women and the bishops have worked to receive the council's teaching. For women religious and bishops alike, this remains the critical question, demanding a willingness to be in "the new situation" and to respond with both fidelity and courage. It is hard to avoid the impression that the bishops and women religious are living out of such different social systems that it is difficult to know if we mean the same thing when we speak of "engaging in dialogue."

Without reducing the complexities at play in any cultural system or settling for facile (and fictive) gender contrasts construing male systems as closed and female systems as open, the fact remains that women religious are recognized leaders in teaching and implementing collaborative processes for both internal governance and for ministry leadership. The various structures and processes of contemplative communal discernment that women religious employ contribute toward cultures of consultation and consensus. One can only wonder what different outcomes the Church might be experiencing today if dialogical structures of consultation and transparency had been more fully realized throughout the presbyteral/episcopal culture and embedded in formation from seminaries to bishops' conferences. Indeed, one could quite plausibly conclude that the sexual abuse crisis was facilitated by a system of distorted institutionalized values; to fail to see this is a form of scotosis that cannot but grieve the Holy Spirit.

Yet that same Spirit continues to make possible the reconciliation needed among us. Scotosis, as an institutional condition, affects all the members of the Body of Christ. At the limits of both vision and charity, the Spirit of God *still* animates this Church. As Yves Congar taught us, this is God's promise, that the "regenerating power that will finally operate is already at work in our world, transiently, precariously, fragmentarily and generally unperceived."[37]

---

conflicting directions. The decisions required by the 'new situation' will be exacting and costly." Ibid., 4 5. See also John Paul II, *Ut Unum Sint* 95.

[36] Quinn, "The Exercise," 27.

[37] Yves Congar, *Lay People in the Church*, trans. Donald Atwater (Westminster, MD: Newman Press, 1957), 86.

Ongoing Reception of Renewal:
The Contemporary Challenge of Emerging Ecclesial Ministries

> It is to the Church's advantage that each institute has its own proper
> character and function. Therefore the spirit and aims of the founder
> should be faithfully acknowledged and maintained, as indeed should
> each institute's sound traditions, for all of these constitute an insti-
> tute's heritage. All institutes should share in the life of the Church.
> They should make their own and should promote to the best of their
> ability, each in a manner suited to its own character, the church's
> initiatives and undertakings in biblical, liturgical, dogmatic, pastoral,
> ecumenical, missionary and social matters. (*Perfectae Caritatis* 2)

The dual Vatican inquiries raise the question of the ecclesial character of
the paths that American women religious, in their lives and ministries, are
charting today. Practically speaking, this leads to the question of how the
Church itself understands and holds the shifts within ministerial identity
and practice, particularly in the areas of institutional leadership and spon-
sorship. Specifically, when considering lay partnerships, what roles and
responsibilities do women religious hold in this nascent arena of ecclesial
life? Our journey toward understanding the problems and possibilities of
these partnerships is a legitimate magisterial concern. Women religious
are accountable to the Church for the decisions made toward the future
of sponsored ministries and should be willing to enter into conversation
with ecclesial authorities to secure this future. But first, a brief overview.

The emergence of lay ministries following Vatican II might be *the* most
under-anticipated outcome of the council. With changes in liturgical form,
new assertions of the centrality of the Scriptures, and, most significantly,
the recovery of the primacy of baptism, the postconciliar Church embarked
on a journey of *aggiornamento*. In a matter of a few years the ordained
priesthood, formerly source of all ministerial responsibility and power,
became "repositioned" within a multitude of newly emerging ministries.[38]
Still, Thomas O'Meara reminds us that "[t]his newness in ministry was in
fact something old: The renewal of various services was a restoration of
aspects of the community to which the letters of Paul witness."[39]

---

[38] Geographically, most Catholics experienced this repositioning in their local
parishes and dioceses as lay leaders began to make a visible presence. In terms of
ecclesiological reflection, Catholic health care as a "site" for emerging lay leadership
has only come into view in the last ten years.

[39] Thomas O'Meara, OP, "Being a Ministering Church: Insights from History," in
Lay Ecclesial Ministry: Pathways toward the Future, ed. Zeni Fox (Lanham, MD: Rowman & Littlefield/Sheed & Ward, 2010), 53–65, at 53.

Women religious were equally caught in this "repositioning" of ecclesial ministries. With the call to renewal came the responsibility to study, pray, and discern both "the signs of the times" and an authentic recovery of the forms of life inspired by the founders. As communities immersed themselves in the historical conditions that birthed their institutions, many came to realize that the expansive vision of their fore-sisters had been domesticated over time. How was Mother McAuley's vision of God's mercy, incarnated among Dublin's poor, sick women and children, to be realized now? What is the contemporary expression of the missionary passion for education found in the legacies of Madeleine Sophie Barat's Society of the Sacred Heart or Anne de Xainctonge's Society of St. Ursula? Renewal called for a revitalized commitment to the poor, the marginalized, and those deemed "untouchable" by society. This "self-examination and experimentation with new expressions of lifestyle and ministry" contributed to a reassessment of women religious' commitment to their established institutional ministries.[40]

New lay partners arrived, then, within a constellation of multiple religious and social transformations in the identity and mission of ministries sponsored by women religious. From the classroom to the board room, women religious found themselves in a new ecclesial moment. Three points stand out. First, decreasing numbers of vowed religious began to impact the personnel available to serve. Lay partners were needed to sustain institutional ministries. Second, renewal exposed the truth that not all members of an institute had been suited for "the corporate apostolate." The days of sending a young sister to the classroom to teach, or to the hospital to nurse, even when these women clearly lacked the talents for such work could no longer be justified. Third, the work of renewal, in some religious institutes, disclosed the founder's original hope to remain *lay* in service to the poor and marginalized; this renewed self-understanding recognized lay partnerships as integral to the original charism. While these three points do not exhaust the forces at work in the early years following the council's call to renewal, they do point toward the significant ecclesial place where the gestation of lay ecclesial ministry and leadership has been actively nurtured. Out of the new, ambiguous, and fertile ground of questions of charism and

---

[40] Doris Guttemoeller, RSM, "Catholic Institutional Ministries: Their History and Legacy" in *Called and Chosen: Toward a Spirituality for Lay Leaders*, ed. Zeni Fox and Regina Bechtle, SC (Lanham, MD: Rowman & Littlefield/Sheed & Ward, 2005), 53–65, at 62.

institution, call and vocation, the role of the laity and lay leadership in ecclesial ministries continues to emerge and mature.

Zeni Fox and Regina Bechtle's 2005 publication *Called and Chosen*, and Fox's more recent book, *Lay Ecclesial Ministry*, offer rich reflections on the emerging vocation of lay ministers and the critical need to form lay leaders for the "new situation" of a globalized world.[41] In an article recounting the history of Catholic institutional ministries, Doris Gottemoeller names an important moment in both the history of institutionalized ministries in the U.S. and the post-Vatican II ecclesial tension being worked out in and through these ministries. In a country historically more hostile than welcoming to immigrant Catholics, ecclesial missions in the U.S. initially provided a "Catholic world" where displaced peoples could find both religious and social support. Today, however, we face a different situation. Gottemoeller asks, "Is a Catholic institution first and foremost a ministry by and for Catholics, or is it an expression of the Catholic mission to the larger needs of society? Is it possible that an institution founded in one era for one purpose may find another focus in a later, more secularized, pluralistic, and ecumenically sensitive era?"[42]

This question lies at the heart of all conversations about the relationship between institutional ministries sponsored by religious congregations and the emergence of lay leaders within these ministries. Focal issues concerning corporate identity, mission, and vitality are important because, in the words of Peter Steinfels, "The Catholic Church can succeed as an institution while failing as a church. But it cannot succeed as a church while failing as an institution."[43] Moreover, Steinfels argues that we hardly know *how* to be the kinds of institutions that are truly Catholic. This is a contemporary work of all the baptized because in the words of Monica Helwig, Catholic institutional identity "is not a matter of something we have lost and must retrieve. It is a matter of discovering how to do something we have never done before."[44] The assertion of my Aquinas Institute colleague, Jean DeBlois, is even more penetrating. It is not so much that our institutions matter in and of themselves. What matters is the *institutionalization of the Gospel*.[45] We need to be actively

---

[41] See Fox and Bechtle, eds., *Called and Chosen*; and Fox, *Lay Ecclesial Ministry*.

[42] Gottemoeller, "Catholic Institutional Ministries," 55.

[43] Peter Steinfels, *A People Adrift: The Crisis of the Roman Catholic Church in America* (New York: Simon & Schuster, 2003), 14.

[44] Quoted in ibid., 161.

[45] I am grateful for ongoing conversations with Jean DeBlois, CSJ, on the subject of sponsored ministries. She is currently researching in this area for future publication.

re-forming our institutional Catholic imaginations. Recognizing that societies are the result of multiple institutions, we sustain our institutional
presence for the sake of incarnating the transformative values of the reign
of God. We live in a world were institutions make the decisions that will
govern how human dignity and the common good will be realized. If
we do not offer and sustain in an *institutional* manner the alternative,
life-transforming values of Jesus, crucified and risen, we cannot make
the gospel difference the world desperately needs.

In the light of the Vatican visitation of women religious in the United
States, could there be some legitimate magisterial concern for the evolving institutional life of our ministries? I raise this question, because in
some cases the answer is "yes." Over the last twenty years of emerging
lay partnerships with women religious in ministry, a consistent refrain
can be heard that sounds more or less like this: "I love ministering with
these sisters. It's the institutional church I cannot take." Often seeded
in women religious' own transformative journey in relation to power,
privilege, and diversity, the frustrated desire for fully flourishing ecclesial
reform contributes to a distancing, even a disconnecting from legitimate
ecclesial structures of authority. In the worse case scenarios, magisterial authority is painted in broad strokes as a monolithic, out-of-touch,
power-jealous episcopacy that attempts to reign in intelligent, compassionate and prophetic believers. From my own experience of working
with lay leaders in leadership formation programs, I do not believe that
I am overstating the characterization. In some cases, women religious
themselves have advocated for "non-ecclesial ministries of the reign
of God." However frustrating and even heartbreaking our historical
journey with our own ecclesial leaders may be, this is a profound mis-
step and calls for correction and remediation. Why? Because strategies
that cut off dialogue cannot claim to be prophetic. If we are truly the
midwives of a new form of graced existence, we must be helping to
birth a new consciousness as *ecclesial persons*. Both James Alison and
John Zizioulas speak of the Christian mystery in terms of becoming
"ecclesial hypostases."[46] Though they offer distinctive descriptions of
this transformation, at the heart of both is the conviction of a metaphysical transfiguring, disclosed by faith, that constitutes a new and particular way of being human. This can only happen if the contemplative,

---

[46] James Alison, *The Joy of Being Wrong: Original Sin through Easter Eyes* (New York:
Crossroad, 1998); and John D. Zizioulas, *Being as Communion: Studies in Personhood
and the Church* (Crestwood, NY: St. Vladimir's Seminary Press, 1985).

prophetic spirituality that has marked much of contemporary reflection on religious life expands to embrace and articulate a robust ecclesial spirituality. If there is a gift waiting to be revealed for us in these dual Vatican inquiries, maybe it will be just this, a reclaiming of a truly inclusive ecclesiology and a deepened commitment to sustain a dialogical stance in the face of misunderstanding, misrepresentation, and even betrayal. The mystery of who we are as Church, as the Body of Christ, is greater than any perceived or real offence. This depth formation in the agapic and paschal patterns of Christian life is both gift and task: the work of the Spirit and our responsibility to communicate in mutual relationship with our partners in ministry, lay and ordained.

Formation toward becoming ecclesial persons is imperative if our institutions are to be instantiations of the reign of God. Our lay partners do not profess the evangelical counsels, or live in apostolic community, or enjoy tax-free status. Most are spouses, parents, and grandparents. Besides being competent professionals in their ministry, they must pay mortgages, put food on the table, nurture and educate their young, and sustain a loving relationship with their life partners. Juliana Casey, IHM, notes that the formation practices that prepared vowed religious for ministry will not serve adequately the formation of lay leaders of ecclesial ministries. She recommends a shift from *transferring* past formation models to *translating* these models so that the gospel values that must characterize any ministry grow integrally from the ground of the life commitments of lay leaders.[47] Focusing on the whole person and the constellation of relationships that constitute their way of holiness in marriage or the single life, lay leaders of Catholic ministries must be adept at leading prayer, discerning the "signs of the times" in their ministries and local church, and implementing the gospel vision of their organization in good and difficult situations. They must be people rooted in faith, hope, and love in such a way that the "multiple demands, multiple cares and multiple loves" of their lives are reverenced and accessed as their "ground of holiness and the primary sacred place of encounter with the divine."[48]

---

[47] Juliana Casey, IHM, "Formation for Lay Ministry: Learnings from Religious Life," in *Lay Ecclesial Ministry*, ed. Fox, 143–55, at 146.

[48] Ibid., 153.

The Gift and Task of Being Ecclesial for a Global World

Yves Congar speaks of the mark of apostolicity as "the mark that for the Church is both a gift of grace and a task."[49] He goes on to describe the mark of apostolicity as the Spirit's gift of sustaining continuity between the Alpha of God's intention for creation and the Omega consummation of the divine initiative in all that is. Apostolicity, as gift, is given to the whole Church and entrusted to all members as the task of "preserving the messianic and eschatological way of living in community that was received from the Lord until he comes again."[50] The distinctiveness of Christian identity is captured in these words. We are a people caught up in the embrace of the God who first moved toward humanity in covenant relationship through the people of Israel and then, in the fullness of time and love, definitively poured out in the life, death, and resurrection of the Beloved, Jesus. Resurrection faith is our ongoing journey into *this* mystery of Divine love and *this particular faith* is the singular experience that lies at the heart of our truth claims and our form of life. The apostolic faith belongs to the Church as both a gift and a task. What we proclaim, we must also live. We must be the difference that Jesus continues to make.

How do we do this in a conflictual, dangerous, and market-driven world? In some sense Vatican II spoke to a modern world that was already going "post-modern." The vision of openness to social movements and to the aspirations of the world's peoples, the dialogical agenda, soon became a much more complex endeavor than any at the council could have imagined. Recovery of our social justice tradition impacted our ecclesial consciousness as both citizens and baptized members. Critical assessment of oppressive social and political systems could not simply remain outside the church door. We had to look at our own exclusive, dehumanizing structures. These difficult questions threatened some of our time-honored self-understandings as a faith community, making dialogue within the Church almost as difficult as dialogue outside the Church.

We recognize that some of the dominant spiritualities represented at the council have funded very different ecclesial visions. The current "contest of interpretation" of the council itself reflects these differences. Each vision holds legitimate concerns and warrants careful, thoughtful consideration. In the fifty years since Vatican II, sociological descriptions

---

[49] Yves Congar, *I Believe in the Holy Spirit*, vol. 2, trans. David Smith (New York: Crossroad/Herder, 1997), 39.

[50] Ibid.

of Europe's dominant religious ethos have shifted from secular atheism to religious pluralism and "detraditionalization."[51] Within this post-Christian and post-secular milieu, the particularity of Christianity as a coherent, unifying form of life appears threatened. Practices of consumption guide "habits of interpretation and use," fueling the deconstruction of traditions and symbol systems.[52] Spiritual seekers freely pick and choose from among a variety of religious repertoires (read commodities) and individually appropriate symbols and practices without much regard for the religious universe that gives these entities their *raison d'être*. In a context of detraditionalization and deep religious pluralism it is naïve not to perceive the grave challenge to Christian particularity. How will future members truly become "ecclesial persons" and enter into the Christian mystery?

Arguments around this situation tend toward construing the challenge as an either/or between *Gospel dialogue* in search of continuity with the context or *Gospel proclamation* as discontinuity over against the context. Lieven Boeve juxtaposes Edward Schillebeeckx and Pope Benedict XVI as contrasting representatives of these perspectives.[53] Schillebeeckx's hopeful assessment of the context's capacity to bear fruit in dialogue with the Gospel echoes the French Dominican contingent at Vatican II (e.g., Marie-Dominique Chenu's "toothing stones"), while Benedict's conviction that the revisionists' dialogue with modernity has failed sounds the caution that both he and Karl Rahner called for at the council: a healthy Christian pessimism in relation to the world.[54] When considering the question of how to adequately communicate the Christian Mystery, we are challenged by contrasting starting points; Schillebeeckx's vision demands the *capacity to translate the mystery*, while Benedict's vision calls for *initiation into the mystery*.[55]

---

[51] Lieven Boeve, *God Interrupts History: Theology in a Time of Upheaval* (New York: Continuum, 2007).

[52] Miller, *Consuming Religion*, 179.

[53] Boeve, *God Interrupts History*, 5–6 and 62–68. Boeve also contrasts the work of Antoon Vergote on the role of experience in Christian faith; see ibid., 68–74.

[54] See Joseph Komonchak's "Is Christ Divided: Dealing with Diversity and Disagreement," *Origins* 33, no. 9 (2003): 140–47, at 143; also see his more substantive essay, "Vatican II and the Encounter between Catholicism and Liberalism," in *Catholicism and Liberalism: Contributions to American Public Philosophy*, ed. Bruce Douglass and David Hollenbach (Cambridge: Cambridge University Press, 1994), 76–99.

[55] Boeve, *God Interrupts History*, 50–56, at 54.

Does this tension speak to the current situation of women religious in the United States? The dilemma described above looks like another zero-sum game: translation undermines and ultimately betrays true conversion while conversion renders translation unnecessary. How might particular uncritical commitments to either of these two starting points participate in the current state of polarization in the Church? More specifically, might recognizing flawed zero-sum thinking reframe these perspectives toward a more complete vision of ecclesial personhood?

In a religiously plural context multiple lifescripts contend for allegiance. If Christianity is to be historically transformative (i.e., a sacrament of the reign of God), it must be seen, recognized, and encountered as a particular and distinctive way of being human, of "being-in-relationship." This form of life is the gift and the task of manifesting the difference that Jesus and his Spirit are making in the world. This is the unique truth claim that makes Christianity a faith community, a claim that must be "recontextualized" if it is to survive the current challenge of detraditionalization.[56] Caught between returning to an insular Christendom or dissembling into vague associations of that "good man Jesus," all the baptized must rediscover and embody the gift and the task of becoming ecclesial persons.

The agapic and paschal form of life revealed in Jesus by the Spirit to the glory of the Father bears concrete witness to the triune Love at the center of all existence, manifesting in time and space a different kind of human history. Shawn Copeland reminds us that we must insist "that the Body of Christ is no metaphor: at bottom, this is a yearning for a metaphysics that recognizes and thematizes (even in the black underground) the reality and luminosity of being."[57] When this metaphysical claim is rendered impotent by triumphalism or untenable by accommodation, we surrender the gift and we fail at the task. We betray our own mystery.

Becoming ecclesial persons is the lifelong work of all the baptized. Christ's mystery becomes our mystery and calls us each individually and all of us communally into the illuminative, purgative, and unitive depths of the paschal mystery. These are not mere words. The reflexive power of the living Gospel acts upon us, and, in a particular way today, grace calls us beyond polarizing behaviors toward a new transparency

---

[56] See ibid., 30–49.

[57] M. Shawn Copeland, "Constructive Proposal: Body, Race and Being," in *Constructive Theology: A Contemporary Approach to Classical Themes*, ed. Serene Jones and Paul Lakeland (Minneapolis, MN: Fortress Press, 2005), 97–116, at 116.

and renewed respect. This brings our reflections back to the profound pain that the dual Vatican investigations have created. Casting suspicion on our commitment to consecrated life accentuated our sense of impasse and confirmed for many the abiding reality of the "dark night of the feminine."[58] In this difficult situation, Constance Fitzgerald's words carry particular power for women religious:

> Contemplation and ultimately liberation, demand the handing over of one's powerlessness and "outsiderness" to the inspiration and power of God's Spirit. How imperative it is that women take possession of their pain and confusion; actively appropriate their experience of domination, exploitation and oppression; consent to their time in history; and hold this impasse in their bodies and their hearts before the inner God they reach for in the dark of shattered symbols. Although the God of the dark night seems silent, this God is not a mute God who silences human desire, pain and feeling, and women need to realize that the experience of anger, rage, depression and abandonment is a constitutive part of the transformation and purification of the dark night.[59]

Women religious need to know and claim this dark night as an *ecclesial* dark night. Women religious cannot distance themselves or step back from *communio*, because if Fitzgerald is right, then by virtue of fidelity to impasse they *are* manifesting "ecclesial being." Clinging to the Crucified in the grace of impasse, women religious have the opportunity to "put all the power of their desire, not in ideology, but . . . before the inner God . . . and purified of violence, they are readied for communion with their God, for sisterhood, equality, liberation and mutuality."[60] This journey into concrete suffering expands faith and deepens hope in the gift, yet to be, gestating for God's glory. What impact might such Gospel fidelity have on the magisterium and the Church as a whole?

---

[58] Beverly Lanzetta, *Radical Wisdom: A Feminist Mystical Theology* (Minneapolis, MN: Augsburg Fortress, 2005).

[59] Constance Fitzgerald, OCD, "Impasse and the Dark Night," http://www.balti morecarmel.org/saints/John%20of%20the%20Cross/impasse%20and%20dark%20 night.htm (accessed September 18, 2011).

[60] Ibid.

Conclusion

> Our profession of the counsels joins us to the Church in a special
> way: we are given to the Bride for the sake of the Kingdom. Yearning
> for her Beloved, the Church walks his road of poverty and obedience,
> service and sacrifice. As religious women, we are called to be the
> ardor of her love, the healing of her dividedness; a sign of her hope
> in the world, comforting and supporting her people as together we
> await Christ's coming in glory. Recipients of God's mercy ourselves,
> we are to witness through service His mercy to His people.[61]

These words captured for me, as a young sister, the heart of religious consecration . . . *to be the ardor of the Church's love.* For many women religious, the dual Vatican visits have questioned the vitality of that ardor. Whether instigated by untoward bias or not, the experience has focused attention not only on consecrated life but on the investigative process itself, raising pertinent questions of the examiners as well of the examined. For religious women, the resulting solidarity has forged new relationships of collaboration that will hopefully serve the future of consecrated life in this country. Charting ecclesial paths in difficult times and contexts demands the best of all of us. The world is well-practiced in the sad arts of exclusion, suppression, and demonization. How are we any different when we allow an insidious scotosis to fuel factions in the Body of Christ and deal out countervailing anathemas? Clinging to the Crucified we are all called to renew our commitment to realizing a dialogical communion that is first and foremost the Spirit's gift and then our task. Resisting pretense, pride, and the seductions of power we hope to seed a truly gracious future.

---

[61] Dominican Sisters of Mission San Jose, Congregation of the Queen of the Most Holy Rosary, Fremont, CA, *Constitutions* (1973), chapter 1, article 3.

Part 2

Theological and Contextual Reflections

Chapter 4

The Prophetic Office in the Church
Pneumatological Perspectives on the *Sensus Fidelium*-Theology-Magisterium Relationship

Ormond Rush

St. Paul's Theological College, Australian Catholic University

When the magisterium intervenes, what fundamental theological prin-ciples are at stake, especially concerning central doctrines such as revela-tion and faith? In a comprehensive interpretation of the spirit and letter of Vatican II, how might one outline a theology of the teaching office of the Church, and in particular a theology of magisterial intervention?

The Catholic position is clear regarding the teaching authority of the magisterium in matters of faith and morals: "The task of authoritatively [*authentice*] interpreting the word of God, whether in its written form or in that of tradition, has been entrusted only to those charged with the church's living *magisterium*, whose authority is exercised in the name of Jesus Christ" (DV 10).[1] The magisterium (the college of bishops with

---

[1] Except where noted, quotations from Vatican II documents in this essay are taken from *Decrees of the Ecumenical Councils*, 2 vols., ed. Norman P. Tanner (Washington, DC: Georgetown University Press, 1990), here corrected. "In modern Catholic usage, the term 'magisterium' has come to be associated almost exclusively with the teaching role and authority of the hierarchy. An even more recent development is that the term 'the magisterium' is often used to refer not to the teaching office as such but to the body of men who have this office in the Catholic Church: namely, the pope and bishops." Francis A. Sullivan, "Magisterium," in *Dictionary of Fundamental Theology*, ed. René Latourelle and Rino Fisichella (Middlegreen, Slough, UK: St Paul, 1994), 614–20. On translating the adverb *authentice* as "authoritatively," see Francis A. Sullivan, *Magisterium: Teaching Authority in the Catholic Church* (New York: Paulist Press, 1983), 26–28.

the pope) is the final ecclesial teaching authority. There are not two magisteria in the Church, in the sense of two formal teaching authorities (theologians equally alongside the college of bishops with the pope). The latter alone have the power for authoritatively determining the faith of the Church, and for overseeing its interpretation. The magisterium, therefore, has the responsibility and right at times of intervening when formulations of individual theologians are perceived to threaten the integrity and unity of the faith of the Church.[2]

Any attempt at a comprehensive theology of magisterial intervention would need to integrate these beliefs regarding the magisterium with other related aspects of Catholic belief. These other aspects relate to the nature of revelation and faith itself, the nature and mission of the Church's teaching office, and in particular the modes and exercise of teaching authority in the Church, including the teaching authority of all believers. It is that fuller range of beliefs that I want to explore in this essay, particularly as it emerges from the spirit and letter of Vatican II. As is typical of any attempt at a Catholic synthesis, this one will include aspects of "both/and" and "yes/but."

Vatican II on the Prophetic Office

We begin with a reflection on theology's role within the Church's "prophetic office," as envisaged by Vatican II. The notion of the three offices of Christ as priest, prophet, and king (the *triplex munus* or the *tria munera*) can be found throughout *Lumen Gentium*.[3] The notion is used to structure the document's discussion of what is common and what is specific to the various roles within the whole People of God. The three offices are: (1) the *munus sacerdotalis* (the priestly office), which is the *munus sanctificandi* (the office of sanctifying); (2) the *munus propheticum* (the prophetic office), which is the *munus docendi* (the office of teaching);

---

[2] For Vatican II's teaching on the magisterium, see particularly *Dei Verbum* 10 and *Lumen Gentium* 25. On the responsibilities and rights of bishops, see National Conference of Catholic Bishops, *Doctrinal Responsibilities: Approaches to Promoting Cooperation and Resolving Misunderstandings between Bishops and Theologians* (Washington, DC: United States Catholic Conference, 1989), 6–7. For a discussion of the magisterium-theologians relationship, see Richard R. Gaillardetz, *Teaching with Authority: A Theology of the Magisterium in the Church* (Collegeville, MN: Liturgical Press, 1997), 241–46.

[3] This marks the conciliar reception of a notion whose use as an ecclesiological rubric begins with John Calvin. See Ormond Rush, "The Offices of Christ, *Lumen Gentium* and the People's Sense of the Faith," *Pacifica* 16 (2003): 137–52.

and (3) the *munus regalis* (the kingly or pastoral office), which is the *munus regendi* (the office of governing).[4] Chapter 2 of *Lumen Gentium*, on the People of God, teaches that all the baptized, the *universitas fidelium* (the whole body of the faithful), participate in the *triplex munus*; the next two chapters of the Dogmatic Constitution discuss the specific ways in which firstly the hierarchy (chapter 3) and then the laity (chapter 4) participate in the three offices of Christ.

A hermeneutical problem arises when interpreting the "spirit" and "letter" of Vatican II on many issues, and it is certainly true for the council's teaching on the prophetic or teaching office of the Church. The "spirit" of Vatican II refers to "the mind of the council," what emerged from all the speeches, written submissions, drafting, and voting, as the final intention of the assembled bishops as a single conciliar body. The "letter" refers to the final form of the sixteen documents through which they expressed their common mind. These sixteen documents of Vatican II do not present systematic treatises. Sometimes a final document might use within it different theological frameworks together to express the same doctrine. One thread might employ the language and particular theological framework of a previous Church teaching, which had presupposed at the time of its original formulation a relevant background theory from a discipline such as philosophy, psychology, or sociology. Another thread might presuppose a newer and different background theory, thereby presenting a shift in theological perspective, and perhaps a "development" in the Church's teaching regarding a particular truth of the faith.

The documents voted on and approved by the whole conciliar assembly represent consensus statements; the council arrived at that consensus through a compromise between different groups among the bishops, a compromise which allowed different theological frameworks to stand in tension. Each group could find their particular perspective affirmed in the document. However, while a continuity is intended between the new and the old, the new often signals the intention of the majority for a shift or "development" in the teaching.[5] This juxtaposition of different

---

[4] For clarification regarding the equivalence of these terms, I am grateful to Hervé Legrand and Ladislas Örsy, in conversation.

[5] Hermann Pottmeyer, while stating that the final compromise position must be the starting point for postconciliar interpretation, believes the position of the majority during conciliar debate should be given greater weight in reconstructing the "spirit" of the council: "Fidelity to the Council also requires that we pay heed to the stress that the Council itself laid on the one or the other thesis, according as a thesis was

theological frameworks to achieve consensus through compromise creates, however, a tension in the final teaching and presents a challenge and task for interpreters of the council.[6]

Pope Paul VI was hinting at this hermeneutical problem and theological challenge when he addressed the assembled bishops on the final working day of Vatican II: "[The council] did not attempt to resolve all the urgent problems of modern life; some of these have been reserved for a further study which the Church intends to make of them, many of them were presented in very restricted and general terms, and for that reason are open to further investigation and various applications."[7] According to Hermann Pottmeyer, the juxtaposition of different theological positions within the final texts calls for a new synthesis by theologians after the council: "the needed synthesis is a task the Council sets for the Church and for theologians; it is a task of reception, which is far from being a merely passive process."[8] Likewise, Walter Kasper, commenting on the final documents emerging from the long drafting process, states: "Admittedly, the harmonization between earlier and later tradition is often not completely successful; for—like most previous councils—Vatican II solved its task, not with the help of a comprehensive theory, but by pegging out the limits of the Church's position. In this sense it was completely in the conciliar tradition for a juxtaposition to remain. As in the case of every council, the theoretical mediation between these positions is *a task for the theology that comes afterwards.*"[9] This is certainly

---

supported by the majority or the minority. The fact remains, however, that the majority and minority alike agreed to both theses and in particular to their juxtaposition." Hermann J. Pottmeyer, "A New Phase in the Reception of Vatican II: Twenty Years of Interpretation of the Council," in *The Reception of Vatican II*, ed. Giuseppe Alberigo, Jean Pierre Jossua, and Joseph A. Komonchak (Washington, DC: Catholic University of America Press, 1987), 27–43, at 39.

[6] Further on the "juxtaposition" of theological theses and the "compromise" nature of many of the final texts noted by various commentators on the documents of Vatican II, see Ormond Rush, *Still Interpreting Vatican II: Some Hermeneutical Principles* (Mahwah, NJ: Paulist Press, 2004), 27–30, 42, 49.

[7] "Address of Pope Paul VI during the Last General Meeting of the Second Vatican Council, 7 December 1965," http://www.vatican.va/holy_father/paul_vi/speeches/1965/documents/hf_p-vi_spe_19651207_epilogo-concilio_en.html (accessed August 11, 2011).

[8] Pottmeyer, "A New Phase in the Reception of Vatican II," 38.

[9] Walter Kasper, "The Continuing Challenge of the Second Vatican Council: The Hermeneutics of the Conciliar Statements," in *Theology and Church* (New York: Crossroad, 1989), 166–76, at 171; emphasis added.

true of the council's teaching on the teaching office. As Hermann Pottmeyer has stated on another matter: "Here again, Vatican II has left us
only with a building site."[10]

Some of the juxtapositions and tensions in the Vatican II documents
regarding the teaching office can be seen when we examine the documents intra-textually and inter-textually.[11] *Intra-textuality* refers to the
relationship of linguistic units (words, sentences, paragraphs, chapters)
within a single conciliar document. *Inter-textuality* refers to the relationship of such linguistic units and documents across the whole sixteen
documents of Vatican II (and indeed the whole tradition of texts and
practices throughout history).

First, there is an *intra-textual* tension in *Lumen Gentium* between certain affirmations in chapter 2 on "The People of God" (art. 9–17) and
those in chapter 3 on "The Hierarchical Constitution of the Church and
in Particular the Episcopate" (art. 18–29). In the earlier chapter (LG 12),
the whole people of God (*universitas fidelium*) is said to participate in
the prophetic office by virtue of baptism,[12] just as the latter chapter
(LG 25) affirms such participation of the bishops by virtue of episcopal

---

[10] Hermann J. Pottmeyer, *Towards a Papacy in Communion: Perspectives from Vatican
Councils I & II* (New York: Crossroad, 1998), 128.

[11] Such a reading would then move on to a (1) reconstruction of the "letter" of
the council, through applying a hermeneutics of the texts; and must, of course, be
complemented by (2) a reconstruction of the "spirit" of the council, through applying
a hermeneutics of the authors (a reconstruction of what the bishops intended through
an examination of the debates and drafting process); and (3) a reconstruction of both
the spirit and letter in the light of new questions that emerge after the council, through
a hermeneutics of reception (a reconstruction of what the teaching means for today's
context). Space and time do not permit such a fuller exposition in this essay.

[12] "*The holy people of God* has a share, too, in the prophetic office of Christ, when it
renders him a living witness, especially through a life of faith and charity, and when
it offers to God a sacrifice of praise, the tribute of lips that honour his name. The
universal body of the faithful [*universitas fidelium*] who have received the anointing of
the holy one, *cannot be mistaken in believing* [*in credendo*]. It displays this particular
quality through a supernatural sense of the faith in the whole people [*sensus fidei
totius populi*] when 'from the bishops to the last of the faithful laity', it expresses the
consent of all in matters of faith and morals. Through this sense of the faith which
is aroused and sustained by the Spirit of truth, *the people of God*, under the guidance
of the sacred magisterium to which it is faithfully obedient, receives no longer the
words of human beings but truly the word of God; it [the people of God] adheres
indefectibly to 'the faith which was once for all delivered to the saints"; it [the people
of God] penetrates more deeply into that same faith through right judgment and
applies it more fully to life" (LG 12, corrected; emphases added).

ordination,[13] without any attempt to integrate the two affirmations. Similarly, the *infallibilitas in credendo* affirmed of the *universitas fidelium* in *Lumen Gentium* 12 is not integrated into the following chapter which addresses the *infallibilitas in docendo* of the magisterium (LG 25). As Karl Rahner notes: "Here an infallibility of faith is attributed to the people of God as a whole, as also to the people of the Church as the recipients of teaching in particular. The Council itself has not attempted to carry this further by relating what it says in these chapters to the statements in chapter III, where it is the hierarchical structure of the Church which is dealt with."[14] This lack of integration is no doubt due in part to the re-positioning of paragraphs and indeed of whole chapters in the long re-drafting process; earlier drafts had used the *tria munera* rubric exclusively with regard to the magisterium and *Lumen Gentium* 25 seems to presuppose that narrower application. A new synthesis is required which can integrate both sets of affirmations.

Second, there is an *inter-textual* tension between the propositionalist and ahistorical model of revelation and truth (presupposed from Vatican I) in *Lumen Gentium* 25 (within chapter 3), and the shift in magisterial teaching effected in *Dei Verbum* to a personalist and historical model of revelation and truth (a shift nevertheless that does not reject the propositionalist notion). The two different models can give rise to very different conceptions of the nature of theology and the nature of magisterial oversight in matters of perceived conflict with church teaching.

Thirdly, there is *intra-textual* and *inter-textual* tension regarding the assistance of the Holy Spirit which calls out for theological synthesis. Only some texts can be cited. *Lumen Gentium* 12 affirms assistance by the Holy Spirit of the whole People of God in believing, and *Lumen Gentium* 25 and

---

[13] "Among the principal offices [*munera*] of bishops the preaching of the gospel is pre-eminent. For the bishops are the heralds of the faith who bring new disciples to Christ. They are the authentic teachers, that is, teachers endowed with the authority of Christ, who preach to the people entrusted to them the faith to be believed and put into practice; they illustrate this faith in the light of the Holy Spirit, drawing out of the treasury of revelation things new and old, they make it bear fruit and they vigilantly ward off errors that are threatening their flock" (LG 25, corrected). The *tria munera* is regularly attributed to the bishops throughout chapter 3. For example, art. 21 states: "Episcopal consecration, along with the office of sanctifying, confers also the offices of teaching and governing."

[14] Karl Rahner, "The Teaching Office of the Church in the Present-Day Crisis of Authority," in *Theological Investigations*, vol. 12 (London: Darton, Longman & Todd, 1974), 3–30, at 5, note 4.

Dei Verbum 9 and 10 affirm it of the magisterium in teaching. *Dei Verbum* 8 states that the apostolic tradition makes progress throughout history with the help of the Holy Spirit and lists the three means through which the Spirit works: the scholarship of theologians, the *sensus fidelium*, and the ministry of the magisterium.[15] Although the word *conspiratio* is used of the relationship between the bishops and the faithful (DV 10), the sense conveyed of the relationship is one of passive obedience, akin to the model of an *ecclesia docens* and an *ecclesia discens*.[16]

These juxtapositions and resulting tensions are left unresolved by Vatican II. They are tensions which still mark both today's differing conceptions of the magisterium-theology relationship and the differing conceptions of the goal of magisterial intervention and the procedures and style with which it should be exercised. For example, The U.S. National Conference of Catholic Bishops document, *Doctrinal Responsibilities* (1989), while it speaks of the responsibilities and rights of bishops explicitly in terms of the three offices of Christ, fails to affirm, explicitly in terms of the *tria munera* rubric, that theologians too participate in all those offices as *fideles*, and in the teaching office in particular by virtue of their Spirit-given charism.[17]

Toward a New Synthesis

I would now like to offer some proposals regarding a way forward to a new synthesis that may overcome and advance the discussion beyond the juxtapositions, compromises, and tensions in the three areas mentioned above.

---

[15] "The tradition that comes from the apostles makes progress in the church, with the help of the Holy Spirit. There is a growth in insight into the realities and words that are being passed on. This comes about through (1) the contemplation and study of believers who ponder these things in their hearts. It comes from (2) the intimate sense of spiritual realities which they experience. And it comes from (3) the preaching of those who, on succeeding the office (*episcopatus*) of bishop, have received the sure charism of truth. Thus, as the centuries go by, the church is always advancing towards the plenitude of divine truth, until eventually the words of God are fulfilled in it" (DV 8, Flannery translation; numbers inserted by author). Commentators see these three as references to (1) theology, (2) the *sensus fidelium*, and (3) the magisterium.

[16] On an active notion of *conspiratio*, see John Henry Newman, *On Consulting the Faithful in Matters of Doctrine* (New York: Sheed & Ward, 1962).

[17] See National Conference of Catholic Bishops, *Doctrinal Responsibilities*, 6–8.

One Office, Three Authorities

The Church's teaching office (the *munus docendi*) involves more than the magisterium. As I have proposed elsewhere,[18] if *Lumen Gentium* 12's affirmation regarding the participation of the *universitas fidelium* in the prophetic office is to be integrated with the affirmations of *Lumen Gentium* 25 regarding the episcopate's participation in that office, then it is important in English-language theological terminology not to continue equating the term "the magisterium" with the term "the teaching office," but rather to speak in terms of the one teaching office (*munus*), which has three distinctive authorities: the *sensus fidelium*, theology, and the magisterium.[19]

Dei Verbum 8 lists these three as the means through which the Holy Spirit directs the apostolic tradition's development through history. Concerning the order of the authorities mentioned in *Dei Verbum* 8, Walter Kasper observes: "[I]t is no accident that the magisterium is only mentioned in third place. The ecclesiality of faith is not exhausted by an attitude of obedience to the Church's teaching authority. That authority is situated within the community of believers and under the authority of the word of revelation. It is not a super-criterion ruling over the Church and its common search for truth in lonely Olympian majesty and issuing condemnations."[20] The three authorities constitute what the International Theological Commission's document on theology and the magisterium (1975) calls "authorities that derive from the Word of God."[21]

The distinctive contribution of and necessarily active relationship among these three ecclesial authorities constitutes the *munus propheti-*

---

[18] See Ormond Rush, *The Eyes of Faith: The Sense of the Faithful and the Church's Reception of Revelation* (Washington, DC: The Catholic University of America Press, 2009), 193–207.

[19] It is to be remembered that, according to *Lumen Gentium* 12, bishops and theologians, as baptized *fideles*, are to be included in the reference *sensus fidelium*. Consequently, "the sense of the faithful" (*sensus fidelium*) is not simply "the sense of the laity" (*sensus laicorum*). Furthermore, theologians can be lay or ordained. For a detailed discussion of these distinctions, see ibid., 241–91.

[20] Walter Kasper, *An Introduction to Christian Faith* (London: Burns & Oates, 1980), 146–47.

[21] International Theological Commission, *Theses on the Relationship between the Ecclesiastical Magisterium and Theology*, Thesis 6, par. 2. Text and commentary can be found in Sullivan, *Magisterium*, 174–218, at 194. For Sullivan's further delineation of those authorities, see Francis A. Sullivan, "Authority in an Ecclesiology of Communion," *New Theology Review* 10 (1997): 18–30, at 19–20.

cum or the *munus docendi*. In their interaction, there is a certain overlap with the *munus regendi*, the office of governance, especially regarding the issue with which we are particularly concerned, that of intervention by the magisterium.[22] But particularly in discussion of this matter of intervention, the two offices should not be disconnected, as if magisterial intervention were only a matter of order, and not also of faith. The very nature of ecclesial faith itself is particularly relevant here. Therefore, a proper perspective emerges, I believe, if we approach the matter firstly from the perspective of the prophetic office, and move then to the matter of governance and the appropriate goal and style of its exercise.

The prophetic office is more than oversight of interpretations and the formulation of doctrine; it is more than official witness, preaching, and teaching by bishops and the pope; it is more than disciplining in cases of perceived threats to the integrity and unity of the faith. It is as much concerned with safeguarding effective transmission of the living faith which saves here and now, as with preservation and safeguarding the one faith's past forms. The whole People of God is to participate in this teaching office, albeit in different ways and with different kinds of authority. (It is important to remember that the *fideles*, referred to in terms such as *universitas fidelium* and *sensus fidelium*, are all the baptized, including the pope, bishops, priests, deacons, religious, and lay people.)

Lay people, within the *fideles*, are informal teachers of the faith in many ways. Above all, they participate in the prophetic office's transmission of the faith by proclaiming the living Word of God through faithful witness. They interpret, apply, transmit, and, indeed thereby, preserve the living Gospel in their daily life in different historical contexts of family life, work, and society. The lay faithful's interpretative sense of the faith as they apply the Gospel to daily life is an important engine in the ecclesial transmission of the faith and, as such, must be allowed to contribute to, in some way, the formal judgment and the official formulation of Church teaching. Discernment by theologians and the magisterium of this application to daily life is vital for an effective and authoritative exercise of the teaching office, especially when the magisterium comes to formulate a *consensus fidelium* on a matter of faith or morals. To speak of the teaching office of the Church only in terms of official formulation, proclamation, and adjudication by the hierarchical magisterium is, therefore, reductionistic.

---

[22] See a discussion of the relationship between the *munus docendi* and the *munus regendi* in the essay by James Coriden which appears above, 43–44.

While only the magisterium can speak for the whole Church as its final teaching authority, the magisterium is nevertheless (1) beholden to the faith of the whole Church, the primary recipient of revelation, and is (2) under the authority of Scripture and tradition.[23] With regards to the former, the *sensus fidelium* is a privileged expression of the lived faith of the whole Church; with regards to the latter, theologians have special scholarly expertise (which not all bishops might have to the same degree) regarding faithful interpretation of Scripture and tradition within new contexts. Therefore, the magisterium is dependent on these two other authorities in the Church for an effective exercise of its formal authority, both *de jure* and *de facto*.

Safeguarding and Accessing the Fides qua Creditur

The next set of tensions that remain and demand synthesis in the Vatican II documents is, firstly, the tension between a propositional and a personalist notion of revelation-faith and truth, and, secondly, the tension between an ahistorical and a historical notion of revelation-faith and truth. They each would give rise to different conceptions of the magisterium-theology relationship, and therefore different conceptions of the purpose and style of magisterial interventions.

---

[23] The classic text is *Dei Verbum* 10. Regarding the first point, Joseph Ratzinger in his commentary notes: "[DV 10] first makes the point that the preservation and active realization of the word is the business of the whole people of God, not merely of the hierarchy. The ecclesial nature of the word, on which this idea is based, is therefore not simply a question which concerns the teaching office, but embraces the whole community of the faithful. If one compares the text with the corresponding section of the encyclical *Humani Generis* (DS 3886), the progress that has been made is clear. . . . This idea of *solo magisterio* is taken up here in the next paragraph, but the context makes it clear that the function of authentic interpretation which is restricted to the teaching office is a specific service that does not embrace the whole of the way in which the word is present, and in which it performs an irreplaceable function precisely for the whole Church, the bishops and laity together." Joseph Ratzinger, "Dogmatic Constitution of Divine Revelation: Origin and Background," in *Commentary on the Documents of Vatican II*, vol. 3, ed. H. Vorgrimler (New York: Herder, 1969), 155–272, at 196. Regarding the second point, and once again contrasting *Dei Verbum* 10 with *Humani Generis* (DS 3886), Ratzinger notes: "For the first time a text of the teaching office expressly points out the subordination of the teaching office to the word, e.g., its function as a servant. One can say, it is true, there could never have been any serious doubt that this was in fact the case. Nevertheless the actual procedure often tended somewhat to obscure this order of things, though it had always been acknowledged in principle." Ibid., 197.

A propositional model will be concerned only with the integrity of faith as *fides quae creditur*. A personalist model of revelation and truth will be just as concerned with the integrity of faith as *fides qua creditur*, a much more elusive but more fundamental form of faith. An ahistorical model would not tend to acknowledge the historically conditioned factors affecting the particular way of expressing truths of faith formally defined in former times.[24] A historical model would see those formulations of the truths of faith as true answers to questions posed to the tradition, but nevertheless conditioned by both the questions, philosophies, and conceptual frameworks operating at the time of formulation, and the ever-changing perspective of the receivers of those formulations throughout history living the faith in new contexts. Not acknowledging and addressing this pervasive historicity, this model would presuppose, could lead to believers misunderstanding the meaning and truth of those formally defined truths of faith.

Both the propositional and ahistorical models would tend to deny that the application of the faith by believers in daily life has any significance for the traditioning of the faith into new contexts and, consequently, for the preservation of the faith. The personalist and historical models would acknowledge the revelatory value and authoritative weight of this informal theologizing and see the *sensus fidelium*, the fruit of the Holy Spirit's activity, as an expression of the community's *fides qua creditur* at work and of their informal and inchoate *fides quae creditur* (what Rahner would call their "concrete catechism").[25]

---

[24] Not all versions of a propositional model of revelation and truth might necessarily presuppose an ahistorical model of revelation and truth. A propositional model may acknowledge the historical conditioning of the original formulation of an officially proclaimed doctrine, but however not acknowledge the historicity of later receivers of such propositions of the faith.

[25] See, for example, Karl Rahner, "What the Church Officially Teaches and What the People Actually Believe," in *Theological Investigations*, vol. 22 (London: Darton, Longman & Todd, 1991), 165–75. Regarding the legitimacy of diverse applications of the faith, Rahner writes: "The differences in the structures that form the concrete framework for faith are quite justifiable, and that applies to the *fides quae* as well as the *fides qua*. It is quite legitimate, since it is absolutely unavoidable, for the truths of faith to be present throughout the world in different ways in the consciousness of faith, sometimes moving to the foreground of this consciousness, sometimes receding to the background, since the persons possessing this faith are themselves different. There are age differences, differences in the times in which they lead their lives, sociological differences, personal differences, and so on." Karl Rahner, "A Hierarchy

Both the propositional and ahistorical models would generally conceive the role of theologians as exclusively concerned with preserving the *fides quae creditur* in its propositional and ahistorical integrity. The personalist and historical models would understand the role of theology as one of exploring the hermeneutical circle between the Church's official *fides quae creditur* as taught by the magisterium and the contemporary *fides qua creditur*, and to see the entry point into that hermeneutical circle as being the discernment of how people are attempting to live the faith in contemporary circumstances (as expressed in the *sensus fidelium*).

Why is the exploration of contemporary *fides qua creditur* a significant starting point for theology? The connection between the figure of the prophet, evoked in *Lumen Gentium*'s reference to the prophetic office, and *Dei Verbum*'s shift to a personalist and historical notion of revelation as God's self-communication in human history is particularly relevant here as we explore the participation of the whole Church in its prophetic office. As Abraham Heschel writes: "[T]he fundamental experience of the prophet is a fellowship with the feelings of God, a *sympathy with the divine pathos*, a communion with the divine consciousness which comes about through the prophet's reflection of, or participation in, the divine pathos. . . . The prophet hears God's voice and feels his heart."[26] This goes to the core of the nature of revelation as God's loving self-gift to human beings, inviting and eliciting a loving response, resulting in an intimate relationship in which humans come to know the very compassionate heart of God, experiencing knowledge of a mystical kind. The prophet-God relationship, as Heschel describes it, exemplifies, then, the fundamental nature of faith as an intimate relationship of love, with a consequent heart-to-heart knowledge (*fides qua creditur*). It is not knowledge of a conceptual or scholarly kind, but something deeper. All the baptized, anointed by the Spirit, are invited into that intimate relationship and receive the deep personal knowledge that mutual loving reveals. This is the kind of knowing which *Lumen Gentium* 12 addresses when it speaks of an "infallibility in believing" emerging from a *sensus fidei* aroused by the Holy Spirit and resulting in a consensus. It is this kind of knowing that is captured in the *sensus fidelium*, making it a particularly authoritative mediator of God's saving revelation. Consequently,

---

of Truths," in *Theological Investigations*, vol. 21 (London: Darton, Longman & Todd, 1988), 162–67, at 165–66.

[26] Abraham J. Heschel, *The Prophets* (New York: Harper & Row, 1969), 1:26; emphasis original.

the *sensus fidelium* should be theological enquiry's starting-point in its study of the faith of the Church. Consequently, the *sensus fidelium* is to be treasured by the magisterium, since it expresses the faith of the Church as it is lived and applied, albeit in its diversity. In this sense, since both theology and the magisterium have an authority that is derived from the authority of the whole Church itself, they each have a certain dependence on the *sensus fidelium* as they fulfill their respective functions in service of the Church and as servants of the living Word of God.

Lumen Gentium 35 reminds us that the prophetic office seeks to continue the work of Jesus the prophet: "Christ is the great prophet who proclaimed the kingdom of the Father both by the testimony of his life and the power of his word. Until the full manifestation of his glory, he fulfills this prophetic office [*munus propheticum*], not only through the hierarchy who teach in his name and by his power, but also through the laity. He accordingly both establishes them as witnesses and provides them with a sense of the faith [*sensus fidei*] and the grace of the word so that the power of the Gospel may shine out in daily family and social life."[27] In his commentary on *Lumen Gentium* 25, Karl Rahner notes that it is significant that the dogmatic constitution chooses the biblical notion of preaching when speaking of the primary role of the hierarchical magisterium. By doing so, *Lumen Gentium* implicitly aligns the *munus docendi* to the *munus propheticum*: "It is noteworthy (and important for an ecumenical theology) that the more doctrinal concept of teaching attributed to the bishops as *doctores* is subordinated to the biblical and more comprehensive or existential concept of preaching."[28] Effective preaching and teaching is a communicative event, involving a speaker, the content to be communicated, and a receiver. An effective preacher and teacher will know his or her listeners, speaking in their language and addressing the complexity of their life situations. Accordingly, in listening to the magisterium's proclamation, the *fideles* should be able to respond: "This is our faith; this is the faith of the church."[29]

A corollary of Vatican II's shift (without forgetting its important propositional dimension) to a personalist and historical understanding of reve-

---

[27] Flannery translation.

[28] Karl Rahner, "The Hierarchical Structure of the Church, with Special Reference to the Episcopate," in *Commentary on the Documents of Vatican II*, vol. 1, ed. Herbert Vorgrimler (London: Burns & Oates, 1967), 186–218, at 208.

[29] Rite of Baptism for Children, 59, in *The Rites of the Catholic Church*, vol.1 (Collegeville, MN: Liturgical Press/Pueblo, 1990), 387.

lation is the theological importance it gives to the *present* saving reality of revelation, not just its foundational occurrence in the past for the early Church and later official ecclesial interpretation in the Church's history. If saving revelation, the deposit of faith with which the whole Church is entrusted, were only an event that happened and was witnessed in the past rather than being also continually active, then the magisterium and theology would need only to be concerned about getting the past right. But revelation, although unsurpassably communicated in the past in the coming of Jesus Christ through the Spirit, is also a saving reality in the present.[30] The same God at work in the Christ event witnessed to in Scripture and tradition is revealing and saving in the present moment. That such revelation is a present reality demands of the teaching office an attentiveness to God's saving activity in the present through the signs of the times.[31]

The very heart of the Catholic claim regarding the inextricable link between Scripture and tradition is the belief that the living Gospel is more than its written witness: it is a power at work in people's lives ("the power of the Gospel"),[32] not just a message. The living Gospel is written onto the hearts of the faithful, all the faithful; it is they who know the faith and are able to recognise its truthful and deviant interpretations and applications. It is this knowledge and ability to discern and apply the Gospel that has been traditionally called the *sensus fidei*, given to all the baptized, regardless of office and ministry in the Church. This active sense is a significant engine of the tradition process. It bridges past and present in a contemporary application of the Gospel. As such, it constitutes a contemporary source for accessing God's revealing and saving power at work in believers. This saving and revealing activity by God, manifest in its active appropriation by believers, provides a lens through which the deposit of faith (the lived apostolic tradition) and its key doctrinal expressions in church history can be faithfully interpreted. Similarly, in a hermeneutical circle of enquiry, the normative apostolic tradition, the deposit of faith, and later official doctrine constitute the

---

[30] On Gerald O'Collins's distinction between "foundational revelation" and "dependent revelation," see his chapter "Revelation Past and Present" in *idem, Retrieving Fundamental Theology: The Three Styles of Contemporary Theology* (New York: Paulist Press, 1993), 87–97.

[31] See *Gaudium et Spes* 4 and 11.

[32] St. Paul: "For I am not ashamed of the gospel; it is the power of God for salvation to everyone who has faith" (Rom 1:16).

lens for interpreting and critically discerning the contemporary lived experiences of the faith. The magisterium, as protector of the faith of the Church, is beholden to the lived faith of the Church, both in its present expressions and in its past formulations. For assistance in that task, so vital for evangelization, the magisterium necessarily turns to the scholarship of theologians. Theologians, for their part, attempt to bring the inchoate and elusive diversity of the *sensus fidelium* to some systematic expression, in the light of Scripture, tradition, etc.[33]

When a particular theologian's personal integration of the *sensus fidelium* on a doctrinal issue is perceived by the magisterium as threatening the integrity and unity of the faith, it is the magisterium's authoritative role to investigate. The process of coming to a judgment, however, itself involves a hermeneutical dimension. For help in making that judgment, in a circle of interdependent rights and responsibilities, the magisterium is dependent on the expertise of theologians, and generally it calls on its own theologians. That dialogue alone, however, does not constitute all dimensions of the magisterium-theology relationship. When the integrity of a particular theologian's interpretation of the faith is finally judged negatively, and the magisterium's consensus judgment is supported by the broad consensus of the wider community of theologians, beyond its own theologians, then intervention is warranted.[34] When the consensus support of theologians is lacking, the necessary principle of *conspiratio* among the three teaching authorities calls for an ongoing dialogue on the issue.

Office of Christ, Office of the Spirit

The third area of tension that remains to be addressed is the lack of integration regarding the assistance of the Holy Spirit. Without interrelating the different modes, the council attributes that same assistance to the magisterium (granting infallibility in teaching, under certain conditions), to theologians, and to the *sensus fidelium* (granting infallibility in believing, under certain conditions).[35] This lack of integration continues to be problematic and could be at the heart of perceived problems with magisterial intervention.

[33] On this role and the complexity of discerning the *sensus fidelium*, see Rush, *The Eyes of Faith*, 215–91.

[34] On some of the complex issues regarding a consensus among theologians and a consensus within the magisterium, see ibid., 261–74.

[35] See DV 8, 23, 24; LG 12 and 25.

The role of the Holy Spirit in the economy of salvation can sometimes be downplayed or ignored. Two examples may be given. First, the current *Code of Canon Law* reflects an ecclesial uncertainty regarding the Holy Spirit, according to the canonist James Coriden:

> The exclusion of the Holy Spirit and charisms from the code was not due to ignorance or casual neglect; it seems to have been a conscious choice. It is difficult to detect the real reasons for this deliberate exclusion. It may have been motivated by a fear of a mysterious charismatic element that might be difficult to verify or control, and that might prove disruptive or dangerous. Or the revisers of the code may have been reluctant to acknowledge any source of authority in the Church other than the exclusively Christocentric and hierarchic sources recognized for centuries. They may have been unwilling to recognize the Spirit who dwells within each one of the Christian faithful and gives them gifts for the building of the Church.[36]

Second, with regard to recent magisterial teaching, the paucity of references to the Holy Spirit in the three encyclicals of Pope Benedict XVI is significant. In the first section of *Deus Caritas Est* (art. 1–18), there is not one single mention of the Holy Spirit.[37] In the first article (19) of the second, practical section of the encyclical, we find five clustered references to the Spirit, and then four other references scattered throughout the rest of the encyclical (art. 21, 28, 37 and 41). In *Spe Salvi*, we find three references to the Spirit (art. 4, 5, and 50). *Caritas in Veritate* has only two references (both in art. 5).

An integrated pneumatology of how the Spirit works in the Church's teaching office and its three authorities must be grounded on a trinitarian theology of the interrelationship between the mission of the Word and the mission of the Spirit and their co-instituting of the Church, and a consequent pneumatologically balanced approach to the three offices of Christ in the Church. The mission of the Word in the economy of salvation is dependent on the mission of the Spirit, and vice versa. The Spirit is the principle of reception of the Word.[38] Without the Spirit the mission

---

[36] James A. Coriden, "The Holy Spirit and Church Governance," *The Jurist* 66 (2006): 339–73, at 372.

[37] It is surprising that in this summary of the Christian tradition on the nature of God as love, the encyclical does not quote Romans 5:5: "God's love has been poured into our hearts through the Holy Spirit that has been given to us."

[38] For a fuller exposition on the Spirit as "the principle of reception," see Rush, *The Eyes of Faith*, 15–36.

of the Word throughout history is ineffective. God's ongoing dialogue with humanity does not stop with the coming of Christ in human time; through the Holy Spirit, God continues to dialogue with the Church and humanity:

> By means of the same [living] tradition . . . the holy scriptures themselves are more thoroughly understood and constantly made effective in the church. Thus God, who spoke in the past, continues to converse with the spouse of his beloved Son. And the Holy Spirit, through whom the living voice of the Gospel rings out in the church—and through it in the world—leads believers to the full truth and makes the word of Christ dwell in them in all its richness. (DV 8)[39]

Furthermore, the offices of Christ in the Church are dependent on the Spirit for their realization. As the principle of the reception of Christ, it is the Holy Spirit who enables the Church to participate fully in, and effectively exercise, the three offices of Christ. The Holy Spirit enables the Church to be a prophetic, priestly, and kingly people. A pneumatological approach to the three offices of Christ enables us to avoid a false dichotomy, and potential conflict, between a purely Christological approach that grounds "ecclesiastical office," "ordination," and "institution" in the intention of Christ, and a purely pneumatological approach that sees charisms coming directly from the Pentecostal Spirit.[40]

The same Holy Spirit assists all three authorities in the one teaching office. "It is the same Spirit who assists the Magisterium and awakens the *sensus fidei*."[41] The Spirit also bestows the charism of theological scholarship upon individuals for the good of the whole Church. John Paul II speaks of "the contribution which theologians and faculties of theology are called to make by exercising their charism in the Church."[42] Likewise, the document *Instruction on the Ecclesial Vocation of the Theologian* (1990) notes:

> In order to exercise the prophetic function in the world, the People of God must continually reawaken or "rekindle" its own life of

---

[39] Flannery translation, corrected.

[40] See Rush, *The Eyes of Faith*, 56–60.

[41] John Paul II, *Ut Unum Sint*, 80, http://www.vatican.va/edocs/ENG0221/_INDEX.HTM (accessed August 13, 2011).

[42] Ibid., 81, in reference to the work of theologians in facilitating the reception of ecumenical dialogues.

faith. It does this particularly by contemplating ever more deeply, under the guidance of the Holy Spirit, the contents of the faith itself and by dutifully presenting the reasonableness of the faith to those who ask for an account of it. For the sake of this mission, the Spirit of truth distributes among the faithful of every rank special graces "for the common good." Among the vocations awakened in this way by the Spirit in the Church is that of the theologian.[43]

Thus the mission of the Holy Spirit guiding authoritative Church teaching (and disciplining) should proceed through a *conspiratio* among the *sensus fidelium*, theologians, and the magisterium. This *conspiratio* should be characterised by both respect and attentiveness. St. Paul urges the Thessalonians to show such respect when dealing with the freedom of the Spirit: "Do not quench the Spirit. Do not despise the words of prophets, but test everything" (1 Thess 5:19-21). In the book of Revelation, we read seven times of the need for such attentiveness to the Spirit: "Let anyone who has an ear listen to what the Spirit is saying to the churches" (Rev 2:7, 11, 17, 29; 3:6, 13, 22). The Church early in its history came to recognise that the Spirit is best respected and attended to by the instrument of council or synod, in dialogue (Acts 15:28: "it has seemed good to the Holy Spirit and to us"). The legitimacy of any exercise of judgment regarding orthodoxy and consequent formal disciplinary action is dependent on the evidence of a dialogic *conspiratio* among all three authorities of the one teaching office.

This essay so far has identified the following as the elements which a new synthesis of Vatican II's emphases would need to hold together: (1) the mission of the Word and the mission of the Spirit; (2) the entire Church (the *universitas fidelium*) as the primary recipient of God's revelation and the magisterium as the official guardian of the faith of the whole Church; (3) "the faith once delivered to all the saints" (Jude 3) and the lived faith of generations of believers throughout history in forever new contexts; (4) the distinctive participation of the *universitas fidelium* in the prophetic office and the magisterium's distinctive participation in that office; (5) the *sensus fidelium* as expressing the lived faith of the Church and the magisterium as expressing the taught faith of the Church; (6) a personalist model of revelation and truth and a propositionalist model of revelation and truth; (7) the model of faith as a living salvific and

---

[43] Congregation for the Doctrine of the Faith, *Instruction on the Ecclesial Vocation of the Theologian* (Vatican City: St. Paul Books and Media, 1990), par. 5–6.

revelatory personal relationship (*fides qua creditur*) and the model of faith as a body of beliefs to which the believer is required to assent (*fides quae creditur*); (8) [paralleling the interrelationship between *fides qua creditur* and *fides quae creditur*] the *infallibilitas in credendo* of the whole people of God under certain conditions and the *infallibilitas in docendo* exercised by the magisterium under certain conditions; (9) the charisms gifted by the Holy Spirit to individuals and the appropriate ordering (not quenching) of those charisms by institutional structures of the Church; and (10) theologians as bearers of the charism of academic scholarship and the magisterium as bearers of "the sure charism of truth" (DV 8).

Some Elements of a Theology of Magisterial Intervention

Presuming such a proposed synthesis of Vatican II on the teaching office, how might legitimate and effective intervention by the magisterium be characterised? What further elements and resources, in addition to those above, might be useful? In addressing those questions, I wish to make six brief points in conclusion.

First, the magisterium-theology relationship should model the spirit of open dialogue which the magisterium officially promotes between the Roman Catholic Church and other Christian churches and ecclesial communities. Something of a model for the *conspiratio* between the three authorities of the teaching office can be found in Pope John Paul II's encyclical *Ut Unum Sint* (1995), in which the *sensus fidelium*, theologians, and the magisterium are portrayed as being in critical interaction, under the guidance of the Holy Spirit. In the passage that follows, the pope is speaking of the process of reception of ecumenical dialogue statements. It is worth quoting in full.

> While dialogue continues on new subjects or develops at deeper levels, a new task lies before us: that of receiving the results already achieved. These cannot remain the statements of bilateral commissions but must become a common heritage. For this to come about and for the bonds of communion to be thus strengthened, a serious examination needs to be made, which, by different ways and means and at various levels of responsibility, must involve the whole People of God. We are in fact dealing with issues which frequently are matters of faith, and these require universal consent, extending from the Bishops to the lay faithful, all of whom have received the anointing of the Holy Spirit. It is the same Spirit who assists the Magisterium and awakens the *sensus fidei*.

Consequently, for the outcome of dialogue to be received, there is needed a broad and precise critical process which analyzes the results and rigorously tests their consistency with the Tradition of faith received from the Apostles and lived out in the community of believers gathered around the Bishop, their legitimate Pastor.

This process, which must be carried forward with prudence and in a spirit of faith, will be assisted by the Holy Spirit. If it is to be successful, its results must be made known in appropriate ways by competent persons. Significant in this regard is the contribution which theologians and faculties of theology are called to make by exercising their charism in the Church. It is also clear that ecumenical commissions have very specific responsibilities and tasks in this regard.

The whole process is followed and encouraged by the Bishops and the Holy See. The Church's teaching authority is responsible for expressing a definitive judgment.

In all this, it will be of great help methodologically to keep carefully in mind the distinction between the deposit of faith and the formulation in which it is expressed, as Pope John XXIII recommended in his opening address at the Second Vatican Council.[44]

Second, the very topic and manner of magisterial intervention within the Catholic Church is itself not a matter unrelated to the Catholic Church's commitment to ecumenical dialogue along the way to full ecclesial communion. It should and will become explicit agenda in these dialogues, as called for by Pope John Paul II in *Ut Unum Sint* 79: "It is already possible to identify the areas in need of fuller study before a true consensus of faith can be achieved: . . . 4) the Magisterium of the Church, entrusted to the Pope and the Bishops in communion with him, understood as a responsibility and an authority exercised in the name of Christ for teaching and safeguarding the faith." In that ecumenical dialogue, the Catholic manner of intervening to exercise authority becomes part of the content for dialogue and open to ecumenical enquiry. Furthermore, along the way Catholics might well need to be open to the "gifts" other Christian denominations wish to "share" with us, in the spirit of a "receptive ecumenism."[45] Among those gifts might be their way of practicing doctrinal oversight, an ecumenical exchange which may challenge our own current procedures.

---

[44] *Ut Unum Sint*, 80–81.

[45] P. D. Murray, ed. *Receptive Ecumenism and the Call to Catholic Learning: Exploring a Way for Contemporary Ecumenism* (Oxford: Oxford University Press, 2008).

Third, in developing a theology of magisterial intervention, further ecumenical learning could well take place by adopting the principle of "differentiated consensus," a term now commonly used to describe the methodology of the *Joint Declaration on the Doctrine of Justification* (1999), though the declaration doesn't use that exact phrase.[46] It does speak, however, of having achieved a "consensus on the basic truths" despite "remaining differences" and "differing explications." The relevant three paragraphs are:

> 5. The present Joint Declaration has this intention: namely, to show that on the basis of their dialogue the subscribing Lutheran churches and the Roman Catholic Church are now able to articulate a common understanding of our justification by God's grace through faith in Christ. It does not cover all that either church teaches about justification; it does encompass a consensus on basic truths of the doctrine of justification and shows that the remaining differences in its explication are no longer the occasion for doctrinal condemnations.

> 14. The Lutheran churches and the Roman Catholic Church have together listened to the good news proclaimed in Holy Scripture. This common listening, together with the theological conversations of recent years, has led to a shared understanding of justification. This encompasses a consensus in the basic truths; the differing explications in particular statements are compatible with it.

> 40. The understanding of the doctrine of justification set forth in this Declaration shows that a consensus in basic truths of the doctrine of justification exists between Lutherans and Catholics. In light of this consensus the remaining differences of language, theological elaboration, and emphasis in the understanding of justification described in paras. 18 to 39 are acceptable. Therefore the Lutheran and the Catholic explications of justification are in their difference open to one another and do not destroy the consensus regarding the basic truths.

While agreement in terms of propositional uniformity was not achieved in the dialogue, there was an agreement arrived at where each partner could nevertheless recognize their own sense of the faith in the sense of

---

[46] The Lutheran World Federation and the Roman Catholic Church, *Joint Declaration on the Doctrine of Justification* (Grand Rapids, MI: Eerdmans, 2000). Also available at http://www.vatican.va/roman_curia/pontifical_councils/chrstuni/documents/rc_pc_chrstuni_doc_31101999_cath-luth-joint-declaration_en.html (accessed August 13, 2011).

the other, despite its different theological framework.[47] Such a principle of "differentiated consensus" could provide an ecumenical opening with rich application to magisterial intervention *within* the Catholic Church where there are "remaining differences" and "differing explications" between a theologian's work and that of the official magisterium.

Fourth, the element of time (significant also for the magisterium in its own assimilation of new ideas) is a factor to be appreciated in the work of any theologian. He or she may not get it "right" every time. Time is needed for the exploration of new ideas by theologians in the search for truth, a search that at times might be unfruitful or lead to wayward speculation that comes close to being beyond the pale. As John Henry Newman asserts, truth is "the daughter of time."[48] Through time, the Church undergoes a continuous *paideia* (education) under God's Spirit with regard to the significance of revelation for new times.[49] The teaching Church is forever learning; "true teaching follows true learning, and true learning is a process that takes time."[50] In referring to the interaction between the magisterium, theology, and the *sensus fidelium*, and the reception of Scripture and tradition by all three, Beinert remarks: "With that [interaction] is brought into play the factor of time. Dialogue and exchange of ideas are processes which can drag on for a long time:

[47] On "differentiated consensus," see Hervé Legrand, "Receptive Ecumenism and the Future of Ecumenical Dialogues: Privileging Differentiated Consensus and Drawing Its Institutional Consequences," in *Receptive Ecumenism and the Call to Catholic Learning: Exploring a Way for Contemporary Ecumenism,* ed. Paul D. Murray (Oxford: Oxford University Press, 2008), 385–98.

[48] John Henry Newman, *An Essay on the Development of Christian Doctrine,* 6th ed. (Notre Dame, IN: University of Notre Dame Press, 1989), 47. Newman cites Crabbe's Tales as the source of the phrase. It is quoted in the context of Newman's discussion of the particular class of development he calls "historical development," which he says is "the gradual formation of opinion concerning persons, facts, and events. Judgments, which were at one time confined to a few, at length spread through a community, and attain general reception by the accumulation and concurrence of testimony. Thus some authoritative accounts die away; others gain a footing, and are ultimately received as truths. . . . Thus by development the Canon of the New Testament has been formed." Ibid., 46–47.

[49] On *paideia,* see Juan Luis Segundo, *The Liberation of Dogma: Faith, Revelation, and Dogmatic Teaching Authority* (Maryknoll, NY: Orbis Books, 1992).

[50] Margaret O'Gara and Michael Vertin, "The Holy Spirit's Assistance to the Magisterium in Teaching: Theological and Philosophical Issues," *Catholic Theological Society of America Proceedings* 51 (1996): 125–42, at 140.

consensus can never and in no way be forced."[51] Likewise, in asserting the "complementarity and necessary interaction" between the cautious pastoral sensitivity of the magisterium (the *cathedra pastoralis*) and the academic rigor and innovative speculation of theologians (the *cathedra magistralis*), Jean-Marie Tillard highlights the virtue of patience as a necessary factor in the teaching of the truth in the Church: "This [complementarity and necessary interaction] needs patience and forbids rapid decisions or short-cuts. But in God's design, time is an essential factor. The Catholic Church knows by experience how difficult it is to correct a too hasty decision. This is why it is its tradition to teach a truth slowly articulated through a consensus of which the *cathedra magistralis* (exegetes, dogmaticians, canonists, moralists) as well as the *sensus fidei* of the whole People of God including 'people in the pews' are the builders, together with the *cathedra pastoralis*."[52] Thus, time should be allowed for the magisterium in its assimilation and testing of new ideas; likewise, time should be allowed for a theologian in the development of his or her proposals.

Fifth, if the mind of Vatican II was to change the style of the Catholic Church, then that style should characterise the manner in which the magisterium intervenes. John O'Malley's fundamental interpretation of Vatican II is well-known: what the bishops of Vatican II set out to achieve was a shift toward a different style of being Church.[53] This is expressed in its recurring call for "dialogue" [*colloquium, dialogus*] at all levels;[54] its use of "horizontal" words such as cooperation, partnership, collaboration, subsidiarity, collegiality; its call for a style of governance focused on service rather than control; its vocabulary of inclusion and participation. Proceeding from such a way of being Church and following Pope John XXIII's injunction at the opening of Vatican II concerning "a magisterium

---

[51] Wolfgang Beinert, "Der Glaubenssinn der Gläubigen in der systematischen Theologie," in *Mitsprache im Glauben? Vom Glaubenssinn der Gläubigen*, ed. Günther Koch (Würzburg: Echter, 1993), 51–78, at 74.

[52] J.-M. R. Tillard, "How is Christian Truth Taught in the Roman Catholic Church?," *One in Christ* 34 (1998): 293–306, at 300.

[53] For one articulation of his thesis, see John W. O'Malley, *What Happened at Vatican II* (Cambridge, MA: The Belknap Press of Harvard University Press, 2008).

[54] Ann Michele Nolan, *A Privileged Moment: Dialogue in the Language of the Second Vatican Council, 1962–1965* (Bern and New York: P. Lang, 2006).

which is predominantly pastoral in character,"[55] a theology of magisterial intervention would want to uphold the truth in love: *veritas in caritate*.[56]

Finally, necessary ecclesial caution in the face of new theological ideas should be tempered by a necessary ecclesial caution and eschatological reserve in the face of the hiddenness and incomprehensibility of God, despite God's revealedness and knowability through the unsurpassable fullness of revelation in Christ through the Spirit. That Spirit has been given precisely in order to lead the Church toward a fullness of truth not yet perceived, a fullness which will only be revealed at the end of time. Ecclesial experience has shown that doctrine does develop and the Church does change, often through the prophetic challenge of theologians. In the concluding sentence of the first chapter "On the Mystery of the Church," *Lumen Gentium* speaks of how, until the clarity of the eschaton, the Church fulfils its mission of revealing the mystery of Christ "in a faithful though shadowed way" (LG 8).[57] In the service of that mission, theologians always work under the shadow of Mystery. The magisterium, in judging them with "the sure charism of truth," peers too through a glass darkly.[58]

---

[55] The speech can be found in Walter Abbott, ed. *The Documents of Vatican II* (London: Geoffrey Chapman, 1966), 710–19, at 715.

[56] See Ephesians 4:15.

[57] The Latin text: ". . . et mysterium eius, licet sub umbris, fideliter tamen in mundo revelet, donec in fine lumine pleno manifestabitur." The above translation comes from National Conference of Catholic Bishops, *Doctrinal Responsibilities*, 3. Tanner has "faithfully . . . albeit amid shadows"; Flannery reads, "faithfully, however darkly."

[58] 1 Corinthians 13:12, KJV. The NRSV reads: "in a mirror, dimly." I am grateful to Richard Lennan and Myriam Wijlens for their helpful comments on this essay.

Chapter 5

Magisterium as a Social Imaginary
Exploring an Old Problem in a New Way

Gerard Mannion

University of San Diego

"If There Are Things Which Should Not Be Questioned, There Are Also Things That Must Be Questioned":[1] Discerning the Problem

Our ways of perceiving and understanding social entities give rise to practices and wider worldviews that can come to dominate the actual life of that social entity and the people within it. Such effects can be negative and positive alike and to varying degrees. Whatever theological explanations of the Church we choose to emphasize and privilege, it is also undeniably a social entity.

This essay seeks to illustrate and emphasize that magisterium can be understood and exercised in qualitatively differing ways vis-à-vis the contribution which such makes to the life and mission of the Church. It will explore one particular approach through which we might help remind ourselves of this fact. In particular, it assesses the impact of how magisterium has been understood and practiced in the period of church history from the aftermath of the Second Vatican II Council down to present times. It will argue that many of the resultant ecclesial perceptions and practices that have followed from one particular yet highly influential way of understanding and exercising magisterium have not been to the Church's benefit in this time. It will seek to suggest possible

---

[1] Yves Congar, "Magisterium, Theologians, the Faithful and the Faith," *Doctrine and Life* 31 (1981): 548–64, at 561.

ways in which alternative ways of viewing and practicing the art of magisterium better suited to these and future times might be agreed upon.

Method and Magisterium: Selecting Some Tools of the Trade

Magisterium Has History:
Church Teaching Authority in Its Developmental Context

So, first, how should we describe and go about investigating, exploring, and explaining Church teaching authority, i.e., magisterium, in our times? What conceptual tools, which methods, and what frameworks might serve us best here? In truth, there are numerous resources available. Perhaps what the most fruitful share in common is a need to stand back and try to transcend the day to day realities of magisterium and its effects. The tools of the social sciences, historical consciousness, organizational analysis, philosophical, and particularly epistemological frameworks could all be employed. The discernment offered by ethics in particular needs to play a major role in any exploration of magisterium.

Our first key point of emphasis is simply that it is important to pay attention to the social contextualisation of and background to the emergence of any particular understanding and ways of exercising magisterium in question. Closely related to this is the need to be equally attentive to the historical backdrop to the same.

It is neither controversial nor even especially novel to state that a plurality of perceptions and ways of exercising teaching authority have always existed within the Church. Comparative and differing perceptions of teaching with authority, the activity itself, as well as different opinions in relation to who could and should be able to perform this activity, are found in many New Testament texts.[2] There are disagreements about such issues right from the outset and church history demonstrates those disagreements never went away.

The Church eventually came to employ "magisterium" as shorthand for "teaching with authority," the teaching function of the Church itself. At differing periods of history, naturally different terms and frameworks have been used to understand this function. In particular, in seeking to understand the disagreements and disputes pertaining to magisterium today, obviously the periods leading up to, during, and following the

---

[2] Of course, this predates any sense of formal offices and notions of magisterium which would gradually emerge in the later Church.

Second Vatican Council are of the utmost importance. It is also especially instructive to look back toward the nineteenth century and beginning of the twentieth century. But we can also point toward the relevance of the Council of Trent and even look beyond the Reformation periods to the conciliarist disputes in seeking to understand the divisions and fault-lines within the Catholic Church in recent decades.

So, from the earliest centuries of the Church, an analogous notion of what came to be termed magisterium existed and differing aspects of this function, as well as differing—indeed fluctuating—understandings of who could, should, and would contribute to the exercising of teaching authority, have been manifested at differing points of church history and in differing places. Francis Sullivan has helped affirm this fact in his many contributions on the subject.[3] Yves Congar also illustrates this so well in a series of essays.[4] I wish to underline the fact that magisterium as we today know it has emerged, developed, and evolved across time and space. It will continue to evolve long into the future. Magisterium has a history; it has a story and that story is an ongoing one.

When church history is written in fifty, one hundred, or more years, the past four decades or so will be listed amongst those periods of church history when disagreement and division over magisterium were at a peak level of divisiveness across the Church. This is one good and important reason to engage in more sustained studies of and conversations concerning magisterium today—not least of all so that the period covered by future church historians will fill but a short chapter and increasingly be reduced to footnotes in subsequent centuries, until tomorrow's learned graduate students begin to dig deep and unearth a mine of sources for new and lengthy historical-critical dissertations in the twenty-third century.

The Social Construction of Ecclesial Reality and the Ecclesially Informed Construction of Wider Social Realities

As well as the historical attentiveness that is required in seeking to understand magisterium today, so also is due attentiveness required to

---

[3] Francis A. Sullivan, *Magisterium* (Dublin: Gill and Macmillan, 1983).

[4] Yves Congar, "A Semantic History of the Term 'Magisterium,'" and "A Brief History of the Forms of the Magisterium and Its Relations with Scholars," in *The Magisterium and Morality: Readings in Moral Theology No. 3*, ed. Charles E. Curran and Richard A. McCormick (New York: Paulist Press, 1982), 297–313 and 314–31, respectively; and "Magisterium, Theologians, the Faithful and the Faith," *Doctrine and Life* 31 (1981): 548–64.

the social context of magisterium. The social construction of reality is a topic that received an increasing amount of attention in the second half of the twentieth century.[5] Such essentially involves a set of theories about the various ways in which we collectively shape and give existence to our shared worlds, our ways and means of relating to one another, the processes and activities, the concepts and forms of knowledge that govern our interactions, and how such become habituated through these processes and thereby become institutionalized over time. This in turn shapes the knowledge and beliefs about our social reality itself. Such theories have been considerably developed in various directions since.

There are numerous ways in which those working within the various theological disciplines and sub-disciplines have sought to make use of such theories. Many of these scholars have embraced and openly utilized the social sciences in a very fruitful and constructive fashion.[6] Other approaches have been more reticent or even diametrically opposed to employing the social sciences in the service of theology.

This essay is an attempt to consider certain implications of the social construction of ecclesial reality and, in turn, the ecclesially informed and shaped social construction of our wider shared reality. By the first of these categories, I mean ways and means of interacting and the accompanying discourse, conceptual frameworks, and knowledge which impact upon how we perceive and therefore how we actually relate to and live out ecclesial life. By the second category, I refer to the ways in which our ecclesial modes of being and our beliefs impact our wider being in the world and our belonging or otherwise to additional social groups and communities.

Although this approach can, of course, be applied to wider ecclesiological viewpoints and modes of ecclesial being, here the focus is narrowed by considering magisterium because I believe in so focusing our attention, we more readily work toward the heart of many serious challenges facing the Church in our times.

---

[5] The classic work is by Peter L. Berger and Thomas Luckmann, *The Social Construction of Reality: A Treatise in the Sociology of Knowledge* (Garden City, NY: Anchor, 1966).

[6] In particular, there have been various applications made of social constructionism in the Church, and theologians such as Gregory Baum have made great use of this and other sociological theories in seeking to make sense of the Church. See, for example, his *Essays in Critical Theology* (Kansas City, MO: Sheed and Ward, 1994). A further example of direct relevance to our discussion topics here is by Michael G. Lawler, *What Is and What Ought to Be: The Dialectic of Experience, Theology and Church* (New York and London: Continuum, 2005).

I believe that one especially fruitful way of seeking to understand and refine magisterium today is through the recent trend for perceiving modes of social discourse and practice through the lens of the concept of the "social imaginary."[7] The notion of social imaginary is settled upon because of its utility and current relevance to promoting a greater understanding of our social relations and processes. It is also one approach that might help us combine the fruits of a number of other methods. I believe that, through building upon and developing further interaction with additional modes of analysis, the concept of "social imaginary" and an appreciation of how such can shape, change, and indeed reflect social and cultural changes, can prove instructive in relation to magisterium. We might better discern that, how, and why magisterium has a history, that is, undergoes change and development, and, at times, radical transformation both in relation to how it is perceived and understood and in relation to how it is practiced. There are many significant ecclesial and wider social consequences to such facts.

We also settle upon the notion of social imaginary here because it takes the theories of social constructionism a stage further. Let us briefly explain the notion. One of the scholars who has helped popularize this concept more than most is the philosopher Charles Taylor.[8] He explains social imaginary in the following, now oft-cited, terms: "I mean something much broader and deeper than the intellectual scheme people may entertain when they think about social reality in a disengaged mode. I am thinking, rather, of the ways people imagine their social existence, how they fit

---

[7] An "imaginary," in its sociological usage and so applied in relation to a social context (as we shall explore further, below), refers to the collective manner in which the shared and/or prevailing values, norms, laws, mores, etc., are envisioned, understood, and related to by particular communities, as well as the symbolic and institutional frameworks that help communities to make sense of, put into practice, and regulate these aspects of shared existence. Theologically speaking, of course, the Church as a community entails much more than what can be explained solely or reductively in social-scientific terms. Nonetheless, the Church is also a community, has variously self-identified as a "society," and has applied to itself the many different ways in which other and wider social groupings have sought to understand, describe, and regulate themselves throughout history. Therefore, to apply imaginary in an ecclesial context is a valid and heuristically informative method to adopt.

[8] On this concept, two of Charles Taylor's most significant works are *Modern Social Imaginaries* (Durham, NC, and London: Duke University Press, 2004); and *A Secular Age* (Cambridge, MA, and London: The Belknap Press of Harvard University Press, 2007), particularly chapter 4, 159–211 (and esp. 164–71, on modern forms of social imaginaries, which largely replicates the earlier book).

together with others, how things go on between them and their fellows, the expectations that are normally met, and the deeper normative notions and images that underlie these expectations."[9] The concept of a "social imaginary" is different from a social theory insofar as it encompasses the less theoretical ways in which ordinary people "'imagine' their social surroundings," such as "in images, stories, and legends," something shared by a much larger group than a theory. Furthermore, "the social imaginary is that common understanding that makes possible common practices and a widely shared sense of legitimacy."[10] The social imaginary is a complex matter: "It incorporates a sense of normal expectations that we have of each other; the kind of common understanding which enables us to carry out the collective practices which make up our social life. This incorporates some sense of how we all fit together in carrying out the common practice. This understanding is both factual and 'normative'; that is, we have a sense of how things usually go, but it is interwoven with an idea of how they ought to go, of what mis-steps would invalidate the practice."[11] Crucially, however, what might begin as the theories of a few can "come to infiltrate the social imaginary"[12] and this "first of elites," and, in time, perhaps spread its influence to become pervasive throughout a given society.

Thanks in large part to Taylor's work, the concept of social imaginary has become something of a buzzword in recent times far beyond the field of the social sciences. Taylor's contribution has led to a great deal of additional debate about social imaginaries, and theologians have sought to apply some of those insights or critically to adapt and supplement them. By and large, it has been a particularly welcome sign to see theologians utilizing the notion of social imaginary, which in itself serves as something of a form of social DNA, toward ecclesiological ends.[13] Ecclesial and moral imaginaries can be understood as part of the broader social imaginaries by and through which we live. But the relationship of influence should never be understood simply in uni-directional terms. All of this builds upon a great deal of work done on imagination crossing between the theological, philosophical, and social sciences in the 1970s, 80s, 90s, and beyond (embracing diverse contributions from, for example,

---

[9] Taylor, *Modern Social Imaginaries*, 23; also *A Secular Age*, 172.

[10] Taylor, Ibid.

[11] Taylor, *A Secular Age*, 172.

[12] Taylor, *Modern Social Imaginaries*, 24.

[13] That is, DNA is a metaphorical way of explaining the actualities of biological existence.

David Tracy's work to Richard Kearney's). So imagination and imaginaries have been to the forefront of much ecclesiologically relevant thinking.

I believe there are a variety of ways in which such a conceptual framework can help us understand developments in the Church since the end of Vatican II. In recent decades, we have seen many developments in the self-understanding of the Church and of its teaching. A number of these developments have not been to the benefit of the Church as it seeks to live out its mission and, in particular, as many in the Church strove and continue to strive to implement as widely and fully as possible the vision of the Second Vatican Council.

In discussing such issues, one is mindful that even to raise the possibility that the present-day prevailing sense of magisterium might not be helping the Church fulfill its mission well and that alternatives are both possible and desirable is to invite the charge of polemics from some quarters. An all-or-nothing mindset prevails in many quarters; a "test the wind," fence-sitting strategy in others. It is sadly true that, in recent times, many shy away from stating in frank terms what they believe to be the more pressing problems facing the Church today. But this was never the case with those such as Yves Congar and Karl Rahner. Their writings are frequently frank—even in their titles—to avoid all ambiguity. Nor was it the case during the conciliar discussions that brought us the inspirational teachings that emerged from Vatican II—and these debates both in session and "behind the scenes." Open, honest, and, where and when necessary, forthright and frank exchanges have always been a part of ecclesial discourse. Blessed John XXIII underlined as much at the beginning of the council when he counseled that the only rule should be that, in all things, charity should prevail.

Francis Sullivan reminds us how the International Theological Commission's 1975 *Theses on the Relationship between the Ecclesiastical Magisterium and Theology* "assigned to theologians a critical role with regard to the magisterium," which Sullivan concludes means that the official hierarchy cannot therefore be the final arbiter of what is truth without wider input from the Church, including theologians.[14] I hope and believe we can rediscover the courage to own doubts openly in the Church today and long into the future. Part of the analysis which follows will seek to offer some reasons as to why such a reserved attitude has come to prevail in parts of the theological community.

[14] Sullivan, *Magisterium*, 207.

Putting the Tools to Work: Exploring and Understanding the Issues

Magisterial Malaises: Discerning the Heart of the Matter

What much of the evidence across the global Christian Church suggests to us today is that certain features and characteristics of older and more repressive social imaginaries are making a comeback across the Church and theology alike—however albeit with distinctly postmodern twists. These social imaginaries accentuate otherness in a pejorative sense. Shunning social visions based upon broader mutuality and interdependence, they likewise perceive difference in a negative light and effectively affirm a retreat from the wider social settings wherein Christians live out their daily forms of existence.

In seeking to make sense of why these challenges have emerged for the Church, it is helpful to survey the scene in the period following the Second Vatican Council, a period during and following which major ecclesial and ecclesiological changes took place. By 1968, an ecclesiological turning point had already been reached by which Catholics increasingly began to position themselves in different ecclesiological and ecclesial "camps." Some embraced and advocated swift change in so many areas of Church life; others wished for a slower pace of reform and renewal; still others began to perceive the changes being implemented in negative terms and with increasing alarm and fear. Such divisions plague the Church to this very day. This had major implications for various aspects of ecclesial, theological, and doctrinal life. So, if one is permitted to paint in broad brush strokes here, the past four decades or so has been a period of shifting "ecclesial imaginaries"—in the one direction trying to make the Church more truly a sacramental presence "in" the world, in the other direction perceiving the need for the Church to swim against the tide of that world.[15] These ecclesial imaginaries have in turn been shaped by, complemented, and in a number of ways reflected shifts in wider social imaginaries of the period.

The group of theologians that came together to form what became openly known as the *communio* program,[16] in particular, would increas-

---

[15] Naturally, a wide variety of different perspectives and practices fall in between these two ends of this continuum. Our focus here is heuristic in intention—we are not dealing in rigid ideal types in any literal sense here.

[16] See Joseph Ratzinger, "Communio—Ein Programm," *Internationale Katholische Zeitschrift* 21 (1992): 454–63 = "Communio: A Program," trans. Peter Casarella, *Communio: International Review* 19, no. 3 (1992), 436–49.

ingly see their vision and prescription for the future of the Church gradually transform so much of ecclesial life, not least of all through the eventual imposition worldwide of a normative understanding of communion ecclesiology.[17] This normative ecclesiological vision has been variously described and characterized by its critics as restorationist, world-renouncing, superioristic, and neo-exclusivistic, and perceived as constituting something very different from the consensus that emerged from Vatican II. I suggest that the astonishing and pervasive success of this *Communio* Project has actually been, to a great extent, due to a parallel transformation in the understanding and exercise of magisterium throughout the Church in the same period.

So, we now turn to the core area of focus. The life of the Roman Catholic Church has been blighted by divisions and disagreements in the last four decades, and too often it has made headline news for all the wrong reasons. Such is well known. One particular set of issues *is linked to* the majority, if not all, of the problems the Church has faced in these times.[18] This is the understanding and exercise of Church teaching authority (i.e., magisterium), in relation to which several developments of concern have arisen. A more restrictive understanding and exercise of magisterium have emerged. There has been a renewed impetus to centralize matters upon Rome. Disagreement, dissent, and even discussion pertaining to "official" teaching on many issues have been dealt with in a stern fashion.

Because such developments have cumulatively influenced and shaped many aspects of Roman Catholic ecclesial life, teaching, formation, and theological inquiry, numerous Catholics today appear to have assimilated such an understanding of magisterium and accept such an exercise of the same as something both normative and apparently "traditional," despite the existence of considerable evidence to the contrary. This apparent conception of magisterium one finds in a wide range of locations, from official pronouncements from Rome, as well as from individual bishops and episcopal conferences, to discourse in theological journals and books, to discussions in the media, and to the vitriol poured out against supposed "liberals" in the blogosphere: "*the* Magisterium" has

---

[17] See Gerard Mannion, *Ecclesiology and Postmodernity: Questions for the Church in Our Times* (Collegeville, MN: Liturgical Press, 2007), esp. chapters 2–4.

[18] Of course, it is readily acknowledged that no single causative factor can explain all difficulties and problems in the Church in these times. But here we seek to identify and discuss one very significant factor behind many such ecclesial challenges.

become a concept that has generated as much controversy, division, and fear as it has misunderstanding.

In the main, theological discussions of such developments pertain to the reception of and appropriate response to what is termed "official" or "authentic" teaching today and who is authorized and/or competent to identify what counts as such; that is to say, the subject-object distinctions. Here we cannot go into lengthy debate in relation to the frequent confusion made between the object of magisterium, i.e., what its purpose and function is, what it addresses and seeks to discern, make sense of, and communicate (in short, the Gospel, the gracious and loving self-communication of God and all the implications of this for our world, or, if one prefers shorthand theological parlance, revelation, the Word of God), and the subject or subjects of magisterium—i.e., the actors or functionaries, those who seek to practice this art, to fulfill this function or purpose in the Church. Needless to say the two are *not* identical. The subject-object debate has always been with the Church, but keeping the focus on the latter as opposed to the former has consistently remained the most important[19] concern for the Church as it strives to fulfill its mission as faithfully as it might.[20]

When Magisterium Brings Division and Discord

If space permitted us, here we could draw upon numerous case studies that would offer much pause for thought in relation to a range of issues that blight ecclesial life today.[21] One of the key problems that the Church across the globe is grappling with today is the tensions and even factions that are bound to emerge when an unswerving, some would say intransigent, perception of the Church and its authority, a perception that, to many, is seemingly impervious to genuine and meaningful

---

[19] As Yves Congar helps demonstrate; see "A Semantic History of the Term 'Magisterium,'" 297–313.

[20] The term "the official magisterium" is employed here when referring to conceptions that center on the role of the "official" Church authorities, particularly Rome, to distinguish them from broader understandings. The primary considerations relate to what (and not "who") magisterium is and who can and should exercise it.

[21] A number of these issues and situations are outlined in Gerard Mannion, "'Defending the Faith': The Changing Landscape of Church Teaching Authority and Catholic Theology," in *The Vision of John Paul II: Assessing His Thought and Influence*, ed. *idem* (Collegeville, MN: Liturgical Press, 2008), 78–106. Cf. also, Bradford E. Hinze, "A Decade of Disciplining Theologians," 12–30, above.

dialogue, permeates much of the life of an ecclesial community. When it is a perception that demands absolute obedience, and this not so much to actual church teaching *per se* but to very particular and time- and context-bound interpretations of church teaching and of church teaching authority, the tensions and factions are compounded further still.

Division and discord are the only outcomes of such a situation and this not simply because of the social developments of recent decades, indeed centuries, but also because of the understanding of church teaching and of the Gospel itself that so many Catholics hold dear, including the primacy of conscience but also the right to play a part in the wider dialogues necessary in important situations—participation and subsidiarity both being fundamental principles of the Catholic social tradition. Conversely, in recent times we have seen a renewed insistence upon the interlocking character of the Catholic faith and therefore of its teaching and therefore of the range and reach of magisterium.

The problem in recent decades is that too many in the Church have allowed an increasing desire for normativity in all aspects of doctrine, theological interpretation, and even ecclesial life in general also to shape and affect the understanding and exercise of magisterium. What all too frequently happens in such a situation is that ecclesiastical politics takes over from genuine teaching authority, with all the messiness and moral questions that are raised when political considerations dictate all other priorities. Power and "territorial" concerns rise to the surface and dictate priorities. Any perceived alternative voices and perspectives are viewed in pejorative terms and deemed to be threats that must be opposed. As with any claim to authority based upon a sense of uniqueness, superiority, expediency, entitlement, or fear, conflict with values that an institution is supposed to cherish and uphold can follow. In promoting, privileging, and defending one particular social imaginary over and against others, morality often falls by the wayside, even to the detriment of the actual social imaginary being promoted itself.

Charles Taylor has illustrated this danger in relation to wider social and political considerations, but when one looks at church history it is obvious that this is as true within the Church as it is without it.[22] Taylor reminds us how overt idealism can eventually morph into its ugly opposite. We have witnessed a range of forms of ecclesial idealism and ideality across the churches and within theology in recent decades.

---

[22] See Taylor, "A Catholic Modernity?," 32–33. Again, Taylor revisits these arguments in *A Secular Age*.

When ecclesiastical politics takes over from more ecclesially life-giving concerns, the Church can only suffer as a result. In this respect, it is instructive today to recall a passage from a further study of the divisions that have beset the Church, which details not simply the dangers of factionism within the Church, but also counsels the necessity to realize and appreciate that, despite the divine institution of the Church that is held as part of Catholic tradition, nonetheless "its humanity is clearly evident in its character as a political institution, a body of people governed by constituted authority towards a common goal."[23] Because of this fact, the author surveys the ecclesial situation through the lens of the political sciences, being himself both a political scientist and a priest. His words again help support the value of understanding the Church's being in general and its magisterium in particular, as prone to giving rise to very particular and often competing and conflicting forms of social imaginary:

> the Church has taken on the appearance of a multipolarized society which at times appears to be on the brink of tearing itself apart over its political differences, not to mention some real theological differences. Whether this factionalism will in fact give rise to actual schisms on a large scale remains to be seen, but that such a possibility is even thinkable indicates the importance of trying to understand this phenomenon in the contemporary Church. Undoubtedly, there always has been a group basis to some extent in the politics of the Church; today it is simply more obvious and more obstreperous. But because it is so apparent, it is also more amenable to analysis as a fact of Church life. . . . The presence of such conflict and the need for adjustment in the Church today is all too apparent. The uneven distribution of decision-making power within the political structures of the Church and the consequent efforts of groups to retain or gain power and influence is at the basis of much of the ecclesial turmoil we are now experiencing. Indeed, the major problems of the Church today are more precisely political than theological in nature. Consequently, any effort at reconciling groups within the Church must fasten itself upon the political realities of the situation.[24]

These words appear in an essay by the late Bernard F. Donahue that was published in 1972 (when the *Communio* Project and its attendant ecclesial

---

[23] Bernard F. Donahue, OSFS, "Political Ecclesiology," *Theological Studies* 33 (1972): 294–306, at 294.

[24] Donahue, "Political Ecclesiology," 305.

and ecclesiological agenda were taking off in earnest). They remain as relevant, if not even more so, today.

In his recent essay analyzing magisterium itself, and of related interest to the issues raised by Donahue here, Charles Taylor is especially concerned to address the now habitual transgression of limits evident in the recent understanding and exercise of magisterium—limits which, for the good of the Church, should really demand faithful observance. One particularly problematic transgression that he discusses, which we might here call the privileging of one social imaginary over and against all others, is in effect a refusal to acknowledge plurality within the Church and theology.[25] Taylor speaks of the transgression enacted by "the sacralization of one philosophical language over other ones equally available for the articulation of Christian faith."[26] Also noting that this was a particularly problematic practice in the anti-modernist campaign and prior to Vatican II, especially in the neoscholastic emphasis in theology and teaching, he states that,

> We could call this move false sacralization, which involves identifying certain modes of thought, certain moral codes, or certain historical periods of the Church's life as essential to the faith and consequently downgrading or even rejecting other philosophies, moralities, and periods. This goes against the spirit of Catholicism itself, which by its very nature is the faith of a universal Church, at once at home in and alien to all times and civilizations.[27]

Taylor sees this transgression especially evident in the "too simple and direct reading of natural law" in recent times.[28] The dangers of suppressing and denying pluralism are here clearly demonstrated.

Acknowledging the Sociopolitical Implications of Contemporary Magisterium

By bringing into focus the wider contexts of magisterium, and particularly in utilizing the notion of magisterium understood as a social

---

[25] Taylor does not explicitly speak in this short essay about understanding magisterium as a social imaginary, but in many ways he, also, is employing such a mode of analysis in relation to the crisis of authority in the Church in an implicit fashion.

[26] Charles Taylor, "Magisterial Authority," in *The Crisis of Authority in Catholic Modernity*, ed. Michael J. Lacey and Francis Oakley (Oxford and New York: Oxford University Press, 2011), 259–69, at 261.

[27] Ibid., 261.

[28] Ibid., 262.

imaginary which can shape and even dictate both the reality of ecclesial life at any given point and the subsequent impact that Catholics and the Church have upon their wider social settings, we might be better placed to find constructive ways of moving beyond the crises and polarizations that have beset the Church for far too many decades now. This approach assists us just as it also necessitates us to treat the intra-ecclesial political ramifications of magisterium in somewhat closer detail. This brings us to T. Howland Sanks's now somewhat eerily prophetic study, which directly addresses the "crisis of magisterium" in the immediate post-conciliar period. Toward the close of that study, he cites with approval Gregory Baum. Writing in 1969, Baum raises similar concerns to those which Donahue would address soon afterward, as well as counseling caution against what I term the "view from nowhere" understanding of magisterium, whereby the cultural, temporal, social, and political backdrop to, and enduring context of, magisterium are overlooked or ignored and forgotten altogether: "There is no objective point of view, abstract and superior, from which questions may be asked. For this reason the theologian must make explicit for himself the reasons for his choice of questions, submit them to a theological critique, and either by keeping, modifying or rejecting them, assume responsibility for the political meaning of his choice."[29]

One of the most serious and growing problems with the crisis of magisterium that has deepened and widened year on year since those words were written—in truth, one of the saddest effects of the prevalence of one particular social imaginary in the Church, viz., the understanding and exercise of magisterium that has been prevalent since the late 1970s—is that an increasing number of theologians have become averse even to acknowledging that their questions along with the answers they seek to discern *have* political ramifications, both within and without the Church.

Indeed, it is a sorry fact that not a few theologians have simply shied away from asking meaningful questions altogether—not simply in ecclesiological terms but increasingly so even in doctrinal terms and, for a large number, even in wider political terms. Expediency has flourished in far too many quarters of the Church in recent times, and ironically so, given the Gospel injunction against naked expediency. To reiterate an important point mentioned earlier: none of this is said in order to be

---

[29] Published the year after, Gregory Baum, "Theology and Ideology," *The Ecumenist* (Jan.–Feb. 1970): 25–31, at 27; as cited in T. Howland Sanks, *Authority in the Church—A Study in Changing Paradigms* (Missoula, MT: Scholars' Press, 1974), 175.

polemical, this must be underlined, but rather to offer a *descriptive* account of the way things have become in the Church. Glance across the contents pages of some of the most widely read journals or catalogues of prominent publishers of theological works in recent times and compare these with the same thirty and forty years ago and one will find some very revealing truths staring one in the face about the impact of this particular conception of magisterium.[30] Whether you then go on to approve or lament such developments is, of course, dependent upon a host of additional factors. But *that* such a sorry and fractious atmosphere has become still more pervasive in the Church of more recent times is confirmed by a description of the ecclesial situation vis-à-vis theological enquiry from the German moral theologian, Klaus Demmer:

> An opinion of one's own is an excessive luxury since theology is subject to the dictates of a "political calculation." This inevitably leads to an attitude of partisanship. Whether or not this is consciously present, there is a process of assimilation to the authorities and the fractions that dispenses the individual theologian from the burden of intellectual autonomy. Usually this is accompanied by an academic overproduction. It is only seldom that one encounters anything original here, and still less anything that genuinely takes the discussion further. It is therefore no cause for astonishment when theological reflection becomes remote from real life.[31]

Such developments in and of themselves offer further compelling evidence of that clear and unavoidable truth that emerges when we seek to examine magisterium as a social imaginary, namely, that magisterium has social and political implications and consequences and is never free from such. The perspectives, beliefs, and actions of those engaged in exercising magisterium therefore have social and political consequences within and without the Church alike. And, just as those involved in secular governance follow a particular political ideology and preferred model of governance and its practice, so also does the same pertain in the Church.

Magisterium does not exist in a vacuum. Those who exercise magisterium do not do so in a moral, social, and political vacuum. The pronouncements,

---

[30] Again, other causal factors are involved here. But I maintain that the prevailing ecclesial atmosphere brought about by the sense of magisterium in question is the most significant factor.

[31] Klaus Demmer, MSC, *Living the Truth: A Theory of Action*, trans. Brian McNeil (Washington, DC: Georgetown University Press, 2010), 61.

results, and consequences of magisterium do not drop from heaven. Magisterium is never exercised in a neutral environment or context. Magisterium is always going to be a process that has social and political connotations—and this, again, in terms of the social and political realities within and without the Church. If one studies the "behind the scenes" history of both the First and Second Vatican Councils, not to mention the long series of ecclesial processes that we today collectively term the Council of Trent, one sees the politicization of magisterium is also nothing new.

If we have, then, succeeded at least in identifying and discerning some of the problems and challenges that need to be faced, can we begin, here albeit briefly, to consider possible ways in which these might be tackled? The evidence suggests that ecclesial change appears key, both in terms of the difficulties and in terms of the solutions required. Back in 1974, Sanks's own reflections upon the "political meaning" of theological undertakings involved looking at the differing ways and perspectives that can predominate at differing times. His preferred response to taking up the challenge set down by Baum was therefore to utilize Thomas Kuhn's work in paradigm analysis in seeking to identify what is taking place when there are shifting intellectual and political sands in both the world of theology and the Church alike. Including, perhaps especially in relation to, magisterium, "The political consequences of any theological position need to be explored, and understanding and explicating the paradigms that are involved in that theology is a step toward this."[32] For Sanks, what the Church requires is clear—the Church needs a "theology of change": "I do not say 'development' because we need to face the fact of change as it is without minimizing it or hiding it by convoluted theological maneuvering. Our historical awareness forces this kind of honesty upon us."[33]

Magisterium and the Social Construction of Contemporary Ecclesial Reality

The foregoing has suggested that we need to examine magisterium both in the context of wider ecclesial life (drawing in wider ecclesiological questions), and also in terms of how these developments vis-à-vis magisterium relate to the wider societal developments during the period in question. In the postmodern era we see new versions of exclusivistic

---

[32] Sanks, *Authority in the Church*, 175.
[33] Ibid.

and authoritarian social imaginaries have come to the fore in numerous religions and wider societies alike. The Catholic Church has not been immune to such developments. The former Master of the Dominicans, Timothy Radcliffe, offered a not dissimilar assessment in 2009:

> Many things often thought of as typically Catholic—an authoritarian style of teaching, centralized control, a legalistic approach to morality, suspicion of the body—are, perhaps, a result of our Church's conformity to the culture of the Enlightenment. As we move into another moment in humanity's history, we may find the Church renewing itself, liberated from the confines of a way of thought that, though hugely beneficial to humanity in many ways, cramped the Church's life and obscured its visibility as a sign of the Kingdom.[34]

I do not share *all* of Radcliffe's judgment here—in particular I believe we should shy away from binary oppositional thinking in relation to the Enlightenment and its legacy.[35] Instead, I believe that the real problem relates more to the Church's postmodern reaction to much of the Enlightenment's legacy—a reaction to both the positive and negative aspects of modernity alike, with the situation being complicated, for sure, by certain hangovers from those periods when the Church adopted some of the more negative traits set in motion by the period known as modernity (including the Enlightenment period). Nonetheless, what Radcliffe does firmly underline here is that the way in which magisterium has been perceived and exercised in the modern and contemporary period is not something that conforms well to how Church teaching authority was understood and exercised across other periods of Christian history.

In this essay, I have been seeking to highlight this fact, for there is much hope for the future of the Church if and when more Catholics realize that if things have not always been thus, then things need not continue to be thus long into the future. And that is good news for the Church in the midst of its struggles and divisions today. This is another key thesis that we need to underline.

Here it is instructive to recall how Taylor, in his treatment of social imaginaries in general, likened their function to the philosophical

---

[34] Timothy Radcliffe, OP, "The Shape of the Church to Come," *America* (April 13, 2009), http://www.americamagazine.org/content/article.cfm?article_id=11565&comments=1 (accessed May 20, 2011).

[35] Although Radcliffe does claim he is not succumbing to such a trend, his words here do lend themselves to such an interpretation.

concept of the "background," that "largely unstructured and inarticulate understanding of our whole situation, within which particular features of our world show up for us in the sense they have. It can never be adequately expressed in the form of explicit doctrines, because of its very unlimited and indefinite nature."[36] And an "implicit grasp" of our social space is very different from a theoretical description of the same.[37]

In *A Secular Age*, Taylor sketches how the modern theory of moral order "gradually infiltrates and transforms our social imaginary." Through such a process "that is originally just an idealization grows into a complex imaginary through being taken up and associated with social practices, in part traditional ones, but often transformed by the contact."[38] When a theory so "penetrates and transforms" the social imaginary, "people take up, improvise, or are inducted into new practices. These are made sense of by the new outlook, the one first articulated in the theory; this outlook is the context that gives sense to the practices. And hence the new understanding comes to be accessible to the participants in a way it wasn't before. It begins to define the contours of their world, and can eventually come to count as the taken-for-granted shape of things, too obvious to mention."[39] This is the way in which, I suggest, the contemporary prevailing understanding of magisterium has come to dominate ecclesial life across recent decades. This social imaginary emerged out of the post-conciliar reactionary ebb and flow and was particularly shaped by, through, and given purchase by the *Communio* Project, and disseminated further and wider through a multitude of policies and intentional actions on the part of first curial, then wider episcopal authorities, aided by various ecclesial movements and not a few theological and philosophical contributions along the way.

The distinctive understanding and exercise of magisterium that has prevailed in recent decades has functioned as a very pronounced form of social imaginary both within and without the Church during this period. The implications of such for ecclesial life in general and Church teaching authority in particular, today and into the future, are numerous and serious. Whether one takes a statement issued by the Doctrinal Commission of the U.S. Bishops' Conference or looks at any blog or "faithful" web site that rails against perceived ecclesial liberals, one finds the presence

[36] Taylor, *A Secular Age*, 173.
[37] Ibid.
[38] Ibid., 175.
[39] Ibid., 175–76.

of this social imaginary of an authoritarian and implicitly "infallible" Church authority (here the term is all too frequently used as it is understood, in a common sense rather than ecclesiological sense). And it is an authority which must be obeyed, and obeyed simply because certain individuals hold Church positions of authority; then what they say also must be obeyed, must be true, and must be "right."

And yet the past again reminds us that the status quo is not normative in any irreversible sense and so need not be how ecclesial being in the future is lived out. Because in so much of the history of the Church the process is the other way around: what provides the authority to a teaching, and therefore to the teachers who pronounce it, is actually the accordance of the teaching with the Gospel, with what is true and right, and this is affirmed collectively through a range of processes and existential and socially enacted endorsements. The model of command and obey and the accompanying threat of punitive sanctions belongs to coercive forms of political ideology; it finds no legitimate place in the Gospel of Jesus Christ. And yet the evidence shows that many features of the contemporary prevailing social imaginary of magisterium finds more in common with coercive political ideologies, and therefore the practices that are resultant from this social imaginary resemble those of coercive political powers in an analogous fashion as well. This is not the first time the Church has faced such a situation, but that it does so just a relatively short period of time after the collective soul-searching and process of discernment that was Vatican II will prove all the more puzzling and disappointing to future church historians.

Whose Defense of Which Understanding of the Faith? The Necessity of Critical Interrogations of Contemporary Magisterium

Just as Alisdair MacIntyre, in his work *Whose Justice, Which Rationality*.[40] sought to demonstrate that there are conceptual schemes at work in any debates pertaining to justice, which in turn presuppose a particular understanding and operative methodology with regards to epistemology and, in particular, to rationality, with such having a marked impact on the sense and practice of justice across differing communities, a parallel might also here be drawn with debates pertaining to magisterium in recent decades. Here we have briefly described how the Church has witnessed the emergence of a particular paradigm shift in the operative

---

[40] London: Duckworth, 1998.

understandings of Catholic teaching authority. And this, along with a real transformation in the understanding of the role of the Catholic theological community and the college of bishops (collectively) in shaping, interpreting, and explicating this teaching authority. So, too, has there been a shift in the prevailing methodological and underlining theological presuppositions informing such a change in understanding and practice with regards to magisterium.

But, if some commentators in recent times speak of theology in a "postliberal age," then one might also chart the reaction to such new developments in relation to magisterium, if not in terms of "postliberal" magisterium, then certainly in terms of a still later development of understanding of Catholic teaching authority that came about in reaction to perceived excesses of "liberal" theologies and theologians and in reaction to further intellectual and cultural trends. So one might tentatively suggest we can, indeed, today speak of the late emergence of a reactionary "postmodern" magisterium. One could even suggest that the contemporary era in some ways mirrors that atmosphere during which the reactionary and centralising understanding of magisterium in the nineteenth century came to dominate the "ecclesial imaginary" for a long period of time.

The Church has always been charged with this discernment of "the signs of the times," and during its most influential and life-giving periods it demonstrably has done so very well. By the same token, in periods of decline and disillusionment, we can see the prevailing pattern is the reverse: intransigence, a refusal to engage with many cultural and societal developments in any fashion, an insistence upon *semper idem* in a way that atrophies the life of the ecclesial community.

In fact, again learning the lessons of history, the prevailing mentalities and strategies that have dominated ecclesial life in recent times might well turn out to be the forces that are actually driving people *away* from the Church, far from preserving it and defending the faith. The time has come for people actually to consider and indeed appreciate how the opening up of the Church at Vatican II gave great life and sustenance to a Church that otherwise might have rapidly entered into grave decline much sooner. Far from hastening the decline in Mass attendance and voluntary commitment to a variety of church-related activities, the so-called "liberal" developments actually kept the Church's vitality going and gave it new life and energy in parts of society it had previously struggled to touch and in parts of the globe where its mission was so desperately needed. And part of such an understanding of recent history must also be to appreciate the effect of the restorationist, neo-exclusivistic, and negative programs, projects, and ecclesial mindsets (as well the revisionist accounts and interpretations of Vatican II) that have prevailed all too widely since: these are among the greatest forces actually turning people away from the Church—including not a few theologians, pastoral workers, ministers, and so many others steadfastly committed to the Gospel.

For many, "the Church" is increasingly ceasing to be of relevance to the world and reality in which they live out their being and in which they struggle to make sense of that being. In some parts of the world and parts of societies elsewhere where the Church appears to be thriving and flourishing, it actually appears to be the case that a sociological and psychological reductivism is prevailing in the organization and governance of the Church. And an endorsement of this reductivism apparently comes from the center. This is something of a great irony, because these are the very reasons why pathways such as liberation theology and the ecclesiology that emerged out of it were opposed.

So, while ecclesial detachment on the part of those alienated and disillusioned is increasing, simultaneously within the Church genuine commitment to the Gospel is waning and what is replacing it in too many places are really postmodern forms of folk religion dressed up as revival and justified with strongly worded injunctions and policies that, at base, communicate merely the message that such "is the only show in town."[41] The "New Evangelization," so prominent in the priorities of ecclesial minds in much of Rome and those wedded to following such an agenda—which might well be termed the culmination of the *Communio* Project hatched all those decades ago—risks becoming the Emperor's new clothes. Beneath the surface of these moves lie all the priorities of the divisive social imaginary we have sought to explicate here. Meanwhile, back in the "world," there is a serious danger that increasing numbers of Catholics—as a direct result of developments within the Church itself in these times—will come to agree with that profound social commentator, Jay Z, that realism dictates that ecclesial and pietistic idealism can achieve little in the face of the harsh realities of contemporary life for so many in contemporary society: "Jesus can't save you, Life starts when the church

---

[41] This is not to denigrate folk religion in any fashion; rather the issue here is that certain forms of it are encouraged, which, in effect, appear to lessen the commitment to the praxis demanded by the Gospel and equally to lessen commitment to the wise injunctions for being Church in the world of our times counseled by *Gaudium et Spes*.

ends."[42] In the heyday of, say, liberation theology, or the Catholic Worker Movement, I suspect no rapper (were such a genre around then) would have thought such a line conceivable.

So the greatest irony is that perhaps the strongest faith in the Gospel in many societies today is held and maintained and defended by many who have serious doubts about the direction in which institutional leaders and policies are taking the Church in these times. There is a profound ambiguity in relation to so much of what passes as Church policy and teaching in these times on the part of so many good people, and, I suspect, among those reading this essay, there are many shuffling uncomfortably because they are seeing descriptions of their own existential and ecclesial place at this time.

The social imaginary that has nonetheless been so influential and has prevailed and predominated across the Church for so long now is demonstrably failing to be persuasive and convincing for an enormous number of Catholics. The solution is neither to shout the essentials of that social imaginary all the louder and to harden opposition against alternative ecclesially informed *weltanschauungen*, nor to devise ever more subtle yet increasingly pernicious campaigns to silence and exclude alternative viewpoints and perspectives while simultaneously skillfully manipulating the media to project an image of the precise opposite of what is taking place.

None of this is to deny that there are not also wider social factors that have brought the Church to its present day situation, nor indeed that there are additional ecclesial factors that feature as causal factors, also. And the wider ecclesiological social imaginary we are here critiquing, of course, emerges out of the specific intentions of those who espouse and shape it—intentions they would say are very positive ones. It seeks to offer the reassurance of unambiguous direction and guidance in a postmodern world of uncertainty, flux, and change; a world of relativism and plurality. Certitude is offered against the fearful state of inertia in the face of limitless choices and options, continuity is projected over and against disruption. But this social imaginary fails to include the necessary checks and balances provided by mechanisms of self-critique and self-discernment. Such an imaginary therefore claims to transcend cultural and temporal as well as contextual boundaries and yet is actually a project of all too specific cultural, temporal, and contextual settings.

[42] Jay Z with Alicia Keyes, "Empire State of Mind," on *The Blueprint 3*, Roc Nation, 520856-2, 2009.

"Not Every Compromise Is Dishonourable":[43] Suggestions for Future Ways Forward

Affirming Magisterium's Inherent Pluralism

A main and straightforward point to emerge from all of the above is to indicate that and how magisterium has always been understood and exercised in diverse ways and forms. It also changes and undergoes the same developments and radical overhauls that other aspects of church life and teaching have undergone throughout the centuries—how could it be otherwise? Indeed, to state such should not be surprising. We have a plurality of ecclesiologies, of Christologies, of understandings of the doctrine of the Trinity, and so on. We have differing forms of understanding and exercising ministry, liturgical variations in practice and interpretation,[44] and numerous different notions of how teachings even are received throughout the Church. Why should teaching authority be any different? It would be most strange if it were the exception to the historically true normative rule of ecclesial life, which, of course, is not a rule in any restrictive sense at all, viz., plurality in doctrinal interpretation and therefore in the practical outworkings of such.

As stated, this should offer us grounds for much hope. It reminds us that the present-day situation in which the Church finds itself is neither unique nor beyond repair. It enables us to appreciate and emphasize further that throughout church history, and perhaps especially so in recent decades, we find a plurality of interpretations of magisterium. For example, a theologian of the mindset of Joseph Kleutgen (who was close to the Curia for a sustained period of his career), and those whom he influenced in the nineteenth century, sought to impose their own understanding of magisterium and how it should be exercised as normative upon the Church. Such was their style, and the style of the times, a style that often brought about the precise opposite outcome to that which it was seemingly intended to bring about. Witness the neoscholastic revolution whereby the works of the Angelic Doctor, Thomas Aquinas, were declared normative to such an extent that many within and without the Church did not actually seriously engage with them as primary sources

---

[43] Karl Rahner, "Theology and the Church's Teaching Authority after the Council," in *Theological Investigations*, vol. 9: *Writings of 1965–67* (London: Darton, Longman & Todd, 1972), 83–100, at 100.

[44] Recent campaigns to bring more uniformity to the same across the Church notwithstanding.

for the best part of a century. Herein lies a further warning against a univocal understanding and model of magisterium and overt claims concerning the "definitive" character of what are unquestionably context-, culture-, and time-bound interpretations of church teachings and of wider tradition.[45]

Being at Home in Postmodernity: Living with Ambiguity

One attempt, in effect if not name, to offer such a theology of change, is the study by John Thiel, who argues that, whether it is the interpretation offered by the systematic theologian or the "unselfconscious" efforts of "any believer" to understand their faith more fully, "unambiguous closure" cannot be the end point of such undertakings insofar as their interpretive efforts "respect the mystery" they are grasping to understand.[46]

This reinforces the need for both ecclesial and epistemological humility in our Church. There is a plurality of interpretations *because* there is a plurality of relations to the divine mystery that is being interpreted, and a plurality of ways in which the gracious self-communication of God (revelation) has been made known (modes of revelation).[47] To state such is simply to work outward from the doctrine of the Trinity, after all—the one God experienced in the distinct modes of divine being, and this God is the same in the depths of divine being as the God whom Christians experience as creator, redeemer, and reconciler and in a host of other ways: the God for us is the same God who is absolute mystery.

Thiel expresses similar sentiments in a passage that helps to explicate the deep theological implications of the plurality that does and must exist within the Church and theology itself and, I would add, therefore in the processes and licit voices of magisterium:

> The ambiguity of interpretation is rooted not only in its inevitable inadequacy to its object but also in the plurality of the means by which God reveals, in both Scripture and tradition: in the plurality

---

[45] And so inherently open to fallibility, reform, and reversal.

[46] John E. Thiel, *Senses of Tradition: Continuity and Development in Catholic Faith* (New York and Oxford: Oxford University Press, 2000), 4. Cf. Taylor, "Magisterial Authority," 259.

[47] What normativity emerges for the Church is due to the consensus that emerges and is tested and eventually affirmed through a multitude of processes but which, throughout history, never excludes differing forms of experiencing and understanding and explaining the same mysteries and treasured relations to the truth.

of meanings that Christians have found and continue to find in Scripture, traditions, and, to an even greater degree in the mutually informative ways that Scripture and tradition together present God's inspired Word. The plurality of both these sacred means and the meanings they offer the faithful imagination becomes more plural and, as a result, more ambiguous still when set in the vast spectrum of possible experience, in which Scripture and tradition are encountered, their meanings are sought, and their mystery is interpreted.[48]

Thiel wishes to discourage "ecclesiastical fundamentalism" in the same way biblical fundamentalism was held in check for so many centuries by the differing senses of Scripture being positively acknowledged in scriptural and theological study and enquiry. Plurality and ambiguity, then, are elements of the faith and ecclesial life that we can and must live with, indeed feel at 'home' with: now we see through the glass darkly.

From a "Morally Impossible Situation" to "Teaching Without Fear"

The situation posed by the present-day understanding and exercise of magisterium at the official level, which has brought about what Charles Taylor terms a "morally impossible" situation[49] is seriously eroding the freedom of Catholic theological and pastoral endeavor, alike. It is draining the life and vitality out of ecclesial being around the globe. For the greater part of the history of the Church, theologians did not traditionally labor so universally under the fear that what they say might jeopardize their careers, livelihoods, and personal as well as families' well-beings. But they have done so for the last two decades or more at least. By and large, those who live in such fear are loyal and faithful servants of the Gospel, not rabid dissenters bent on bringing about some Da Vinci Code-esque radical overhaul of the fundamentals of the faith. Rather, they seek to see the Gospel influence and shape and have a positive influence upon our lives and wider world in a fuller and more wide-ranging fashion. So something is wrong. The magisterial malaises are very real and something has to change. Taylor ultimately pleas for a "Teaching without Fear."[50] Can we find a pathway toward this?

---

[48] Thiel, *Senses of Tradition*, 1 5.
[49] Taylor, "Magisterial Authority," 266.
[50] Ibid., 268.

Concluding Reflections

We do not necessarily have to privilege the concept of social imaginary in exploring the magisterial malaises of our times. We could employ a range of alternative or complementary tools, methods, and concepts. For example, one could also explain the malaises in terms such as the intransigent and anti-dialogical magisterial system having colonized the ecclesial life-world. Nor do we have to agree that the issues here are the only causal factors behind present-day ecclesial difficulties.

Here I have simply sought to utilize one notion that may offer us a way of transcending the divisions that are quite obviously not in the best interests of the Church, its members, and the Christian mission. By understanding magisterium as a social imaginary, we come to appreciate that differing perceptions of what teaching authority is and how it should be exercised, as well as who should be involved (participate) in its exercise, have an enormous impact on the day to day life of the Church, upon ecclesial existence itself. Therefore we can come to realize that there can be a different way to that which has prevailed in recent decades, and that the divisions and polarizations can be transcended.

An understanding and exercise of magisterium that relies upon coercive fear and the rejection of all dissenting perspectives and voices, which in turn shapes the entire governance and teaching structures throughout the Church, which imposes exclusionary perspectives and further practices upon the life of the Church local and universal alike, which shuns the world and so hastens the withdrawal of the Church apace on what Karl Rahner termed the long "march to the ghetto,"[51] is but one, admittedly very powerful, successful, and wide-reaching social imaginary in the Church. But it is *one* nonetheless, and this demonstrably so in both synchronic and diachronic terms.

However, the Second Vatican Council—including in and through the divisions and disagreements throughout the conciliar process—helped demonstrate that alternative and more ecclesiologically fruitful social imaginaries are possible. But many suggest this conciliar exercising of magisterium differs markedly from the spirit and letter of many pronouncements of the official exercise of magisterium in recent times. We must ask ourselves why this is so, and what should be done about this situation of ecclesiological cognitive dissonance that currently exists in relation to the council.

If all theology is really about is explaining and affirming the teachings of central Church authorities in a given time (as today's prevailing under-

---

[51] Karl Rahner, *The Shape of the Church to Come*, trans. and intro. by Edward Quinn (London: SPCK, 1974), 93.

standing of magisterium clearly seeks to suggest), then at least three, probably four, generations of Catholic theologians have been operating under a totally delusional understanding of what their craft is all about. Their vocations have been misheard. But such cannot be the case. Again, both synchronically and diachronically, the weight of evidence is clear that theology is about much more than this, and the role of the theologian is far broader and deeper than such a confirmatory undertaking. Despite protests to the contrary by some of those wedded to the model of magisterium we have been examining here, the prophetic charism within the Church so often finds expression in the form of what today would be termed dissent; indeed, it is proper to speak of "the virtue of dissent," when one surveys the interventions of so many theologians throughout the story of the Church from the very earliest Christian centuries.[52]

Furthermore, if there is something to be said for the theories concerning the social construction of reality, of our being in the world, the world that is God's own creation, then those social imaginaries that accentuate otherness in a pejorative sense, which, rather than mutuality and interdependence, affirm qualitative difference from and a retreat from the wider social settings wherein Christians live out their daily forms of existence, cannot be viable visions for building up the life of the Church and fulfilling its mission. Christ sent the disciples out *into* the world. He did not command them to retreat into an exclusivistic form of existence. The experiences of the early Church confirm quite the opposite.

All of this helps us to appreciate how we can never really, in these times, live according to a single, uniform social imaginary, but rather we live in terms of a series of multiple-belongings and through a mosaic of differing social imaginaries—sometimes these prove complementary, sometimes they do not. Within the churches the same is also true. We also need to come to a renewed appreciation of unity through diversity, as well as of the sense of catholicity itself, and this understood in qualitative, rather than crudely quantitative terms. The Church desperately requires a more existentially oriented and humble (both in existential and epistemological terms) account of what the quest for Christian truth entails and, therefore, an understanding and exercise of magisterium complementary to this.

---

[52] See "A Teaching Church That Learns? Discerning Authentic Teaching for Our Times," in *Crisis of Authority in Catholic Modernity*, ed. Michael J. Lacey and Francis Oakley (Oxford and New York: Oxford University Press, 2011), 161–91, at 183–84.

Chapter 6

Quaestio Disputata
The Magisterium in an Age of Digital Reproduction

Anthony J. Godzieba

Villanova University

Introduction

The small question that I want to raise here has implications for the ways we think theologically about magisterium. Indeed, it could be an indicator of how the role of authority within the ecclesial *communio* has already developed in a way that mirrors the operations of contemporary consumer and managerial culture, thus drawing the Church farther away from the very *communio* it intends to promote. The reader shrewd enough to catch the echoes of Walter Benjamin in my title will sense the direction of my argument.

Here is the question: does the immediate availability of a wide variety of papal statements via electronic media and the internet change the perceived level of authority that they carry? Even more fundamentally, does this "digital immediacy" influence the reception of these statements, which in turn shapes the statements' truth-value and their influence on the development of the Roman Catholic tradition, the reality of *communio*, and the very character of "teaching authority"?

My reflections are occasioned by a discussion in the journal *Theological Studies* several years ago regarding the assisted nutrition and hydration (ANH) of severely brain-damaged patients. This discussion was a reaction to the very pointed statement made by Pope John Paul II in his 2004 allocution "Life-Sustaining Treatments and Vegetative State," to the effect that the allocution had on the development of the Catholic moral tradition, and to the subsequent reception of the pope's comments by bishops, by those involved in Catholic health-care situations, and by Catholic ethicists who deal with end-of-life issues. These reactions were most intense while the United States was in the throes of controversy over the care of Terri Schiavo, who had been diagnosed as being in a persistent vegetative state and who eventually died in March 2005.[1] In his allocution, the pope insisted that "the administration of water and food, even when provided by artificial means, always represents a *natural means* of preserving life, not a medical act. Its use, furthermore, should be considered, in principle, *ordinary and proportionate*, and as such morally obligatory, insofar as and until it is seen to have attained its proper finality, which in the present case consists in providing nourishment to the patient and alleviation of his suffering."[2]

In this essay, I will steer clear of the complex ethical issues.[3] Rather, I want to discuss the effect that the immediate accessibility of magisterial

---

[1] Pope John Paul II, "Address to the Participants in the International Congress on 'Life-Sustaining Treatments and Vegetative State: Scientific Advances and Ethical Dilemmas'" (March 20, 2004), http://www.vatican.va/holy_father/john_paul_ii/speeches/2004/march/documents/hf_jp-ii_spe_20040320_congress-fiamc_en.html (hereafter "Allocution"); Thomas A. Shannon and James J. Walter, "Assisted Nutrition and Hydration and the Catholic Tradition," *Theological Studies* 66 (2005): 651–62; John J. Paris, James F. Keenan, and Kenneth R. Himes, "Did John Paul II's Allocution on Life-Sustaining Treatments Revise Tradition?," *Theological Studies* 67 (2006): 163–68; Thomas A. Shannon and James J. Walter, "Reply to Professors Paris, Keenan, and Himes," *Theological Studies* 67 (2006): 169–74. Regarding the unprecedented nature of the allocution's particular teaching, see Thomas A. Shannon and James J. Walter, "Implications of the Papal Allocution on Feeding Tubes," *The Hastings Center Report* 34, no. 4 (July–August 2004): 18–20, where the authors note that "the reason the papal statement is so startling to many is that it came out of the blue."

[2] "Allocution," 4.3.

[3] I will also avoid the most recent developments in the ANH discussion, namely, the response by the Congregation of the Doctrine of the Faith (CDF) to two questions posed to it by the U.S. Catholic bishops regarding ANH in cases of a patient in a persistent vegetative state ("Responses to Certain Questions of the United States Conference of Catholic Bishops Concerning Artificial Nutrition and Hydration" [August 1, 2007], http://www.vatican.va/roman_curia/congregations/cfaith/documents/rc_con_cfaith_doc_20070801_risposte-usa_en.html) and the ensuing discussion surrounding the CDF's response. For examples, see John J. Hardt and Kevin D. O'Rourke, "Nutrition and Hydration: The CDF Response, In Perspective," *Health Progress* 88, no. 6 (November–December 2007): 44–47; and Justin F. Rigali and William E. Lori, "On Basic Care for Patients in the 'Vegetative' State: A Response to Dr. Hardt and Fr. O'Rourke," *Health Progress* 89, no. 3 (May–June 2008): 70–72. For the wider context necessary for interpreting the CDF statement, see Daniel P. Sulmasy, "Preserving Life?

statements has on the hierarchy of truths, an essential tool in evaluating the development of doctrine in Roman Catholicism. Along with this fundamental theological topic, I also want to ask a closely connected ecclesiological question: whether such digital immediacy has the side-effect of promoting a distorted understanding of *communio*, where the pope functions more as CEO, bishops as corporate vice presidents, and theologians as explicators of already-established decisions, sidelined from being participants in the developing tradition.

The Discussion

In the September 2005 issue of *Theological Studies*, Catholic ethicists Thomas Shannon and James Walter argued that over the previous quarter-century there had occurred "four unacknowledged shifts" in the Catholic method of determining moral obligation toward the dying: shifts in method, in context (to a focus on the immediate situation of imminent dying), in degree of certainty of use (from appropriateness to a presumption in favor of use of ANH), and in degree of obligation (from presumption to necessity of use). Together these have contributed to what the authors believed to be a significant alteration of a Catholic tradition of moral discernment stretching back to the sixteenth century to an unprecedented "revisionist" position that they see exemplified in the 2004 allocution: "Thus, in a series of statements from various ecclesial commissions and magisterial authorities, the tradition has been moved recently from both a patient-centered focus and obligations determined through the use of proportionate reason to a technology and intervention-centered focus with obligations being determined by deontological principles."[4]

In the March 2006 issue, John Paris, James Keenan, and Kenneth Himes took exception to this interpretation, arguing that Shannon and Walter were "mistaken in attributing magisterial authority to a speech that is inconsistent with the church's traditional position on end-of-life care."[5] To arrive to this judgment, they relied on the guide to interpretation laid out in *Lumen Gentium* 25 as well as on what they considered to be the

---

The Vatican and PVS," *Commonweal* (December 7, 2007): 16–18. For the current state of the question, see Patrick Guinan, "Is Assisted Nutrition and Hydration Always Mandated? The Persistent Vegetative State Differs from Dementia and Frailty," *National Catholic Bioethics Quarterly* 10, no. 3 (Autumn 2010): 481–88.

[4] Shannon and Walter, "Assisted Nutrition and Hydration," 653.

[5] Paris, Keenan, and Himes, "Did John Paul II's Allocution," 168.

non-reception of the allocution's particular teaching by bishops' conferences and by the consensus in the recent moral literature.[6] Thus, they were reluctant "to concede magisterial authority to what was not a dogmatic pronouncement on faith or morals promulgated to the universal Church," since "as *Lumen Gentium* makes clear, it is by official doctrinal statements proclaimed to the universal church—not by comments made to private groups—that the Church teaches. Those teachings, particularly those having long-standing reception within the Church, are not abandoned or significantly 'revised' by an unadorned papal allocution."[7]

In the same issue, Shannon and Walter replied that their colleagues had misunderstood their central argument, which was not focused on the magisterial authority of the allocution alone but rather on their claim that "among a variety of documents written during John Paul's papacy, including and possibly culminating in the papal allocution itself, four significant and unacknowledged shifts occurred that cumulatively appeared to *challenge, not alter,* the long-standing Catholic tradition on the use of some technologies to preserve life."[8] As evidence of this challenge, they cited various episcopal statements as well as a statement by the U.S. Catholic Medical Association that all appear to grant the allocution a definitive status in settling the issue by its suggestion "that the removal of ANH is euthanasia by omission."[9]

Analysis: What Is Left Unthought?

Throughout this discussion, it is clear that all the authors seemed to have missed a fundamental point regarding the process of reception and the strange outcome of this particular case—namely, that a one-off papal speech was viewed by some prominent ecclesiastics as a definitive

---

[6] They point specifically to the latter half of this passage in article 25 of the "Dogmatic Constitution on the Church" (*Lumen Gentium*): "The religious assent of will and intellect is to be given in a special way to the authentic teaching authority of the Roman pontiff even when he is not speaking *ex cathedra*; in such a way, that is, that his supreme teaching authority is respectfully acknowledged, and sincere adherence given to decisions he has delivered, in accordance with his manifest mind and will which is communicated chiefly by the nature of the documents, by the frequent repetition of the same doctrine or by the style of verbal expression" (trans. in *Decrees of the Ecumenical Councils*, ed. Norman P. Tanner, 2 vols. [London: Sheed & Ward / Washington, DC: Georgetown University Press, 1990], 2:869).

[7] Paris, Keenan, and Himes, "Did John Paul II's Allocution," 164, 168.

[8] Shannon and Walter, "Reply," 170.

[9] Ibid., 171.

settlement of a contested moral issue. The question raised is this: why was the allocution received as having a "definitive" status, especially by those who should know better in the light of the traditional hierarchy of truths as well as the canons for evaluating the authority of magisterial statements?

In their essay, Paris, Keenan, and Himes focus on the isolated case of the allocution itself and deny it any definitive character. Their judgment is due to the fact that, in their view, its particular genre did not live up to the commonly held standards of universal magisterial authority. That is, John Paul II's address had no discernable effect on the course of the developing tradition regarding life-sustaining ANH treatments. In this judgment they are joined by James Bretzke, who in a carefully argued essay claims that "the main thrust of the address is not aimed at reversing the centuries-old tradition of ordinary and extraordinary means," but rather that the pope was targeting "the notion of euthanasia on demand" and the wider "culture of death" which supports this.[10]

Shannon and Walter, for their part, did hint at the issue of reception within an ongoing tradition. The allocution, they argued, could be considered part of a trend to steer the tradition in a deontological direction. They sketch out what they consider to be the crucial elements involved in this development:

> The past 25 years have been characterized by a growing centralization of church authority in the papacy, by a continual quoting of the pope's previous writings as a justification for current teachings (note the recently issued *Compendium of the Social Doctrine of the Church*—in which John Paul II's writings have a place of primacy—and the term "doctrine" rather than "teaching" in its title), and by a willingness of many in the Church simply to repeat what the pope said as a way of resolving complex questions. The allocution was read within the context of a heightened sense of centralization of authority in the papacy.[11]

But they failed to ask precisely *why* this particular allocution, despite its minor genre, was granted near-absolute, "deal-clinching" status by those who cited it in the heat of the Schiavo case, and why some who

---

[10] James T. Bretzke, "A Burden of Means: Interpreting Recent Catholic Magisterial Teaching on End-of-Life Issues," *Journal of the Society of Christian Ethics* 26, no. 2 (2006): 183–200, at 194.

[11] Shannon and Walter, "Reply," 173.

know the different levels of papal teaching "used this papal allocution to promote a position that most theologians know is inconsistent with the long-standing tradition."[12] While claiming that their intent "was not to assess the magisterial authority of John Paul II's allocution," Shannon and Walter do indeed raise this issue by pointing out that the "definitive" force of the allocution's claim had already been conceded in some influential commentaries on end-of-life care.[13] They provide evidence of how certain members of the hierarchy, the deputy director of the Secretariat for Pro-Life Activities of the U.S. Catholic Conference of Bishops, and both the Catholic Health Association and the Catholic Medical Association in the United States, viewed the principle enunciated in the allocution as trumping all others in advocating a presumption in favor of ANH intervention.[14] And so, whether or not the allocution meets the criterion for a "definitive" magisterial statement, in quite a number of venues it was treated as such. Again, the question remains: what accounts for this particular and peculiar reception?

A number of factors no doubt contributed to the "absolutizing" of the pope's statement. In addition to the systemic ones mentioned by Shannon and Walter, we might add John Paul II's personal charisma (which led commentators to note his "rock star" status among youth), his role as an uncompromising moral icon (at least until the mishandling of certain scandals late in his papacy), and his canny use of the media, all of which endeared him to those who felt that under Pope Paul VI the Church had lost its moral compass in the immediate aftermath of Vatican II. But one other probable factor should also be considered: the immediate availability of papal and other official Vatican statements through various

---

[12] Ibid.

[13] They address the question of the authority of the statement more directly in their article "Implications of the Papal Allocution on Feeding Tubes," but rather inconclusively, in my opinion.

[14] For example, Cardinal Javier Lozano Barragan, president of the Pontifical Council for Health Care; Cardinal William Keeler, chairperson of the U.S. Bishops' Committee for Pro-Life Activities; Archbishop Raymond Burke of St. Louis, MO; Richard Doerflinger, deputy director of the U.S. bishops' Secretariat. Doerflinger is quoted in an interview as saying that "before the pope made his statement about feeding-tube cases at a conference last year [2004] there was enough uncertainty about the church's position that Catholics could remove feeding tubes without fear of committing a sin. No one could fairly have said to you that you were dissenting from clear Catholic teaching. Now you would have to say, 'Yes, you are.'" Cited by Shannon and Walter, "Assisted Nutrition and Hydration," 652–53.

electronic media—what I am calling "digital immediacy"—and the precise determination of the form of that availability in our aestheticized culture, a culture saturated with images and constituted by a primacy of the visual. Here Walter Benjamin's classic essay "The Work of Art in an Age of Mechanical Reproduction" can help us identify the important issues.

The main thrust of Benjamin's argument deals with the work's loss of authenticity in the operation of reproduction. Authenticity presupposes "the presence of the original" and exists "outside technical . . . reproducibility."[15] "The authenticity of a thing," he says, "is the essence of all that is transmissible from its beginning, ranging from its substantive duration to its testimony to the history it has experienced."[16] On being reproduced and reduced to a set of "likenesses," the work of art loses the "aura" of its uniqueness and originality—it becomes an aesthetic object that has lost its substance and becomes detached "from the domain of tradition," from the historical flow of which it is an expression and to which it testifies. Reproducibility bestows upon a work a spatial "closeness" that we desire, a closeness that also obliterates the uniqueness revealed in distance and hence causes "the contemporary decay of the aura." The decay and the dispersal of authenticity, then, is due both to the workings of mechanical reproduction *and* to the acquisitive desires of the consumer of the reproduction. The work becomes in effect a homeless object, infinitely repeatable in an infinite number of contexts. Such an object is in a position to be self-interpreting and create its own tradition. Therefore, the work is not the only thing affected by this "detachment." The historical tradition from which it comes is "shattered," resulting in "the liquidation of the traditional value of the cultural heritage."[17] Benjamin concludes his analysis of this process with a fundamental insight: "For the first time in world history, mechanical reproduction emancipates the work of art from its parasitical dependence on ritual. . . . But the instant the criterion of authenticity ceases to be applicable to artistic production, the total function of art is reversed. Instead of being based on ritual, it begins to be based on another practice—politics."[18]

---

[15] Walter Benjamin, "The Work of Art in the Age of Mechanical Reproduction," in *Illuminations*, ed. Hannah Arendt, trans. Harry Zohn (New York: Schocken, 1969), 217–51, at 220.

[16] Ibid., 221.

[17] Ibid., 221, 223.

[18] Ibid., 224.

Benjamin's paradigmatic examples of reproduction are film and pho-tography. But his quite prophetic analysis is transferrable to the kind of immediate and all-consuming imaging that he could never have envi-sioned: the digital immediacy of incessant cable news (and its 24/7 news cycle), YouTube, blogs, and quickly updated institutional web sites. His argument takes on an additional urgency in our aestheticized Western culture where image equals reality.[19] The exhilarating shock of imme-diacy that reproduction creates—that is, the perceptual and conceptual appropriation of once-distant images and texts *seemingly* without me-diation—is even more severe in a world where electronic media enable both the immediate access to information and images by the consumer (known a decade ago as "pull" technology) and the direct and immediate presentation/representation of information and images by the producer ("push" technology—literally "in your face"). The truncation of time and distance, the "closeness" that we crave, the immediacy of access to ap-parently autonomous aesthetic objects, confirm their isolated authority as absolute, their ability to "be" and to "mean" on their own without needing or even hinting at the tradition from which they have developed.

What I want to suggest is that the contemporary *form* that the papal teaching took, rather than its content, was the crucial determining fac-tor in its reception as definitive. By "form," I do not mean any of the standard genres of allocution, apostolic letter, encyclical, etc., but rather the digital immediacy that constitutes the "norm" of our aestheticized contemporary culture. This norm, closely linked with commodification, is the grid within which the allocution appeared and was understood by its hearers and readers. In the midst of the image storm, this norm bestows on any official statement an absoluteness that allows it to be presented as an inevitably authoritative *fait accompli* that, in a very real sense, disallows any real reception history—a true "conversation stop-per." The immediately available aesthetic object is tradition-less and self-interpreting. Immediacy equals authenticity equals authority.

In his book on interpreting magisterial documents, Francis Sullivan suggests five criteria that the theologian should use in interpreting

---

[19] As Richard Kearney has noted, "now the image *precedes* the reality it is supposed to represent. Or to put it another way, reality has become a pale reflection of the image. . . . At the level of artistic culture there is a growing awareness that images have now displaced the 'original' realities they were traditionally meant to reflect." *Idem, The Wake of Imagination: Toward a Postmodern Culture* (Minneapolis: University of Minnesota Press, 1988), 2.

doctrinal texts: (1) familiarity with the historical context of the text; (2) performing a close exegesis of the text itself; (3) an analysis of how the text interprets Scripture and integrates with its revealed truth; (4) an examination of the subsequent history of the doctrine that is expressed in the text; and (5) an expression of the doctrine in terms of contemporary understanding.[20] There can be no arguing with the trustworthiness of these suggestions, reflecting as they do the long commonly held tradition of the hermeneutics of magisterial teaching. However, this traditional process of discernment is undercut by a world of digital immediacy. The "shearing-off" of both context and ongoing reception that is intensified with digital reproduction has already undermined the force of steps one and four, as demonstrated by the reactions to the allocution catalogued by Shannon and Walter. And since "contemporary understanding" is already aestheticized and fragmented in the twenty-first century, step five is undermined as well. Thus it appears that authority need no longer be discerned and either conceded or denied by the receiving community. Rather, magisterial statements as representations now assert themselves as fully formed, self-interpreting objects that might hint at their roots in a tradition of theological conversation but no longer depend on a her- meneutical "thickness" for their power to settle the issue. Their origin in authority is represented to us—performed, if you will—in the terms of an autonomous aesthetic object, which looks, functions, and is perceived as being just as "authentic" as every other autonomous aesthetic object we encounter. The resulting unilateralism shatters standards of discernment and gradations of "theological certainty."[21]

There was a name for this in Washington, DC, political circles during the George W. Bush administration: "catapulting the propaganda"—that is, hurling a message couched in the rhetoric of inevitability over the heads of all intermediaries (interpreters, commentators, and pundits) with the intention of communicating directly to "the people"—as if the message, its promoters, and its receivers were not already saturated with cultural presuppositions. In this particular context, bishops as well as theologians become mere reporters of what appears to be an already fully formed, self-interpreting message. Bishops take on the role of corporate

---

[20] Francis A. Sullivan, *Creative Fidelity: Weighing and Interpreting Documents of the Magisterium* (New York/Mahwah, NJ: Paulist, 1996), 109–10.

[21] For the traditional "grades of certainty," see Ludwig Ott, *Fundamentals of Catholic Dogma*, trans. Patrick Lynch, ed. James Bastible (1955; reprint, Rockville, IL: Tan Books, 1974 [Ger. orig., 1952]), 8–9.

vice presidents, conveying the CEO's edicts, and theologians are called on merely to restate the message in simpler terms for the news media and the company's newsletter.

Thus John Paul's proclamation on ANH was understood (by both theological initiates and those outside the guild) according to the "canons" of a digitally immediate culture as yet another self-interpreting image, another autonomous aesthetic object. And it was granted the same kind of authority of authenticity. The danger, of course, is that digital immediacy levels out all such objects to appear the same (note, for example, how radically different events are reduced to identical news items in a parade of images on 24/7 cable news). The seduction of immediate availability is that it grants the same authenticity of authority (and the authority of authenticity) to every image in the grid.

It is unlikely that the Vatican's webmasters ever had Benjamin's theory in mind while crafting the Vatican web site. However, the concrete reality of that site is an exemplary performance of Benjamin's fundamental political insight: each page on the site has the same "parchment" background, giving every document of whatever level of authority an "antique" patina that connotes an importance that demands serious respect, if not outright submission. The site, to no one's surprise, is a celebration of the papacy. And—again to no one's surprise, if one has read Benjamin—it is a celebration of the power of representation in the high modernist mode of the finest corporate web sites, complete with smiling and waving pontiff, mission statements, departmental documents, even videos and photo albums (e.g., Pope Benedict XVI on vacation in Val d'Aosta or visiting the Lateran University) that humanize the organization and its CEO. The fact that Joseph Ratzinger has left such an extensive pre-papal paper trail, and that there are numerous students of his in important teaching posts throughout the world, make it difficult for the Vatican to completely control his image. However, this was not the case with John Paul II. Before his papacy he was known only within certain ecclesiastical circles, and the Vatican web site, constructed during his papacy, was one source that carefully controlled his image. It constantly reminded us of his extensive theological and moral interventions, made available to anyone with an internet connection and existing as substantive aesthetic objects in their own right.

The immediate availability of self-interpreting representations, however, violates the critical role that temporality and temporal distance have always played in the constitution of Christian identity and in the theological evaluation of statements concerning this identity and the practices that constitute it.[22] One traditional theological test of authentic authority is to gauge the impact of a magisterial statement over time, to see whether it has been discussed and substantially repeated.[23] It takes time to discern the basic non-negotiables of Christian identity in certain practices and reflections. In the past, contested theological positions were discussed over decades if not centuries. More recently, *dubia* were proposed to official Vatican offices as the start of a protracted conversation on authenticity and authority of Catholic teaching, leading to the goal of a specific decision. This was done until either a consensus was reached or the magisterium intervened to judge whether or not a consensus indeed exists in certain long-contested cases (the centuries-long debate over the Immaculate Conception is one example, the ongoing debate over the reception of the encyclical *Humanae Vitae* another). However, as Benjamin argues, reproduction dissolves both spatial distance and extended temporality to render the object immediately graspable, or, in our terms, self-interpreted to the degree that it closes down the conversation of reception. The norm of immediacy as applied to images (the immediate is the true) also becomes the norm of evaluation of the worth and authority of ecclesial representations.

Pope Benedict XVI seems to be aware of this power of immediacy. He expressly noted in the first volume of his series *Jesus of Nazareth* that the book "is in no way an exercise of the magisterium, but is solely an expression of my personal search 'for the face of the Lord' (cf. Ps 27:8). Everyone is free, then, to contradict me."[24] He thus attempted to blunt the force of digital immediacy by suppressing the book's veneer of au-

---

[22] For an explanation of such ongoing constitution, see Francis Schüssler Fiorenza, "The Crisis of Hermeneutics and Christian Theology," in *Theology at the End of Modernity*, ed. Sheila Greeve Davaney (Philadelphia: Trinity Press International, 1991), 117–40; Anthony J. Godzieba, "Method and Interpretation: The New Testament's Heretical Hermeneutic (Prelude and Fugue)," *The Heythrop Journal* 36 (1995): 286–306.

[23] Cf. Paris, Keenan, and Himes, "Did John Paul II's Allocution," 165–66. See also Sullivan, *Creative Fidelity*, 108, with regard to infallible teaching: "When one is dealing with a controversial issue, I believe one rightly applies two principles: 1) that the consensus required for infallible teaching of the ordinary magisterium must be a constant and enduring one; 2) that no doctrine is understood as being infallibly taught unless this fact is clearly established, and this fact can hardly be clearly be established if there is no consensus among Catholic theologians that the doctrine has indeed been infallibly taught."

[24] Joseph Ratzinger (Pope Benedict XVI), *Jesus of Nazareth: From the Baptism in the Jordan to the Transfiguration*, trans. Adrian J. Walker (New York: Doubleday, 2007), xxiii–xxiv.

thority. At other times, though, circumstances have slipped out of his control: for example, after having made a comment on his flight to Brazil in 2007 on the excommunication of politicians who support abortion, the statement was absolutized immediately in the media. On landing, his spokesman had to seriously qualify it, "walking it back" from its absolute status.[25] The 2009 affair surrounding Bishop Richard Williamson, the Levebvrist bishop known and denounced for his anti-Semitism, also escaped Vatican control, leading to the pope's unprecedented apology to the world's bishops and a promise to check internet news sources more thoroughly.[26] Digital immediacy also affects the impact and the intent of documents issued by Roman curial offices. In 2007, the CDF proposed as a settled issue a rather narrow interpretation of Vatican II's use of *subsistit in* ("the unique Church of Christ . . . subsists in the Catholic Church), reading *subsistit* as equivalent to *est* and thus asserting as the only adequate interpretation "the full identity of the Church of Christ with the Catholic Church."[27] This was presented without any hint that this is clearly a minority opinion, running contrary to the intent of the doctrinal commission charged with preparing the draft of Vatican II's Constitution on the Church that took over Sebastian Tromp's suggested terminology (*subsistit in*) but not his definition, and also contrary to the intentions of the majority of council fathers who voted in favor of the commission's more expansive explanation.[28] The CDF's intent was to settle the issue; its document is clearly presented as an autonomous

[25] "Pope Arrives in Brazil with Tough Abortion Stance," *USA Today* (9 May 2007), http://www.usatoday.com/news/ world/2007-05-09-pope-brazil_N.htm.

[26] "Letter of His Holiness Pope Benedict XVI to the Bishops of the Catholic Church Concerning the Remission of the Excommunication of the Four Bishops Consecrated by Archbishop Lefebvre" (March 10, 2009), http://www.vatican. va/ holy_father/benedict_xvi/letters/2009/documents/hf_ben-xvi_let_20090310 _ remissione-scomunica_en.html.

[27] Congregation for the Doctrine of the Faith, *Responses to Some Questions Regarding Certain Aspects of the Doctrine on the Church* (June 29, 2007), http://www.vatican. va/roman_curia/congregations/cfaith/ documents/rc_con_cfaith_ doc_20070629 _responsa-quaestiones_en.html, q. 3. See also esp. q. 2.

[28] See Francis A. Sullivan, "*Quaestio disputata*: A Response to Karl Becker, S.J. on the Meaning of *subsistit in*," *Theological Studies* 67 (2006): 395–409, esp. 400–402. Sullivan notes that Becker has been a consultor to the CDF since 1986 (395). The CDF responses substantially reproduce Becker's main thesis. Sullivan disputes (successfully, in my view) Becker's interpretation of the documentary evidence. See further Karim Schelkens, "*Lumen Gentium*'s 'Subsistit in' Revisited: The Catholic Church and Christian Unity after Vatican II," *Theological Studies* 69 (2008): 875–93. See also the

object that nods to an ongoing theological discussion but intends to allow no ongoing reception. The CDF document stands in isolation, never in conversation with forty years of discussion of *subsistit in*—a digital representation *par excellence.*

Conclusion

What remains unthought in the *Theological Studies* discussion, then, is the cultural factor of digital immediacy, how it shapes our perception and appropriation of ecclesial statements, and how it can obliterate both the hermeneutical thickness of the theological tradition and the necessary temporal constitution of the ecclesial community if theological care is not taken. Within the grid of digital immediacy there can be no "classics" in the sense proposed by Hans-Georg Gadamer, since reproduced aesthetic objects are, by their nature, devoid of a "history of effects" *(Wirkungsgeschichte).*[29] When speaking of our relation to these representations, I have deliberately used "perception" and "appropriation" rather than "reception," since reception indicates the striving for understanding, interpretation, and application that is carried out over time. The productive force of time and temporal distanciation, however, are precisely what is truncated and eliminated from a world of autonomous aesthetic objects, all of them authoritative because they are authentic and authentic because they are immediate.

I see two consequences of this situation. First, a digitally immediate culture reinforces the development of structures of Church authority along the lines of contemporary managerial culture. The centralization of power and authority in Rome is no new phenomenon.[30] The specific managerial arrangement of power within the present exercise of *communio,* however, is new: the pope appears more and more like a CEO, bishops like corporate vice presidents (or even branch managers), and theologians as writers for the corporate newsletter. With power and authority arranged under the pressure of immediacy, *communio* now

---

important update by Francis A. Sullivan, *"Quaestio disputata*: Further Thoughts on the Meaning of *Subsistit In," Theological Studies* 71 (2010): 133–47.

[29] Hans-Georg Gadamer, *Truth and Method,* 2nd rev. ed., trans. rev. Joel Weinsheimer and Donald G. Marshall (New York: Continuum, 1989), 285–307.

[30] Such an arrangement of "power vectors" has roots as far back as Pope Nicholas I (858–67). See J. Derek Holmes and Bernard W. Bickers, *A Short History of the Catholic Church* (New York/Ramsey, NJ: Paulist, 1984), 60–61.

replicates a contemporary business model that ignores history and is oriented toward short-term gains. This, however, is a fall from the more dynamic, historically situated view of *communio* rooted in the patristic period and retrieved by twentieth-century Catholic ecclesiology.[31] In this latter understanding, the local church is a full participant in the development of Christian identity, and this role must be retrieved anew in an age of digital reproduction, differently than in the twentieth century, if the effectiveness of the whole Church as sacrament of salvation is to be actualized.[32]

Second, the traditional hierarchy of truths and the methods of magisterial discernment have been exposed as inadequate to cope with the flood of ecclesial representations in a digital storm. The traditional methods of evaluation were bypassed by those who granted John Paul's allocution definitive status. New methods of evaluation, based on the insight that *communio* is a narrative constituted by historically situated practices and reflections, must be crafted that insist on the historical thickness of the theological discussions into which the magisterium intervenes, and by which the magisterium is already influenced. The fundamental task of the theologian—faith-seeking-understanding as incarnated in conversation with other theologians and with the Church at large—must be robustly asserted in a culture of reproduction that prefers disembodied, de-temporalized certainties to the hard work of coming to consensus. Here, theologians must be countercultural and promote the culture of embodied discipleship and interactive conversation as the more likely story of Church development and moral decision-making, as well as a more detailed analysis of the intersection of faith and aesthetics.[33]

[31] Cf. Ludwig Hertling, *Communio: Church and Papacy in Early Christianity*, trans. Jared Wicks (Chicago: Loyola University Press, 1972 [Ger. orig. 1943, 1962]); Dennis M. Doyle, *Communion Ecclesiology: Vision and Versions* (Maryknoll, NY: Orbis, 2000).

[32] See also the important debate over the relationship between the universal Church and the local churches that occurred around a decade ago between Joseph Ratzinger and Walter Kasper. For citations of the literature and a summary of the issues, see Kilian McDonnell, "The Ratzinger/Kasper Debate: The Universal Church and Local Churches," *Theological Studies* 63 (2002): 227–50.

[33] On this latter point, see my argument regarding the sacramental imagination in "The Catholic Sacramental Imagination and the Access/Excess of Grace," *New Theology Review* 21, no. 3 (August 2008): 14–26.

Chapter 7

When Mediating Structures Change
The Magisterium, the Media, and the Culture Wars

Vincent J. Miller

University of Dayton

Introduction

Even a passing consideration of the endless social and cultural revolutions being worked by contemporary media raises the question of their likely effects upon the Church. In his essay in this volume, Anthony Godzieba argues that papal use of modern media gives rise to a new form of magisterial authority—"digital immediacy"—that radically centralizes authority in the Church foreclosing reception and theological debate. I agree that modern media contribute to a centralization of authority. I argue, however, that the effect is more complex. Contemporary media produce multiple, simultaneous, and contradictory cultural effects that both centralize and erode magisterial authority.

These new mediations place the magisterium in different contexts, impacting its reception. Believers are more likely to bring to Christian doctrine the habits of interpretation and use they employ in commercial popular culture. This renders religious traditions open to appropriation willy-nilly. Reception is not foreclosed. On the contrary, it is given greater latitude. It is common to assume that such relativizing of the tradition tends toward individualistic and therapeutic interpretations. This is but one aspect of the cultural *zeitgeist* that pulls at the Church. Another cultural dynamism is widely observable: an obsession with contrastive identity and boundary drawing. "Countercultural" has become a cultural default. Prophetic stances, for all their claims of standing against the tide, swim right along with the current of the age.

The second half of the essay turns to an analysis of the contemporary cultural ecology that is emerging from revolutions in communications technologies and globalization. This will help us understand the cultural needs to which religion will likely by yoked, and the default models of authority to which the papacy and the episcopate will likely be scripted. It considers the problems posed by heterogenization and deterritorialization, as choice penetrates deep within our religious communities, rendering them enclaves of the like-minded detached from geographical connections to other communities and responsibility for particular locations.[1] The "special agenda organization" is the paradigmatic form of association in this cultural ecology. This form's impact upon the episcopate and the Church is analyzed via study of the relative media impact of episcopal interventions in the 2008 presidential campaign.

This cultural ecology poses a profound challenge to the Church. It threatens to reduce the episcopate to a special agenda organization spokesperson, and to rupture the catholicity of the Church, so that it conforms to the divides of the culture war.

Digital Immediacy

Godzieba's exploration of the "unthought" effects of mediation helps us think critically about the transformation of the nature and function of magisterial statements and authority. His argument that the "form" of magisterial statements no longer refers to "allocution, apostolic letter, encyclical, etc., but rather the digital immediacy that constitutes the 'norm' of our aestheticized contemporary culture" is enormously insightful.[2] The contrast is abundantly evident in his central example: between the relatively low level of authority embodied in a papal allocution and the near definitive status John Paul II's brief statements about artificial hydration and nutrition have been accorded.

Before they were options within a formal range of magisterial utterances, encyclicals, allocutions, and bulls were themselves particular mediations developed in varied organizational and technological contexts

---

[1] Robert M. Bellah, et al., *Habits of the Heart: Individualism and Commitment in American Life* (Berkeley: University of California Press, 1985), 71, 186.

[2] Anthony Godzieba, "The Magisterium in an Age of Digital Reproduction," above, 143–52, at 147.

(e.g., medieval bureaucracies dependent upon scribal publication and irregular communication, modern bureaucracies that employed the printing press and regular travel, etc.). Thus, our contemporary media context represents not the rise of mediation, but simply a newer form of it that will perhaps one day be added as a formal genre to the range of traditional magisterial forms.

Godzieba's analysis, like Benjamin's that inspires it, can be described as "productivist." That is, it finds the ideological effects to be largely a consequence of the content and form of production. Studies of consumer culture have long sought to balance such analyses with approaches that can better attend to the active agency of consumers who are quite active in the appropriation of cultural material, interpreting and using it in ways that surprise both clerical elites and mandarin Marxist critics. Thus, for all the value of Godzieba's preference for "perceiving" and "appropriating" over the more hermeneutically and theologically rich term "reception," there is more to be considered here. Entire schools of the study of consumer culture (e.g., Michel de Certeau, cultural studies as begun in Birmingham, England and developed in the United States) find ample evidence that consumers are profoundly active in the reception and use of material received through the channels of commercial popular culture. For this reason, I find his argument about the effects of digital immediacy upon the Church to be insightful, but incomplete.

The Papacy and the Media: Centralization and Erosion of Authority

In *Consuming Religion,* I argued for a more dialectical assessment of the effects of the papacy's attempt to employ contemporary media.[3] Godzieba argues that digital mediation contributes to the further centralization of authority in the Church and reduces ecclesial *communio* to a "managerial arrangement of power." There is certainly much to this concern. John Paul II's charisma made him enormously effective in modern visual media. Dr. Joaquin Navarro-Valls, then director of the Vatican Press Office, oversaw modernization of the Vatican communications office—the *Sala Stampa*—making it into a proactive communications office that actively manages the Vatican's message and the papal image. The Catholic faithful learned of papal decisions, encyclicals, and allocutions not from their parish pulpit or diocesan paper, but on television,

---

[3] Vincent J. Miller, *Consuming Religion: Christian Faith and Practice in a Consumer Culture* (New York: Continuum, 2004).

secular newspapers, and the internet. This enabled John Paul to speak directly to the people in the pews, in a manner unimaginable for most of his predecessors. As a result, John Paul's message was much less mediated by traditional Catholic structures such as diocesan bishops and their theological staff or seminary faculty. Olivier Roy finds here a distinctly modern form of post-traditional religious authority (he includes John Paul's distinctive efforts to appeal to youth as part of the same dynamic).[4]

But such "immediacy" comes with a cost. It does not simply free the papacy from the inertia of traditional media structures; it recontextualizes the pope as well. Traditional interpretive frameworks for receiving the papal message are replaced with the hermeneutics believers learn within commercial popular culture. The papacy is scripted into models of authority common in the media. The ecclesial structures that modern media can "catapult" over are the very ones that give the papacy local authority. They are the places where the faithful learn the particular (and often tacit) hermeneutics and pragmatics for interpreting and acting upon magisterial teaching. These are replaced by the more consumerist habits of interpretation and use that believers are formed in by commercial popular culture.

Dr. Navarro-Valls illustrated his understanding of the success of the Vatican media strategy by telling the story of an encounter between a young boy and the pope in Bogotá, Colombia. The boy called out to John Paul, "I know you; you're the pope. You're the same one I saw on television." For Navarro-Valls, the boy's recognition shows that the policy has not achieved mere "ephemeral celebrity," but a "ministry of global presence from the Church and from the priesthood."[5] Recognition is good, but the context matters. For the boy, John Paul would share the company of the Colombian equivalents of Barney and Spongebob Squarepants; for his parents, Oprah and Dr. Phil.

That company tells us much about the costs exacted by digital immediacy. Religious authority is contextualized in the role of the "New Cultural Intermediary" (NCI). Pierre Bourdieu identified these as serving the needs of a new bourgeois.[6] NCIs produce symbolic goods such as

[4] Olivier Roy, *Globalized Islam: The Search for a New Ummah* (New York: Columbia University Press, 2004), 28–35.

[5] George Weigel, *Witness to Hope: The Biography of Pope John Paul II* (New York: Harper Collins, 1999), 491.

[6] Pierre Bourdieu, *Distinction: A Social Critique of the Judgement of Taste*, trans. Richard Nice (Cambridge, MA: Harvard University Press, 1984), 359.

marketing, advertising, public relations, radio and television program-
ming, and magazine lifestyle journalism. They are members of the helping
professions (social workers, marriage counselors, sex therapists, dieti-
cians, etc.).[7] In addition to providing knowledge for developing personal
taste in the maelstrom of consumption options they also provide guidance for life choices in the post-traditional culture where the heads of
each nuclear family are expected to make their own choices concerning
sexuality, child rearing, meaning, etc.[8] NCIs possess great influence, but
have no normative authority. They inform consumers of lifestyle options
and spiritual techniques. It is left to the consumer to choose which are
best. Although there may be consistent interests and values represented,
the NCIs do not concern themselves with, and their viewers do not expect
attention to, such matters as coherence and consistency that mark being
a believer and practitioner of a traditional religion.

Thus, although digital immediacy partners well with the centralization
of authority in the Church, it simultaneously erodes magisterial authority.
The much less charismatic Benedict XVI seems to be strategically aware
of this predicament. A vignette from the first World Youth Day of his
papacy conveys its intractability. In reaction to celebratory acclaim—"Ben-
e-det-to!"—Benedict turned away from the adoring assembly to face the
Eucharist displayed in a monstrance for Benediction. Benedict's gesture
challenged the logic of spectacle that would place him at the center of
attention. He modeled an alternative logic, one where the gaze is turned
toward the transcendent. An observer notes the unfortunate response of
many in the crowd. They turned their gaze not to the reserved Eucharist,
but to the concert-sized video screens displaying a montage of Benedict's
adoration juxtaposed with an image of the monstrance. Benedict's gesture
was defeated precisely by the crowd's response. This conformed to the
ritual practices inculcated by the medium, more than those of the osten-
sible rituals of Eucharistic Exposition and Benediction.[9]

These erosions go far beyond the reduction of the papacy and episcopate to celebrity or new cultural intermediary. As I have argued in
Consuming Religion, the consequences are twofold. Religious traditions
are engaged with the habits of interpretation and use learned in con-

---

[7] Mike Featherstone, *Consumer Culture and Postmodernism* (London: Sage, 1991),
43–44; Bourdieu, *Distinction*, 359–69.

[8] Miller, *Consuming Religion*, 94–106.

[9] Yves De Maeseneer, "Dialectics of Adoration: World Youth Day, Shopping Malls,
and the Return of the Baroque," *Bulletin ET* 17, no. 1 (2006): 126–39.

sumer culture. On the hermeneutical level, we lose tradition-specific interpretive habits, and an awareness of the reinforcing, elaborating, and correcting interconnections among symbols, doctrines, and values. On the level of practice, such meanings are shorn from shared community practices that enable them to inform a particular form of life.

Theology as a discipline presumes aspects of the past organizational and communication infrastructures that may no longer exist. However revisionist it may be, theology often implicitly assumes the location of the seminary professor: in some formal relationship with the episcopate, teaching seminarians who will one day preach and minister in ways informed by theologians' research. The five criteria for interpreting magisterial statements Godzieba cites from Sullivan are a legacy of the neoscholastic textbook (in which Sullivan likely wrote the earliest version of his schema). Theology's specialized role in the Church enabled it to develop such complex interpretive frameworks and pursue concerns such as coherence and consistency. When contemporary media become the default communicative infrastructure of the Church, those criteria are lost as well.

The erosion of religion by popular mediation and commodification opens it to a broad range of consumerist reception that complexifies the centralizing effect of digital immediacy. For this reason, in order to fully understand the predicament of contemporary magisterial authority, we must consider reception in greater detail. The thrust of the commodification critique is that religious traditions are engaged by believers as collections of discrete elements that can be understood and employed willy-nilly. Thus, digital mediation and commodification do not tell the entire story. We must explore the dominant cultural needs, which will provide meanings around which religious material is reinterpreted and the uses to which it is likely to be put.

The Contemporary Cultural Ecology

When religion is shorn of its complex theologies and practices by new forms of mediation and commodification, what replaces them? The literature on religion and consumer culture is dominated by concern about the default to narcissistic and therapeutic spiritualities of the sort warned of by Phillip Reiff and Christopher Lasch.[10] Bourdieu's and

---

[10] Philip Rieff, *The Triumph of the Therapeutic: Uses of Faith after Freud* (New York: Harper and Row, 1966); Christopher Lasch, *The Culture of Narcissism* (New York: Norton, 1978). For an exemplary theological engagement with these issues see

Featherstone's accounts of the new cultural intermediaries also focus on such concerns. No doubt there is no shortage of therapeutically minded narcissists about, but this is not a necessary outcome of the loss of complex traditional modes of interpretation and practice. It is but one set of cultural needs that can pull religious traditions in a retrograde direction. A survey of the contemporary cultural scene reveals many other cultural needs that threaten to draw religions away from their traditional goods and logics. There are also other problematic roles into which religious leaders are likely to be scripted.

The cultural changes being worked by new communication and information technologies and consumer culture are profound. They form part of a larger set of transformations that are fundamentally reworking the nature of social and cultural space. Globalization is driven significantly by new forms of communication, but also by transportation, organizational, and economic innovations. It is allied with other cultural dynamisms long underway: urbanization, pluralization, individualization, and detraditionalization. Here I will focus on two cultural dynamisms discussed in the literature on globalization that are particularly germane to the exercise and reception of magisterial authority: heterogenization and deterritorialization.

a. Heterogenization

Homogenization has long been the most frequently expressed concern about the cultural effects of globalization. This sees the cultural diversity of the world under threat by a tide of consumer-driven cultural uniformity. For that reason, it may seem surprising to speak of heterogenization, the increasing differentiation of cultures and communities as an effect of globalization, but this has long been a topic of discussion in sociological literature. Roland Robertson observes that one of the surprising "universal" effects of globalization is precisely that it creates an imaginary in which cultures are seen as species of a larger genus. As a result, people generally have a more reflexive understanding of their own cultural particularity than in ages past. Robertson terms this the

---

L. Gregory Jones, "A Thirst for God or Consumer Spirituality?," in *Spirituality and Social Embodiment*, ed. L. Gregory Jones and James J. Buckley (Oxford: Blackwell, 1997), 3–26. Bourdieu's and Featherstone's accounts of the new cultural intermediaries also focus on such concerns.

"universalisation of the particular."[11] No longer buffered from difference by the impassability of space or by national borders, we now imagine ourselves as particular precisely because of our imagination of diversity. This imaginary gives rise both to cosmopolitan comfort with diversity and a xenophobic anxiety about the existence of others whose decisions and lives affect us. In the words of Ulrich Beck, a world of "glass boundaries" engenders both pity and hatred.[12]

A second cause of heterogenization gets us closer to the topic of new media and community. Benedict Anderson's seminal argument about the nation-state held that large-scale national identities depended upon the communication infrastructures of "print capitalism" which could support national-scale literature and widely read newspapers. These provided linguistic and cultural uniformity that enabled people to imagine themselves in solidarity with millions of others whom they would never know. Myriad localities, dialects, and cultures could now be understood as variations on a larger national culture. Arjun Appadurai argues that advances in communications technologies and media tend to fragment these large-scale solidarities.[13] The internet is the current cutting edge of technological advances which have plebeianized cultural production. The profound exclusion of the global digital divide notwithstanding, the cost of media production has dropped to near zero. (Indeed the crisis of the current moment focuses on well-established and highly capitalized media such as newspapers unable to find profitability in the maelstrom of the internet, where anyone can start a blog or YouTube channel.) Such a "media ecology" (to use Neil Postman's terminology) allows ever more differentiated communities to flourish.[14] The evolution of television provides a useful analogy. Once the only alternatives to the big 3 networks were PBS and the backwater of the UHF channels. With the advent of cable and then digital cable, a spectrum was now available for a host of specialized networks, from the obvious—news, weather, sports, classic film—to the unforeseen—animals, home renovation, and knife sales.

[11] Roland Robertson, *Globalization: Social Theory and Global Culture* (London: Sage, 1992), 27, 97, 175.

[12] Ulrich Beck, *Cosmopolitan Vision*, trans. Ciaran Cronin (Cambridge: Polity Press, 2006), 8.

[13] Arjun Appadurai, *Modernity at Large* (Minneapolis: University of Minnesota Press, 1996), 161.

[14] Neil Postman, "The Reformed English Curriculum," in *High School 1980: The Shape of the Future in American Secondary Education*, ed. A. C. Eurich (New York: Pitman, 1970), 161.

The new media ecology allows myriad communities to flourish; all they need to attract is enough participants to maintain a conversation in a comments section of a blog or link to others in a blogroll.

Heterogenization is at work on the ground outside of media spectrum and the blogosphere. We face not merely a *media* ecology, but a shifting *cultural* ecology. Numerous recent works in demographics point to the increasing separation of our communities into clusters of similar demographics.[15] The automobile has proven a great solvent to the geographical glue of communities. Having long expected commutes to work from our communities, we now commute to communities as well. The territorial parish is quickly becoming congregationalized as people travel to ones best suited to their needs and tastes. Technology from the automobile to the latest form of internet social networking invented this morning renders social belonging increasingly a matter of choice.

b. Deterritorialization

The same technologies that enable ever smaller communities to flourish and render social belonging a matter of choice also allow such shared cultures to float free of geographical space. If, as William Cavanaugh argues, the nation-state was a universalizing project that had to eliminate the particularities of local cultures and communities that stood in the way of its centralizing power structure, the further unfolding of media technology described by Appadurai does not necessarily return community to the local; on the contrary, it enables culture to float free of it.[16] Ethnic diasporas are fundamentally changed when they have the means to continue their culture regardless of their location. Saskia Sassen questions whether the term "immigration" is too wed to narratives from earlier historical periods to describe the economic and cultural location of contemporary migration.[17] Global satellite networks and the internet allow cultures to thrive across and through national boundaries. Likewise on a more micro level, virtual communities have become a significant form of voluntary association, replacing local clubs and social groups as sources of socialization and formation.

---

[15] James Gimpel and Jason E. Schuknecht, *Patchwork Nation: Sectionalism and Political Change in American Politics* (Ann Arbor: University of Michigan Press, 2003); Bill Bishop, *The Big Sort: Why the Clustering of Like-Minded America Is Tearing Us Apart* (Boston: Houghton Mifflin Harcourt, 2008).

[16] William Cavanaugh, *The Theopolitical Imagination* (London: T & T Clark, 2002), 100ff.

[17] Saskia Sassen, *The Sociology of Globalization* (Norton, 2007), 112.

To these technological advances, we should include the transformations of the nation-state as a factor in deterritorialization. Many argue
that the term "decline" is an inadequate descriptor for the relationship
between states and globalization. The "global," as it is currently emerging, is precisely the result of decades of intentional policy decisions to
create the economic structures and practices that underpin it (free trade
agreements, currency markets, the WTO, etc.).

Zygmunt Bauman observes that one consequence is that the nation-
state surrenders control of one of the traditional legs of national sovereignty—the domestic economy.[18] The economy is depoliticized, and as
a consequence, politics floats free from the concrete demands of policy.
Voters do not expect their choices to have much impact on their economic
lives. Industrial workers in rustbelt states know that the factories are
gone and neither party is going to bring them back. According to Bauman, the only aspect of traditional sovereignty that remains is national
identity. Appadurai offers a dark analysis of what happens when national
identity floats free from the collective project of maintaining the domestic
economy, and the other traditional role of the nation-state—security—is
undermined by non-state threats. Identity becomes an ever more neurotic
concern driving xenophobic, ethnic, and religiously driven obsessions
with purity that often issue in violence against real or imagined enemies
within.[19] Short of that, it creates an atmosphere where identity becomes
an overriding cultural concern, forced to do the work once covered by
more capacious practices and concerns.

c. The Problem with Identity

These two cultural dynamisms have effects that are directly relevant
to the way in which magisterial authority is exercised and received.
Heterogenization allows myriad communities to prosper, but it also
encourages sectarianism and contrastive identities. Deterritorialization
changes the relationship between communities and territory. Communities that float free of space don't have to directly encounter and coexist
with others, they are more free to define themselves against what they
imagine others to be. Deterritorialization abstracts beliefs and values
from accountability for their consequences. Established religions have

---

[18] Zygmunt Bauman, *Globalization: The Human Consequences* (New York: Columbia
University Press, 1998), 65.

[19] Arjun Appadurai, *Fear of Small Numbers* (Durham: Duke University Press, 2006).

to answer for the shortcomings of their societies. In a deterritorialized world, every group, no matter how much it may be in the demographic majority, can imagine itself a minority with no responsibility for their influence over the status quo.

This cultural ecology encourages sectarian forms of community. Communities become ever more homogenous, held together only by what they believe in common—negotiated not with a global *ecumene* of believers, but within the bounds of small "elective fraternities" or focused movements.[20] Communities are sustained by their ability to offer clear identities. Thus, we turn to religious traditions not for their complex wisdom, but for "sentiments, whose greatest force is in their ability to ignite intimacy into a political state and turn locality into a staging ground for identity."[21]

Indeed, "identity" may turn out to be a bad thing. The task of projecting an identity is as different from fidelity to tradition, as today's wedge issue politics is from building a broad political coalition. This conflict of tasks was evident in an exchange I witnessed at Georgetown some years ago between the president of an influential Catholic watchdog group who had no formal theological training, and John Collins Harvey, a senior Catholic bioethicist and member of the Pontifical Academy of Life. During the controversy of the Schaivo case, the group had targeted Harvey in one of its press releases as a "Professor of Death" who did not support John Paul II's teaching on artificial hydration and nutrition. Harvey demanded to know on what grounds this charge was made. The organization's leader replied with his evaluation of the inadequacy of an interview Harvey had given on the history of Catholic teaching on end-of-life care. Harvey responded using the complex professional hermeneutics of his field—a style of language quite different from the activist's heated press-release discourse. The exchange illustrated that the complexities and nuances that mark a lived tradition of moral reflection do not translate easily into the rhetorical needs of identity projection. Attempts to plumb the significance of the clause "in principle" in the all-important passage in John Paul's allocution, which are so essential for practicing ethics in a Catholic healthcare setting, appear at best as overly rigorous hairsplitting, and at worst, as casuist sophistry for those whose primary task is establishing a clear identity. The two were speaking different languages yoked to fundamentally different tasks.

---

[20] Danièle Hervieu-Léger, *Religion as a Chain of Memory*, trans. Simon Lee (New Brunswick, NJ: Rutgers University Press, 1993), 149–56.
[21] Appadurai, *Modernity At Large*, 41.

"Identity," for all the integrity evoked by its rhetorical use, is a very limited cultural practice. Far from preserving the complex orthodoxy and orthopraxis of a tradition, it shears off what does not serve its limited needs. The complex hermeneutics and casuistry of living traditions with responsibility for putting their beliefs into practice do not fit well in this new identity-focused culture. Nuance, complexity, and the demanding task of holding multiple beliefs and commitments in tension do not fulfill the cultural work of identity. Thus, it is not surprising that identity watchdog groups seldom address a broad range of issues in their evaluations of orthodoxy.

d. Special Agenda Organizations

This exchange points to a new form of organization that thrives in this ecology. This form has increasingly colonized American religious institutions over the past century. Robert Wuthnow termed these "special purpose groups." James Davison Hunter considered more political forms of these organizations, which he termed "special agenda organizations" in his study of American culture wars.

Wuthnow argued that special purpose groups are one of the most significant factors in the restructuring of religion in the United States at the end of the twentieth century. These exist independently of traditional denominations. While they are religious movements, they are not directed at the formation of local religious communities such as sects or new denominations. They are instrumentally oriented toward specific objectives and membership is organized through mobilization to meet these objectives.[22]

Special purpose groups are highly focused and adaptive. They allow for high levels of commitment to a focused cause, while not disturbing other commitments and associations. These groups do not compete with denominations, they work around and within them. Churches continue to gather people in traditional worship settings, but the engaged practice of faith within these communities takes place within special purpose groups focused on spirituality such as Bible study and charismatic prayer groups; or focused on matters of justice such as civil rights, peace and justice, or pro-life groups; or simply focused on the common concerns of professions or hobbies such as organizations of Christian drag racers or church secretaries.[23]

---

[22] Robert Wuthnow, *The Restructuring of American Religion* (Princeton, NJ: Princeton University Press, 1990), 101–5.

[23] Ibid., 130.

Wuthnow believes that such groups contribute much to the vitality of American denominations. Nevertheless, their tendency to attract homogenous membership may cause these groups to contribute to "the development of cultural cleavages. . . . Like weeds in the cracks that only a few decades ago consisted of nothing more than hairline seams." They sort out allegiances within denominations and congregations and thus lessen the ability of religious communities to sustain the complex unities their traditions demand. New forms of prayer (e.g., charismatic, meditative) split off from the shared liturgical tradition, while social action groups shear apart into justice and peace and pro-life concerns. The growth of such groups brings "heightened potential for religious communities to become fractured along the lines of larger cleavages in society."[24] Wuthnow's concern has proved prescient.

Their effects go far beyond religious communities. Hunter's study of the culture war focuses on special agenda organizations, "a wide variety of religiously based public affairs organizations, political lobbies, and associations" which are "concerned with promoting a particular social or political agenda in the public domain."[25] These have become increasingly influential in the public sphere and within the churches. Special agenda organizations thrive by focusing on a single issue or cluster of issues. Lacking the responsibility to address the full range of issues in public life of concern to the Church, they are able to develop arguments and frames, issues and policy analyses, and to insert them into the media and public life.

Special agenda organizations likewise do not need to balance the interests of a complex constituency. Their memberships are composed entirely of people concerned enough about their issues to be active members. Consistent with the contemporary cultural ecology, their appeals and media messaging often speak more to their committed members than to the broader public who presumably must be convinced of their causes. Although their *raison d'être* is advocacy, their survival depends upon attracting committed supporters. Thus they employ rhetoric of denunciation and outrage to move their supporters to action and donation. Indeed the fundamental genre of communication has remained constant through changes in technology—the targeted direct mail, email, or web ad. These usually warn of some dire action about to be accomplished

---

[24] Ibid.

[25] James Davison Hunter, *Culture Wars: The Struggle to Define America* (New York: Basic Books, 1991), 90.

by enemies of the cause (whose own special agenda organizations are no doubt issuing similar letters), include a token advocacy action (a survey, a postcard, or click-through email message to a legislator), and offer a chance to donate to the organization so that it may continue its noble fight for the cause.

It is important to note how this cultural ecology systematically favors extreme rhetoric and contrastive identities. John O'Malley and Cathleen Kaveny have written extensively about prophetic rhetoric in ecclesial and public life.[26] This is a venerable moral stance and rhetorical form in both the Western tradition and American history. As a part of the cultural repertoire it has been employed in various situations through time and across cultures. It is particularly attractive at the present moment. Prophecy's use of dichotomy and demand for clarity are perfectly suited to the identity needs of the contemporary cultural ecology.

Deterritorialization contributes to extreme rhetoric as well. The abstraction of community from particular territories results in a decline in participation in shared public life. Whereas local churches, synagogues, and mosques are likely to work together on matters of relevance to their shared community, when such communities are located primarily in cyberspace they have no obvious location to ground cooperative efforts and no obvious others with whom they must get along. This is true on the intraecclesial level as well. The more that ecclesial formation and reflection is carried out in the heterogenized spaces of cyberspace and congregationalized parishes, the less likely believers are to have the skills and desire to speak beyond their enclaves.

Jose Casanova has argued that the profound deterritorialization of the loss of the Papal States led the Vatican to reconfigure its power as doctrinal authority.[27] Gradually, this authority was broadened from the Church to the entire world as the papacy developed into a global moral authority. In this regard Casanova points to John XXIII's embrace of human rights language, but the universal moral perspective can certainly be traced in the modern development of social teaching from Leo XIII onward. This was a role that John Paul II exercised in a historic manner. It is worth noting however that this transformation was not simply a

[26] John O'Malley, *The Four Cultures of the West* (Cambridge, MA: Harvard Belknap, 2004). M. Cathleen Kaveny, "Prophecy and Casuistry: Abortion, Torture, and Moral Discourse," *Villanova Law Review* 51, no. 3 (2006): 499–580.

[27] Jose Casanova, "Religion, the New Millennium, and Globalization," *Sociology of Religion* 62, no. 4 (2001): 431.

response to deterritorialization, it was a move onto a different territory. Having lost temporal power, the Church repositioned itself as a moral voice within national and global civil societies.

As heterogenization fragments these spaces of shared discourse, optimism regarding the project of moral witness fades, and with it the rhetorical task of convincing others in this shared space. With no temporal power of its own, with members formed in communities that by their very nature imagine themselves as countercultural, in the midst of the decline of the project of civil society, the Church might increasingly feel both pessimistic about the state of the world, and powerless to impact it in any way. In such a situation, one would expect the Christian heritage of apocalyptic rhetoric to find resurgence. It is has long flourished among extreme groups, and it is increasingly finding its way into episcopal discourse.

Through targeted messaging and mass media presence, special agenda organizations are able to reach beyond and through traditional religious communications infrastructures such as: seminaries and colleges, denominational print media, and journals of opinion. They can reach a much broader audience: members of traditional churches, newer evangelical communities, and people with little or no religious affiliation. This broad reach enables these organizations to forge broad, trans-denominational religious, cultural, and political movements. This change in communicative infrastructure is tremendously important. Not only can this movement reach into existing religious communities to address their members, it possesses the cultural power to challenge their traditional authorities and to reframe their theological discourses.

The Religious Right has had enormous success utilizing this new form of organization. Dr. James Dobson's career charts the rise of this form of religious authority. His earliest work was much more in the mold of a conservative evangelical New Cultural Intermediary. He gained national prominence in 1972 with the publication of *Dare to Discipline*, which wove from the proverb "spare the rod, spoil the child" both a parenting manual and a repudiation of the perceived moral laxity of the 1960s.[28] Yet his conservative message was still very much focused on the lifestyles and choices of individual families: an evangelical Dr. Benjamin Spock. Throughout the 70s, his influence in evangelical circles grew through his

---

[28] James Dobson, *Dare to Discipline* (Chicago: Gospel Light, 1972). See Robert Wuthnow, *After Heaven: Spirituality in America since the 1950s* (Berkeley: University of California Press, 1998), 90–93.

radio program. He only achieved national prominence, however, in the 1980s, after his message became more overtly political and he incorporated a separate lobbying arm, the Family Research Council.

In this cultural ecology, collective identities are no longer sustained by local community contacts or by the complex beliefs and practices guided by an authoritative tradition with an extensive system of formation (primary socialization, religious education on primary, secondary, and higher education levels) and authority (theologians, local pastors, bishops). Instead, collective religious identities are now formed under the leadership of religious intermediaries leading special agenda organizations communicating through mass and targeted media. Key here is Appadurai's insight, discussed above, that constructing a shared identity in such an undifferentiated, deterritorialized setting favors elements of traditions and practices which elicit strong emotions or set a community apart from others. Attachment to tradition may remain strong, but it is not practiced in a comprehensive manner. Rather, elements are lifted from it that sustain a clear identity.

This identity-focused ecology is almost identical to the conditions Scott Appleby describes for the emergence of ethno-nationalist religious extremism in situations of high levels of religious commitment and low levels of religious literacy. Identity is not only too narrow a social function to support the richness of religious belief and practice; it also risks fueling conflict by depriving believers of the elements of their traditions they need to resist the exploitation of religion to fuel cultural conflict and violence.[29]

The Episcopate and the Special Purpose Organization: The 2008 Presidential Election

The consequences of this new, politicized cultural ecology were particularly evident in the Catholic debate during the 2008 elections. The United States Conference of Catholic Bishops issued its quadrennial statement on faith and public life, *Forming Consciences for Faithful Citizenship*. This document, which passed by a vote of 221 to 4 in November of 2007, displayed the tensions Catholics face in the American political context, where both of the two major parties hold positions significantly at odds with Catholic social teaching. It repeatedly described ending

[29] R. Scott Appleby, *The Ambivalence of the Sacred: Religion, Violence, and Reconciliation* (Lanham, MD: Rowman & Littlefield, 2000).

abortion as a fundamental moral obligation that cannot be reduced to "one issue among many," yet simultaneously rejected a single-issue focus that uses abortion to dismiss or ignore other "serious threats to human life and dignity." It specifically addressed the political divisions within the American Church, noting that "not every Catholic can be involved" in all pressing issues, and calling for mutual support among those working on different issues. "We are not factions, but one family of faith fulfilling the mission of Jesus Christ."[30] The document clarified the relationship between the exercise and formation of conscience, and retrieved the traditional concept of prudence for political decisions.

The document was distributed through an impressively wide range of media: printed copies were distributed in parishes and made available on a dedicated web site: FaithfulCitizenship.org. Abridged versions were produced as bulletin inserts. A novena was prepared and offered online, as were a series of webcasts by Conference staffers and issue experts. Despite these impressive communications structures, the meaning and application of the document were decided not within ecclesially sanctioned spaces and debates, but within broader media and political space.

Special agenda groups struggled to support or marginalize the document. On the right, groups like the Catholic Answer Education Fund and Randall Terry (founder of Operation Rescue) produced their own competing voter guides. The group Fidelis produced an extensive web site (CatholicVote.com). Randall Terry was particularly egregious in his challenge to the USCCB. His organization leafleted Catholic parish parking lots with "Faithful Catholic Citizenship" designed to mimic the graphics of the Conference's voter guide. All of these groups suggested or asserted that a candidate's support for abortion rights is an insurmountable obstacle for Catholic voters. Progressive organizations such as Catholics in Alliance for the Common Good sought to keep the full range of Catholic social concerns in play, including life issues.[31] Media coverage tended to reduce both sides to the question of whether or not Catholics could vote for candidates that support abortion rights.

The bishops' role in the debate concerning the document is telling. Many discussed the election in their diocesan papers and encouraged members of their dioceses to employ *Faithful Citizenship*. This garnered

---

[30] United States Conference of Catholic Bishops, *Forming Consciences for Faithful Citizenship* (Washington, DC: USCCB, 2007), #28, 29.

[31] Disclosure: I have served on an advisory board for Catholics in Alliance for the Common Good.

little press attention. Blogger Rocco Palma ran a story that claimed 50 bishops had made public statements defining abortion as the fundamental moral concern of the election.[32] This story in turn received media coverage, which seldom noted that 148 ordinaries had not made such statements.

Those bishops who were most effective in the debate were those who augmented their episcopal role and resources with those of the special agenda organization, working through secular media and the networks of special agenda organizations. Archbishop Charles Chaput of Denver stands out as the most effective in this regard. He published a book with a secular press on political responsibility that appeared around the time of the political conventions in late summer.[33] He argued repeatedly that no prudential argument could be made to vote for a candidate that supports abortion rights in the face of more than a million abortions performed each year in the United States. A LexisNexis search returns 94 hits for *Faithful Citizenship* from June through the election; Archbishop Chaput received 97—3 times that of Cardinal Francis George, who was USCCB President at the time.

Other bishops openly rejected the document. Bishop Joseph Martino of Scranton (a small rustbelt town, albeit the birthplace of the Democratic vice presidential candidate) voted against it and declared it inapplicable in his diocese. His actions garnered national attention with 21 hits, nearly equal that of Cardinal George.

The contrast between the USCCB strategy regarding *Faithful Citizenship* and the bishops who pursued the strategies of special agenda organizations is illuminative. It shows that the new communicative structures overwrite the old. The USCCB's expansion into new media space did not rewrite these rules. The episcopal task of conveying the entire range of Catholic concerns in public life is hard to sustain in this cultural ecology.

Bishops who function according to the rules of special agenda organizations are much more effective in the mediascape. This space reaches far beyond their own dioceses, into all others. As then-Archbishop Donald Wuerl noted in 2005, while the decisions of some bishops to publicly deny communion to Catholic politicians who supported abortion rights presumed the autonomy of the Ordinary to interpret canon law in his

---

[32] Rocco Palmo, "Fifty Bishops Say US Election Is about Abortion," *The Tablet* (October 25, 2008), http://www.thetablet.co.uk/article/12189 (accessed November 10, 2008).

[33] Charles J. Chaput, OFM Cap, *Render unto Caesar: Catholic Witness and American Public Life* (New York: Doubleday, 2008).

own diocese, the "ubiquity and influence" of the media cause a local bishop's actions and statements to "have immediate national impact and affect the bishops of the rest of the dioceses throughout the country."[34] Increasingly, the Church is "in" media space, which does not respect diocesan boundaries.

The 2008 election is a helpful example because of the USCCB's unprecedented efforts to use a range of new media. The differential impacts illustrate the ways in which the media structure reception. They are not well suited for communicating a comprehensive range of issues. Bishops are granted a much greater hearing insofar as they supplement their episcopal role with that of the special agenda advocate. Insofar as this complements their episcopal work within their own diocese, it is not necessarily a problem. Speaking out nationally on one issue does not preclude teaching the fullness of the faith in one's own diocese. However, as we have noted, media space is increasingly the place within which the ecclesia is constituted. Parishes, liturgies, sacraments, and CCD classes are in no danger of disappearing, but believers' formation in the faith, their sense of its most important principles and commitments comes not from their family, parish, or diocese, but from the presentation of Catholicism in the media sphere. Thus, when bishops are drawn into the role of the special agenda organization, they may not be "supplementing," but rather, reducing their episcopal authority. They may end up narrowing the Church's understanding of its faith even if they are good stewards of comprehensive orthodoxy in their own dioceses through more traditional channels.

It is worth returning again to the reception of John Paul's allocution on end-of-life care from the perspective of this analysis. While Vatican use of new media certainly contributed to the reception of John Paul's teaching, it is abundantly clear that the special agenda organizations were massively involved in communicating and interpreting the significance of John Paul's teaching. How many other allocutions of his have received so much (or any) discussion? New forms of media may communicate magisterial teaching in a much more direct manner. The "catapult" however requires the active cooperation of new ecclesial actors—special agenda organizations—to put it into play in the media sphere. Note the stunning contrast of John Paul's repeated statements of critical hesitation

---

[34] Jerry Filteau, "Bishop Cites 'National Impact' of Denying Politicians Communion," *Catholic News Service* (August 18, 2005), http://www.catholicnews.com/data/stories/cns/0504718.htm (accessed November 10, 2008).

concerning the invasion of Iraq. These statements critical of the Bush administration enjoyed no power of digital immediacy and no ability to catapult themselves into American ecclesial consciousness. The USCCB voiced hesitations and critiques of the rapid run up to war similar to John Paul's. All of these magisterial statements were actively downplayed and interpreted away by many of the same pundits and special agenda organizations that consistently amplified John Paul's teachings on life issues.[35] Conservative pundits and special agenda organizations with their profound media savvy controlled the message.[36] The capital of orthodoxy these conservative figures had developed over the decades was deployed to marginalize the voice of the magisterium.

Conclusion

Transformations in the structures and forms through which authority is exercised and communicated will likely transform the nature, exercise, and reception of authority. This is the case with the hierarchy's embrace of modern forms of communication and the new technologies of the internet. While these new media can contribute to the centralization of authority in the Church, they also place magisterial statements in new contexts in which they are subject to different interpretive practices. Control over the meaning of teaching is simultaneously centralized and distributed. The latter dynamism requires us to examine the broader cultural ecology to consider the likely uses to which magisterial statements will be put. Here we find a tendency toward fractiousness, a need for clear and distinct identities, and an abstraction of doctrine and community from responsibility for particular territory. This media ecology supports a new form of cultural intermediary: the special agenda organization. Their focus on a narrow range of issues and ability to marshal committed activists makes them very effective at influencing the media sphere. As the secular media replace traditional ecclesial communication networks, such activists and pundits increasingly influence believers' understanding of Catholicism.

---

[35] Peter Dula, "How Catholic Conservatives Got Iraq Wrong," *Commonweal* 131, no. 21 (December 3, 2004): 12–21.

[36] Perhaps a bit of hesitation is warranted regarding the conclusion that this power is the result of new forms of media. Gary Wills discusses the "cult of the encyclicals" among liberal American Catholics in the 1950s and 1960s. "Those who cited them so blithely loved to inflate their authority, but had not bothered to find out what (if anything) made them compelling." *Why I Am a Catholic* (Boston: Houghton Mifflin Harcourt, 2002), 44–45.

All of this presents a profound challenge to the catholicity of the Church.[37] Bishops and theologians must work to preserve and to communicate the fullness of the faith in a context where the media systematically disadvantage such comprehensive concerns, and in a culture where believers are likely to prefer clear identities to the less gratifying work of holding the complex whole of the faith together. Those who teach the faith must struggle against the script of the special agenda organization while finding a way to speak in the media space that rewards it. The entire Church must find new ways to cultivate Catholic unity in an environment that encourages fractiousness and division.

---

[37] For a discussion of these issues using catholicity both as a principle of diagnosis and basis for responding, see Vincent J. Miller "Where Is The Church? Globalization And Catholicity," *Theological Studies*, 69 (2008): 412–32.

Part 3

Recent Developments

Chapter 8

The Elizabeth Johnson Dossier
Introduction to the Johnson Dossier

Richard R. Gaillardetz

As we indicated in the introduction to this volume, the final section of our collection is dedicated to the 2011 investigation of Prof. Elizabeth A. Johnson's 2007 book, *Quest for the Living God: Mapping Frontiers in the Theology of God*. Bradford Hinze's opening essay in this volume offered a comprehensive survey of magisterial interventions in the work of theology at the national and international levels. To complement that survey, this final section will focus on a single example of magisterial intervention in the work of a contemporary theologian.

Prof. Elizabeth Johnson is one of America's most respected and influential theologians. She has published critically acclaimed volumes on Christology, the Trinity, Mary, and the communion of saints. She has made important contributions to contemporary feminist theology while resolutely working within the mainstream Catholic theological tradition. She is a past president of the Catholic Theological Society of America (CTSA) and is a recipient of that society's prestigious John Courtney Murray award. It is understandable, then, that the USCCB Committee on Doctrine's decision to issue a statement condemning her most recent work would have garnered so much attention.[1] In order to explore this case in more detail, we are including the complete text of six documents related to her investigation which appear in chronological order: (1) the USCCB Committee on Doctrine's "Statement on *Quest for the Living God: Mapping Frontiers in the Theology of God*, by Sister Elizabeth A. Johnson"; (2) a second statement, "Bishops as Teachers," offered by Cardinal Wuerl

---

[1] Of course, as Hinze notes in his essay, she is hardly the only prominent theologian in the United States to come under investigation.

177

on behalf of the Committee on Doctrine which sought to clarify the teaching responsibilities of the bishops; (3) Prof. Johnson's extended response, "To Speak Rightly of the Living God: Observations by Dr. Elizabeth A. Johnson, CSJ on the Statement of the Committee on Doctrine"; (4) an additional appendix to her original observations that Johnson sent to Cardinal Wuerl in July; (5) the Committee on Doctrine's final statement, "Response to Observations by Sr. Elizabeth A. Johnson, C.S.J., Regarding the Committee on Doctrine's Statement about the Book *Quest for the Living God*"; and (6) Johnson's concluding public statement. However, it may be helpful to reconstruct a detailed chronology of the Johnson case to date.

In some sense, of course, the case begins with the publication of Johnson's book, the latest in a distinguished list of publications by Johnson on various aspects of the doctrine of God. Johnson's comprehensive grasp of contemporary theological "frontiers" and her engaging writing style made the book immediately popular among scholars and other educated readers. It was the popularity of the book that spurred the investigation which transpired over some unspecified period and without Johnson's knowledge. On March 30, 2011, the USCCB Committee on Doctrine publicly issued a document titled, "Statement on *Quest for the Living God: Mapping Frontiers in the Theology of God*, by Sister Elizabeth A. Johnson."[2] In an accompanying letter addressed to the bishops, Cardinal Donald Wuerl, chair of the Committee on Doctrine, offered a brief rationale for the statement. In the letter, Wuerl reported that the investigation was instigated by "requests from bishops concerning the pastoral implications" of Johnson's work and he suggested that Johnson could have avoided the investigation if she had chosen to seek an *imprimatur*. Finally, Wuerl expressed the committee's openness to engage Prof. Johnson in dialogue. The first that Johnson heard of the investigation was a day earlier on March 29, at a meeting with Archbishop Timothy Dolan and the president of Fordham University, Fr. Joseph McShane. Dolan had brought the committee statement with him to the meeting. The next day, Prof. Johnson offered a brief public statement, writing:

> It is heartening to see the Bishops Conference give such serious attention to the subject of the living God. I appreciate how this

---

[2] http://old.usccb.org/doctrine/statement-quest-for-the-living-god-2011-03-24 .pdf. The document was apparently approved by the committee on March 24, 2011. The publication was delayed for a few days at the request of Archbishop Timothy J. Dolan of New York, president of the USCCB, in order to allow him time to contact Prof. Johnson with news of the statement.

statement acknowledges the laudable nature of the task of crafting a theology of God, and the number of issues on which the statement judges that I am "entirely correct." The book itself endeavors to present new insights about God arising from people living out their Catholic faith in different cultures around the world. My hope is that any conversation that may be triggered by this statement will but enrich that faith, encouraging robust relationship to the Holy Mystery of the living God as the church moves into the future.

I would like to express two serious concerns. First, I would have been glad to enter into conversation to clarify critical points, but was never invited to do so. This book was discussed and finally assessed by the Committee before I knew any discussion had taken place. Second, one result of this absence of dialogue is that in several key instances this statement radically misinterprets what I think, and what I in fact wrote. The conclusions thus drawn paint an incorrect picture of the fundamental line of thought the book develops. A conversation, which I still hope to have, would have very likely avoided these misrepresentations.

That being said, as a scholar I have always taken criticism as a valuable opportunity to delve more deeply into a subject. The task of theology, classically defined as "faith seeking understanding," calls for theologians to wrestle with mystery. The issues are always complex, especially on frontiers where the church's living tradition is growing. Committed to the faith of the church, I take this statement as an occasion to ponder yet further the mystery of the living God who is ineffable.

At this time I will make no further statements nor give any interviews.[3]

What soon followed was a groundswell of criticism leveled at the committee's treatment of Johnson. On April 8, the Catholic Theological Society of America (CTSA) executive board issued a public statement expressing their concerns on three issues related to the committee statement: "1) the fact that, in this matter, the bishops did not follow the procedures set forth in their own document, *Doctrinal Responsibilities*; 2) a misreading of Professor Johnson's work in the statement; 3) the troubling implications the statement presents for the exercise of our vocation as theologians."[4] The officers and board of directors of the College Theology Society (CTS)

---

[3] The text of this statement appeared on *NCROnline.org* at http://ncronline.org/news/johnson-bishops-condemnation-came-without-discussion.

[4] Available on the CTSA web site: http://www.ctsa-online.org/johnson.html.

almost immediately endorsed the CTSA statement. Somewhat surprisingly, the response from prominent conservative Catholic groups was muted.[5] The many criticisms, along with rumored complaints from several bishops themselves, led Cardinal Wuerl to publish a follow-up document on April 18 titled, "Bishops as Teachers."[6] This attempt to clarify and reinforce the teaching obligations of the bishops did nothing to quell the criticism.

The Faculty Senate of Fordham University sponsored a letter addressed to the bishops' committee protesting the treatment of Prof. Johnson. The letter, sent on April 19, would eventually include 180 signatories, including university faculty and administrators. This letter elicited a far more conciliatory response from Capuchin Fr. Thomas Weinandy, executive director of the Committee on Doctrine. On April 28 he sent a letter to the Fordham Faculty Senate in which he insisted that the committee was taking their concerns seriously and that the committee's action "in no way calls into question the dedication, honor, creativity, or service" of Prof. Johnson.[7] A separate letter from Fr. Weinandy, also dated April 28, was sent to Johnson, expressing the committee's openness to further dialogue. Weinandy wrote: "To underline the seriousness of this offer, Cardinal Wuerl has directed me to write to you and to reiterate the willingness of the Committee to receive any written observations that you may wish to provide with regard to its statement."[8]

Prof. Johnson accepted the invitation and on June 1 sent her extended response to the committee's criticisms of her work, a response that was initially made public without her immediate knowledge.[9] She titled her response, "To Speak Rightly of the Living God: Observations by Dr.

---

[5] However, Fr. Joseph Koterski, SJ, president of the more conservative organization, Fellowship of Catholic Scholars, did publish a statement on the society's web site expressing surprise at the criticism of the bishops' committee and stating his support for the action of the committee. Available on the FCS web site: http://www2 .catholicscholars.org/Default.aspx?pageId=1016346. As regards professional associations for Catholic theologians, the CTSA has almost thirteen hundred members and CTS over five hundred. The Fellowship of Catholic Scholars has a membership of approximately 750 but it is an international organization with membership from throughout the world.

[6] Available on the USCCB web site: http://old.usccb.org/doctrine/BISHOPS -AS-TEACHERS-%20CARDINAL-WUERL-4-18-11.pdf.

[7] Quoted in an *NCROnline.org* article dated May 13, 2011: http://ncronline.org/ news/faith-parish/bishops-committee-reaches-out-catholic-scholars.

[8] The letter itself was made available to the author by Prof. Johnson.

[9] The response was published by *NCROnline.org*, June 6. It was subsequently published in *Origins* 41, no. 9 (2011): 129–47.

Elizabeth A. Johnson, CSJ on the Statement of the Committee on Doctrine of the United States Conference of Catholic Bishops about her book *Quest for the Living God: Mapping Frontiers in the Theology of God.*" The response itself, a sixteen-thousand-word essay, offered a clarification of her views and a meticulous, point-by-point rebuttal of the committee's criticisms.

In the meantime, reactions to the committee's original censure continued. On June 10, at their annual convention business meeting, the CTSA membership approved the following resolution:

> The Catholic Theological Society of America regrets deeply that the provisions established by the American Bishops in the document *Doctrinal Responsibilities: Procedures for Promoting Cooperation and Resolving Disputes Between Bishops and Theologians* were ignored in passing judgment on *Quest for the Living God* by Professor Elizabeth A. Johnson, C.S.J. These provisions came from the CTSA and from the Canon Law Society of America. After six years of deliberation, debate, and consensus, they were submitted to the Congregation for the Doctrine of the Faith and obtained its review and concurrence. Then they were presented to the entire body of American Bishops at the regular meeting of the Conference and approved overwhelmingly for use in the United States. They were not imposed upon any diocese as an obligation of law but presented as careful provisions and directions in order to avoid precisely the situation in which we find ourselves.
>
> In light of this, the CTSA recommends to the American Bishops that they establish a committee that would evaluate the procedures of the Committee on Doctrine that led to their statement (147 in favor, 1 opposed, 2 abstentions).[10]

CTSA president, Prof. John Thiel of Fairfield University, immediately wrote to the president of the USCCB, Archbishop Timothy Dolan, informing him of the society's resolution. He reiterated the society's concerns while adding that neither the resolution nor the earlier board statement should be read as a "challenge to the charismatic authority of the magisterium." In a letter dated July 7, Archbishop Dolan responded to Prof. Thiel, expressing gratitude for the society's acknowledgement of the legitimate role of the magisterium. He then responded to the criticism raised by the CTSA that the committee had failed to observe the guidelines set out in *Doctrinal Responsibilities.* He noted that the 1989 document did not directly apply to the Johnson case, since it was intended to deal with conflicts between theologians and individual bishops, but he did

---

[10] Available on the CTSA web site: http://www.ctsa-online.org/resolutions.html.

concede that "we bishops should always be mindful of improving the manner in which we engage theologians in a necessary discussion of their work."[11] Dolan also added that the larger Administrative Committee of the USCCB had debated the Committee on Doctrine's statement and had unanimously approved its publication.

About this time (mid-summer), Prof. Johnson had been receiving disturbing letters from various individuals who had complained to the bishops' committee about their treatment of Johnson. Apparently, Fr. Weinandy had written them extensive responses, outlining further accusations against Johnson that went beyond those contained in the committee statement. The recipients of these letters, disturbed by both the caustic tone of Weinandy's comments and the fact that new criticisms were being raised, sent copies of his letters to her. Johnson feared that these further criticisms might become part of the committee's delibera-tions and concluded that they too merited a direct response. On July 14 Johnson sent to Cardinal Wuerl a document that responded to the new criticisms that Weinandy was disseminating, and asked that the docu-ment be treated as an appendix to her initial response. Wuerl responded with a brief letter (July 22) indicating that the document would be sent to the committee members but that it would *not* be considered as part of her formal response by the committee. He informed her that the committee would be meeting in September to discuss her response and he gave the impression that the committee would not be considering the additional criticisms that Weinandy had been offering in private correspondence.

During the last week of October, Johnson received a copy of the com-mittee's final statement. It was made public on the USCCB web site a few days later on October 28. The statement offered a comprehensive reaffirmation of the committee's original condemnation. Particularly troubling was the fact that the committee did in fact take up one of Wein-andy's added criticisms (even though Wuerl had indicated to Johnson that they would not), namely that Johnson rejected the claim that any expression for God could be taken literally. The committee returns to this criticism in its final statement without taking into account Johnson's clarification in her appendix. For that reason we have decided to include Johnson's appendix in the documentation of her case. On the same day that the committee released its final statement, Johnson also released a brief public statement. Both are included in the dossier.

---

[11] The correspondence is published on the "members only" section of the CTSA web site.

24 March 2011

Statement on *Quest for the Living God: Mapping Frontiers in the Theology of God*, by Sister Elizabeth A. Johnson

Committee on Doctrine

United States Conference of Catholic Bishops

The Committee on Doctrine of the USCCB has undertaken an examination and evaluation of the book *Quest for the Living God: Mapping Frontiers in the Theology of God* (Continuum, 2007) by Sister Elizabeth Johnson, C.S.J., a professor at Fordham University. The Committee has concluded that this book contains misrepresentations, ambiguities, and errors that bear upon the faith of the Catholic Church as found in Sacred Scripture, and as it is authentically taught by the Church's universal magisterium. Because this book by a prominent Catholic theologian is written not for specialists in theology but for "a broad audience" (2), the Committee on Doctrine felt obliged, as part of its pastoral ministry, to note these misrepresentations, ambiguities, and errors.

This statement will first consider the importance of the topic and the method proper to Catholic theology. It is here, at the level of method, that the book rests upon a false presupposition, an error that undermines the very nature of the study and so skews many of its arguments, rendering many of its conclusions theologically unacceptable. The statement will then examine various topics addressed in *Quest for the Living God*, following the order of the chapters and noting the misrepresentations, ambiguities, and errors.

A False Alternative:
"Modern Theism" or Radical Reconstruction of the Idea of God

The heart of Christian theology is the study of God not simply as one, but also as a Trinity of persons—the Father, the Son and the Holy Spirit. "The mystery of the Most Holy Trinity is the central mystery of Christian faith and life. It is the mystery of God in himself" (*Catechism of the Catholic Church*, no. 234). It is laudable then that Catholic theologians undertake such studies, especially when their writings advance the

Church's understanding and appreciation of the mystery of God, and build up and confirm the faith of all believers. Because the mystery of God as a Trinity of persons is the foundational mystery of the Church's faith, it is all the more important that those theologians who do embark on the study of this mystery do so from within the very heart of the Church's faith. Pope John Paul II stated in his encyclical, *Fides et Ratio*:

> Theology is structured as an understanding of faith in the light of a twofold methodological principle: the *auditus fidei* and the *intellectus fidei*. With the first, theology makes its own the content of revelation as this has been gradually expounded in Sacred Tradition, Sacred Scripture and the Church's living Magisterium. With the second, theology seeks to respond through speculative inquiry to the specific demands of disciplined thought. (no. 65)

Theologians must, therefore, first lay hold of the content of God's revelation, the *auditus fidei*, as proclaimed in Scripture and taught within the Church, through an act of personal faith.[1] Only then are they properly equipped to enquire into the content of that faith, the *intellectus fidei*, seeking a greater understanding and clearer expression of it. By means of the theologians' reaffirmation of the Church's corporate confession of the Father, Son, and Holy Spirit, their service is conformed to the mystery of their Baptism and their incorporation into Trinitarian communion through Jesus Christ.

Sr. Johnson, however, begins with a critique of the Church's faith, or, rather of what she terms "traditional theology" or "classical Christian theology." In response to the distortions she claims are there and to the challenges posed to faith in the contemporary cultural situation, she offers a thoroughgoing reinterpretation of the doctrine of God. She makes this move plausible by presenting the unappealing portrayal of God to be found in what she labels "modern theism." According to Sr. Johnson, modern theism models God as "a monarch" who is at the "peak of the pyramid of being." The best theology can do is portray him "as benevolent." "'He,' for it is always the ruling male who stands for this idea, is essentially remote" (14). While loving he is "uncontaminated" by the world. "And always this distant lordly lawgiver stands at the summit of hierarchical power, reinforcing structures of authority in society, church, and family" (14). According to Sr. Johnson, this portrayal follows from the

---

[1] St. Thomas Aquinas points out that just as other sciences accept as a given the first principles of their particular science, Christian theology "does not argue in proof of its principles, which are the articles of faith" (*Summa Theologiae* I, q. 1, a. 8).

conviction that God is immutable, incorporeal, impassible, omnipotent, omniscient, and omnipresent (see 15). This is modern theism.

In contrast to such an unappealing notion of God, Sr. Johnson offers an alternative based on new and thoroughgoing reinterpretations of the traditional conception of God: "[t]he theologies traced out in this book, in contrast to modern theism, are deeply concerned with God's relationship to the world" (16). She claims that "we are witnessing nothing less than a 'revolution' in the theology of God" (1, see also 13-14), a revolution that is necessary because "modern theism" has thrown the Christian faith "into crisis." "Thinking people questioned what it all meant, this old, rather creaky tradition of luxuriant doctrines and rituals and hierarchy and pious customs, and whether any of it was true" (27).

What Sr. Johnson calls "modern theism" is actually an Enlightenment deist notion of God that contains some elements, though now misrepresented, of a traditional Catholic understanding of God. She acknowledges that modern theism is the result of the distortion of the Christian tradition by Enlightenment ideas and that it does not represent "classical Christian theology" (15). At some points, then, she claims to be retrieving the authentic tradition of "early Christian and medieval theology" (17). At other points, however, she seems to regard "modern theism" as interchangeable with "traditional Christian doctrine" and "traditional preaching and theology," for she reproaches the latter for the same faults as the former (73, 80). While some ideas that she identifies as distortions due to the Enlightenment are in fact distortions of the Christian theological tradition, other ideas that she identifies as characteristics of modern theism, such as God's immutability, incorporeality, impassibility, omnipotence, etc. (15, 52, 54), are not distortions at all but integral and essential elements of that tradition. In any event, by associating traditional Christian theology with modern theism, she seeks to justify the need for her own proposals.

Sr. Johnson states correctly that God can, at times, be misrepresented as an arrogant monarch who acts in a tyrannical and dictatorial fashion. However, traditional Catholic teaching does not do this. Rather, it understands that God the Father is all-loving, and as such, he providentially cares for his creation. Jesus is indeed the Lord of lords and King of kings, not in the sense of pompously lording it over his subjects, but rather as the servant who lays down his life for his sheep. Jesus' name is above every other name and every knee must bend before him and every tongue proclaim him "Lord" because he humbled himself "accepting death, even death on a cross" (Phil 2:6-11). The Holy Spirit empowers Christians to act after the manner of Jesus and so bear the fruit of charity, joy, peace, patience, and endurance (Gal 5:22-23). This traditional Catholic understanding of God bears no resemblance to Sr. Johnson's monarchical deity of "modern theism."

Moreover, God is not at "the peak of a pyramid" as if he had no concern for those whose manner of existence is lower than his own. Likewise, God is not at "the peak of a pyramid," as if God existed in manner similar to all else that is, the only difference being that he is on the top. Within traditional Christian theology, God is indeed the supreme being, but that means that he actually exists in a manner that is uniquely his own and so his manner of existence radically differs in kind from all else that exists. Existing in such a manner does not make God remote. Rather, it allows him lovingly to employ his almighty power to bring into existence other beings and, in so doing, he is intimately related to them, especially to human beings, as the good Creator. Sr. Johnson recognizes that God's radical transcendence and radical immanence go together (16, cf. 43). As will be shown later, however, her panentheism (p. 188), as well as her rejection of divine omnipotence and impassibility, does not preserve transcendence. Furthermore, for God to be immutable, incorporeal, impassible, etc. does not mean that God is static, inert, distant, and uncaring. Rather, such attributes assure that he is supremely loving, good, and perfect. God, then, is actively involved in the world of sin, evil, and suffering. In the history of salvation he has demonstrated that he is involved, the Incarnation being the supreme culminating instance. While God is active in this world contaminated by sin, evil, and suffering, he himself is not contaminated, nor complicit, for this would deprive him of his perfect goodness and love and hinder his salvific activity within time and history.

Sr. Johnson is correct that some notions of God do wrongly portray him as a "distant lordly lawgiver" who "stands at the summit of hierarchical power, reinforcing structures of authority in society, church, and family." This may be the view of "modern theism," but it is not the view of traditional Church teaching. God is indeed the supreme giver of law, such as the Ten Commandments, but such laws are not arbitrary and capricious. Rather, they are laws that instruct human beings on how they are to live truly authentic human lives, godly lives of love, justice, and righteousness. While the exercise of authority in society, the Church, and the family may be flawed at times, yet the lack of structures of authority within society, the Church, and the family would cause untold injustice and suffering. The exercise of authority that flows from the traditional Christian notion of God fosters truth, justice, equity, peace, and right order.

From the above, it is evident that *Quest for the Living God* contaminates the traditional Catholic understanding of God, which arises from both revelation and reason and which has been articulated by the Fathers and the Scholastics, especially Thomas Aquinas, and taught and professed by the Church, with Enlightenment deism. Such a notion of God may conform to what is termed "modern theism," and so be in need of reform as the book suggests. However, to give the impression that "modern theism," is virtually identical with the traditional Catholic notion of God is seriously to misrepresent the tradition and so to distort it beyond recognition. Nonetheless, as seen in the above analysis, this is what *Quest for the Living God* has done at its very onset. It is this misrepresentation that Sr. Johnson takes as a warrant for articulating her many models of God, models that she proposes as more attractive than "modern theism."

Quest for the Living God speaks of a crisis within the Church, a crisis reflected in the disjuncture between "modern theism" and a more contemporary understanding of God based upon secular experience. The real crisis, however, the one that this book illustrates, is reflected in the disjuncture between a proper and authentic understanding of the traditional notion of the Christian God and an understanding of God that no longer comports with Christian revelation and the Church's profession of faith.

A False Presupposition: All Names for God are Metaphors

Sr. Johnson also justifies her radical revision of the traditional Christian understanding of God by asserting that the Church's names for God are metaphors that arise from religious experience and that consequently can be replaced by human ingenuity if that experience undergoes a change. For Sr. Johnson, theology begins with an acknowledgment that God is a mystery beyond all human understanding and that human language about God reflects human understanding and not the divine reality. "The first and most basic prescript is this: the reality of the living God is an ineffable mystery beyond all telling" (17). It is the "beyond all telling" that is key to Sr. Johnson's understanding of God. This is her first "ground rule."

The second ground rule is that no expression for God can be taken literally. She explains as follows:

> Our language is like a finger pointing to the moon, not the moon itself. To equate the finger with the moon or to look at the finger and not perceive the moon is to fall into error. Never to be taken literally, human words about God proceed by way of indirectness. They set

> off from the spare, original, strange perfections of this world and turn our face toward the source and future of all without capturing that essence of the mystery. (18)

Sr. Johnson is entirely correct on this: the Catholic theological tradition affirms that no human language is adequate to express the reality of God. Catholic teaching maintains that human concepts apply to God only in an analogous fashion. As the *Catechism of the Catholic Church* points out, "We can name God only by taking creatures as our starting point, and in accordance with our limited human ways of knowing and thinking" (no. 40). All creatures in some way resemble God, who is the source of any perfection found in them. Creatures possess only some perfections, and these only in a limited way. God possesses all perfections infinitely. From our knowledge of creatures we can come to understand a perfection such as goodness, but when we would attribute the perfection of goodness to God we must remember that God is good in a way far surpassing the way that creatures are good. Our language does apply to God, but only by analogy. "Admittedly, in speaking about God like this, our language is using human modes of expression; nevertheless it really does attain to God himself, though unable to express him in his infinite simplicity" (no. 43).

While Sr. Johnson is well within the Catholic theological tradition when she maintains that human language is never adequate to express the reality of God, she departs from that tradition when she makes the more radical claim that human language does not attain to the reality of God. For her, the meaning of the concept "good" derived from our knowledge of creatures is "lost" when it is applied to God. "We literally do not understand what we are saying. Human comprehension of the meaning of 'good' is lost, for we have no direct earthly experience of anything that is the Source of all goodness" (19).

While God is a mystery that cannot be fully comprehended and thus fully articulated, nonetheless, according to the Catholic theological tradition it is possible to make statements about God that are true even if they do not express the fullness of the mystery. That tradition acknowledges that there is a difference between God's being incomprehensible and God's being unknowable. To say that God is not comprehensible is to say that he cannot be completely known and understood.[2] On the other hand, God is knowable in the sense that human concepts do reflect some real if limited knowledge of God. For Sr. Johnson, if God is incompre-

---

[2] See St. Thomas Aquinas, *Summa Theologiae* I, q. 12, a. 7.

hensible he is also unknowable. This is incorrect. The Catechism of the Catholic Church states:

> We do not believe in formulas, but in those realities they express, which faith allows us to touch. "The believer's act [of faith] does not terminate in propositions, but in the realities [which they express]."[3] All the same, we do approach these realities with the help of formulations of the faith which permit us to express the faith and to hand it on, to celebrate it in community, to assimilate and live on it more and more. (no. 170)

The doctrines of the Trinity or the Incarnation, for example, state truly what the mystery of God is even if they do not and cannot express fully the mystery. The mysteries of the Trinity and the Incarnation are known even if they are not completely comprehended. These doctrines are not merely fingers pointing one in the direction of an unknowable mystery. They actually allow one to know the truth of what the mystery is.

By defining "mystery" in this way, Sr. Johnson defends her freedom to offer all sorts of statements about God that may point in the direction of the mystery; she simultaneously admits that they do not say anything literal about God. This is her third ground rule. Quoting Aquinas, she argues that there are many names for God employed throughout history within many different cultures and religions (see 21-22). Aquinas did say that there are many names for God, but for him these names are derived either from the use of reason or from divine revelation, and all express some truth about the reality of God; they are not mere pointers to a mystery that can never be known in itself.

Despite Sr. Johnson's critique of Enlightenment theism, her understanding of the unknowability of God has more in common with Enlightenment skepticism about the possibility of knowing metaphysical realities than with the apophaticism of the Church Fathers. The Church Fathers, most prominently the Cappadocians, were well aware that God is incomprehensible, but they founded this judgment on what God had truly revealed about himself as found in Scripture and Tradition. This revelation provides true knowledge of God as a trinity of persons, who create and redeem in love, a revelation that manifests not the unknowability of God, but his incomprehensibility. The theology of the Cappadocians, like all authentic Catholic theology, is governed by the truth of biblical revelation and its linguistic expression.

---

[3] St. Thomas Aquinas, *Summa Theologiae* II-II, q. 1, a. 2, *ad* 2.

Sr. Johnson's notion of the unknowability of God bears a strong resemblance to that of the Enlightenment philosopher Immanuel Kant, who argued that human knowledge and concepts do not attain to the reality of things in themselves, but only express how things appear to our minds. Sr. Johnson faces a problem similar to that of Kant: since all names for God are merely metaphors that we use to point to the divine reality but that never actually lay hold of it, there appears to be no objective means for judging among metaphors for God as to which are closer to the truth. Indeed, as we shall see below, for Sr. Johnson, metaphors for God are to be evaluated not on the basis of their accuracy with regard to the nature of God, but primarily in terms of how they function in human society.

The false presupposition on which this book is founded, then, is the conviction that all names for God are metaphors. It is important to evaluate how this false presupposition influences the various notions of God discussed in the book.

A God Who Suffers

In the light of the Holocaust and other horrendous evils, modern theism found itself unable to defend belief in its "omnipotent, omniscient Supreme Being" (52). Sr. Johnson acknowledges that Metz and Schillebeeckx believe that God stands in solidarity with those who suffer (see 56 and 65), but do not suggest that suffering affects the divine nature. Moltmann and Soelle, however, propose that God does indeed suffer as God. "They developed the powerful symbol of the suffering God who endures and is defeated with those who suffer. This symbol opens up the idea that God takes the pain of the world into the divine being in order there to redeem it" (56). This stands in stark contrast to the modern theism which was influenced by Greek philosophy. "Possessing all perfections in an unimaginable way, the divine nature has no possibility for change, cannot be affected by the world, and, of course cannot suffer. Divine dignity depends on this" (57).

In her antipathy for this latter position, Sr. Johnson gives the impression that she finds nothing wrong with Moltmann's understanding of the cross, namely, that on the cross the Son suffers not only in his human nature but also in his divine nature (see 60-62). She looks very favorably, moreover, on Soelle's rejection of divine omnipotence: "Soelle makes a major contribution to the question of suffering with her work on divine power" (63). Sr. Johnson might say in her defense that she is only presenting the thought of Moltmann, Soelle, and other theologians, and not actually subscribing to it herself. She has selected the ideas of these particular theologians, however, as well as those of the other theologians that she presents in the book, as representing what she considers to be the most important and most praiseworthy developments in recent theology, those that she considers provide the basis for the future of Christian theology. Certainly, the reader is given the impression that a God who suffers as God is far better than one who does not.

It is her understanding of "mystery" and "symbol," moreover, that allows Sr. Johnson to present this understanding of God as a viable alternative to traditional Catholic teaching. In her view, all statements about God, whether hers or those of the theological tradition, are metaphorical and do not express any literal truth about the "mystery" of God. With the metaphor of the suffering God, however, she believes that she and other theologians are saying something that is important for contemporary human beings.

Later in her book, Sr. Johnson advocates an understanding of God that implies that the finite order is ontologically constitutive of God's being. It is this view of God, which she identifies as "panentheism," that allows her to predicate suffering to God as such. It is only because God partakes of the finite order that the suffering within the finite order redounds to him. However, such an understanding undermines God's transcendence in that God's manner of existence, as Creator, would no longer differ in kind, but only in degree, from that of all else that exists.

New Names for the Unknown God

Sr. Johnson argues that women "have experienced strong discomfort with the dominant images of God as father, lord, and king" (96) and that female language for God is not only permissible but necessary. For Sr. Johnson, language for God should be analyzed not primarily in terms of its adequacy for expressing the reality of God—all human language fails to attain the reality of God—but in terms of its socio-political effects. She sees God-language as a human construction that is created in a particular socio-political context and reflects socio-political power relations. In her view, the traditional Christian language for God arises from a patriarchal social structure in which men possess the preponderance of power. The male imagery of God is a device used by the patriarchal power structure to perpetuate itself. "As hallowed by tradition and currently used, all-male images of God are hierarchical images rooted in the unequal relation between women and men, and they function to maintain this arrangement" (96). Now that society has begun to change, the traditional images of God have become "religiously inadequate" (96). "Instead of evoking the reality of God, they block it" (96).

As part of the effort to complete the overthrow of unequal and unjust power relations, she argues that it is necessary to replace the traditional language and concepts of God with new language and new concepts of God that will serve the purpose of promoting the socio-political status of women both in society and in the Church. Instead of as the "patriarchal lord who required their obedience," women have begun to envision God in "non-authoritarian ways" (96-97). Moreover, this replacement of the patriarchal system requires the use of female imagery for God.

> Holy mystery who is source, sustaining power, and goal of the world cannot be confined to any one set of images, but transcends them all. Should femaleness be an obstacle to naming the divine? Or can women's reality function as a sacramental sign of God's presence and action? If God created women in the divine image and likeness, theologians reasoned, then can we not return the favor and employ metaphors taken from women's lives to point to the living God? Can the living God not be spoken of in female terms? (97)

Sr. Johnson discusses feminine images of God found in the Bible – "mother" and "Holy Wisdom (Sophia)." "A veritable symphony of images in addition to mother and Wisdom enables women and girls to recognize themselves in language about God. The Spirit of God, named with the feminine noun *ruah* in Hebrew, is often depicted in Christian art as a dove, the ancient symbol of the goddess of love" (106). Sr. Johnson seeks to avoid a dualism where male images denote "reasonableness, power, justice-making, and headship" and female images denote feminine traits.

> In other words, women reflect God not only as mothering, nurturing, and compassionate, although certainly that, but also as powerful, taking initiative, creating-redeeming-saving, wrathful against injustice, in solidarity with the poor, struggling against and sometimes victorious over the powers of this world. Reorienting the imagination at a basic level, these female images open up insight into the maternal passion, fierce protectiveness, zeal for justice, healing power, inclusive hospitality, liberating will, and nonhierarchical, all-pervading relationality that characterize divine love. In the process, they carry back to women the stamp of the divine likeness. (109)

What is lacking in the whole of this discussion is any sense of the essential centrality of divine revelation as the basis of Christian theology. The names of God found in the Scriptures are not mere human creations that can be replaced by others that we may find more suitable according to our own human judgment. The standard by which all theological assertions must be judged is that provided by divine revelation, not by unaided human understanding. God does use human, and thus limited, means in revealing himself to the world. The only way, however, that one can reliably discern what is fallible and thus revisable is by first adopting and appropriating the standard of divine truth which has been received by revelation. Unfortunately, the point of departure for *Quest for the Living God* is not the divine revelation, accepted in faith by the Church, but non-theological norms, which are used to critique the Catholic theological tradition. In fact, it is Sr. Johnson's radical position on the unknowability of God that has prepared the way for this. By reducing all theological language and concepts to mere metaphors, Sr. Johnson has effectively eliminated as a criterion both divine revelation, to which Scripture and the Apostolic Tradition bear witness, and the Church's teaching which interprets them; she thus opens the way for other criteria that would evaluate theological affirmations as social and political phenomena.

The Presence of God in All the Religions

While Sr. Johnson states on a number of occasions that Jesus provides a unique encounter with God (see 155), yet she also wants to argue that there is more to God than that which is revealed through Jesus. Again, this is in keeping with her understanding of "mystery." No metaphor or symbol embodies the whole truth of who God is.

Sr. Johnson argues that the Church has grown in its understanding and appreciation of other religions. The Church went from a negative evaluation of other religions to a more positive assessment at Vatican II, although the Council was working with a "fulfillment model." "According to the fulfillment model that shaped the council's thinking, all religions are meant to reach their true fulfillment in the one church of Jesus Christ" (157). However, John Paul II did speak in *Redemptoris Missio* of the Spirit being present in other religions. The conclusion could then be drawn ("not definitive," though "heading in the direction of yes") that "thanks to the presence of God's own Spirit, people are saved through the practice of their religion, not despite it" (158). What Sr. Johnson is doing here is setting the stage to argue that the Spirit of God is at work in other religions in the same manner that the Spirit is working within Christianity and thus other religions are equally salvific.

Sr. Johnson is critical of *Dominus Iesus*. "This declaration met with a decidedly mixed reception" (160). Some applauded the document for upholding the centrality of Jesus. "But the torrent of criticism from religious leaders and scholars across a broad spectrum shows that something essential was seriously missing" (160). If the Spirit of God can be found in the sacred texts of other religions, then these "cannot be mere human inventions, as the declaration also asserts" and thus to declare that such religions are "'gravely deficient' redounds to insult the divine manner of acting in the world" (161). The conclusion to be drawn from this is simple.

> As the argument over *Dominus Iesus* shows, there is no consensus on the vital issue of what God intends by the existence of multiple religious paths. *Dominus Iesus* is one way to interpret the religions in the light of faith in Jesus Christ, but people in dialogue who themselves confess Christ as the Way have experienced a reverence for other religions that points to a broader, deeper, wider play of God's merciful ways. (161)

It appears that, for Sr. Johnson, the Spirit has inspired the sacred texts of other religions in a way that is similar to that of the Bible, and thus is working in a similar manner within those religions as well. In developing this argument, Sr. Johnson undermines the uniqueness of Biblical revelation and even denies the uniqueness of Jesus as the Incarnate Word. Moreover, she places the teaching of the magisterium on a par with the opinions of "other" theologians.

The heart of the issue here comes down once more to Sr. Johnson's understanding of "mystery" and "metaphor/symbol." In her view, because God is the primordial mystery "there is no end to the being and fullness of God" (161).

> At the outset it opens the possibility that others might have distinct encounters with the divine that can be new resources for Christian exploration into the overabundance of God. To put it simply, the living God is not a Christian. Rather, the incalculable mystery, which the Christian scripture dares to call love (1 John 4:8 and 16) is not constrained in loving but freely pours out affection to all and each one. (162)

While "in Jesus Christ, God's saving activity reaches its greatest intensity in history in the concrete" (162, see 174); while "the crucified and risen Word of God and the church that proclaims God's mercy in him are normative and constitutive for the salvation of all"; still, "the manifestation of God's presence and activity in the religions cannot be limited to what has been revealed in Jesus Christ and proclaimed by the church" (162-3). The Spirit of God does not simply repeat what "she" has revealed in Jesus, otherwise these religions would not be different from Christianity (see 163). Because the mystery of God is so full it is not exhausted by any one religious tradition.

Sr. Johnson's position on that matter is not in keeping with the Christian understanding of Jesus as the fullness of truth. For the fullness of "truth," according to Sr. Johnson's argument, one needs Jesus + Hinduism, Buddhism, Islam, etc. (see 174-79). Sr. Johnson's conclusion is contrary to Church teaching. "Disputes about how to reconcile core Christian affirmations about the salvific role of Jesus Christ with the validity of other religions are numerous. There is as yet no theological consensus" (175).

Creator Spirit in the Evolving World

There are two problematic concerns in Sr. Johnson's chapter on evolution. First, how does one conceive of a transcendent God who is equally immanent within the world and history?

> The mental model that allows for the most intelligible interpretation of this presence is panentheism (all-in-God). In recent centuries theology worked mainly with the model of theism. This construal infers God to be the highest member of the order of being. It insists on God's difference and distance from the world while paying little attention to divine nearness. Its opposite model is pantheism (all is God), which erases the difference between created and uncreated, thereby collapsing God and the world into each other. Unlike either of these patterns, panentheism envisions a relationship whereby everything abides *in* God, who in turn encompasses everything, being *"above all and through all and in all"* (Eph 4:6). What results is a mutual abiding for which the pregnant female body provides a good metaphor. (188)

The panentheism presented in *Quest for the Living God*, however, lacks any characteristic that would constitute a real difference between it and pantheism. "Mutual abiding" is not an adequate description of the

Biblical conception of Creator and creation, according to which God as Creator exists in a different ontological order than that which he creates.

In fact, it is only because God is self-existent, and thus radically distinct from creation, that he is able to bring into existence, out of nothing, other beings. It is precisely the act of creation that establishes both the transcendent otherness of God as well as his intimate relationship to creation, for creation only exists by being related to God as its Creator. "[B]ecause he is the free and sovereign Creator, the first cause of all that exists, God is present to his creatures' inmost being: 'In him we live and move and have our being.' In the words of St. Augustine, God is 'higher than my highest and more inward than my innermost self'" (*Catechism*, no. 300). The panentheism espoused by Sr. Johnson, however, fails to respect not only the transcendent integrity of God, but also the integrity of the created order, for in this view the finite created order finds its value not in its own created being, possessing its own inherent created value, but in being ontologically constitutive of God's own being.

The second concern is over the evolution of human beings.

> Modern forms of theism assume that God intervenes in the world at will to accomplish divine purpose apart from natural processes. But the scientific picture of the universe indicates that this is not necessary. Nature is actively organizing itself into new forms at all levels. Even the emergence of life and then mind can be accounted for without special supernatural intervention. (192)

For Sr. Johnson, material forces and their self-organizing processes can account for the human spirit with both intelligence and free will. She writes: "Human thought and love are not something injected into the universe from without, but are the flowering in us of deeply cosmic energies, arising out of the very physical dynamism of the cosmos, which is already self-organizing and creative" (185). Even on a purely philosophical level, however, such claims are subject to refutation. The physical cannot account for the non-physical, and the self-organization of created realities does not explain itself. Moreover, "[t]he Church teaches that every spiritual soul is created immediately by God – it is not 'produced' by the parents – and also that it is immortal" (*Catechism*, no. 366; see also Pope Pius XII, *Humani Generis*, no. 36). It is the spiritual nature of the human soul that allows human beings, through their bodily senses, intellectually to know the truth and freely to will the good and so act upon it.

Trinity: The Living God of Love

Sr. Johnson wishes to limit our understanding of God to the economy of salvation. In her view, we can grasp the economic expression of God within the finite order of time and history, but we do not know God as he immanently exists as a Trinity of persons.

> At the outset and all through this chapter [chapter 10] it is crucial to keep this point in mind: the point of trinitarian language is to acclaim the living God as the mystery of salvation. Whether found in scripture, creed, liturgy, doctrine, or theology, it is Christian code tapping out the belief that the living God made known through Jesus and the Spirit is dynamic Love encompassing the universe who acts to save. At the most basic it is saying, very simply, *"God is love"* (1 John 4:16). (202-3)

Sr. Johnson's presentation of the teaching of the Council of Nicaea is ambiguous. According to her, by its teaching the Council aimed to protect "the church's faith that Jesus is God's self-revelation, the true Wisdom of God sent to save and set free" (205). This minimalist interpretation of the Council, however, conceals the fact that it is one thing to say that "Jesus is God's self-revelation," which could simply mean that through Jesus God provides us a human image of who he is, and quite another to say that Jesus is ontologically the eternal Son of the Father. Only the second understanding affirms a true metaphysical Incarnation.

Sr. Johnson also faults the later theological development of the Nicene Creed for separating the God for us (*pro nobis*) from God in himself (*in se*). "Theologians started to make a real distinction between God revealed in the history of salvation, otherwise known as the economy of salvation, and God who exists apart from the world in an eternal, divine realm" (206). In Sr. Johnson's view, such a distinction has spawned trinitarian speculation that borders on the bizarre and the completely irrelevant.

> Today this school of thought's laborious explanation of various fine points in the trinitarian construct elicits a host of criticisms. The fundamental problem lies in the fact that reflection lost touch with the historical story of redemption, where all trinitarian meaning has its roots, ending up with a description of God that had little or no contact with Christian life. It presented its thinking in highly obtuse prose; scholars today take issue with its "abstruse analysis," "irrelevant abstractions," "philosophical mazes," "elaborate theological maneuverings," "complex celestial mathematics," and "obscure language," along with its "sheer long-windedness." For all

its abstraction, furthermore, this theology presented its findings as if they were a literal description of a self-contained Trinity of three divine persons knowing and loving each other. This, of course, is not the case, no such literal description being possible. (207-8)

According to Sr. Johnson, "the biblical story of encounter with God—the story of the personal God of Israel encountered in the concrete life and destiny of Jesus of Nazareth and present through the Spirit in the life of the church and the world—was transposed into an abstract, complex, literal, and oppressive trinitarian theology" (209). Theology lost sight of the fact that the "intent of this trinitarian symbol is not to give literal information but to acclaim the God who saves and to lead us into this mystery" (209).

Once again, it is evident that, according to Sr. Johnson, language about God, even Trinitarian language, does not actually provide knowledge of and truth concerning God and the manner of his existence. For her, God remains mysteriously unknowable. This position, however, completely undermines the Gospel and the faith of those who believe in that Gospel, for it supposes that the Church does not proclaim what is actually true, but only the symbolic expression of what ultimately cannot be known, and the faithful do not believe what is actually true, but only some symbolic expression of that which can never be identified. In contrast the *Catechism of the Catholic Church* states:

> Faith is first of all a personal adherence of man to God. At the same time, and inseparably, it is a *free assent to the whole truth that God has revealed*. As personal adherence to God and assent to his truth, Christian faith differs from our faith in any human person. It is right and just to entrust oneself wholly to God and to believe absolutely what he says. (no. 150; see also no. 144)

Conclusion

In some ways, *Quest for the Living God* presents itself as a retrieval of the authentic Christian theological tradition. Against the contamination of Christian theology after the Enlightenment by modern theism, Sr. Johnson claims to be retrieving fundamental insights from patristic and medieval theology. As we have seen, however, this is misleading, since under the guise of criticizing modern theism she criticizes crucial aspects of patristic and medieval theology, aspects that have become central elements of the Catholic theological tradition confirmed by magisterial teaching. Similarly, she claims to be retrieving the classical under-standing of the incomprehensibility of God. Again, as we have seen, her understanding of this is not that of the Catholic theological tradition, for it effectively precludes the possibility of human knowledge of God through divine revelation and reduces all names and concepts of God to human constructions that are to be judged not on their accuracy (all are deemed inaccurate) but on their social and political utility.

The basic problem with *Quest for the Living God* as a work of Catholic theology is that the book does not take the faith of the Church as its starting point. Instead, the author employs standards from outside the faith to criticize and to revise in a radical fashion the conception of God revealed in Scripture and taught by the Magisterium. While the book at times displays an engagement with the Catholic theological tradition and remains in continuity with it, it also departs from that tradition at a number of crucial junctures. For these reasons, combined with the fact that the book is directed primarily to an audience of non-specialist read-ers and is being used as a textbook for study of the doctrine of God, the Committee on Doctrine finds itself obligated to state publicly that the doctrine of God presented in *Quest for the Living God* does not accord with authentic Catholic teaching on essential points.

USCCB Committee on Doctrine
Donald Cardinal Wuerl
Archdiocese of Washington
Chairman

Most Reverend Leonard P. Blair
Bishop of Toledo

Most Reverend Daniel M. Buechlein, OSB
Archbishop of Indianapolis

Most Reverend José H. Gomez
Archbishop of Los Angeles

Most Reverend William E. Lori
Bishop of Bridgeport

Most Reverend Robert J. McManus
Bishop of Worcester

Most Reverend Kevin C. Rhoades
Bishop of Fort Wayne-South Bend

Most Reverend Arthur J. Serratelli
Bishop of Paterson

Most Reverend Allen H. Vigneron
Archbishop of Detroit

✦ ✦ ✦ ✦

April 18, 2011

Bishops as Teachers
A Resource for Bishops

Dear Brother Bishop,

On behalf of the Committee on Doctrine, I am pleased to be able to offer you this pastoral resource concerning the Committee's recent statement on Sr. Elizabeth Johnson's book, *Quest for the Living God: Mapping Frontiers in the Theology of God*.

Within the Catholic Church the bishops have a very clear and defined role as the authentic teachers of the faith. In a recent statement, the leadership of the Catholic Theological Society of America seems to misread the legitimate and apostolic role of bishops in addressing the right relationship of theologians and bishops. As a further service to you in your solicitude for the teaching of the faith, the members of the Committee on Doctrine want to provide this resource should any questions arise concerning the ancient and long recognized episcopal "munus docendi." Such clarity is also necessary before addressing procedural issues such as how to nurture dialogue and what processes best serve the overriding need for a clear and faithful proclamation of the faith.

This resource speaks to the teaching office and the NCCB document *Doctrinal Responsibilities*.

Apostolic Tradition: Handing on Revelation

In the New Testament, the followers of Jesus marveled that, unlike other teachers, he taught with authority (e.g. Mt 7:29). Saint John's Gospel relates the trial of Jesus before Pontius Pilate, during which Pilate asks Jesus, "Then you are a king?" and Jesus responds, "You say I am a king. For this reason I was born and for this reason I came into the world, to testify to the truth. Everyone who belongs to the truth listens to my voice" (Jn 18:37). Christ earlier declares himself to be "the way, the truth, and the life" (Jn 14:6). In his being, his deeds, and his words, Christ is the perfect revelation of the Father. In him, we have received our greatest knowledge of the living and true God; through him, we have learned how we should live.

In order for this revelation to be known, however, it must first be heard, which immediately implies the necessity of a structured teaching organism to proclaim it. As Saint Paul tells the Romans, "How are men to call upon him in whom they have not believed? And how are they to believe in him of whom they have never heard? And how are they to hear without a preacher? And how can men preach unless they are sent?" (Rom 10:14-15). Christ himself taught his disciples to preach the good news while he was still among them in the flesh, sending them out two by two to the towns that he would visit (Lk 10:1). After his resurrection and the descent of the Holy Spirit upon the apostles at Pentecost, they continued that ministry of preaching the gospel at the cost of their very lives, and appointed others to continue, in turn, their own ministry of preaching the word after they had gone.

It is only through this uninterrupted tradition, stretching back to the time of the apostles and continued by their successors, the bishops, that we can be sure of the integrity and validity of the Christian faith. The Church is called "apostolic" precisely because she alone can trace her origins to the deposit of faith entrusted to the apostles, the Twelve chosen by Jesus and charged, together with their successors, with the responsibility of teaching the true faith, making sure that it is presented clearly, and applying it to the problems and needs of every age. In this way, we have a guarantee that what is taught today is what Jesus actually taught and intended as guidance for his followers, that nothing is forgotten, misunderstood, or lost from century to century, from generation to generation, from person to person.

The Bishop as Teacher

The privilege of handing on the faith, of course, is not limited to bishops. The joy and excitement of the New Evangelization is in no small part found in the efforts of every disciple to share the good news of Jesus, his Resurrection, his gospel, and life in his Church. All the faithful are called to participate in the evangelization and sanctification of the temporal order. It is not enough to rely on the hierarchy alone to address serious social and moral problems in our society. The voice and the engagement of the laity will ultimately determine the direction of our society. Bishops have the responsibility to teach but it falls to the laity to apply that teaching.

Nevertheless, it is the specific competence and responsibility of bishops to teach the faith in its entirety. On the 25th anniversary of his election as bishop of Rome and chief shepherd of the universal Church, Venerable John Paul II wrote in the apostolic exhortation *Pastores Gregis* that bishops are to exercise the ministry of leading the Church "as pastors and true fathers." In doing so, he wrote, "we have the task of gathering together the family of the faithful and in fostering charity and brotherly communion." That unity is fostered by handing on the faith authentically. As Saint Paul reminds Timothy, "[P]reach the word, be urgent in season and out of season, convince, rebuke and exhort, be unfailing in patience and in teaching" (2 Tim 4:2).

In addition to teaching directly, however, bishops also teach indirectly by their oversight of what is presented as authentic Catholic teaching. The Committee on Doctrine in *The Teaching Ministry of the Diocesan Bishop* (1992) observes that Catholic bishops, in addition to communicating knowledge of revelation and exhortation in virtue, "are to determine authoritatively the correct interpretation of the Scripture and tradition committed to the Church . . . and they are to judge for the Church the accuracy of the presentation of this revelation by others." If "the common faith of the Church is to survive from one generation to the next," the document notes, "the Church must possess the internal resources to distinguish for the entire community what is true from what is false in these translations and developments of the gospel message . . . It is a necessary condition that the word of God be continued in its authentic meaning into every culture and into every century." The National Conference of Catholic Bishops (now the United States Conference of Catholic Bishops) in *Doctrinal Responsibilities* likewise affirms, "Theologians also acknowledge that it is the role of bishops as authoritative teachers in the Church to make pastoral judgments about the soundness of theological teaching so that the integrity of Catholic doctrine and the unity of the faith community may be preserved."

The prophetic mission of the College of Bishops cannot be grasped, though, exclusively as a pragmatic need for internal organization and theological coherence. Ultimately it can be understood only in the context of revelation itself, when revealed truth is perceived as salvific and the reliable transmission of that truth as a precious gift from the Lord entrusted to the Church. Only the Holy Spirit, dwelling within the Church, can make possible the teaching ministry of the bishop. As the Committee on Doctrine states in *The Teaching Ministry of the Diocesan Bishop*, "Only within the command of Christ to preach the gospel—with all the continual challenge to interpretation and application inherent in that command—can the ministry of the bishops be understood. The bishops are called to embody and to effect the Church's consistent witness to Christ in their care for orthodoxy. The magisterium is to continue and to serve the presence of the teaching Christ." In continuing the mission of Christ the Teacher, the bishops in union with the Pope are therefore ministers of a free and wonderful gift of God, the assurance that we adhere to the true faith. It is the source of our conviction that what we hold by faith is authentic, a conviction that so grasps the believer that he or she would be willing to die rather than deny it.

The Theologian as Teacher

Our understanding of the faith, however, is not limited to the explicit teaching and preaching of the bishop. The *Catechism of the Catholic Church* enumerates two other ways that "the heritage of faith is able to grow in the life of the Church" (CCC 94). One such way is through the spiritual experience of believers, particularly through their exposure to Sacred Scriptures and their interior life of prayer. Another is through "the contemplation and study of believers who ponder these things in their hearts" and in particular "theological research which deepens knowledge of revealed truth" (ibid.).

It is the privilege of theologians to delve more profoundly and systematically into the meaning of the faith, according to the ancient adage, *fides quaerens intellectum*. Since this faith is handed on by the Church through the ministry of the magisterium, the bishop and the theologian have a special relationship that can and should be reciprocally enriching. "The Church cannot exist without the teaching office of the bishop," *The Teaching Ministry of the Diocesan Bishop* states, "nor thrive without the sound scholarship of the theologian. Bishops and theologians are in a collaborative relationship. Bishops benefit from the work of theologians, while theologians gain a deeper understanding of revelation under the guidance of the magisterium. The ministry of bishops and the service rendered by theologians entail a mutual respect and support."

As in every academic discipline, theologians enjoy a legitimate autonomy defined by the standards of their field and the boundaries of what constitutes spurious or fruitless investigation. There is a broad field for theological exploration and critique, for instance, from the "underlying assumptions and explicit formulations of doctrine . . . to questions about their meaning or their doctrinal and pastoral implications, to comparison with other doctrines, to the study of their historical and ecclesial context, to translations into diverse cultural categories, and to correlation with knowledge from other branches of human and scientific inquiry" (*The Teaching Ministry of the Diocesan Bishop*). These investigations are not made in isolation from the received faith of the Church, though, but are made presuming that faith, and in light of that faith.

By taking the truth of revelation as a starting point, it should be pointed out that theological inquiry is not diminished but in fact enhanced, since it is only—as in every other discipline—by building on what is confidently known that deeper and fuller investigation can be pursued. Prior to his election as Pope, Cardinal Ratzinger wrote in *The Nature and Mission of Theology* that natural science "has achieved its great successes thanks, not to a free-floating creativity, but to the strictest adhesion to its object. Naturally, it must constantly probe the object on all sides with anticipatory hypotheses and seek new methods of penetrating it with questions which will elicit answers. Once given, however, none of the answers can simply be cleared away. On the contrary, the more they increase in number, the more possibilities of inquiry are disclosed and the more concrete space is won for real creativity. I mean the sort of creativity which does not forge ahead into the void but connects the already existing paths in order to open up new ones. It is not otherwise in theology."

It is essential for the health and progress of theology, then, that it take place within the context of a clearly articulated community of faith, that its creativity be channeled and maximized by boundaries delineated by the received revelation. Identifying these boundaries of the authentic faith constitutes the bishop's contribution to the flourishing of the theological sciences. Saint Paul often uses examples from the realm of sports, and perhaps one would serve us well here. In any sporting match, football, tennis, baseball, there are referees and umpires. The game can only proceed with the supervision of a referee. In a tennis match, it is not the player who calls the ball "out of bounds" but the referee. The player may object that it was not his or her intention to hit the ball out of bounds. He or she may even question whether the ball is out of bounds. But it is the referee who must make the call. Otherwise, there can be no coherent game, no enjoyment of the match, no sense of progress in learning the sport: in short, the "tennis game" would devolve into a fruitless exchange of individuals hitting the ball at will.

So it is in academic, theological investigation. If it is to be directed towards a fruitful deepening of our understanding, then it cannot be an exchange of individuals hitting the ball randomly. Once ideas are written and published by a theologian, they must stand on their own; it is the bishops who are entrusted with the office of referee, who must call the play. To be sure, as in other disciplines the most effective check on fruitless investigation is the vigorous exercise of peer review, critique, and dialogue, as once was a strong tradition in the theological disciplines. When that peer review is absent or ineffective, however, it is the responsibility of the bishop to make the call and to declare, if necessary, certain notions out of bounds, the bounds of Christian revelation.

Dialogue between Bishops and Theologians

The *Catechism of the Catholic Church* teaches that the "Magisterium is not superior to the Word of God, but is its servant. It teaches only what has been handed on to it. At the divine command and with the help of the Holy Spirit, it listens to this devotedly, guards it with dedication and expounds it faithfully. All that it proposes for belief as being divinely revealed is drawn from this single deposit of faith" (CCC 86). As shepherds of God's flock, bishops have the responsibility to teach the faith and to preserve it as it has been received and passed on. Theirs is the duty to see that the noble enterprise of theology is integrated into the overall mission of the Church to transmit the good news. Both bishop and theologian serve the Word of God and cooperate in building up the community of faith.

The legitimate academic freedom of Catholic theologians, then, is understood like any other freedom, with its own appropriate limits and its own ordering to human flourishing. At times it may seem to conflict with the pastoral freedom and, in fact, the pastoral obligation of the bishop to protect the authenticity of the faith and the spiritual good of the faithful. Nevertheless, when good will is present on both sides, when both are committed to the truth revealed in Jesus Christ, their relationship can be one of profound communion as together they seek to explore new implications of the deposit of faith.

The Church, therefore, encourages a respectful dialogue between and among theologians and bishops. Such a dialogue, however, can only thrive in the context of faith, since it is through faith that we know of the divine institution of the Church and the continuing guidance of the Church, including the magisterium, by the Holy Spirit. The personal faith of the theologian is thus an essential prerequisite of this important dialogue. In *The Nature and Mission of Theology* Cardinal Ratzinger observed that as "there is no theology without faith, there can be no theology without conversion . . . the opportunity for creative theology increases the more that faith becomes real, personal experience; the more that conversion acquires interior certainty thanks to a painful process of transformation; the more that it is recognized as the indispensable means of penetrating into the truth of one's own being." As a person of faith, the theologian understands and appreciates the charism of teaching entrusted to his or her bishop, and willingly submits personal theological ideas for the bishop's evaluation.

One recognized starting point for this dialogue is the request for an *imprimatur*. Books that treat the sacred sciences and are intended to be used as the basis for instruction in Catholic institutions are required to have the *imprimatur* (*Code of Canon Law*, can. 827, §2). Even for texts that do not require the *imprimatur*, it is still recommended (*Code of Canon Law*, can. 827, §3). It is a very helpful way for the theologian to initiate a process of dialogue through which theological ideas may be evaluated in light of the deposit of faith. Once a theological work is published, however, it is *ipso facto* open to response. It is like the ball that has been hit in a tennis match. It is already in play. If it is called out of bounds, it is not an adequate response to say that the referee did not enter into dialogue with the player beforehand. When a work is published and, particularly, if it is being used and accepted as authentic Catholic teaching, the bishop has an obligation to address it. Thus the initiation of dialogue by an author is not only welcome but recommended, before the work is published and the bishop may be constrained to make a public appraisal of it. The Committee on Doctrine's 2004 resource, *The Permission to Publish*, outlines the rights and responsibilities of diocesan bishops, and the many options presented to them in this regards under canon law.

Communion in the Church

The sense of communion with the Church and the awareness of what this means is at the very heart of a profound harmony between the bishops, the authoritative teachers of the faith, and theologians who have the task of investigating and penetrating more deeply the meaning of the faith. When this communion is appreciated and sought, theologians perceive the magisterium as intrinsic to their work. Natural scientists are grateful for the existence of physical laws since their work is only sound, only fruitful, when it respects the foundational truths of those concrete boundaries. In a similar way, the Church's teaching office, when grasped in the context of faith, is a great assistance to the scholarly research of theologians since its judgments are determinative of good theology.

The alternative is the principle of private judgment, which Blessed John Henry Newman labeled "a principle of disunion," conceived in opposition to the judgment of the magisterium. When a theologian does not understand his or her role within the communion of the Church, the role of a servant—like that of the bishop—to the truth, he or she risks usurping the bishop's central role of leading people to salvation. Isolated from the community of faith, the theologian seriously endangers the faithful by proposing "a different gospel" (2 Cor 11:4) which is no longer salvific.

On the other hand, when a theologian strives to serve the truth revealed by God, the truth that Jesus insisted upon during his interrogation by Pontius Pilate, the truth that he entrusted to the protection of his Church, the theologian becomes a vital member of the body of Christ, an agent of communion and of faith in an age hungering for both. Nineteen centuries ago, Saint Ignatius of Antioch praised the Church of Philadelphia in Asia as "a source of everlasting joy, especially when the members are at one with the bishop and his assistants, the presbyters and deacons, that have been appointed in accordance with the wish of Jesus Christ, and whom he has, by his own will, through the operation of His Holy Spirit, confirmed in loyalty." Theologians contribute powerfully to the rich teaching of our faith, and when they pursue their vocation to assist "faith seeking understanding" with honor and commitment, always in union with the Church and her teaching authority, they enrich the very communion that Saint Ignatius admired so many centuries ago. And that, perhaps, is their most important contribution of all.

The Process of Dialogue

The USCCB Committee on Doctrine's recent statement on the book by Sister Elizabeth Johnson, C.S.J., *Quest for the Living God: Mapping Frontiers in the Theology of God,* has to be seen in the light of the bishops' obligation to provide for the spiritual good of the faithful. Responding to this book presents new challenges in the light of the circumstances of our day.

The book in question is an already published work not primarily directed to professional theologians for theological speculation, but rather one used as a teaching instrument for undergraduate students, many of whom are looking for grounding in their Catholic faith. The background against which the bishops must exercise their teaching responsibility today is the generally recognized catechetical deficiencies of past decades beginning with the 1970s. The result is a generation or more of Catholics, including young adults today, who have little solid intellectual formation in their faith. It is in this context that books used in religious studies/ theology courses at Catholic colleges and universities must be seen as *de facto* catechetical and formational texts. While the content of a book may be highly speculative and of interest for trained theologians, when it is used in a classroom with students often ill-prepared to deal with speculative theology the results can be spiritually harmful. The bishops are rightly concerned about the spiritual welfare of those students using this book who may be led to assume that its content is authentic Catholic teaching. The Committee on Doctrine expresses serious concern about the pastoral implications of the teaching in this book.

Moreover, the circumstances involving the teaching of theology within Catholic Universities and Colleges have significantly changed. Undergraduates are now offered a variety of texts within introductory theology/religion courses. While many of the texts can be quite helpful in presenting the faith and teaching of the Catholic Church, there are others that cause confusion and raise doubt among students. Some texts can even be understood as offering an alternative pastoral and spiritual guidance to students in contrast to the teaching magisterium. This is especially a concern given the current diminished level of catechetical preparation of so many young students. In the light of this changed academic situation special attention must now be given as to how to address theological works that are aimed at students and yet do not meet criteria for authentic Catholic teaching.

Reference has been made to the 1989 NCCB document *Doctrinal Responsibilities* which was intended to promote cooperation in resolving misunderstandings between individual diocesan bishops and theologians. *Doctrinal Responsibilities* did not address the special responsibilities of the Committee on Doctrine of our national episcopal conference. In addition the document is presented for consideration as one way of proceeding but not as obligatory. Furthermore, the statement makes it clear that these suggested guidelines "can only serve if they are adapted to the particular conditions, of a diocese, its history and its special needs."

In the past several years, some bishops within the Conference have requested that the Committee on Doctrine examine various writings and offer an assessment because of their theological and pastoral concerns. The Committee on Doctrine, as a service to individual bishops and to the Conference as a whole, and in keeping with the mandate entrusted to the Committee on Doctrine by the Congregation for the Doctrine of the Faith, has tried to comply with such requests. It did so knowing that such requests were timely and important. Since the issues and books were in the public domain, the Doctrine Committee felt obliged in certain cases to issue public statements so as to address the urgent theological and pastoral needs of Bishops and for the wellbeing of all the faithful. It may even turn out that the desired dialogue is sometimes facilitated when the position of both parties is public. The Doctrine Committee does not wish to stifle legitimate theological reflection or to preclude further dialogue, but it does want to ensure that the authentic teaching of the Church, concerning doctrine and morals, is clearly stated and affirmed. While dialogue between theologians and bishops is very important it should work along side of the bishops' primary teaching and sanctifying mission.

The Committee on Doctrine recognizes the legitimate vocations of the theologian as well as of the bishop. The Committee hopes that the discussion generated by its statement will help lead to a renewal and foster a proper and fruitful relationship between the bishops and the whole theological community.

> Faithfully in Christ,
> Donald Cardinal Wuerl
> Archbishop of Washington
> Chairman, Committee on Doctrine

✦ ✦ ✦ ✦

To the Committee on Doctrine of the United States Conference of Catholic Bishops:

Cardinal Donald Wuerl, Washington DC

Bishop Leonard Blair, Toledo OH

Archbishop Daniel Buechlein, Indianapolis IN

Archbishop José Gomez, Los Angeles CA

Bishop William Lori, Bridgeport CT

Bishop Robert McManus, Worcester MA

Bishop Kevin Rhoades, Fort Wayne–South Bend IN

Bishop Arthur Serratelli, Paterson NJ

Archbishop Allen Vigneron, Detroit MI

In the cover letter to the U.S. Bishops on March 30, 2011 that accompanied the Committee on Doctrine's criticism of my book *Quest for the Living God*, Cardinal Donald Wuerl stated that the Committee was always open to dialogue with theologians and would welcome an opportunity to discuss my writings with me. In my one public statement on the matter, released April 1, 2011, I also expressed a willingness to dialogue over these matters.

In a letter dated April 28, 2011, I was informed that Cardinal Donald Wuerl reiterated this openness to dialogue, and expressed the willingness of the Committee on Doctrine to receive any written observations that I would wish to make with regard to its Statement about my book. The observations which follow are in response to this invitation.

I write these observations in the spirit of the Egyptian bishop Athanasius. I've always appreciated his words, written during the conflict that ensued after the Council of Nicea when three groups contended vociferously over the right way to express Jesus Christ's divine identity. Athanasius, who upheld the *homoousios* (one in being) teaching of the Council, noted that his party and the *homoiousios* party (similar in being), originally perceived as opponents, were actually on the same side as compared with the subordinationist Arian position. In the effort to forge unity, he wrote:

> those, however, who accept everything else that was defined at Nicea, and doubt only about the *homoousios*, must not be treated as enemies; nor do we here attack them as Ario-maniacs, nor as opponents of the Fathers; but we discuss the matter with them as

brothers with brothers, who mean what we mean, and dispute only about the words. (*De Synodis* 41)

The Committee on Doctrine's Statement declared that my book contains misrepresentations, ambiguities, and errors with regard to Catholic teaching. My statement spoke of misrepresentations, misinterpretations, and an incorrect picture of my book in the committee's Statement. I also expressed regret that a prior conversation had not taken place to perhaps allay these difficulties. In view of our common concern for the church and for the richness of its teaching, I hope in these observations to discuss the matter with you as sister with brothers, "who mean what we mean, and dispute only about the words."

Thank you for this invitation to dialogue.

Peace,

> Dr. Elizabeth A. Johnson, C.S.J.
> Distinguished Professor of Theology
> Fordham University
> June 1, 2011

Cc. Fr. Thomas Weinandy, O.F.M., Cap., Executive Director

✦ ✦ ✦ ✦

To Speak Rightly of the Living God
Observations by
Dr. Elizabeth A. Johnson, CSJ,
on the
Statement of the Committee on Doctrine
of the United States Conference of Catholic Bishops
about her book
Quest for the Living God:
Mapping Frontiers in the Theology of God

Introduction

The first observation I would like to make underscores the obvious: *Quest for the Living God* is a work of theology. It is not a catechism, nor a compendium of doctrine, nor does it intend to set out the full range of church teaching on the doctrine of God. Rather, it presents areas of Christian life and study where the mystery of the living God is being glimpsed anew in contemporary situations. Hence the subtitle, *Mapping Frontiers*.

To be specific: Listening to theologies emerging within distinct contexts in the church, *Quest* presents ideas and images of God surfacing, being tested, spiritually prayed, and ethically lived out in eight different conversations: in transcendental, political, liberation, feminist/womanist, black, Latino/Latina, interreligious, and ecological theologies. Each of these conversations wrestles with the word of God amid, respectively, the onslaught of atheism; massive public suffering; the oppression of poverty, sexism, racism, and ethnic prejudice; respectful encounter with other religions; and the amazing discoveries of science. The book culminates, quite deliberately, in a chapter on the Christian belief in God as Trinity, to which I suggest all these different discourses have been contributing rich angles of understanding. *Quest* is offered to readers as an invitation to think about their own idea of the living God in view of this new scholarship.

As a whole, it seems to me, the book illustrates the dynamic process described by the Second Vatican Council's *Dogmatic Constitution on Divine Revelation* (*Dei Verbum*):

For there is growth in understanding of the realities and the words
which have been handed down. This happens through the contemplation and the study made by believers, who treasure these things
in their hearts (Lk 2:19, 51), through the intimate understanding
of spiritual things they experience, and through the preaching of
those who have received through episcopal succession the sure
gift of truth. (§8)

Precisely this type of activity is illuminated in each chapter of *Quest*; for
example, the idea of the liberating God emerging through the experience of struggle, prayer, and study done by the church of the poor in
Latin America.

It appears that part of the present difficulty stems from the Statement's
reading my book as if it belonged to a genre other than theology. Theological research does not simply reiterate received doctrinal formulas
but probes and interprets them in order to deepen understanding. To do
this well, theology throughout history has articulated faith in different
thought forms, images, and linguistic expressions. Its work employs all
manner of methods and ideas taken from other disciplines in order to
shed light on the meaning of faith.

In a reflection encouraging a vital interchange between theology and
science, Pope John Paul II expressed a hope for this work:

Just as Aristotelian philosophy, through the ministry of such great
scholars as Thomas Aquinas, ultimately came to shape some of
the most profound expressions of theological doctrine, so can we
not hope that the sciences of today, along with all forms of human
knowing, may invigorate and inform those parts of the theological
enterprise that bear on the relation of nature, humanity, and God?
(*Message to the Vatican Observatory*, 1988).

It is critically important, he continued, that each discipline should enrich,
nourish, and challenge the other for the future good of humanity. Theology, of course, should not take on all ideas from science or other disciplines indiscriminately. "As these findings become part of the intellectual
culture of the time, however, theologians must understand them and test
their value in bringing out from Christian belief some of the possibilities
which have not yet been realized." After adducing examples from the
Middle Ages, the pope seems to chide today's theologians for being too
timorous: "Theologians might well ask, with respect to contemporary
science, philosophy, and other areas of human knowing, if they have

accomplished this extraordinarily difficult process as well as did these medieval masters." The options, he urged, do not include isolation, fear, or "every regressive tendency to a unilateral reductionism." Rather, "The vitality and significance of theology for humanity will in a profound way be reflected in its ability to incorporate these findings."

I bring forward this message not simply because I participated to my benefit as a younger theologian from the resulting dialogue with scientists sponsored by the Vatican Observatory, and not only because the fruits of that exchange form a chapter of *Quest*, but because of the message's vision of what theology is supposed to be doing: engage with the world; dialogue critically with all forms of human knowing; bring that wisdom to bear on faith; invigorate understanding of the relation of humanity and God; bring out new possibilities in Christian expression of the revelation God has given; for the common good of all.

Quest for the Living God presents theologies from around the world which are doing precisely this. The Statement faults the book for not being in accord with church teaching because it does not repeat established doctrinal formulas. Simply because things are said in a different way, however, does not mean that traditional formulas of faith, let alone the core understanding of faith they convey, are being rejected. It is of course not the case that everything that theology says is correct, and here the episcopal teaching office has its proper role. But let me underscore the fact that this book does not deny, either explicitly or implicitly, any central doctrine of the church derived from scripture and creed. Rather, it represents how contemporary believers are seeking to express the ancient wisdom with new relevance. In this, it accords with the view of Pope John XXIII whose memorable opening speech to the Second Vatican Council called for formulation of doctrine in the literary forms of modern thought, since "the substance of the ancient doctrine of the deposit of faith is one thing, and the way in which it is presented is another."

My initial observation, which governs all the rest, is that *Quest for the Living God* is a work of theology. It presents the dialogue of faith with ideas beyond the ecclesiastical circle, exploring new possibilities in Christian belief and practice coherent with people's lives today, as did the ancient and medieval theologians for their day. It is a work of theology and it would be good to read it on those terms.

The following observations are divided into two parts of five sections each, roughly paralleling the committee's Statement. The first part deals with fundamental issues; the second, with insights into the mystery of God arising from particular theologies.

1. The Faith of the Church

The committee's Statement rightly asserts (2) that those who embark on the study of the mystery of God should do so from within the very heart of the Church's faith. It judges, however (20), that the basic problem with *Quest* is that the book does not take the faith of the church as its starting point. This is the first point on which we might dialogue, because I find this judgment baffling. Not only does *Quest for the Living God* begin with the faith of the church, but it also ends there as well.

On the first page I note that around the world "different groups of Christian people, stressed by particular historical circumstances, have been gaining glimpses of the living God in fresh and unexpected ways." This does not mean they are discovering a novel God, the text continues, but are gaining a deeper appreciation of what previous generations believed, in line with Augustine's acclamation, "O Beauty, ever ancient, ever new, late have I loved you." The second page of *Quest* reiterates this starting point, explaining further how on different continents Christians struggling with atheism, injustice, and other weighty issues have sensed and been grasped by God's presence. Theologians in these communities articulate the insights arising from the faith-filled insights and practices of these people, which in turn open up challenging paths of discipleship for the whole church. The "Introduction" ends with the invitation to readers to think about their own idea of God, and perhaps discover something more in what has already been found to be life-giving and true by others in the church. "The result can be a greater richness of faith that cleaves to the living God and shows itself in passionate care for the world" (5). In the "Epilogue" *Quest* states that the ideas presented have arisen as a result of faith's encounter with the living God amid changing, life-or-death circumstances. It notes that in every instance the theology presented is substantiated by scripture, tradition, and/or church teaching and buttressed by cogent lines of reasoning. The destructive power of sin, it continues, risks ruining God's good creation. "In face of this risk, the active presence of the living God in the world, *regardless*, is one of the oldest and most enduring of biblical promises. By listening with people to where the Spirit is moving in their lives today, by attending to what this signifies, by interpreting it creatively in terms of the treasure of biblical faith, and by calling for the praxis of universal solidarity in suffering and hope, these theologies shed light on ways in which that ancient promise does not disappoint" (227).

Explicitly, then, this book starts and finishes with the faith of the church, defining itself in that light. In trying to figure out why the committee's Statement concludes the opposite, I recalled Avery Dulles' classic work *Models of the Church*. Here he describes different ways of thinking about the church: as institution, as people of God, as sacrament, as herald, as servant, and later, as community of disciples. Each model has its advantages and disadvantages; while different, they are complementary; all are needed for full understanding. Is it possible that the Statement is working out of one model of the church and *Quest* from another?

The church in whose faith this book finds its home is delineated in the Second Vatican Council's *Constitution on the Church* (*Lumen Gentium*). Following its first chapter on Christ as the Light of the Nations, and prior to delineating the roles of hierarchy and laity and the witness of religious orders which may belong to either group, this constitution, after heated conciliar debate, positions the church as all the people of God. This is the whole community of believers who, blessed with the baptismal gifts of the Spirit and sharing in the mission of Jesus Christ, cling to the faith handed on by the saints, penetrate it more deeply by accurate insights, and apply it more thoroughly to life. Carrying forward this teaching, the *Catechism of the Catholic Church* states simply: "The faith of the faithful is the faith of the Church, received from the apostles" (§ 949). Such is the understanding of the faith of the church that frames my book. It is the faith of the people of God.

I remember being profoundly instructed upon first reading the essay by John Henry Newman (subsequently Cardinal, now Blessed), *On Consulting the Faithful in Matters of Doctrine*. One of his key examples is the situation of the post-Nicene controversy, when the laity clung to the council's teaching on the divinity of Christ while many of the bishops went back to teaching Arianism. Newman notes that this is "as striking an instance as I could take . . . that the voice of tradition may in certain cases express itself, not by Councils, nor Fathers, nor Bishops, but the *communis fidelium sensus*." This sense of the faithful, he explains, a sort of practical wisdom (*phronema*) deep in the heart of the mystical body of Christ, can be taken as a direction of the Holy Spirit which gives "testimony to the fact of the apostolical dogma" not only in the fourth century but as a basic characteristic of the church. Please note that I am not saying the church is currently in a similar situation of crisis over doctrine. My point is that Newman's understanding underscores the legitimacy, with all due critical discernment, of consulting the faithful in matters of the doctrine of God. Such consultation requires taking the insight and practice of the faithful into account both critically and creatively. *Quest* has sought to show how contemporary theologians have done just that.

In light of the above sources, I respectfully submit that *Quest for the Living God* does indeed start with the faith of the church. It is written from faith for faith in the context of the church. The need for clarification on this point could well form the first talking points of dialogue: does the Statement take one model of the church and its faith and measure *Quest* against it in exclusionary rather than complementary terms? Simply put, what does the committee's Statement mean by "the faith of the church"?

2. God's Self-Disclosure

The faith of the church which frames this book is not self-initiated but arises in response to God's own loving self-disclosure. By the end of the 19th century, the existence and dynamic of this radically free gift had been studied and organized in a systematically operative theology of revelation. This affirms that God has communicated God's own self to human beings; that this self-communication has a noetic character; that it discloses the divine plan of loving goodness to save all human-kind. This happens through historical events and persons together with their interpretations, culminating in the whole event of Jesus Christ. Responding to this historically given divine revelation, faith, itself a grace, is the believing response to this word which enables people to entrust themselves wholly to God and to assent to the saving truth which God has revealed.

In several places (pp. 6, 9, 13, 14) the committee's Statement declares that the ideas of God proposed in *Quest* do not comport with revelation, "to which scripture and the apostolic tradition bear witness, and the church's teaching which interprets them." As with the issue of the faith of the church, these statements puzzle me. The reason is because at the core of every idea of God presented in this book is a biblical insight lifted up, newly recognized, and freshly received by some group of faithful people in the church, an insight which sheds new light on the revealed self-giving love of God and the divine plan of salvation.

Quest's understanding of revelation is shaped by the teaching of the Second Vatican Council in *Dei Verbum*. There it is described as God's loving choice to speak to human beings as friends, showing forth and communicating God's own self and the hidden purpose of the divine will to save. Through the interplay of deeds and words in history this plan is realized, starting with our first parents, moving through the call of Abraham and the formation of the chosen people, and culminating in Jesus Christ. The historical nature of the process is further delineated by the narrative of how revelation is transmitted in the centuries after Christ. Handed on to all generations through the apostolic preaching and the written scriptures, preached and spread in tradition, transmitted in the church through its teaching, life, and worship, and interpreted by the teaching office of the church which serves the word of God, revelation is God's way of sharing "those divine treasures which totally transcend the understanding of the human mind" (§6).

In keeping with this view, the constitution instructs that theology's soul should be the study of the sacred page, whose word powerfully rejuvenates the quest for understanding (§24). *Dei Verbum* furthermore underscores the necessity of interpreting scripture, including the gospels, according to the genre of their historical composition, thus forestalling any kind of fundamentalism of the text. In dealing with the dilemma that some biblical passages present scientific or historical data inconsistent with contemporary knowledge, *Dei Verbum* further clarifies the council's account of revelation. "The books of Scripture must be acknowledged as teaching firmly, faithfully, and without error that truth which God wanted put into the sacred writing for the sake of our salvation" (§11). The official footnote quotes a text from Aquinas arguing that things which do not affect salvation do not belong to revelation in the doctrinal sense. As commentaries on this document note, the Bible was not written to teach natural science or political history; it treats of these insofar as they are involved in matters of salvation, which is the heart of what is being revealed. Salvation thus functions as a formal hermeneutical principle for the interpretation of scripture. This is underscored by the very first paragraph of *Dei Verbum*, which desires that by hearing the message of salvation "the whole world may believe; by believing it may hope; and by hoping, it may love." (§1)

In trying to figure out why the Statement found my book deficient in cohering with revelation, I turned again to Avery Dulles and his insight that in the postconciliar church there is a pluralism of theologies of revelation. In his *Models of Revelation* he presents six models being used in contemporary theology, namely revelation as doctrine, as history, as inner experience, as dialectical presence, as new awareness, and, presenting in the end his own preferred understanding, revelation as symbolic mediation. While agreeing on the teaching of the council about revelation delineated above, might the committee's Statement and *Quest* be working out of different models of revelation?

Let me illustrate this observation with the Statement's assessment of female images of God (to which I will return below). The Statement rightly acknowledges that the images which *Quest* discusses, namely those clustered around divine maternity, Wisdom (Sophia), and Spirit (*ruah*), are found in the Bible. But then the Statement criticizes the book's account of how these ways of speaking about God are being used by feminist, womanist, *mujerista* and Latina theologies in the United States and around the world, saying:

> The names of God found in the Scriptures are not mere human creations that can be replaced by others that we may find more suitable according to our own human judgment. The standard by which all theological assertions must be judged is that provided by divine revelation, not by unaided human understanding.

What is vastly puzzling is that far from being created by unaided human understanding, these female ways of envisioning God are part of inspired scripture. Therefore, by the Statement's own criteria, they are deserving of being considered part of revelation. Whence, then, comes this criticism? The critique states that I have eliminated as a criterion divine revelation to which scripture bears witness. This is a fundamental misunderstanding of my work. In fact what I have done is bring forth from scripture some precious images of God, long-neglected, but filled with the potential of revealing the saving love of God.

Upon re-reading my book I see one place where I could perhaps have been clearer. Before launching on the above criticism, the Statement quotes from *Quest* (109) the following summary:

> In other words, women reflect God not only as mothering, nurturing, and compassionate, although certainly that, but also as powerful, taking initiative, creating-redeeming-saving, wrathful against injustice, in solidarity with the poor, struggling against and sometimes victorious over the powers of this world. Reorienting the imagination at a basic level, these female images open up insight into the maternal passion, fierce protectiveness, zeal for justice, healing power, inclusive hospitality, liberating will, and non-hierarchical, all-pervading relationality that characterize divine love. In the process, they carry back to women the stamp of divine likeness.

Perhaps it would have been helpful if the second sentence here had reiterated that all these female images of God can be found in the Bible. I presumed this was obvious from the previous seven pages of examples (100-106), but maybe not. If the text had read "these female images *from scripture* open up insight . . . ," would the charge that their use eliminates revelation still have arisen?

My observations here underscore the need for clarification on this matter and raise up another point about which it would be fruitful to dialogue: what does the committee's Statement mean by revelation? Does this meaning render biblical female imagery for God invalid?

3. The Craft of Theology

Within the framework of the faith of the church arising in response to the treasure of God's historical self-disclosure or revelation, theology, in Anselm's classic description, is the effort of faith seeking understanding, *fides quaerens intellectum*, or the praxis of faith seeking understanding, in some more recent methodological approaches. The present participle *quaerens* signals that this is an ongoing project. The church moves forward in history, encountering new cultures and philosophies, grappling with new difficulties, benefitting from new discoveries, gaining new insights, all of which make necessary a conscious and methodical reflection on the meaning of faith from age to age. This disciplined reflection can be likened to a craft. It fashions a way of thinking that employs thought forms and linguistic terminology suitable to the era in which it works, in order to bring out faith's meaning afresh. For "even if Revelation is already complete, it has not been made completely explicit; it remains for Christian faith gradually to grasp its full significance over the course of the centuries" (*Catechism* §66).

Standing in this tradition, *Quest*'s chapters reflect how our era continues to contribute to the remarkably rich pluralism that characterizes the history of theology as a whole:

~ Theology is crafted in historical periods: early Christian, medieval, modern, postmodern.

~ It reflects geographically distinct cultures: East and West, as in trinitarian thought of Cappadocians and Augustine.

~ It is dotted with schools of thought, sometimes clashing: Jesuits and Dominicans on grace and free will.

~ Theology is connected with persons: Hildegard of Bingen, Edward Schillebeeckx.

~ It is connected with topics: christology, theology of peace.

~ It is connected with persons and topics together: John Paul II's theology of the body.

~ It works in different parts of the vineyard: biblical, historical, systematic, moral, spiritual, practical, ecumenical, apologetic, philosophical.

~ It is pervaded with different passions: for mystical union, for intellectual clarity, for social justice.

~ It is rooted in different imaginations: analogical, dialectical, liberationist.

~ It works with different methods: deductive, inductive, transcendental, correlation, hermeneutical.

~ It employs different philosophies: Aristotelian, Neo-Platonic, process, analytic, while not being tied to any one.

~ It dialogues with the wisdom of different arts and sciences: literature, history, psychology, political theory, critical theory, ideology critique, cosmology, biology.

This description is not exhaustive. Indeed, university courses on the history of theology or the history of Christian thought cannot do justice to two thousand years of this work in one semester or even two. Lest the diversity seem chaotic, it should be noted that, as Karl Rahner writes in his essay "Pluralism in Theology and the Unity of the Creed in the Church" (*Theological Investigations XI*), the goal is always the same: within the community of the church, to seek the meaning of faith in order to believe, hope, and love more deeply.

I further observe that at times theology develops ideas that not only sustain the inquiring minds and committed praxis of the people of the church but also influence official church teaching itself. John Courtney Murray's writings on the dignity of the human person whose individual conscience in religious matters should not be coerced, for example, helped shape the Second Vatican Council's *Declaration on Religious Freedom*, which shifted centuries of teaching to the contrary. The best example in our day is the liberation theology of Latin America. As one of its esteemed originators, Gustavo Gutiérrez, has noted, seldom has an insight moved so quickly from the faith of the people to theology to church teaching as has the idea of God's preferential option for the poor, now present in magisterial documents as a challenge to the church's own practice. It is interesting to observe that this is one of the theologies presented in my book with which the Statement finds no fault. I wonder what other theologies in *Quest* may eventually have similar influence. For example, the *Catechism of the Council of Trent* (written 1566) says nothing about female images of God; the post-Vatican II *Catechism of the Catholic Church* (written 1992) indeed does (see below), reflecting new insights in theology which may or may not in time lead to the development of doctrine.

Standing on the shoulders of many giants, *Quest for the Living God* is a work of theology. Each of the insights presented emerges from "faith seeking understanding" in the particular vexing circumstances of a group of believers in the church. Each takes its bearing from scripture and refers in significant ways to Jesus Christ and the Spirit. Some are particularly interesting in that they bring new voices with their subjugated knowledge to the table, expanding the ranks of the theological guild. In my judgment, they all offer a rich fare for those who want to think about their faith. There are other contemporary developments in theology of God which for reasons of time and expertise I did not include. But I wager that one hundred years from now when the history of theology in our era is written, these eight theologies will be included.

In view of this thick description of theology and the identity of *Quest* as a work of theology, I submit two further observations.

~ In our day with its intellectual practice of historical consciousness and ideology critique, theology at times asks about the relationship between the religious ideas of any era and the political constitution of its societies. In the face of massive suffering in the world, there is danger that a community's talk of God will ignore its implications for those being crushed, becoming privatized or triumphalistic. The Statement criticizes *Quest*'s discussion of this issue, in particular its critique of monarchical notions of God, declaring that "the exercise of authority that flows from the traditional notion of God fosters truth, justice, equity, peace, and right order" (6). Indeed it should, and often, of course, it does. But the Jewish people killed during the Crusades, the women burned as witches by the Inquisition, the African slaves held in bondage in the Americas with church approval and participation, these and other examples make clear that the exercise of authority in the traditional name of God has not always been beneficial. As part of the church's millennium observations, Pope John Paul II felt moved to confess repentance for these and other such misdeeds. But a theologian may be permitted to ask: What was there in the prevailing idea of God that allowed and did not resist the violence? Convinced that the symbol of God functions, *Quest* traces the ethical practice that flows from each theology of God it presents in order to ascertain if justice, peace, and right order really are the result. The Statement (12) criticizes the book for testing the socio-political effects of God-talk. I suggest that in this regard theology has lost its innocence.

~ The Statement persists in identifying each theology presented in this book as "her own proposals." Would that I were that creative! As clarified above, this book reports about and explicates theological insights about God that have arisen in different sites of struggle around the world. In that sense, as the president of my university, Joseph McShane S.J., explained to our local ordinary, Archbishop Timothy Dolan, when he graciously met with us over this matter, "it is her Avery book." Unlike Cardinal Dulles, I do not seek to make a synthesis of the various models but let them play out in their uniqueness. Like him, however, since I have judged these insights worthy of consideration, I do try to explain their context and rationale in the best possible manner. Unfortunately, the Statement configures my exposition of these views as though I had embarked on a grand conspiracy to destroy the church's faith and substitute my own proposals. Far from it. In truth, what *Quest* does is show how various theologies are expressing faith in God in a rich symphony of ideas and images.

This, then, brings up another set of questions for discussion: what does the committee's Statement understand theology to be? And how does the Statement interpret the pluralism of theologies that has existed historically and exists around the world today? And how does the Statement envision safeguarding the freedom of the theologian to explore, so that understanding of faith may continue to grow? If the Statement's conception of theology is different from that of *Quest* and those it presents, does that difference necessarily invalidate the way these theologies work or might they be complementary?

4. Modern Theism

Given the distinctions in the three prior sections between faith, revelation, and theology, it is important to flag the Statement's discussion of modern theism. Right at the start, the Statement declares that *Quest* "begins with a critique of the Church's faith, or, rather of what she terms traditional theology" (2). It is the *'or, rather'* that creates the subsequent misreading. For right here the Statement conflates faith with theology, which should be held distinct. The Statement then proceeds with the presupposition that the book wants to wipe out the faith of the church and replace it with radical new theological ideas. If that were truly the case, then I could see why the Committee on Doctrine would want to criticize the book. But nothing could be further from the truth.

As I present it in the book, "modern theism" is the name for a specific kind of *theology*. It arose in Europe during and after the Enlightenment when theologians used the kind of reasoning forged by Enlightenment philosophers to argue for the existence of God. Modern theism splits Aquinas's *quinque viae*/five ways of demonstrating the existence of God (*Summa* part I) from his treatment of the *via veritatis* who is Christ (*Summa* part III), ideas which Aquinas kept intact under the rubric of *sacra doctrina*. Consequently, it sketches a truncated metaphysical knowledge about God, drawing conclusions about God's relation to the world from concepts of divine qualities that have been obtained in the abstract, apart from revelation. Rightly stressing a fundamental separation between God and the world, it does not incorporate into its basic view how God relates to the world in incarnation and grace. One finds this kind of theology in the manuals which formed the major textbooks of theology prior to the Second Vatican Council.

As it developed in the 17th century and was then transposed into different keys, modern theism brackets revelation in its argument about the existence and attributes of God. In his distinguished study of the origins of this kind of theology (which *Quest* lists as one of its sources), Michael Buckley concludes, "It is not without some sense of wonder that one records that the theologians bracketed religion in order to defend religion." A critical self-contradiction then developed within this kind of theology: "The unrecognized violence of this contradiction thus lay not only between the religious content and the philosophic form but also between the Christian god and the impersonal content that was counted as his primary evidence." The Christian God is defined without Christ. "Christianity, in order to defend its god, transmuted itself into theism" (*At the Origins of Modern Atheism*, 345-46). It is this view of God delineated by modern theism that modern a-theism attacked.

During this period the faith of the church flourished in its spirituality, piety, devotion and ritual care, even while it was under stress from a growing culture of atheism. There were outstanding exceptions among theologians who thought differently. At its best, the preaching and teaching of the church also presented a more adequate notion of God. But the prevailing pattern of thought associated with modern theism is judged by many today to be inadequate. As Karl Rahner has observed, if one were to remove the Trinity from theological treatises of this era, it would barely make a difference.

Quest for the Living God (14-17) describes this development in brief, pinpointing what the book means by "modern theism." It laments the way this view of God has gone on to become trivialized in contemporary popular culture, including its cavalier rejection by the so-called new atheists. It then alerts the reader that the theologies traced out in this book are departing from the method used by modern theism. Incorporating religious belief and practice at the outset, they are attempting new articulations of the belief that "God is Love" (1 Jn 4:8), closer to the history and mess of the world than modern theism allowed. *Quest*'s critique of modern theism is a critique of a curtailed theology in favor of a more vibrant tradition.

As the Statement notes (3), *Quest* rightly does not think modern theism represents classical Christian theology. The Statement also agrees with *Quest* that when the prevailing view of God resulting from modern theism presents a distant lawgiver who "stands at the summit of hierarchical power, reinforcing structures of authority in society, church, and family," it is in need of reform. The book's consistent appeal to scripture and theological tradition, however, contradicts the Statement's judgment that I think modern theism is identical with the traditional Catholic understanding of God. Modern theism is the theology of one historical period.

I offer, then, this observation. The committee's Statement conflates faith with theology. More specifically, it mistakenly attributes to *Quest* an equating of faith with a theological pattern known in the literature as modern theism. In doing so, it misreads at the outset what my book is about. It takes criticism of one particular school of thought—modern theism—as if it were a criticism of the ancient and medieval forms of faith, which it is not. Consequently, it attributes nefarious intent to the author. And it employs this error throughout the rest of its reading of the book.

It would be interesting to discuss whether the Committee on Doctrine agrees or not with the assessment that modern theism is inadequate. This would be an historical judgment, in any case, and not subject to the criticism that one's view is against church teaching.

To bring this issue to questions for dialogue: What distinction does the committee recognize between the faith of the church and particular patterns of theology? What if any value does the committee see in theologians making critical judgments about past ways of doing theology? I myself learn from the strengths and weaknesses of past ways

of doing our craft, as I expect theologians of the future will learn from
the strengths and weakness of our era. How else can theology, like any
intellectual discipline, advance?

5. Speaking about the Living God: Religious Language

To guide the discussion to come, *Quest* presents ground rules for language about God, norms synthesized mainly from Aquinas' writings but
with backing in scripture. These are: first, God is infinite holy Mystery
who can never be fully comprehended by our human minds; second,
no human language is adequate to express this divine reality; and third,
there need to be many names for God, each one opening up a different
angle of vision. The Statement declares its agreement with all three, even
observing that *Quest* is "entirely correct" about the second.

It is vastly puzzling, then, that the Statement concludes that as a result of these three ground rules, I personally think it is impossible to
know God or to make statements about God that are true. It claims that
I maintain that any language about God will do; we can choose words
for God haphazardly; none of it means much anyway, because like a
Kantian skeptic I think our words do not attain to God.

Please allow a clarification which is in truth a correction of the committee's Statement. I state categorically that I do not hold this position.
I do not think this and never wrote it. Nowhere in the book can one find
this stated either explicitly or implicitly. Indeed, the whole book is written with the opposite intent, to present the knowledge of the living God
arising from different insights and practices of the faith in the church,
knowledge which I judge to be true.

The Statement (6-10) begins its criticism with the heading "False Presupposition: All Names for God are Metaphors." Again, to be absolutely clear: the book never makes this statement. To be sure, to say that
all names for God are metaphors is one way to paraphrase the second
ground rule in ordinary, everyday language (but the book does not say
this). Biblical scholars, too, generally hold to the metaphorical character
of words for God in scripture. In systematic theology, however, a layer
of technical analysis exists regarding the nature of religious language,
and here the above heading palpably misrepresents *Quest*.

To step back from the book for a moment: my position on the nature of
religious language has from my early years followed the Catholic tradition on analogy. I did my doctoral dissertation on analogy, criticizing
Wolfhart Pannenberg's Barthian interpretation of analogy as always

and everywhere collapsing into univocity. I have claimed analogy as the theory guiding my work in several scholarly publications translated into numerous languages. I have even debated the analogical nature of God-talk with a process theologian in open sessions at annual meetings of the Catholic Theological Society of America and the American Academy of Religion. So what I state here is no secret or sleight of hand. The heading stated above attributes to me a position I have simply never held. The proper heading would be: "True Presupposition: All Names for God Are Analogies."

But the book must stand on its own feet. What do I write there? On pp. 18-19 *Quest* states that Catholic theology typically explains the indirect play of God-language by the theology of analogy, which I then go on to explain. On pp. 19-20 *Quest* then presents the more typical Protestant position that God language is metaphor, which I also explain. On p. 20 I bring forth the more recent theory of symbol as discussed by Tillich and others. The conclusion is that whichever theory is used, they are all working with the second ground rule, using good, true, and beautiful aspects of creation to speak of the infinite Mystery who dwells within and embraces the world but always exceeds our grasp. To be sure, I do not claim analogy as my own position in these pages. But neither do I claim the metaphorical position. In any event, the point was not to argue one theory of religious language over against another, but to explain how all theories converge in affirming the limited nature of human language about God.

In trying to fathom why the Statement takes such umbrage at *Quest's* discussion of religious language, I wondered if at root it has to do with the way the book in fact describes analogy. Unlike Cajetan and other commentators on Aquinas who interpreted his work so as to give a substantialist meaning to God-language, twentieth century methods of reading Aquinas in his pre-nominalist, pre-Cartesian historical context have resulted in a strong recovery of the complexity of analogy including its negating moment. As seen in the work of David Burrell, William J. Hill, Eric Przywara, Herbert McCabe and others, this retrieval stresses the apophatic character of all concepts used analogously of creatures and God, thereby bringing Thomistic scholarship into accord with a genuine and long-standing Christian tradition. Could the Statement and *Quest* be working out of two different interpretations of Aquinas?

As I understand it, Aquinas positions analogy between univocity, where words have the exact same meaning for creatures and God, and equivocity, where they have no meaning at all in common. Since the creaturely world reflects something of its Creator, there is similarity but not identity in the same words used of creatures and God. Honoring this relationship of Creator and creation, Aquinas describes a supple movement of mind in which we first affirm a creaturely perfection of God; then negate the finite way we know that quality; and then reaffirm the creaturely perfection as belonging to God in a supereminent or excellent way.

Drilling down deeper as to how this works, scholars make a distinction between the perfection itself, *res significata*, and the mode in which it is known, *modus significandi*. At the end of the analogical process we attribute the *res* to God in an infinite way while acknowledging the finite *modus*, or the limited way of knowing commensurate with our earthly experience. Hence our mode of representing what we are talking about, our concept of the perfection, does not match its mode of being in the reality of God. The concept is inadequate. And yet having used it, our minds arrive at insight via a judgment that this perfection is true of God superlatively. It is a judgment that breaks out of the finite mode of apprehension endemic to our creaturely way of knowing.

When performed within the context of faith, the analogical process does not lead to agnosticism. Its knowing is a dynamic kind of relational knowing, pervaded with religious awareness. It intuits an unspeakably rich and vivifying reality opened up by the intelligible content of the concept, even though at the same time God remains in essence conceptually inapprehensible. It is like when you love someone. No words can ever adequately express the mystery of the other person whom you love. If this is the case between two creatures, how much more of human words about the living God who is Love? Thus Aquinas can write:

> The perfection of all our knowledge about God is said to be a knowing of the unknown, for then supremely is our mind found to know God when it most perfectly knows that the being of God transcends everything whatever that can be apprehended in this life (*In Boeth. de trin.* 1, 2).

Indeed, "we cannot know of God what He is, and thus we are united to Him as to one unknown" (*ST* q.12, a.13).

Returning to *Quest*: the text discusses how analogy "affirms, negates, and then negates the negation itself. This third step brings the mind through to a new affirmation of God, who transcends both assertion and negation" (18). Note that the book explicitly states that our words do affirm something of God. Then, after illustrating the process with the example 'God is good,' *Quest* writes about the result: "Human comprehension of the meaning of 'good' is lost, for we have no direct earthly experience of anything that is the Source of all goodness. Yet the very saying of it ushers our spirit toward the presence of God who is good, a reality so bright that it is darkness to our mind. In the end the play of analogy brings us to our knees in adoration" (19).

Having stated that I am incorrect in this, the Statement cites the *Catechism* as presenting the right teaching: "We do not believe in formulas, but in those realities they express, which faith allows us to touch." And the quote continues, citing Aquinas: "The believer's act of faith does not terminate in propositions but in the realities which they express" (§170). But this is just what I present in different words but with the same meaning. Nowhere does *Quest* claim, as the Statement asserts it does, that human language does not attain to the reality of God. Rather, in its own words it reiterates the *Catechism's* teaching that "Since our knowledge of God is limited, our language about him is equally so" (§40).

Still trying to figure out what the issue is here, I wondered if the Statement thought the three ground rules applied only to words about God arrived at by reason but not to those given by revelation. Again, this could not be the case. Describing the import of the revelation of the divine name YHWH to Moses, the *Catechism* writes: "This divine name is mysterious just as God is mystery. It is at once a name revealed and something like the refusal of a name, and hence it better expresses God as what he is—infinitely above everything that we can understand or say" (§206). Precisely.

In a similar vein, speaking of Jesus' revelatory way of calling God *Abba*-Father, John Paul II writes that this name "points indirectly to the mystery of the eternal generating which belongs to the inner life of God. . . . this generating has neither masculine nor feminine qualities. . . . God is spirit and possesses no property typical of the body, neither feminine nor masculine. Thus even fatherhood in God is completely divine and free of the masculine bodily characteristics proper to human fatherhood." Jesus' calling God his Father is meant in an "ultracorporeal, superhuman, and completely divine sense" (*Mulieris Dignitatem* §8). I dare say that by this point no one has a clear, fixed concept of the fatherhood of God.

In writing about this subject at the beginning of *Quest*, I thought it was good and useful to alert readers to these ground rules. They awaken us to the awesome nature of the subject of the book. They inculcate intellectual humility. And they guard us from grasping, defining, or otherwise arrogantly presiding over the reality of God with our concepts. Nowhere does the book say, as the Statement alleges, that these ground rules mean that we cannot know God. Rather, they explicate the truth that we must "purify our language of everything in it that is limited, image-bound, or imperfect, if we are not to confuse our image of God—the inexpressible, the incomprehensible, the invisible, the ungraspable—with our human representations. Our human words always fall short of the mystery of God." (*Catechism* §42)

To conclude this observation: the Statement takes exception to *Quest*'s words that "the reality of the living God is an ineffable mystery beyond all telling." Yet in speaking of sacred art, the *Catechism* states that "truth can also find other complementary forms of human expression, above all when it is a matter of evoking what is beyond words: the depths of the human heart, the exaltations of the soul, the mystery of God" (§2500). The mystery of God is beyond all telling (*Quest*) or beyond words (*Catechism*)—where is the difference? I suggest there is none. I am still at a loss to understand, in light of *Quest*'s actual presentation, what triggered the Statement's misconstrual of my position.

This surfaces another talking point for dialogue, perhaps best phrased this way: what does the Statement understand to be the nature of our language about God? I suspect we have a great deal of common ground here. Pressing the issue further, how does the committee's Statement think to distinguish analogy from univocity? Here there might be technical differences.

6. A Suffering God

The Statement takes issue with *Quest*'s discussion of the contemporary, post-Holocaust question about whether and to what extent God suffers with the agony of the world. On the one hand, *Quest* presents those like Edward Schillebeeckx and Johannes Baptist Metz who hold that while God is compassionate toward those who suffer, suffering does not touch the being of God. On the other hand, it also presents thinkers such as Jürgen Moltmann and Dorothee Soelle who hold in their different ways that God indeed suffers, on the cross and beyond. I find this one of the most important and fascinating discussions in contemporary theology. For many years my own mind, formed by the tradition of impassibility, assumed the former position. But then something happened that made me question this teaching as an absolute beyond some qualification. Let me tell you the story.

In 1987 I was invited by the South African Catholic Bishops' Conference to be the lecturer in their annual Winter School aimed at updating clergy on some aspect of theology. My subject was christology, and the project entailed delivering the same set of lectures for a week at a time in six different locations. To crush opposition to apartheid, the government at the time had declared a state of emergency. Many priests had been detained in prison, some interrogated under torture for their pastoral activity. Some had presided at funerals where mourners were shot by the military. Even to preach a homily in a black township on the theme of God's love was to incur the wrath of the government, for such words gave dignity to the people. Fear was in the air; violence an ever-present reality. During Q & A periods as priests and bishops spoke of their experiences, and during liturgies when laments poured out, I became aware that here was a church of confessors and martyrs akin to that of the early church.

Toward the end of the first week I delivered a lecture on the cross, including contemporary views *pro* and *con* the idea of the "crucified God." In the lively discussion that followed, I asked for a show of hands as to which position made more sense to them, Schillebeeckx's or Moltmann's. Every hand but one went up for Moltmann. I was dumbfounded. I had gone to South Africa assuming that the tradition of impassibility was unquestionably right. The judgment of bishops and priests who suffered for the gospel in ways I could hardly imagine made me stop and ask what was going on here in these people of faith. For them, as for the imprisoned Dietrich Bonhoeffer, "only a suffering God can help" (*Letters and Papers from Prison,* July 16, 1944). This result was repeated in subsequent weeks, with passionate affirmations. I returned from this beloved country with a new question, born of the suffering and spiritual experience of these good men.

Subsequent study made it clear that the Bible has no hesitation in attributing *pathos* to God ~ grief, weeping, lament. The key event of the revelation of the divine name to Moses at the burning bush begins with YHWH's words: "I have seen the affliction of my people who are in Egypt; I have heard their cry because of their taskmasters; I know well what they are suffering; therefore I have come down to deliver them . . ." (Ex 3:7-8). Biblical scholars point out that the Hebrew verb 'know' in this text is the same used in Genesis where we read, "And the man knew his wife Eve, and she conceived and bore Cain" (4:1). Here and in many other instances the Hebrew verb indicates something more than simply rational knowing, something akin to an experiential kind of knowing. YHWH sees and hears the pain, and feels it, and so comes to liberate. This is the narrative in which the sacred name is revealed, and with which it is forever connected.

Christianity's encounter with the philosophy of Hellenism brought with it the idea of impassibility, necessitating that early church theologians try to figure ways to marry Hebrew and Greek perspectives. This they did with greater or less success. Could there not be a way, I asked myself, to reclaim the biblical view of divine *pathos* while still safeguarding the transcendence of God which the concept of impassibility rightly aims to protect?

I found that the work of Abraham Heschel, which *Quest* presents (56-58), offers one way. To protect divine freedom, Heschel reflects that *pathos* is not a *necessary* divine attribute, one that belongs to the eternal God as infinite. But in view of Israel's history it is *in fact* how God freely chooses to respond to the human dilemma, namely, with sympathetic engagement. *Pathos* has the quality of an ethical category, a stance of living care. To say that God is compassionate, feelingly and concretely concerned, is to say that God freely cares about human well-being for all, which includes especially those ground down as victims of historic injustice. Hence to call God a God of *pathos* is not a psychological claim but a theological one. Like all theological language it is inadequate. But it is not false as a way to illuminate God's compassion.

The Statement criticizes *Quest*'s presentation of the suffering God which proceeds along these lines. It says I am presenting it as a viable alternative to traditional Catholic teaching. Here an interesting fact presents itself. At the very time that my book was under review, Cardinal Walter Kasper, at that time President of the Pontifical Council for Promoting Christian Unity (now *Emeritus*) and himself a distinguished theologian, gave a public lecture on God at the Aquinas Center at Emory University in Atlanta, Georgia. Counterposing the challenge to faith posed by modern atheism with the trinitarian doctrine of God who is Love, he raised the question of the suffering God. Traditional theology, he said, has understood suffering as a deficit and thereby excluded the possibility that God could suffer. But, he continued, on this point a shift has occurred in a large part of modern theology, citing here half a dozen major Catholic theologians including Hans Urs von Balthasar. In Kasper's words on behalf of the suffering God, available online:

> Self-evidently, if God suffers he does not suffer in a human but in a divine manner. For God's suffering cannot be something external that befalls him. God's suffering cannot be a passive accident, nor can it be the expression of a deficiency, but only the expression of sovereign self-determination. God is not passively affected by the suffering of his creatures; he allows himself in freedom to be affected

by the suffering of his creatures; he allows himself to be moved by sympathy (Ex 34:6); indeed, as the prophet says, his heart recoils in the face of the misery of his creatures (Hos 11:8). He is not an apathetic but a sympathic God, i.e., a God who can *sym-pathein*, who suffers with us.

The Cardinal is affirming God's suffering and at the same time protecting God from being limited because of it: divine suffering is part of and flows out of God's infinite active loving.

Quest's presentation of the God who suffers is well within the parameters of this contemporary Catholic theological discussion, which seeks alternative ways of preserving the import of divine impassibility without making it sound as if God were apathetic. In truth, I myself am inclined toward a both-and position on this question rather than an either-or, seeing value in the tension between biblical God-language and Greek metaphysics, as the text of *Quest* itself indicates.

Thus we arrive at another point for dialogue: in view of the biblical witness, might not the doctrine of divine impassibility admit of more nuanced interpretation, the likes of which we find in Cardinal Kasper's thelogical reflections? Could it not be that due to the insight and practice of people in the church including pastors and bishops, the reflection of theologians over these past decades, and especially the re-rooting of theology in scripture, we are witnessing a development in this area of doctrine?

7. Female Images of God

The Statement criticizes *Quest* for saying that traditional masculine language and concepts of God should be *replaced* by feminine ones. Please allow a clarification which is in truth a correction of the committee's Statement. I state categorically that I do not hold this position. I do not think this and never wrote it. Nowhere in the book can one find such a substitution called for either directly or indirectly. To the contrary, in presenting female images of God, *Quest* affirms: "This is not to say that male metaphors cannot be used to signify the divine. Men, too, are created, redeemed, and sanctified by the gracious love of God, and images taken from their lives can function in as adequate or inadequate a way as do images taken from the lives of women" (99). Instead of wanting to *replace* the church's traditional language for God, *Quest* is suggesting ways in which it can be *expanded*.

The book's discussion takes its cue from a pair of parables told by Jesus in Luke's gospel. In the first, a shepherd with 100 sheep loses one, leaves the 99 to search for it, and rejoices with neighbors when he succeeds (15:3-7). In the other which immediately follows:

> Or what woman having ten silver coins, if she loses one of them, does not light a lamp, sweep the house, and search carefully until she finds it? When she has found it, she calls together her friends and neighbors, saying, "Rejoice with me, for I have found the coin that I had lost." Just so, I tell you, there is joy in the presence of the angels of God over one sinner who repents (15:8-10).

After analyzing the shepherd story, the *Jerome Biblical Commentary* writes that the parable of the lost coin "has the same lesson as the first." These two are "parables of mercy," having in common the teaching of God's redeeming search for sinners. As *Quest* observes (106), both of these parables are imaginatively crafted by Jesus to depict the work of God the Redeemer, one using a male and one using a female figure. Despite the fact that tradition has favored the shepherd, the sweeping woman is just as revelatory of divine compassion. Would the church not benefit by expanding its repertoire of beloved images of God to include this searching woman? The Statement's criticism of *Quest* for supposedly wanting to *replace* the church's traditional language for God simply misses the mark. It attributes to me a position that I reject in *Quest* and in every other writing I have done on the subject.

The Statement further criticizes the book's discussion of female images for God for lacking "any sense of the essential centrality of divine revelation as the basis of Christian theology." Here I reiterate and expand upon my puzzlement already stated in section 2 above. The Statement rightly acknowledges that *Quest*'s discussion of feminine images of God focuses on those found in the Bible, in particular images that cluster around maternity, Holy Wisdom (Sophia), and *ruah* (Spirit). Insofar as scripture conveys the word of God revealed for the sake of our salvation, is it not the case that biblical language, narratives, and imagery communicate divine revelation? And if female images of God are part of that testimony, as *Quest* demonstrates, are they not legitimate witnesses of revelation? And is it not permitted that they form part of the repertoire of language about God within the community of faith? Is the church not permitted to use the language of Jesus when speaking about God?

Reflecting theologically on this language in his apostolic letter *Mulieris Dignitatem—On the Dignity and Vocation of Women*, Pope John Paul II explained that the Genesis stories of the creation of man and woman teach that "both man and woman are human beings to an equal degree, both are created in God's image" (§6). Indeed, thanks to the personal character of human being, "both man and woman are like God" (§7). This identity is key for understanding biblical revelation, he continues, which uses characteristics of both men and women to speak about God. This anthropomorphic language has limits, of course, because God is in essence totally other. Still, citing passages from the prophets and the psalms, the Pope declares that texts that speak of God with masculine or feminine qualities give "indirect confirmation of the truth that both man and woman were created in the image and likeness of God" (§8).

This insight comes to more succinct expression in the *Catechism* which, likewise citing prophets and psalms, states that "God's parental tenderness can also be expressed by the image of motherhood" (§239); and again, "In no way is God in man's image. He is neither man nor woman. God is pure spirit in which there is no place for the difference between the sexes. But the respective 'perfections' of man and woman reflect something of the infinite perfection of God: those of a mother and those of a father and husband" (§370).

As an example of good use that takes biblical language and applies it in a new setting, *Quest* (102) adduces the remarks of Pope John Paul I on the occasion of the Camp David peace talks taking place between Israeli and Palestinian representatives. Comparing war to a fevered illness, the Pope observed:

> God is our father. Even more God is our mother. God does not want to hurt us, but only to do good for us, all of us. If children are ill, they have additional claim to be loved by their mother. And we too, if by chance we are sick with badness and are on the wrong track, have yet another claim to be loved by the Lord. With a mother's love the living God keeps vigil through the long night of war, trying everything to break the violent fever and bring about peace.

The puzzling thing is that female images found in scripture are criticized as being against church teaching, while other non-biblical images, such as the African American image that 'God is black,' are not so criticized. I have tried to fathom why the Statement finds this female language so objectionable, and wonder if it is due to the fact that these images have come newly into speech mainly by the efforts of women. I could be wrong about this. But this is indeed a new phenomenon in the history of Christianity. Long silent and invisible in shaping the public culture of the church, baptized members of the community of the church who are women are trying to reclaim the fullness of their theomorphic and christomorphic identity. Some among them have joined the theological guild. In their work of seeking to understand faith, they have re-discovered biblical passages that speak about God in female terms, and have found in prayer the power of this language to affirm the human dignity of women who are "like God." It is a beautiful discovery. And since the symbol of God functions powerfully in the faith community, this usage can both enrich the church's appreciation of the mystery of the living God and encourage efforts to promote the flourishing of women made in the divine image. Thus does *Quest* present the spiritual discoveries made by many good women, and the scholarship that backs them up.

In light of the presence of female images for God in scripture, I am truly at a loss to understand why the Statement writes, "The names of God found in scriptures are not mere human creations that can be replaced by others we find more suitable according to our own human judgment" (13). That is clearly not what this book is doing, for it is bringing forth female ways of speaking about God found in scripture. And in the light of the use of female images for God by popes and the *Catechism*, I cannot fathom the Statement's criticism that *Quest* eliminates divine revelation, to which scripture and the apostolic tradition bear witness, and the church's teaching which interprets them. The Statement appears to be writing about some other book.

This leads to another point for dialogue. Is it permissible to use female imagery, along with male, animal, and cosmic imagery, for the incomprehensible God, or not? By what criteria would the Statement make this decision?

8. The Generous God of the Religions

The Statement declares that *Quest* holds the position that all religions are equally salvific. Please allow a clarification which is in truth a correction of the committee's Statement. I state categorically that I do not hold this position. I do not think this and never wrote it. Nowhere in the book can one find this stated either explicitly or implicitly. Yes, following church teaching since the Second Vatican Council, the book affirms the presence of the Holy Spirit in other religions, resulting in "spiritual and moral goods" (*Declaration on the Relation of the Church to Non-Christian Religions—Nostra Aetate* §2). But nowhere does the text predicate an equivalence between Christianity and any other religion.

In addition, while noting that *Quest* indeed affirms that Jesus provides a "unique" encounter with God and is "normative" and "constitutive" for salvation, the Statement criticizes the text for denying the uniqueness of Jesus as the Incarnate Word. Contrary to this misreading, let me draw attention to the constructive section of this chapter. This begins by staking out the position that "sees Jesus as the incarnate Word, crucified and risen" and explains:

> In Christian faith, Jesus Christ is *the* sacrament of this two-way encounter. Wishing to unite with the human race in its joys, sinfulness, and terrible suffering in order to save, the Word became flesh and dwelt among us as a human being. Through his life, death, and resurrection God has forged a saving bond with the human race that cannot be broken. The cross brings God's love into the depths of our death; Christ's risen humanity is the pledge of life for all into the eternal future. God thereby posits the incarnate Word in history in order to signal a broader economy, the presence of God's saving will coextensive with the history of humankind. (176)

Nor is this mere window dressing. The heart of the argument is that this revelation is a "treasure," and the text continues: "Christians need not, indeed must not, abandon the faith that Jesus is in person Wisdom made flesh whose advent holds saving significance for the whole of humankind, nor stop explaining to others the beauty of the gospel and its effect on our lives" (177). I am wondering how much more explicit the Statement requires a text to be.

But perhaps the difficulty is not that the book denies that Jesus Christ is the Word made flesh, which it does not, but that it goes on to suggest that the incarnation in Jesus Christ does not mean that others are deprived of God's gracious presence and action. This position, however, is in accord with church teaching. Starting with the Second Vatican Council every church document that deals with the religions in fact affirms the presence of God at work outside the boundaries of the institutional church. *Nostra Aetate* famously declared, "The Catholic Church rejects nothing which is true and holy in these religions"; rather, the church looks with sincere respect on their beliefs and practices which, though different, "nevertheless often reflect a ray of that Truth which enlightens all people" (§2). The council's *Decree on the Church's Missionary Activity (Ad Gentes)* likewise affirms salvific "elements of truth and grace" in the religions "as a sort of secret presence of God" (§9), noting that Christians themselves "can learn by sincere and patient dialogue what treasures a bountiful God has distributed among the nations of the earth" (§11).

On the 25th anniversary of these decrees, Pope John Paul II's encyclical letter *Redemptoris Missio* explicitly states that God "does not fail to make himself present in many ways, not only to individuals, but also to entire peoples through their spiritual riches, of which their religions are the main and essential expression" (§55). Even *Dominus Iesus,* which strongly posits the centrality of Christ in the face of relativism, avers that various religious traditions "offer religious elements which come from God" (§21). The documentation could go on and on. Clearly, according to church teaching, belief in Jesus as the incarnate Word does not cancel out the presence of God in the other religions. The Statement describes negatively the idea in *Quest* that the church has grown in understanding and appreciation of other religions. But on what basis would the Statement want to argue the opposite?

Here is where the church in Asia, thanks to its experience as a little flock amid majority religions, is leading the theological conversation, giving the rest of the church a glimpse of what I call the generous God of the religions. *Quest* cites episcopal conferences of India, Korea, and the Philippines regarding the sense of the Sacred found in Asian traditions; it presents insights these conferences gain as they explore the mystery of God's self-revelation, known in Jesus Christ, at work in the different ways of the religions. The book recounts my own startling encounter with the power of Hindu symbols used in an approved Eucharistic rite during a conference in India on Christ and the savior figures of other faiths sponsored by the Vatican's Pontifical Council for Interreligious Dialogue (173). That liturgy, and the whole experience of the church in India which I discovered during that conference, rearranged the furniture of my mind, casting more sharply the question of how to reconcile the centrality of Jesus Christ with God's work in other religions.

On one level, the issue is fascinating in an intellectual sense. As an avowed westerner who thinks in a linear line of logic, I stretch to understand the Asian way of inclusive thinking that holds: Rather than saying 'A is true so B must be false,' the Asian tends to say 'A is true and B is also true in some sense.' For the westerner, that would imply that truth is relative. But such is not the case, suggests the Theological Commission of the Federation of Asian Bishops' Conferences in their document on theological method (2000). Rather, truth is one but multidimensional: "There is but one Truth; but Truth is a Mystery which we approach reverently while seeking to understand its various aspects and dimensions." Instead of either-or, one hopes to understand both-and, and in different ways. *Quest* presents a series of models in which these options are being worked out in contemporary theology.

On another level, this question is also fascinating because it stretches the heart to be attuned to God's action in the world in places where we had not previously noticed, as with the poor, with victims of genocide, with women. The Statement criticizes *Quest*'s way of engaging with this issue as being due to my idea of God as Mystery whose being and fullness are without end. For one thing, I thought the Statement had agreed on the first ground rule that God is indeed infinite Mystery (section 5 above). But more importantly, this issue arises from the faith of the church as believers in Jesus Christ and their pastors encounter the wideness of God's mercy in the people of other faiths.

This surfaces another vital point for dialogue: how does the Statement interpret the universal saving will of God and the presence of the Spirit of God in other religions? Might it not be that "there is growth in understanding of these realities" (DV §8), as witnessed in church documents of the last half century? By what criteria should this be adjudicated?

9. Creator Spirit in the Evolving World

In this chapter *Quest* reaches the frontier where theology is engaging contemporary science. The Statement levies two criticisms against its discussion, one concerning panentheism, the other dealing with evolution and human persons.

Regarding the first, the Statement rightly observes that the book underscores both the transcendence and immanence of God vis-à-vis the world. But then it judges that by introducing the model of panentheism to illuminate the God-world relationship, *Quest* makes the world "ontologically constitutive of God's own being." Let me make a clarification that is also a correction of the committee's Statement in the strongest possible terms. I do not think this and never wrote it. Nor does the mental model of panentheism necessitate such a conclusion. Certain instances of process theology which operate with the panentheistic model do make the world necessary for God and might warrant this critique. But while learning a great deal from this school of thought, I am not a process theologian. Formed by scripture as interpreted by Aquinas, my understanding has always posited the ontological distinction between God and the world.

The category panentheism (all-in-God) has been developed precisely to delineate and demarcate a view different from pantheism (all [is] God). As used in contemporary theology, it provides a third option between theism and pantheism, one which gives stronger play to divine immanence than does modern theism, while maintaining the absolute transcendence of God which pantheism does not. By definition, panentheism is "the belief that the being of God includes and penetrates the whole universe, so that every part of it exists in Him, but as against pantheism, that his being is more than, and is not exhausted by, the universe" (*Oxford Dictionary of the Christian Church*). Karl Rahner's *Dictionary of Theology* notes further that panentheism is heretical only if it denies creation and the distinction of the world from God, which *Quest* obviously does not do.

As the title of this chapter indicates, my main interest lies in bringing pneumatology back into the discussion of the relation of God and the world, to ask about divine presence in the evolving world. It seems to me that the doctrine of God the Holy Spirit is a largely untapped resource that could help theology think through the doctrine of creation in light of recent scientific discoveries. Panentheism as a model lends itself to this retrieval. *Quest* (188) declares that "The mystery of the living God, utterly transcendent, is also the creative power who dwells at the heart of the world sustaining every moment of its evolution." The book goes on to suggest that the Spirit not only dwells within the world but also surrounds our emerging, struggling, living, dying, and renewing planet of life and the whole universe itself. It illustrates this with Luther's great image of God in and around a grain; with Augustine's magnificent image of the whole creation like a finite sponge floating in an infinite sea, necessarily filled in its every pore with water; and with the beautiful image of the pregnant female body (backed up by Moses' reprimand of the Israelites' infidelity: "you forgot the God who gave you birth"—Deut 32:18). These are all heuristic images that help theology explore divine immanence. As *Quest* explains, they increase understanding of the utterly transcendent God who yet is not far from us, being the One "in whom we live and move and have our being" (Acts 17:28). It is interesting that the Statement also cites this biblical text but neither credits *Quest*'s exploration of its meaning nor presents its own understanding of this text. But the "in whom" opens the door to the model of panentheism: God in the world and the world encircled by God who infinitely transcends the world.

Examining this chapter again, I see that perhaps it would have forestalled its misunderstanding of panentheism if *Quest* had stated explicitly that creation is God's free gift, a gratuitous act of love and thus not necessary. I assumed this, given the book's basic understanding of God, as this excerpt indicates:

the Creator Spirit dwells at the heart of the natural world, graciously energizing its evolution from within, compassionately holding all creatures in their finitude and death, and drawing the world forward toward an unimaginable future. Throughout the vast sweep of cosmic and biological evolution, the Spirit embraces the material root of life and its endless new potential, empowering the cosmic process from within. The universe, in turn, is self-organizing and self-transcending, energized from the spiraling galaxies to the double helix of the DNA molecule by the dance of divine vivifying power (191).

Far from making the world ontologically necessary to God, *Quest's* discussion of the Spirit's presence and activity explores the transcendent God's free and intimate relation with the world.

The Statement criticizes *Quest* for its brief treatment of the evolution of human beings. Let me reiterate that the text never takes issue with anything the church teaches on this point. What it does is bring this belief into dialogue with the contemporary theory of evolution, a dialogue encouraged by Pope John Paul II: "Does an evolutionary perspective bring any light to bear upon theological anthropology, the meaning of the human person as *imago Dei*, the problem of Christology, and even upon the development of doctrine itself?" (*Message to the Vatican Observatory*, 1988). *Quest* has listened carefully to the scientific account of the evolution of the human species. This account sees human emergence as being of a piece with the whole story of the evolution of life on this planet, *scientifically speaking*. Matter evolves to life and then to consciousness and then to self-consciousness, and this can be accounted for without positing divine intervention, *scientifically speaking*.

What to make of this, theologically? If one has a radically dualistic idea of matter and spirit, a way forward is difficult. However, Rahner's work in his book *Hominisation* and elsewhere argues for the idea that matter has been gifted by its Creator with the power of active self-transcendence. This means that "a development of the material in the direction of spirit and the self-transcendence of the material into the spirit is, both philosophically and in the Christian sense, a legitimate conception" ("Unity of Spirit and Matter in the Christian Understanding of Faith," *Theological Investigations VI*). I myself think it would be fruitful to pair this idea with primary and secondary causality, so that God accomplishes the creation of the human species in and through the processes of nature itself. But I am still thinking about this.

In any event, the point of this chapter is not to resolve this question. Rather, it is to present the scientific account which establishes an unbreakable biological and historical link between human beings and the rest of the natural world. Human beings are created by God as an indigenous part of the community of life. We need to see ourselves as truly earthlings, "a unique strand in the cosmos, yet still a strand *of* the cosmos" (185). The goal in view is ecological responsibility.

My observation here is that once again the Statement has taken texts of *Quest* out of context. Ignoring the issue being discussed, the Statement criticizes the book because it does not articulate all of church teaching on a given point. Certainly, there is a time and place for doing just that. But I respectfully suggest that an exploration of the presence and activity of God in light of new scientific knowledge is not that place.

Another question for dialogue now presents itself. How does the Statement envision theology being invigorated and informed by scientific discoveries of today?

10. Trinity: The Living God of Love

The last chapter of my book sums up the preceding ones by exploring theology of the Triune God, whose salvific engagement with the world they all recount in some way.

Citing the connection *Quest* makes between the Trinity and the salvific mystery that "God is love" (1 Jn 4:16), the Statement judges that I wish to limit our understanding of God to the economy of salvation. Let me state categorically that here again the Statement attributes to me something foreign to my understanding. I do not think this and never wrote this, in *Quest* or any other publication. I am simply following one of the great developments in contemporary trinitarian theology and returning to scripture in order to root this doctrine of God precisely in the history of revelation which gave rise to it. To start with the economy of salvation in no way means that theology cannot move to consideration of the immanent Trinity, the two being deeply intertwined. Such is an unwarranted conclusion, as Rahner's axiom which guides my own thinking underscores: "the Trinity of the economy of salvation is the immanent Trinity, and vice-versa." That *Quest* does not in fact discuss the immanent Trinity coheres with its purpose as a work of theology aiming to tease out the existential significance of belief in the Trinity for readers from whom this meaning is largely hidden.

Again, noting the book's use of biblical language about Jesus Christ, such as Jesus is God's self-revelation, the true Wisdom of God sent to save and set free, the Statement judges that this language is inadequate.

Instead, it argues: "Jesus is ontologically the eternal Son of the Father. Only the second understanding affirms a true metaphysical Incarnation" (18). Certainly, if the purpose here were to affirm the incarnation within certain philosophical presuppositions, then the Statement's point would be well-taken. However, this section of the chapter is tracing the historical origin of the doctrine of the Trinity from early Christians' appreciation of Jesus' relation to his Father up through the Arian controversy, culminating in the Nicene confession "God from God, light from light, true God from true God," which *Quest* quotes (204-206). In such a context, using biblical and creedal language about the divinity of Christ, I submit, is entirely appropriate. Stated another way, if the phrase "ontologically the eternal Son of the Father" is the only way to affirm "a true metaphysical incarnation," then none of the New Testament authors affirms such a truth. Even classic Christian theologians who are considered doctrinally orthodox, for example Athanasius, upholder of Nicea, would not pass this test.

The Statement's criticism at this point, however, is telling. In working with it I began to glimpse more clearly what perhaps has been the Statement's main problem with the book all along. Certainly, the teaching of councils such as Nicea, Constantinople I, and Chalcedon is authoritative. The trinitarian and christological confessions of these councils have provided a touchstone for centuries of theological interpretation ever since, and nothing *Quest* presents departs from their meaning. It appears, however, that the Committee on Doctrine holds that certain formulas such as "Jesus is ontologically the eternal Son of the Father" must be explicitly used and a specific metaphysical system adopted in order for any discussion to pass muster. This assumption has the effect of a drowned continent swirling all the currents above it while remaining itself invisible. No matter what the context or the question under review, the basic truth must be expressed in an explicitly determined set of words, words assumed to have a certain a-historical, unchanging meaning, or it is judged to be not in accord with Catholic teaching. These precise phrases themselves, such as the one above, are not biblical, creedal, or conciliar. Could it be said that this demand presented by the Statement is like neo-scholastic theology insofar as it focuses on certain propositions as the litmus test for right-thinking theology? If this is really the case, it would be a form of fundamentalism, not of the Bible, nor of doctrine, but of one later hermeneutic of doctrine.

I could be wrong, and would be happy to be disabused of this assessment. The Statement's declaration that only certain language is acceptable in a work of theology, however, suggests otherwise. In which case, I would like to respectfully ask: why? The *Catechism* and other compendia are there for all to see and learn from. The purpose of theology is not necessarily to repeat these formulas in every instance, but to explain them, to unpack their meaning, to find ways to express their meaning in new conceptual frameworks. Besides everything already said in these observations about the craft of theology and its hermeneutical function, I cite here John Paul II's words in the encyclical *Fides et Ratio*: "As an understanding of revelation, theology has always had to respond in different historical moments to the demands of different cultures, in order then to mediate the content of faith in a coherent and conceptually clear way. Today too . . ." (§92). This entails more than the simple repetition of formulas, true though they be. Such confinement of theology's language to set formulas would fly in the face of the whole history of theology, stopping in its tracks theology's work of seeking understanding in *this* historical moment. To borrow a metaphor, insisting on such a norm would be akin to a referee changing the rules in the middle of the game.

Regarding the doctrine of the Trinity itself, the Statement reiterates its previous critique that I think trinitarian language does not provide actual knowledge of God. However, this whole chapter is written with the contrary assumption. It begins and ends with the Pauline greeting, "The grace of our Lord Jesus Christ, the love of God, and the fellowship of the Holy Spirit be with you all" (2 Cor 13:13), and in between spends every effort to explain how the Trinity is the Christian form of monotheism. *Quest* discusses the name of God as "the Father and the Son and the Holy Spirit," noting how this articulation stabilizes Christian understanding of God, and affirming its value for liturgical use (217-18). It is true that *Quest* discusses how classical authors warned against taking trinitarian language as literally descriptive: one and three do not refer to numbers in the usual sense; 'person' does not give a complete explanation but allows us not to remain silent (Augustine); they are "three I-know-not-what" (*tres nescio quid*—Anselm). This is not to deny Christian knowledge of God. But it does remind the reader that language about God, while disclosive and true, can never be commensurate with the Mystery it finitely and beautifully seeks to express.

Quest's position finds interesting affirmation in the *Catechism*. In the eleventh century the church split into Eastern and Western branches over the disputed question of the *filioque* ("and the Son"). This term expressed the Western view that the Spirit proceeds from the Father and the Son, as distinct from the Eastern view that the Spirit proceeds from the

Father alone. Writing about these different ways of formulating the inner trinitarian relations, the *Catechism* teaches that both are acceptable. "This legitimate complementarity, provided it does not become rigid, does not affect the identity of faith in the reality of the same mystery confessed" (§248). Even with regard to such a momentous matter as the inner life of the Trinity, i.e. the relations between the trinitarian persons themselves, different manners of expression are permitted, a clear indication that trinitarian formulas are not exact definitions. I would like to ask the Committee on Doctrine: on what basis is *Quest* being held to a different standard?

Hans Urs von Balthasar's statement about the status of knowledge expressed in trinitarian language sums up Catholic tradition and my own position:

> the statement therefore that God is 'triune', all this is and remains discourse about incomprehensible mystery. It is only analogously (where the similarity is overruled by a greater dissimilarity!) that we can speak of persons in God; only analogously (where the similarity is overruled by a greater dissimilarity!) that we can speak of 'begetting' and either 'spiration' or 'breathing forth'; only analogously (where the similarity is overruled by a greater dissimilarity!) that we can speak of 'three', for what 'three' means in relation to the absolute is in any case something quite other than the inner worldly 'three' of a sequence of numbers. (*Reader*, 186)

Even in revelation the Triune God is greater than human language, which speaks truthfully but not exhaustively. Rejoicing in this holy Mystery, *Quest*'s stated aim in this chapter is the theological one of explaining how this language is meaningful "for the sake of our salvation" (DV 11).

This brings up one more pertinent question for dialogue. Does the Committee on Doctrine really hold that works of theology must always and everywhere express their thinking in certain predetermined formulas taken from neo-scholasticism? If so, it would be helpful to clarify who decided this, and when, and by what criteria. If so, it would also be important to discuss how such a requirement departs from the whole time-honored history of theology, whose mandate is to seek understanding in different cultures in coherent and conceptually clear ways.

Conclusion

These final observations step beyond the texts of the Statement and *Quest for the Living God* and consider several wider issues.

By now it has become clear what my brief public statement meant when it referred to misrepresentations, misinterpretations, and an incorrect picture of my book in the committee's Statement. At the outset the Statement makes several erroneous moves that jeopardize the accuracy of its judgment: deciding that the book did not start with the faith of the church; interpreting my critique of the theological position known as modern theism as criticism of the faith of the church; and misconstruing my position on religious language as leading to Kantian skepticism. In addition, overlooking the fact that this book shares with readers the fruit of different avenues of scholarship developing in the church today, the Statement presents each succeeding view of God as "her radical revision" (6). Given these initial misreadings, what follows was almost bound to miss the mark. Ideas are taken out of context and twisted to mean what they patently do not mean. Sentences are run to a conclusion far from what I think or the text says. False dilemmas are composed. Numerous omissions, distortions, and outright misstatements of fact riddle the reading. As a work of theology, *Quest for the Living God* was thoroughly misunderstood and consistently misrepresented in the committee's Statement. As a result, the Statement's judgment that *Quest* does not cohere with Catholic teaching is less than compelling. It hangs in the air, untethered by the text of the book itself.

To use a judicial metaphor: the fact that *Quest for the Living God* was brought up on charges by person or persons unknown, put on a year-long trial, and found guilty before I was ever informed adds to the problematic aspect of the Statement's appearance. In my view, it would have been better to have this dialogue prior to the release of the Statement. Then, if the Committee on Doctrine still wished to make a statement, it would at least be based on an accurate reading of what the book actually says.

Simple human courtesy would indicate that springing such a public critique without warning is neither a generous nor respectful way to treat an adult. Were it not for the graciousness of Archbishop Timothy Dolan, my local bishop, I would have found out about the Statement online or in the newspaper. It is no disparagement to the episcopal office to suggest that the committee might have garnered less criticism from scholars and the reading public if it had followed a more dialogical procedure.

Furthermore, in a letter to the Fordham University faculty cited in the press, Thomas Weinandy, O.F.M. Cap., Executive Secretary of the Committee on Doctrine, wrote that the critique of the book "in no way calls into question the dedication, honor, creativity, or service of its author." This is interesting to know, because the Statement's harsh tone, disparaging words, ridicule, and rhetoric of fear certainly created that impression in my own mind and in the view of the public at large. A better path, it seems to me, would have been for the Statement to follow the common saying cited by John XXIII in his first encyclical: "in essentials, unity; in doubtful matters, liberty; in all things, charity."

As a result of these observations, I admit to curiosity about the process followed by the Committee on Doctrine to arrive at the Statement. Did each of the nine bishop members or their theologians read the book and draw up notes? Did they discuss the points to be made and debate them *pro* and *con*? Did they vote on the final document? I ask because of my work on faculty and professional committees, where factual distortions are called into question and positions change as people hear each other's arguments. The numerous misreadings of *Quest* flagged in these observations makes me query if the committee might not find a more satisfactory way of proceeding to assure more accurate outcomes.

I am glad to know the Committee on Doctrine did not ban my book. Over-zealous editors with a love for alliteration created variations of the headline "Bishops Ban Book," but Thomas Weinandy O.F.M. Cap. is cited in the *New York Times* as saying that the bishops have no authority to mandate that books be removed from college classrooms.

That being said, it is interesting to note that I did not write *Quest for the Living God* to be used as a textbook. If that were the goal, the book would have been written differently. As stated in its Introduction, *Quest* is written for a broad audience of thinking, seeking, committed, teaching, preaching adults as nourishment for their own mature faith. The fact that it is being used in whole or part in college and university courses indicates a professorial judgment that young adults could benefit from critical engagement with theological conversations actually taking place in the church today. College curricula typically include critical literary hermeneutics, complex economic and political theory, postcolonial accounts of history, sociological analysis, pragmatic philosophical approaches, gender theory, and the practice of scientific methods. In view of the sophisticated study students make in other disciplines, presenting religion in a simplistic way would be deadly. Rather than simply imparting information to be appropriated, theology in the college and university setting aims to *think*: it invites students to discover Christian faith critically and appreciatively by raising questions, offering interpretations, making comparisons, evaluating, and testing new thought forms, all to encourage growth in understanding. For students to engage with theological investigations guided by a competent professor is not only *not* harmful but can be positively beneficial, promoting intellectual and frequently spiritual growth. Students are much better prepared to face the world in flux if they have grappled with faith in this way.

With regard to the originally intended adult readers, no one can live in our wired society without being exposed to ideas of every stripe, including religious ones. *Quest*'s presentation of glimpses of God arising in different contexts opens windows on the rich mystery of faith. It presents issues that many readers are already thinking and talking about in any case. The Statement seems to think that controversies which in fact exist, such as over the suffering God or the activity of the Spirit in other religions, should not be presented to the thinking public. I am reminded of the delightful anecdote told by Gregory of Nyssa when debate raged in the church over the divinity of Christ: "even the baker," he reported, "does not cease from discussing this, for if you ask the price of bread he will tell you that the Father is greater and the Son subject to him." If a 4th century baker can discuss theology of God, 21st century educated persons are up to the task, it seems to me. It is *their* faith that is at stake, and if they choose to search for understanding, they may benefit from this book intellectually and spiritually.

In its conclusion the Statement says that *Quest* misleadingly "presents itself as a retrieval of the authentic Christian tradition." Insofar as the book presents glimpses of God emerging out of the religious belief and practice, suffering and study of groups of people struggling to live out their faith today, the retrievals presented are actually signaling something new going forward in the living tradition, "toward the fullness of divine truth" (*DV* 8). New dimensions of the mystery of faith in the living God revealed in Jesus Christ through the Spirit are coming to light. In its suggestions for further reading at the end of each chapter, the book names close to 175 authors whose ideas are represented in its pages. Almost none of them make formulaic metaphysical statements. But all, like Jacob wrestling with the angel, try to bring to expression something of the truth and beauty of God come to heal, redeem, and liberate the questing world of today. Unless certain true but limited language is taken to be the equivalent of the expansive breadth and depth of Catholic teaching—and this may be the heart of the matter—then I respectfully submit that *Quest for the Living God* with its map of frontiers accords with the Catholic tradition and its time-honored tradition of seeking understanding of faith.

Thank you for this invitation to offer my observations on the Committee on Doctrine's Statement. Once again I declare my willingness to continue to dialogue about these important matters.

✦ ✦ ✦ ✦

July 14, 2011

Cardinal Donald Wuerl
Archbishop of Washington
5001 Eastern Avenue
Washington, DC 20017

Dear Cardinal Wuerl,

Thank you for your letter of June 22, 2011 informing me that the Committee on Doctrine has decided to review and respond carefully to my Observations on the Committee's March Statement on my book *Quest for the Living God: Mapping Frontiers in the Theology of God.* It is good to be informed of what is going on.

Germane to the Committee's review, another matter has come to my attention. In a letter dated May 24, 2011, Fr. Thomas Weinandy, O.F.M., Cap., Executive Director of the Committee on Doctrine, wrote to an individual who had communicated with the Committee about my book. A copy of this letter was passed on to me. In it, Fr. Weinandy in his own voice makes new, specific criticisms of my book that do not appear in the March Statement of the Committee on Doctrine. Once again, as in the Statement, these criticisms are inaccurate. Since this letter is written on the letterhead of the Committee on Doctrine, I am concerned that it may be taken to reflect the views of the Committee on Doctrine.

In the spirit of the Committee's invitation to respond to its Statement, I include here an Appendix that offers observations about this letter. I ask that this be attached to my Observations sent to the Committee on June 1st.

My continuing concern is that in reviewing and responding to my Observations, the Committee will bring up new criticisms as Fr. Weinandy does in this letter, and do so as before in a way that misrepresents the argument of the book. To prevent this from happening, I respectfully suggest that should there now be new criticisms made of my book, I be informed before they are issued for the sake of clarification.

I am fully prepared to take responsibility for what I wrote and to correct it if can be shown to be against the teaching of the church. But as a scholar I am not prepared to be held accountable for what I did not write and do not mean.

New York and Washington are not far apart. I assure you explicitly of my willingness to meet face-to-face to clarify these matters, and in fact would like to do so, should you deem that helpful. With kind regards and best wishes,

Peace,

Dr. Elizabeth A. Johnson, C.S.J.
Distinguished Professor of Theology

Cc. Committee on Doctrine
Archbishop Timothy Dolan, Archbishop of New York
Joseph McShane, S.J., President of Fordham University
Jean Amore, C.S.J., President of Sisters of St. Joseph, Brentwood

✦ ✦ ✦ ✦

July 11, 2011

To Speak Rightly of the Living God
Appendix

Dr. Elizabeth A. Johnson, C.S.J.

It has come to my attention that additional criticisms of my book *Quest for the Living God: Mapping Frontiers in the Theology of God* have been raised in a May 24, 2011 letter to a private individual written by Fr. Thomas Weinandy, O.F.M., Cap., Executive Director of the Committee on Doctrine. I add this Appendix to my Observations of June 1, 2011 by way of clarification, presuming that the goodwill of the committee, which invited me to submit written observations regarding its March Statement, continues. The letter in question brings up several issues. I deal here with two that did not come up in this form in my original Observations.

Language about the Mystery of God

Fr. Weinandy writes in his May 24 letter:

"You will probably not be surprised to learn that I believe that you overestimate the continuity of thought of Sr. Johnson with that of traditional theologians such as Augustine and Aquinas. Sr. Johnson frequently refers to the great authors of the tradition, but there are points she departs in crucial ways from their thought. For example, while Sr. Johnson is correct that the great theologians such as Aquinas were very careful to point out the limitations of human language when applied to God, she departs from the thought of Aquinas when she insists that "no expression for God can be taken literally. None" (p. 18). Aquinas held that certain names do apply to God literally, *proprie* (*Summa theologica* I, q. 13, a. 3). He explicitly rejects the idea that all names apply to God only metaphorically, *metaphorice* (ad 1).

"Admittedly, it is a tricky business to explain how our language does and does not apply to God. Still, Sr. Johnson should understand the subtle distinctions made by Aquinas. It seems that Sr. Johnson rejects the idea of some names applying literally to God as part of her project to displace traditional masculine names for God. Only when all names for God are reduced to metaphors, will one be free to choose the names which best serve one's purpose."

Sed contra: Having taught Aquinas' views on God-language for decades, I presumably have some understanding of the subtle distinctions his position stakes out. In a nutshell, the Latin word *proprie*, so crucial to Aquinas' argument in question 13, does not mean the same as 'literally' in the vernacular sense. The following should serve to clarify the lack of accuracy expressed in this letter.

~ *Quest for the Living God* was written for a broad audience. Its purpose is to make accessible to interested people several key discussions going on in theology today about the mystery of the living God. The Committee on Doctrine rightly noted this fact in its original statement. In keeping with its genre, such a book uses vernacular language that regular readers will understand. Thus, when *Quest* says that no word for God can be taken literally, it is using ordinary American English to say that no word for God means exactly what it means when said of creatures, definitively, without remainder; all our words have limitations. Should one consult the dictionary for confirmation, 'literally' means exact or verbatim, according to the letter, or reproduced word for word (*Webster's New Collegiate*); it means taking words in their usual sense, in a literal manner, exactly copied (*New Oxford American*).

A book written about contemporary theology for a broad audience is not one in which the finer points of scholastic discussion need be brought to the fore. Even if they were, 'literally' would not mean the same thing in Aquinas and ordinary modern English. Reading *Quest* according to the genre in which it was written, one can see that the statement "no expression for God can be taken literally" is correct in the vernacular meaning of the term.

~ This letter cites Aquinas' *Summa*, question 13, article 3 and its use of the Latin word *proprie*. To begin with, this word is sometimes but not always translated 'literally.' Even with such a translation, *proprie* does not mean 'literally' in the ordinary vernacular sense. Placing the text in context will allow its precise meaning in Aquinas to come to light.

Aquinas has already established in question 12 that natural human reason, which begins from sense experience, cannot know the essence of God; and that the revelation of grace, while strengthening our minds to know God more fully, does not remove this human condition: "by the revelation of grace in this life we cannot know of God what He is, and thus are united to him as to one unknown" (q. 12, a. 13). Given this view, the obvious question arises: if God is unknown, what do our words about the divine actually mean? Question 13 proceeds to give an answer. First, to counteract those who would say we cannot speak of God at all, Aquinas argues that we can: "It is the knowledge of creatures that enables us to use words to refer to God" (article 1), although the divine essence is beyond the meaning of the names we use. Next, Aquinas bores down further into the meaning of positive words such as 'good' or 'wise,' arguing that such language can be predicated of God substantially insofar as good or wise creatures share in divine perfection and represent God, however imperfectly (article 2).

In article 3, at issue here, Aquinas asks whether all such words are to be interpreted metaphorically, *metaphorice*, or whether some might be said properly, *proprie*. On the one hand, God is likened to a rock or a lion; these are clearly metaphors, because their meaning is tied to a certain bodily likeness. On the other hand, the words 'being, good, living,' and the like are also predicated of God. Aquinas argues that these latter names are not metaphors, for while our understanding of them is indeed taken from creatures, they belong to the essence of God in a proper sense (*proprie*). He begins the body of his argument by quoting Ambrose, who contrasts words said of God by way of a certain likeness, *per similitudinem* or metaphorically, and words which clearly show forth what is proper to divinity, *proprietatem Divinitatis*. Aquinas then offers his own explanation of how the latter terms function, making the distinction between the perfections themselves (*res*) and the way they are signified (*modum*) which I explained in my original Observations pp. 17-18. This distinction allows words to affirm attributes of God while preserving divine incomprehensibility. The article concludes that words which do not have bodily conditions as part of what they mean but "simply mean certain perfections without any indication of how these perfections are possessed—words for example like being, good, living" are not metaphors but can be said of God *proprie*, that is, in a proper sense, appropriately, accurately, in a way that belongs to his essence, or, if you like, 'literally,' though always with the proviso that they fail to represent adequately what God is.

~ The Latin word *proprie* is rightly open to many translations other than 'literally.' It means what is characteristic of a person, belonging to oneself, in a proper sense (*Cassell's New Latin Dictionary*), and this is clearly Aquinas' meaning in article 3. It is interesting to note that *The Latin-English Dictionary of St. Thomas Aquinas* compiled by Roy Deferrari does not even list 'literally' as one of the meanings of *proprium*, the adjective from which the adverb *proprie* is derived, offering instead: not common with others, one's own, special, particular, proper, true, real, genuine, the opposite of *similitudinarius*. Again, these also cohere with Aquinas' meaning in article 3.

~ Reading *Quest* side-by-side with the *Summa* q. 13 makes one thing clear. *Quest*'s denial of literal language for God does not contradict Aquinas's use of *proprie* because "literal" in contemporary English and "*proprie*" in 13th century Latin have significantly different senses. "Literally" in ordinary vernacular parlance means exact correspondence; "*proprie*" in Aquinas' technical discussion means not metaphorical, not said by way of bodily similitude, but proper to God's own essence.

To summarize: in my Observations of June 1, 2011, I made clear that I adhere to the analogical interpretation of language about God, and do not think all language of God is metaphorical. With regard to the letter cited above, I reiterate this position. I also add this observation: reading Aquinas' text in context countervails Fr. Weinandy's criticism regarding *Quest*'s use of the term. According to the best practice of book-reading, it is neither scholarly, accurate, nor fair to transport the *Summa*'s technical discussion of the difference between saying 'God is a rock' and saying 'God is good' into *Quest for the Living God*'s generalized discussion of the limits of God-language. The word *proprie* in question 13, article 3 is simply not the equivalent of 'literally' in vernacular English. If it were, God-language would collapse into univocity.

Suffering and God

Fr. Weinandy writes in his May 24th letter:

"You will notice that in the *Commonweal* article that you cite [June 3, 2011], Prof. Haught does not dispute the basic accuracy of the Committee on Doctrine's description of her position on the issue of divine suffering and panentheism. In his view, the problem is not that she envisions God suffering as God, but rather that the Committee insists on the traditional view that God cannot suffer as God (that the Second Person of the Trinity suffered as man was widely acknowledged by the Church Fathers and the subsequent theological tradition). I recommend the incisive rebuttal of Haught's article by the philosopher Brian Davies, who points out the insuperable difficulties involved in asserting both that God is the creator of all that is and that God suffers."

I recognize that this letter was written before the Committee received my invited Observations in early June. Still, I wish to underscore that there I did indeed dispute the basic accuracy of the Committee on Doctrine's description of my position (pp. 20-23).

The question of how best to understand divine compassion for the world is not a new one, but it has been raised anew in recent decades by members of the church from lay persons to theologians to bishops. Mapping this frontier, *Quest* presents representatives of the two sides of the debate for thinking people to consider. I cite Cardinal Walter Kasper and other Catholic luminaries to demonstrate that the issue of how God might suffer is very much an open theological question.

If any further evidence is needed that bringing this issue to the fore is not against the teaching of the church, one need but consult Pope John Paul II's 1986 encyclical *Dominum et Vivificantem*. Speaking of the Holy Spirit who will convince the world of sin, he asks:

> Therefore, will not "convincing concerning sin" also have to mean revealing suffering? Revealing the pain, unimaginable and inexpressible, which on account of sin the Book of Genesis in its anthropomorphic vision seems to glimpse in the "depths of God" and in a certain sense in the very heart of the ineffable Trinity? . . . The concept of God as the necessarily most perfect being certainly excludes from God any pain deriving from deficiencies or wounds; but in the "depths of God" there is a Father's love that, faced with man's sin, in the language of the Bible reacts so deeply as to say: . . . "I am sorry that I have made them" (Gen 6:5-7). But more often the Sacred Book speaks to us of a Father who feels compassion for man, as though sharing his pain. In a word, this inscrutable and indescribable fatherly "pain" will bring about above all the wonderful economy of redemptive love in Jesus Christ . . . the Holy Spirit will enter into human and cosmic suffering with a new outpouring of love which will redeem the world. And on the lips of Jesus the Redeemer, in whose humanity the "suffering" of God is concretized, will be heard a word which manifests eternal love full of mercy: "*Misereor*" (Mt 15:32, Mk 8:2).

What distinguishes this papal teaching from the *Commonweal* article written by my esteemed colleague, the philosopher Brian Davies, O.P., is the use of Scripture as a source. Following the path of reason alone, philosophy does not consult Scripture. Theology, however, does. It cannot rest content with what philosophy, without recourse to inspired texts, has established to be the case. An exclusively philosophical approach to theology is precisely what Vatican II sought to overcome in its insistence that Scripture, not metaphysics, is the soul of theology. If theology's soul is the study of the sacred page which powerfully rejuvenates understanding (*Dei Verbum* 24), then classical philosophy's relegating biblical texts that portray the suffering of God to the category of mere metaphor seems inadequate. I myself am still contemplating this question, trying to think through a both-and position, one that would honor the transcendence of God safeguarded in the classical position while at the same time doing more justice to the texts of scripture which portray God as affected by the world. The "insuperable difficulties" that a Creator God who suffers presents to philosophical thought become less onerous to thought once the God of revelation, engaged with history, enters the picture. In terms of what I think and what *Quest* actually says, the letter's view that I simply envision 'God suffering as God' is incorrect.

A Final Reflection

In a June 22 letter, Cardinal Wuerl has informed me that the Committee on Doctrine intends to review and respond to my Observations submitted in early June. I look forward to this response, with the hope that the members will resolve the misunderstandings that I, and many others, have found in the Committee's reading of my book. There is a great need for fairness and accuracy here, because serious charges have been leveled. For the good of the church, for the relationship of bishops and theologians, and for the enlightenment of the thousands of people reading the book, the true problems that *Quest* presents, if any, need to be clarified.

Quest for the Living God presents the work of theologians around the world who, walking with the belief and practice of the people of God, try to bring the saving reality of the living God into the language and conceptual forms of our day. I respectfully suggest that mapping these frontiers is a legitimate thing for a theology book to do. This is not contrary to the faith of the church. Rather, it is an exercise of that faith. The fact that this book could present so many new avenues of reflection on God signals, I think, the presence of the Spirit, alive and nourishing the church. For the living God is the holy mystery of Love who cannot be comprehensively expressed or contained in any words, no matter how beautiful, sacred, official, or true. There is always more for us to discover, in prayer and in service with and for the suffering world. It would be a blessing if the Committee on Doctrine and I could find common ground for dialogue on at least this point.

✦   ✦   ✦   ✦

Response to Observations by
Sr. Elizabeth A. Johnson, C.S.J.,
Regarding the Committee
on Doctrine's Statement about the Book
Quest for the Living God

Committee on Doctrine
United States Conference of Catholic Bishops

On 24 March 2011, the USCCB Committee on Doctrine published a "Statement on *Quest for the Living God: Mapping Frontiers in the Theology of God*, by Sister Elizabeth A. Johnson." In June 2011, the Committee received a letter from Sr. Elizabeth Johnson dated 1 June 2011, which accompanied a thirty-eight page text entitled, "To Speak Rightly of the Living God: Observations by Dr. Elizabeth A. Johnson, CSJ, on the Statement of the Committee on Doctrine of the United States Conference of Catholic Bishops about Her Book *Quest for the Living God: Mapping Frontiers in the Theology of God.*" Both the letter to the Committee on Doctrine and the accompanying Observations were published immediately in the *National Catholic Reporter* and a month later in *Origins*. In the intervening months the Committee on Doctrine carefully studied the Observations. Having completed its study, the Committee herewith presents its conclusions.

The Committee on Doctrine acknowledges that in the Observations Sr. Elizabeth Johnson agrees that theological investigation should begin and end with the faith of the Church. The Committee commends Sr. Elizabeth Johnson for her stated intention to help the Church progress in her understanding of divine realities as described by the Second Vatican Council in *Dei Verbum*, no. 8:

> For there is a growth in the understanding of the realities and the words which have been handed down. This happens through the contemplation and study made by believers, who treasure these things in their hearts (see Luke, 2:19, 51) through a penetrating understanding of the spiritual realities which they experience, and through the preaching of those who have received through Episcopal succession the sure gift of truth.

While recognizing the legitimacy (and, indeed, the necessity) of such a theological endeavor, the Committee on Doctrine remains convinced that the book *Quest for the Living God* in fact fails to fulfill this task, because it does not sufficiently ground itself in the Catholic theological tradition as its starting point. The Observations insist repeatedly that all the ideas in the book flow from the faith of the Church and that the bishops have misinterpreted the book. In defense of the book, the Observations discuss the nature of theological research and contain many true assertions about what theology is supposed to be, citing a number of authoritative sources, from St. Augustine to Pope John Paul II to Second Vatican Council to the *Catechism of the Catholic Church*. The Observations insist that *Quest for the Living God* expresses the same faith in a new way, "in different words but with same meaning" (Observations, 19).

It would seem, however, that the multiple readings of the words themselves point at least to serious ambiguity in the book. When it examined the particular points at issue, the Committee on Doctrine was confirmed in its judgment that these "different words" do not in fact adequately express the faith of the Church. We wish to emphasize that just as in its March statement, the Committee on Doctrine is offering an assessment of the words of the book, *Quest for the Living God*, but no judgment of the personal intention of the author. Just as in its March statement, however, the Committee finds itself coming to the same conclusion, that although "the book at times displays an engagement with the Catholic theological tradition and remains in continuity with it, it also departs from that tradition at a number of crucial junctures," and that "the doctrine of God presented in *Quest for the Living God* does not accord with authentic Catholic teaching on essential points."

While it is not possible here to address all the issues raised in the Observations, we shall treat a few prominent examples. Since the understanding of analogous and metaphorical language is a crucial topic both in the book and in the statement by Committee, we shall address this in some detail and other matters more briefly.

Analogy and Metaphor

The Observations maintain that the *Quest for the Living God* upholds the Church's conception of analogy and that the Committee has misunderstood and misrepresented the book. They point out that the book never states that all names for God are metaphors. It is true that this is never stated explicitly. Nevertheless, whatever the intention may have been, the argument of the book in fact leads the reader to conclude that all names for God are metaphors or the functional equivalent.

The book's "Second Ground Rule" reads as follows: "no expression for God can be taken literally" (*Quest*, 18). The Observations object to the subheading in the Committee's statement, "A False Presupposition: All Names for God Are Metaphors," pointing out that this statement never appears in the book (Observations, 16). The Observations concede, however, that "to say that all names for God are metaphors is one way to paraphrase the second ground rule in ordinary, everyday language" (Observations, 16). The Committee's interpretation is not artificial, but is in fact the natural reading of the text.

The context of the book as a whole supports this interpretation. Throughout the book the terms "literal" and "literally" are repeatedly used to describe the way in which our names *do not* apply to God. The book's rejection of the terms "literal" and "literally" naturally leads the reader to assume that what the author means is "metaphorical" and "metaphorically."

There is nothing in the text that would lead the reader to a different conclusion. When analogical and metaphorical God-language are discussed, they are treated as equivalent. The crucial difference between them is never explained. In the book, three ways of understanding God-language are presented in succession, namely, those based on analogy, metaphor, and symbol (*Quest*, 18-20). The book indicates no preference for any of these ways. As the Observations concede, the author does not claim analogy as her own position (Observations, 17). Rather, all three are presented as various ways of adhering to the "Second Ground Rule." The reader, not only the non-specialist, for whom the book is written, but even one well versed in theology, can be forgiven for concluding that according to the book there is no significant difference among analogy, metaphor, and symbol.

The Observations fail to clarify the position on analogy and metaphor contained in the book. The Observations maintain that the understanding of analogy presented in the book is indebted to twentieth-century Thomistic scholarship that "stresses the apophatic character of all concepts used analogously of creatures and God" (Observations, 17). It is true that every analogous concept has an apophatic character in that it involves negation, namely, of the *modus significandi*. Yet the *apophasis*, the negation, is not the essence. Beyond the negation there is the positive element, the *res significata*. A crucial function of analogy is to provide a way of expressing knowledge about God that is not just negation of what is unsuitable to God. We know that God is good, not just that God is not bad. The focus on negation with no recognition that some names can be said properly (*proprie*) of God only reinforces the impression that all names are reducible to metaphor.

The assertion in the Observations that "God remains in essence conceptually inapprehensible" (Observations, 18), without proper qualification, is more reflective of the thought of Kant than that of Aquinas. Aquinas indeed affirmed that a creaturely intellect cannot comprehend the essence of God, even in the beatific vision. Human concepts certainly cannot *comprehend* the essence of God. To assert without qualification that concepts do not even *apprehend* the essence of God, however, seems to imply that we have no knowledge at all about God. Here again the focus is only on negation and without the necessary reference to the positive element in analogy.

It is true that a clear recognition of role of negation in analogy is crucial to avoid the temptation to be too satisfied with our concepts. Yet there must also be a clear recognition of the positive element in analogy in order to help differentiate analogy from metaphor and to distinguish a salutary acknowledgment of the limits of creaturely knowledge from metaphysical agnosticism. This recognition is provided neither in the book nor in the Observations.

The Observations point out that the book does acknowledge that our words do affirm something of God on page 18 where it asserts that analogy "affirms, negates, and then negates the negation itself. This third step brings the mind through to a new affirmation of God, who transcends both assertion and negation 'in the brilliant darkness of a hidden silence' (Pseudo-Dionysius)." The next paragraph applies analogy to the example of goodness and indeed reaches the correct conclusion: "God is good; but God is not good the way creatures are good; but God is good in a supereminent way as Source of all that is good" (*Quest*, 18).

In the following sentence and paragraph, however, this affirmation is again negated: "At this point our concept of goodness cracks open. We literally do not understand what we are saying. Human comprehension of the meaning of 'good' is lost, for we have no direct earthly experience of anything that is the Source of all goodness" (*Quest*, 19). If there is no human comprehension of the concept that is affirmed of God, then the affirmation is meaningless and there is no analogy. According to the Catholic understanding of analogy, we do in fact know what "good" means and that "good" applies to God. The way in which God is good, however, surpasses our understanding because God is good in a way that surpasses that of all creatures.

The same problem appears in the next paragraph, where the example of the personhood of God is discussed. "At this point we've lost the literal concept. We don't really understand what it means to attribute person-hood to God" (*Quest*, 19). With such repeated negation, however, the book fails to recognize that analogy expresses some kind of knowledge of God. We must have at least some understanding of the concept that we are affirming of God for there to be an analogy.

In the book's description of analogy, negation always has the final word. The book never explains to the reader the positive and affirmative aspect of analogy that separates it from both metaphor and metaphysi-cal agnosticism. The Observations cite the teaching of the *Catechism* on this subject and claims that the book is presenting this very teaching "in different words but with the same meaning" (Observations, 19). The Committee on Doctrine finds itself obligated to point out that here, as on other matters, the Observations fail to acknowledge important dif-ferences between the position presented in the book and the Catholic theological tradition.

Names for God

The Observations assert that the Committee has misunderstood and misrepresented the book by failing to recognize that the intention behind the book was not to *replace* the Church's traditional masculine language for God but only to *expand* it to include female images. It is true that the book does not assert that male metaphors should never be used. Indeed, it acknowledges that it is possible for male metaphors to signify the divine (*Quest*, 99). When the book speaks of the traditional masculine language for God, however, it is to denounce it as a tool of patriarchal oppression "religiously inadequate" for our times (*Quest*, 96). According to *Quest*, when this language is used exclusively, it is taken literally and becomes an "idol" (*Quest*, 98-99, 110). The counterpart to the critique of male names and metaphors is the extended discussion of the theological fittingness of female names and images and the importance of using them in order to release "divine mystery" from "its age-old patriarchal cage so that God can be truly God" (*Quest*, 99). Is it unreasonable for the reader to find in these pages a call to replace inadequate, though traditional, language for God with feminine language?

While one could say that the book does not call for the replacement of traditional language in the narrow sense of proscribing the use of male imagery at any time and in any context, it clearly advocates the replacement of traditional masculine language in certain unspecified, but evidently important, contexts. The problem is that there is no recognition of the central role that the names of "Father," "Son," and "Holy Spirit" play in the divine revelation given to us about the relationship among the three Persons of the Trinity.

The Observations ask whether the Committee believes it is permissible to use female imagery for God. In its statement, the Committee does not exclude all possibility of using feminine imagery. The concern of the Committee was not the use of female or feminine imagery but the insinuation that traditional language based on divine revelation, such as "Father," obscures the truth about God. Certain language belongs to the deposit of divine revelation and may not be replaced, even if human reason might find some indications that to do so might be socially useful.

Perhaps in its statement the Committee could have given a fuller treatment of the question of what language cannot be replaced and in what contexts. The names mentioned in the book are father, lord, and king (*Quest*, 96). All three figure prominently in Scripture, in the sacred liturgy, and in the teaching of councils and popes. Such names cannot be discarded as "religiously inadequate" and replaced with other names judged to be more suited.

The term "Father" is particularly important, as it reflects the usage of Jesus himself. There are contexts in which it simply cannot be replaced. For example, in the eyes of the Church, a baptism is not valid unless it is done in the name of the "Father and the Son and the Holy Spirit." Names such as "Father," "Son," and "Holy Spirit" have a special place among the names given by divine revelation because they refer to the relationship among the three Persons within the Trinity. These terms are different from names such as "good" and "wise" that tell us of the attributes of God and from names such as "Lord" and "King" that tell us of the relationship between God and creatures. Indeed, they function as proper names for the Persons of the Trinity and cannot be replaced with other names of human devising. They tell us who God is: The one God *is* Father, Son, and Holy Spirit. These are not humanly created analogies for which other names can be substituted at will. Rather, God has provided names that by analogy truly reveal who he is.

Neither in the book nor in the Observations is there an acknowledgement that there is a crucial issue of the theology of revelation at stake here. The reader is given no indication that certain names cannot be replaced in critical contexts because of their origin in divine revelation.

Modern Theism

The Committee agrees that modern theism, strictly defined, does not represent classical or traditional Catholic theology. The book, however, does not offer a precise and clear definition of modern theism and is confusing about the relationship of modern theism to the longer Catholic theological tradition going back to the patristic and medieval theologians. At some points the book acknowledges that modern theism results from ideas from certain Enlightenment thinkers. At other points, however, it describes "traditional Catholic doctrine" and "traditional preaching and theology" as having the same faults that are attributed elsewhere to modern theism (*Quest*, 73, 80).

Most importantly, in the book certain concepts are ascribed to modern theism that in fact belong properly to the core of the Catholic theological tradition, concepts such as divine omnipotence, omniscience, immutability, and impassibility (*Quest*, 15, 52, 54). These concepts are discredited as being associated with modern theism, when in reality they have been constants in the tradition since the time of the Fathers of the Church and founded not on Greek philosophy but on what they considered to be a right reading of Scripture.

This confusion of modern theism with the Catholic theological tradition serves to make the alternative ideas proposed in the book seem more attractive. In the book only two alternatives are presented, modern theism or the new trends celebrated by the book. This is a false alternative. Furthermore, the true extent of the discontinuity between these new theological proposals and the Catholic theological tradition is obscured.

The Evolution of Human Beings

The Observations maintain that the book "has listened carefully to the scientific account of the evolution of the human species. This account sees human emergence as being of a piece with the whole story of the evolution of life on this planet, *scientifically speaking*" (Observations, 31). This is true in that science by its very nature has no other way of looking at the evolution of human beings than as the result of the interplay of material forces. The next sentence, however, repeats the same misunderstanding that the Committee found in the book, namely, that about what can be explained in scientific terms and what cannot be explained in scientific terms: "Matter evolves to life and then to consciousness and then to self-consciousness, and this can be accounted for without positing divine intervention, *scientifically speaking*" (Observations, 31). Science could account for life, consciousness, and self-consciousness, however, only if these were wholly the result of the interplay of material forces. While an adherent of a materialist philosophy would readily agree that material factors account for all reality, this accords neither with Catholic teaching, nor with sound philosophical argumentation.

Although a scientific explanation of life in purely material terms already presents considerable difficulties that could be discussed, the crucial issue is that of self-consciousness. Simply put, human self-consciousness cannot be wholly explained as the result of material causes. The multiple neurons of the physical brain cannot account for the unitary self-consciousness of the human person. The functioning of the brain cannot of itself explain human acts of knowing and willing. This has been amply demonstrated by various philosophical arguments. There is therefore one stage in evolution that cannot be fully accounted for by scientific explanation, that of the appearance of self-conscious intelligence and free will.

Human beings necessarily come to be as part of the material universe. Bodily existence is an intrinsic part of human nature. Consequently, scientific investigation has a great deal to teach us about the human person and human society. At the same time, there is something about the human person that transcends material realities and that escapes the grasp of scientific investigation. There must be another, a non-material explanation for the existence of this aspect of the human person. There is a range of philosophical attempts to provide an explanation. The Catholic Church teaches that the human soul is not the result of material forces, such as the bodies of the parents, but is created immediately by God.

Neither in the book nor in the Observations is there any recognition of these philosophical and theological issues.

The Transcendence of God

The Observations assert that the "panentheistic" model advocated by the book was not intended to make the world ontologically constitutive of God's own being: "Examining this chapter again, I see that perhaps it would have forestalled its misunderstanding of panentheism if *Quest* had stated explicitly that creation is God's free gift, a gratuitous act of love thus not necessary" (Observations, 30). While such a clarification would have been helpful, it would not have resolved the question as to whether or not the panentheism proposed in the book is adequate for preserving the transcendence of God. Both the book and the Observations assert that this is the case, yet neither provides solid grounding for this claim. The metaphors offered in explanation, such as the "mutual abiding" represented by the "pregnant female body" (*Quest*, 188) or the "finite sponge floating in an infinite sea, necessarily filled in its every pore with water" (Observations, 30; see *Quest*, 198), are based on material relationships and are insufficient to express the transcendence of God.

Furthermore, the metaphor of the sponge, taken from Augustine's *Confessions* and presented as an example of panentheistic thought in the heart of the Catholic theological tradition, is not advocated by Augustine as a suitable image of God. In this passage Augustine is recounting his earlier inadequate conceptions of the divine. At this point a major representative of the Catholic theological tradition is presented as an advocate for a position which he rejects.

Similarly, in the section on "Divine Agency" Thomas Aquinas is presented as endorsing a view according to which "it is incoherent to think of God working in the world apart from secondary causes, or beside them, or in addition to them, or complementary to them, or even in competition with them" (*Quest*, 193). While Thomas certainly rejected the idea of creaturely and divine agency being in competition with each other and viewed the ordinary exercise of divine providence as being through secondary causes, he argued that precisely because of God's relationship to the world as creator, God can produce the effects of secondary causes without these causes or effects beyond those of secondary causes (*Summa theologiae* I, q. 105, a. 6). This is the case of a miracle. Thus Thomas does not argue that it is always the case that "events both ordinary and extraordinary take place according to the rhythms and dynamisms of nature's own capacities" (*Quest*, 193). Here Thomas's actual position is dismissed as belonging to Modern Theism. "Modern forms of theism assume that God intervenes in the world at will to accomplish divine purpose apart from natural processes" (192). It is Thomas's recognition of the transcendence of God vis-à-vis creation that prevented him from tying all divine agency to secondary causes and his recognition of the transcendent end of creation that prevented him from limiting divine purpose simply to what nature can produce by its own inherent processes and causes.

In both the book and the Observations the full extent of the divergence between the description of panentheism advocated therein and the Catholic theological tradition is obscured for the reader.

Suffering In God

In its statement, the Committee pointed to the book's willingness to posit suffering in God as another example of the failure to uphold the divine transcendence with respect to creation. The Observations claim that the book's "presentation of the God who suffers is well within the parameters of this contemporary Catholic theological discussion" (Observations, 23). The book focuses on three German theologians, Jürgen Moltmann, Dorothee Soelle, and Johann Baptist Metz. The book makes no choice among the three positions and presents them all as viable alternatives. The chapter ends with the following: "Whether one adopts the symbol of the crucified God [Moltmann], or the silent cry of life [Soelle], or the compassionate God of promise to whom one laments [Metz], their work brings divine presence indelibly into the darkness of suffering that cries to heaven" (*Quest*, 68). Yet of the three only Metz upholds traditional Catholic teaching by rejecting the idea of a suffering God or of suffering in God.

The book points out quite correctly that "Christian reflection has always held that there is a real sense in which the cross reveals a crucified God. Insofar as Jesus who is crucified is the Word incarnate, his suffering is the suffering of God with us" (*Quest*, 60). The key distinction is that the Word suffers not as God but as man. The Second Council of Constantinople taught that Jesus Christ, one of the Trinity, was crucified "in the flesh" (*sarki*). Continuing on, the book brings out clearly how Moltmann denies this distinction: "But this same theology also traditionally holds that the Word of God suffered only in his human nature, the divine nature being infinitely beyond such passion. Moltmann pushes beyond this limitation to locate suffering in the very being of God" (*Quest*, 60-61). The book is misleading by presenting this position as a viable alternative for a Catholic theologian.

Trinity

The Committee criticized the book for having effectively limited our understanding of God to the economy of salvation and for being ambiguous about the relationship among the three Persons of the Trinity. The Observations contend that the Committee has misinterpreted the book. It is true that the book never explicitly states that theologians can speak only of the economic Trinity, and not of the immanent Trinity. The Observations assert: "To start with the economy of salvation in no way means that theology cannot move to consideration of the immanent Trinity, the two being deeply intertwined" (Observations, 32). The book, however, contains no consideration of the immanent Trinity at all, as the Observations concede (Observations, 32). This omission renders the presentation of the economic Trinity inadequate, as the economic Trinity cannot be understood in isolation from the immanent Trinity. There is only one Trinity. In the economy God reveals himself to us as Trinity, as Father, Son, and Holy Spirit. To speak of the economic Trinity presupposes that one has learned that God in his inner being—immanently—is Trinity, is Father, Son, and Holy Spirit. To speak of "Three" whom we encounter in the economy of salvation, while refusing to speak of "Three" who truly belong to the very being of God, leaves the door open to modalism, the view that the Father, Son, and Holy Spirit are merely three ways or "modes" in which the one God expresses himself in the economy. The omission of a consideration of the immanent Trinity renders *Quest for the Living God* seriously deficient as a presentation of the doctrine of God.

Furthermore, while there are no positive discussions of the immanent Trinity, the book emphatically rejects traditional theological concepts and terminology for the immanent Trinity, lumping them together with "neo-scholastic theology," which is itself chiefly characterized by infection from "Modern Theism." "While it gave lip service to divine incomprehensibility, Catholic neo-scholastic theology done according to this method engaged in luxuriant technical description of God's inner self-differentiation through relationships of origin, employing specialized terms" (*Quest*, 207). According to the book, this theology "presented its thinking in highly obtuse prose; scholars today take issue with its 'abstruse analysis,' 'irrelevant abstractions,' 'philosophical mazes,' 'elaborate theological maneuverings,' 'complex celestial mathematics,' and 'obscure language,' along with its 'sheer long-windedness'" (*Quest*, 208).

The chief grounds for such criticism is that this type of thought pays only "lip service to divine incomprehensibility" and presents "its findings as they were a literal description of a self-contained Trinity of three divine persons knowing and loving each other. This, of course, is not the case, no such literal description being possible" (207, 208). Here again we see an emphasis on negation that rules out any analogy that would truly apply to God. Moreover, we also see again ideas being dismissed as being infected by Modern Theism that are in fact integral parts of the Catholic theological tradition.

It does not infringe on divine incomprehensibility to attempt to describe "God's inner self-differentiation through relationships of origin." The only way to speak of a Trinity is in terms of the relationships of origin among the three Persons. The Council of Nicaea speaks of Jesus Christ as the Son of God, the "only-begotten generated from the Father." The Council of Constantinople adds that the Holy Spirit "proceeds from the Father." Theological discussion of the relationships of origin among

Father, Son, and Holy Spirit did not begin with Post-Enlightenment neo-scholasticism, under the influence of Modern Theism.

Even more fundamentally, such discussion is not an example of human hubris, a foolish attempt to capture the infinite God in finite concepts, but is made possible because of divine revelation. Jesus Christ has revealed himself as Son of the Father, who will send the Holy Spirit to dwell in the hearts of believers. To speak of the Son as generated by the Father is to use an analogy, but an analogy provided by divine revelation.

While the book never asserts that the analogy of generation—that of the Father and the Son—is entirely untenable, it never uses this analogy to describe the Trinity. Even when reporting the confession of faith from the Council of Nicaea, the affirmation that Jesus is the only-begotten Son of God, generated from the Father, is omitted (*Quest*, 205). Instead, the book mentions this analogy at another point only in order to dismiss it as belonging to a defective neo-scholastic theology that neglected divine incomprehensibility (*Quest*, 207). The same is true of the other main analogy for the Trinity used in the Catholic tradition, that of knowing and loving, based on the New Testament description of Jesus as the *Logos* (*Quest*, 207).

The book's misunderstanding of the incomprehensibility of God has effectively ruled out even divinely revealed analogies for the relationship among the Persons of the Trinity. The result is that the book can only speak in vague terms about the Trinity, for example, as "the living God made known through Jesus and the Spirit" (203) or as the God who acts in history "through incarnate Word and renewing Spirit" (210). It is not possible to give an adequate account of the Trinity without recourse to the revealed analogies of Father, Son, and Holy Spirit. Moreover, it is likewise impossible to understand who Jesus is as pre-existent *Logos*, as ontologically the eternal Son of the Father, and what the incarnation means without an understanding of the relations among the persons of the Trinity.

Conclusion

The Observations "To Speak Rightly of the Living God" argue that in its statement the Committee on Doctrine has "thoroughly misunderstood and consistently misrepresented" the book *Quest for the Living God* (Observations, 36). "Ideas are taken out of context and twisted to mean what they patently do not mean. Sentences are run to a conclusion far from what I think or the text says. False dilemmas are composed. Numerous omissions, distortions, and outright misstatements of fact riddle the reading" (Observations, 36). After studying these Observations, however, the Committee has found that they have not in fact demonstrated that the Committee has misunderstood or misrepresented the book. Rather, the Committee on Doctrine finds itself confirmed in its judgment about the book.

The Observations propose that the Committee's chief objection to *Quest for the Living God* is that the book does not repeat certain traditional formulas (see Observations, 3-4, 33-35, 38). "Theological research does not simply reiterate received doctrinal formulas but probes and interprets them in order to deepen understanding" (Observations, 3). It is true that the task of theological reflection is never accomplished by the mere repetition of formulas. The real issue is whether or not new attempts at theological understanding are faithful to the deposit of faith as contained in the Scriptures and the Church's doctrinal tradition. All theology is ultimately subject to the norm of truth provided by the faith of the Church. It is the responsibility of bishops to judge works of theology by that standard, in terms of how adequately they express the faith of the Church. As Pope John Paul II explained, since theology seeks an understanding of revealed truth whose authentic interpretation is entrusted to the Bishops of the Church, it is intrinsic to the principles and methods of their research and teaching in their academic discipline that theologians respect the authority of the Bishops, and assent to Catholic doctrine according to the degree of authority with which it is taught (*Ex Corde Ecclesiae*, no. 29).

The Observations argue the Committee has failed to appreciate the accord of the book with the faith because the Committee was operating with a narrow neo-scholastic conception of theology, whereas *Quest for the Living God*, along with the theologies presented therein, operates with a different "model" of Church and of divine revelation. In fact, however, it is not the position of the Committee that "works of theology must always and everywhere express their thinking in certain predetermined formulas taken from neo-scholasticism" (Observations, 35).

The problem is not that the book attempts to express the faith of the Church in terms that have not previously been used and approved, rather than repeat traditional formulas word-for-word or use the language of a particular theological "model." The problem is that the language used in the book does not adequately express the faith of the Church. On several points, as the Committee has noted, the "different" language used in the book does not in fact convey the faith of the Church.

The Committee on Doctrine wishes to make it clear that its statement concerned only the text of the book and involved no attempt to judge the intention of the author. Nevertheless, the Committee is convinced that a careful investigation of the case reveals the soundness of its decision to issue a statement about the book *Quest for the Living God*. For bishops, the book is a particular pastoral concern because it is written for a "broad audience" rather than a more narrow scholarly audience (*Quest*, 2). Furthermore, whether or not the book was originally designed specifically to be a textbook, the book is in fact being used as a textbook for the study of the doctrine of God.

Having examined both the book and the Observations in detail, the Committee on Doctrine believes that it is its duty to state publicly that on several critical points the book is seriously inadequate as a presentation of the Catholic understanding of God.

USCCB Committee on Doctrine
Donald Cardinal Wuerl
Archbishop of Washington
Chairman, Committee on Doctrine

Most Reverend Leonard Blair
Bishop of Toledo

Most Reverend Daniel Buechlein
Archbishop of Indianapolis

Most Reverend José Gomez
Archbishop of Los Angeles

Most Reverend William Lori
Bishop of Bridgeport

Most Reverend Robert McManus
Bishop of Worcester

Most Reverend Kevin Rhoades
Bishop of Fort Wayne–South Bend

Most Reverend Arthur Serratelli
Bishop of Paterson

Most Reverend Allen Vigneron
Archbishop of Detroit

October 11, 2011

✦ ✦ ✦ ✦

October 28, 2011

Statement of Elizabeth A. Johnson, CSJ

It is with sadness that I read the October statement of the Committee on Doctrine about my book, *Quest for the Living God: Mapping Frontiers of the Theology of God* (Continuum, 2007). My disappointment focuses on three issues: process, content, and result.

First, process. In April the committee invited me to submit observations on their original statement (dated March 24, 2011), which had been composed without any discussion or foreknowledge on my part. My response was entitled "Observations" (printed in *Origins* 7/7/11). In it I posed important questions about the nature of faith, revelation, biblical language, and theology itself, figuring that discussion on these fundamental matters might clarify the content of the book and where it had been misrepresented. Both publicly and privately I made clear my willingness to meet with Cardinal Wuerl and the committee to discuss these matters at any time.

The committee did not engage these questions. No invitation was forthcoming to meet and discuss with the committee in person. Moreover, in its new document the committee addresses none of these issues—not a single one. The opportunity to dialogue was bypassed. Despite the protocol "Doctrinal Responsibilities" (1989) approved by an overwhelming majority of the U.S. Conference of Catholic Bishops after consultation with the Holy See, this committee for a second time has shown a lack of willingness to dialogue about such an important matter as the living God in whom we believe. It could have been so interesting and beneficial for the church.

Second, content. As a result of the lack of process, the October statement mainly reiterates the points made in the committee's original statement. I appreciate that the new statement distinguishes between its criticism of the book and the intent of the author. It does correct some errors made in the committee's original reading of my book, and the vituperative rhetoric has been toned down. Yet there is little movement in understanding.

For example, pointing to Jesus' parable of the woman searching for her lost coin (Lk 15:8-10), my "Observations" ask: is the church not allowed to use the language of Jesus, who casts God the Redeemer in this female image? While admitting the "possibility", the October statement draws from this question the "insinuation" that calling God "Father" obscures the truth about God, something the book never says. It further criticizes *Quest* for not making the trinitarian language of Father, Son, and Holy Spirit more central, noting how necessary this is in the formula of baptism. What is so baffling here is that *Quest* agrees with the validity of trinitarian language. It spends a whole chapter describing how this language came about, exploring its meaning, and affirming its use in liturgical ritual. True, *Quest* also points out that scripture offers a multitude of other ways to speak of God, such as the above parable. For some reason, this is not acceptable.

Remaining with what is apparently a propositional notion of revelation and faith, the statement reaffirms its earlier judgment. But as scripture itself demonstrates and my simple Observations try to make clear, there is so much more richness to the picture. The content of the statement disappoints insofar as it ignores the breadth and depth of God's self-gift in history (revelation) and the people's living response (faith).

Third, result. This statement, like the first, continues to misrepresent the genre of the book, and in key instances misinterprets what it says. It faults *Quest* for what it does not say, as if the book were a catechetical text aiming to present the full range of Christian doctrine. It takes sentences and, despite my written clarifications to the contrary, makes them conclude to positions that I have not taken and would never take. The committee's reading projects meanings, discovers insinuations, and otherwise distorts the text so that in some instances I do not recognize the book I wrote. This October statement paints an incorrect picture of the fundamental line of thought the book develops.

I am responsible for what I have said and written, and stand open to correction if this contradicts the faith. But I am not willing to take responsibility for what *Quest* does not say and I do not think.

To restate what I have maintained all along: the aim of this book is to explore many ways to think about the living God. Like the householder who brings out of the storeroom things new and old (Matt 13:52), theologians over the centuries have labored to seek understanding of faith that keeps pace with history. In that tradition, *Quest for the Living God* presents contemporary theologies from around the world which, listening to the belief and practice of people of the church, try to connect the truth of the living God with the thought forms and critical issues of our day. The book's chapters clarify the new avenues of insight, rooted in scripture: God as gracious mystery who is ever greater, ever nearer; the crucified God of compassion; the liberating God of life; God who acts womanish; who breaks chains of slavery; who accompanies the people in *fiesta*; the generous God of the religions; the Creator Spirit indwelling the evolving world; and Trinity, the living God of love.

I respectfully suggest that mapping these frontiers is a legitimate theological undertaking. Far from being contrary to the faith of the church, it is an exercise of that faith. **I want to make it absolutely clear that nothing in this book dissents from the church's faith about God revealed in Jesus Christ through the Spirit.** The many new avenues of reflection signal, I think, the presence of the Spirit, alive and active, nourishing people in their hunger for God in our day. Of the thousands of messages I have received, one of the most poignant is from an elderly Catholic man who read it as part of a parish book club. The result? "Now I am no longer afraid to meet my Maker," he said—a stunning testimony to the non-violent appeal of the truth of the theologies presented in *Quest*.

To conclude: this book affirms that the living God is the holy mystery of Love who cannot be comprehensively expressed or contained in any words, no matter how beautiful, sacred, official, or true. There is always more to discover, in prayer and in service with and for the suffering world. It would have been a blessing if the Committee on Doctrine and I could have found common ground for dialogue on at least this point.

I lament that this is not the case.

At this time I will make no further statements nor give any interviews.

Chapter 9

Reflections on Key Ecclesiological Issues Raised in the Elizabeth Johnson Case[1]

Richard R. Gaillardetz

Boston College

The Johnson dossier offers an instructive case study regarding the exercise of teaching authority in the Church. By the exercise of authority I mean not only the actions of the Committee on Doctrine but also those of Prof. Johnson. The exercise of an ecclesial teaching authority does not lie exclusively with the magisterium, that is, the doctrinal teaching authority of the pope and bishops. A careful study of the teaching of Vatican II reveals a much broader consideration of the Church's teaching office. The Australian theologian, Ormond Rush, has called attention to the ecclesiological significance of the council's employment of the three-fold offices of Christ (priest, prophet and king) and the functions that correlate to them (sanctifying, teaching, governing) as a framework for reflecting on the life and mission of the Church.[2] Although the council was not entirely consistent and did not work out every detail of this correlation, the clear logic of its overall use of the *tria munera* suggests

---

[1] This essay is a significantly expanded version of a shorter piece that appeared in *Horizons* 38, no. 2 (Fall 2011).

[2] See both Rush's essay in this volume, 89–112 above, and his book-length work, *The Eyes of Faith: The Sense of the Faithful and the Church's Reception of Revelation* (Washington DC: Catholic University of America Press, 2009), esp. part 3.

that we can no longer assign these offices, as John Henry Newman once did,[3] to certain subsets within the membership of the Church.

The council's ecclesiological vision leads us in a different direction. The entire baptized share, albeit in distinctive ways, in the exercise of these three offices. Just as the council teaches of a common priesthood of the faithful and a ministerial priesthood (LG 10), so too there are distinctive participations in the Church's one prophetic (teaching) office, and each form of participation has its own proper "authority." Rush identifies three fundamental "authorities" in the Church's teaching office: the *sensus fidelium*, the community of theologians, and the magisterium.[4] Each authority draws from diverse sources. The proper authority of the *sensus fidelium* is grounded in baptism and the supernatural instinct for the faith (*sensus fidei*) offered to each believer by the Holy Spirit.[5] The theologian's authority presupposes her own exercise of the *sensus fidei* but draws additionally on both academic expertise and a charism for theological reflection. The teaching authority of the bishop draws on both the exercise of the *sensus fidei* and the charism for pastoral leadership that presumably led to his episcopal ordination. That ordination, in turn, provides the special grace of the sacrament which can assist the bishop in his distinctive responsibility to preserve the integrity of the apostolic faith. Each of these authorities has a role to play in the exercise of the Church's teaching office and no one authority can properly fulfill its responsibilities apart from the others.

The documentation provided in the Johnson case draws our attention to the exercise of two of these three "authorities": the authority of theologians (reflected initially in Johnson's book and subsequently in her responses to the committee) and the authority of the bishops (reflected in the original statement of the Committee on Doctrine, Cardinal Wuerl's subsequent document, "Bishops as Teachers," and the Committee on Doctrine's final statement). Let us consider these two authorities in turn.

---

[3] Newman seems to locate the priestly function of the Church in the ministry of the priest and the laity in the parish community, the prophetic function in the *schola theologorum*, and the governing function in the ministry of the bishops. See John Henry Newman, *Via Media of the Anglican Church* (1877), ed. H. D. Weidner (New York: Oxford University Press, 1990), 1:xl. See also *idem, An Essay on the Development of Christian Doctrine*, 6th ed. (Notre Dame, IN: University of Notre Dame Press, 1989), chapter 2, 2, 76–77.

[4] Rush, *Eyes of Faith*, 175.

[5] See *Lumen Gentium* 12.

Assessing the Theologian's Exercise of the Church's Teaching Office

What are some essential characteristics of the participation of the theologian in the teaching authority of the Church? I would propose the following:

1) The teaching authority of the theologian must be undertaken within the heart of the Christian tradition and in fidelity to the apostolic faith.

The theologian must undertake the theological task in fidelity to the Christian tradition. The committee's March statement develops this in reference to Pope John Paul II's discussion of the *auditus fidei,* the "hearing of the faith" in his encyclical, *Fides et Ratio* (FR 65).[6] To do theology within the heart of the Christian tradition means attending carefully to the testimony of Scripture, the fundamental creedal expressions of the Church's faith as normative (but not exhaustive) articulations of the apostolic faith, the witness of the liturgy, the work of the great theological voices of the tradition, the distinctive witness of saints and mystics, and the more ordinary witness of believers past and present. Since the great tradition is a dynamic, living reality, theologians must also attend to new voices and theological currents which may reflect the movement of the Spirit in our Church today. For theologians, this fidelity does not preclude a certain experimental and provisional dimension to their work. Theologians do not merely excavate the great tradition; they participate in its ongoing development. Likewise, theologians must not be relegated to the role of mere expositors of magisterial teaching. They engage in the work of theology in part by bringing that tradition into conversation with the questions and issues facing our world today and the new insights the Spirit brings to God's people as they seek to live the Gospel in an ever changing world. The theologian best serves tradition not by functioning as a kind of museum curator but by the ongoing work of reinterpreting the tradition in ways that respond to the needs of our times, thus keeping alive the transformative power of the Gospel. As the late Cardinal Avery Dulles put it in one of his earlier works:

---

[6] USCCB Committee on Doctrine, "Statement on *Quest for the Living God: Frontiers in the Theology of God* by Sister Elizabeth A. Johnson." The committee statement is included in this volume but can also be found on the USCCB web site at: http:// old.usccb.org/doctrine/statement-quest-for-the-living-god-2011-03-24.pdf. This reference to *Fides et Ratio* is found on p. 2 (pagination here refers to the online version).

> The theologian . . . cannot be rightly regarded as a mere agent of the hierarchical teaching authority. His task is not simply to repeat what the official magisterium has already said, or even to expound and defend what has already become official teaching, but even more importantly, to discover what has not yet been taught. . . . The theologian . . . is concerned with reflectively analyzing the present situation of the Church and of the faith, with a view to deepening the Church's understanding of revelation and in this way opening up new and fruitful channels of pastoral initiative. To be faithful to his vocation, the theologian often has to wrestle with unanswered questions and to construct tentative working hypotheses which he submits to the criticism of his colleagues.[7]

2) The exercise of the teaching authority of the theologian must be undertaken with a proper eschatological humility.

The theologian should undertake theological reflection and investigation with a profound spirit of humility in the face of the Holy Mystery of God. As *Dei Verbum* 8 taught, the Church is always moving "toward the plenitude of divine truth." Divine revelation is eschatologically conditioned. This means that the Church does not so much possess the truth as it lives within revealed truth, a truth that will always elude a final and comprehensive articulation in history. Honoring the eschatological character of divine revelation means renouncing any arrogance that would suggest that the theologian's views are above critique and represent the "final word" about the God of the Christian faith.

3) The theologian must exercise her vocation within the communio *of the Church.*

This *communio* is manifested at multiple levels. Proceeding from Christian faith and baptism, this *communio* is manifested most basically by the theologian's active participation in the life of the Church, that is, in its worship and in its mission in the world as a sacrament of the reign of God. For many Catholic theologians, the preeminent expression of their *communio* in the Church does not lie in the taking of some oath or the granting of a *mandatum* but in the act of participation in the Sunday Eucharist, a liturgical act that always includes the profession of the Creed.

---

[7] Avery Dulles, *The Survival of Dogma* (New York: Crossroad, 1982), 98, 101.

Participation in this mission is reflected as well in practices of Christian charity and the work for justice. Of course the theologian's life of faith is difficult to assess from the outside and ought to be presumed unless there are clear signs that would call into question the theologian's sharing in the life of faith.[8] At a second level, that which applies most directly to the teaching authority of the theologian, *communio* in the Church will include an attitude of respect toward the doctrinal teaching authority of the bishops and a determination to sustain communion with the bishops through practices of dialogue and mutual learning. Such communion may find juridical expression (e.g., through application for the *mandatum* or an *imprimatur* for one's work) but these expressions are by no means the only or even the best way to express this communion.

These characteristics are concerned with the proper *exercise of the teaching authority* of the theologian. This is not the same thing as judging the adequacy of a theological work. In other words, one could argue that a theologian has properly exercised his teaching authority and still take issue with the adequacy and/or coherence of a given theological argument. Theologians do not enjoy the charism of infallibility. In light of these characteristics of an authentic teaching authority for theologians, what might we say regarding Prof. Johnson's exercise of that authority?

Let us begin with the first characteristic. As regards the book under investigation, although Johnson's intention was to privilege new voices and "new frontiers" in her reflections, her book is clearly an exercise in theology undertaken by a scholar deeply immersed in our mainstream Catholic theological tradition. This was particularly evident in her responses to the committee. Although scholars are free to challenge her conclusions, and *Quest* is certainly foregrounding newer theological developments, there can be little doubt of Johnson's indebtedness, in particular, to the Thomistic theological heritage. *Quest* mostly presupposes the fundamental creedal commitments of the faith rather than explicitly engaging them, not because they are unimportant but because the book is dedicated to mapping new developments that challenge a series of theological devolutions that she refers to as "modern theism." Johnson

---

[8] This inability to judge the theologian's interior dispositions in the life of faith explains the negative reaction of many theologians to the address of Fr. Weinandy to the Academy of Catholic Theology, in which he consistently called into question the sincerity of faith of many theologians today. See Thomas Weinandy, "Faith and the Ecclesial Vocation of the Catholic Theologian," *Origins* 41, no. 10 (2011): 154–63.

insists that in *Quest* the term "modern theism" is not synonymous with the received apostolic faith of the Church.[9]

This brings us to the committee's fundamental criticism of her work, namely her failure to use the faith of the Church, the *auditus fidei*, as a necessary starting point for the theological task.[10] This point is particularly important because, as we shall see, both theologians and the magisterium share this obligation to begin with the apostolic faith. But, where do we look for this "hearing of the faith"? While there is no evidence that Johnson rejects the normative value of Church doctrine, she carefully avoids a reduction of revelation to formal doctrinal pronouncements and catechism definitions by including in the *auditus fidei* the witness of the whole people of God, the *sensus fidelium*. In her response to the committee, Johnson explicitly invokes the example of Blessed John Henry Newman on the importance of consulting the faithful on doctrinal matters.[11]

Regarding the second characteristic, Johnson's work certainly appears to be undertaken in a spirit of humility. Although she does not hesitate to offer her own judgments on the wisdom and helpfulness of various theological trajectories, she does not offer her reflections as the final word on the doctrine of God. Rather, she offers the reader, with a tentativeness appropriate to such new developments, a wide array of emerging theological insights. Her initial public statement expressed openness to criticism and willingness to dialogue with the bishops.

Finally, Johnson recognizes the importance of preserving *communio* within the Church by eschewing any academic elitism in favor of drawing on the insights of ordinary believers (manifesting a *communio* with God's people) and by acknowledging the legitimate authority of the bishops. In fact, as one considers her long response to the committee, what becomes apparent is the way in which she models respectful interaction among the three authorities discussed above: the authority of theology, the authority of the *sensus fidelium,* and the authority of the bishops. With regard to the latter, although it is evident that she strongly disagrees with both the process of the investigation pursued by the committee and the substance of its judgments, at no point does she reject the committee's

---

[9] Elizabeth A. Johnson, "To Speak Rightly of the Living God," *Origins* 41, no. 9 (July 7, 2011): 129–47, at 136. Although this statement is included in this volume, future references to this statement will use the pagination from the *Origins* edition.

[10] Committee on Doctrine, "Statement," 2–3.

[11] Johnson, "To Speak Rightly of the Living God," 132–33. See John Henry Newman, *On Consulting the Faithful in Matters of Doctrine* (Kansas City, MO: Sheed & Ward, 1961).

legitimate authority. Indeed, her patient and careful response exhibits her tacit acceptance of the bishops' magisterial authority.

Assessing the Committee on Doctrine's Exercise of the Church's Teaching Office

Now we turn to the Committee on Doctrine's distinctive participation in the Church's teaching office. Here too we can affirm certain features that ought to characterize the authentic exercise of the teaching authority of the bishops.[12]

1) The teaching authority of the bishops must be undertaken within the heart of the Christian tradition and in fidelity to the apostolic faith.

This first characteristic is shared by both bishops and theologians. With respect to the bishops, this constitutes a reminder that they are to teach what they have received. Their teaching must be drawn from prayerful reflection on the biblical witness, the fundamental creedal expressions of the Church's faith, the witness of the liturgy, the work

---

[12] A clarification regarding the authoritative status of the Committee on Doctrine's statement might be helpful. Pope John Paul II's apostolic letter *Apostolos Suos* granted a doctrinal teaching authority to documents issued by an episcopal conference in either of two situations: (1) the document is approved unanimously by the entire conference; or, (2) the document is approved by a two-thirds majority and receives a *recognitio* from the Holy See. (The document can be accessed on the Vatican web site at http://www.vatican.va/holy_father/john_paul_ii/motu_proprio/documents/hf_jp-ii_motu-proprio_22071998_apostolos-suos_en.html.) Article 2 of the Complementary Norms issued in that document explicitly rejects the possibility of a body of the episcopal conference outside the plenary assembly issuing a document as a properly magisterial teaching act. Rather, the March committee statement appears to come under article 3, which refers to "statements of a different kind" which are offered by the conference's "doctrinal commission" and only when "authorized explicitly by the permanent council of the conference." This authorization is referred to in the letter of Archbishop Dolan to the president of the CTSA (mentioned in the introduction to part 3 of this volume). The precise manner in which such "statements of a different kind" are to be seen as exercises of the bishops' teaching office is not clear. They can certainly be interpreted as an exercise of the bishop's disciplinary authority. However, I think there can be no question, but that the Committee on Doctrine would consider their statement, even if lacking the authority of a positive magisterial teaching act, as a broader expression of the responsibility of the bishops to protect the integrity of the apostolic faith. My thinking through this question was assisted by several helpful conversations with Francis Sullivan.

of the great theological voices of the tradition, the distinctive witness of saints and mystics, and the more ordinary witness of believers past and present. Since much of this is mediated through the work of theological scholarship, it should go without saying that they must also attend to the contributions of theologians.

2) The teaching authority of the bishops is fundamentally conservative in character.

Unlike theologians, the bishops are *not* charged with exploring new and provisional formulations of the faith. Rather, their task is to assess whether new formulations are reconcilable with the received faith of the Church. Consequently they are to be concerned with assessing theological works with regard to the integrity of Christian doctrine. Again, Dulles writes: "The bishop's task is to give public expression to the doctrine of the Church and thus to lay down norms for preaching, worship, and Christian life. His concern, therefore, is primarily and directly pastoral."[13] This task is quite different from assessing the adequacy and coherency of theological developments. The conservative nature of their ministry demands a clear distinction between theological and doctrinal judgments.

3) The bishops must exercise their teaching authority within the communio *of the Church.*

The bishops too must recognize that their ministry has to be undertaken within the Church's *communio.* They do not function as an external governing board but rather must manifest *communio* first of all with the people of God. The *communio* proper to the bishops as teachers demands that they adopt the attitude of an attentive listener, eager to identify the unique contributions of the *sensus fidelium.* One thinks immediately of the injunction of St. Cyprian of Carthage: "a man is teachable if he is meek and gentle and patient in learning. It is thus a bishop's duty not only to teach but also to learn. For he becomes a better teacher if he makes daily progress and advancement in learning what is better."[14] This also requires that they maintain *communio* with theologians, seeking their expertise in relationships characterized by mutual respect. The Committee

[13] Dulles, *The Survival of Dogma,* 101.
[14] *Epistle* 74.10.

on Doctrine affirms this in their guide to the teaching responsibilities of the bishops: "the bishop and the theologian have a special relationship that can and should be reciprocally enriching."[15]

How well do the recent actions of the Committee on Doctrine reflect these basic characteristics of authentic episcopal teaching authority? What is not questioned here is the right and responsibility of the bishops to preserve the integrity of the apostolic faith through normative judgments. Johnson herself acknowledges this authority.

The first characteristic is concerned with fidelity to the apostolic faith, and it is a concern, understandably, that the Committee on Doctrine takes very seriously. Indeed, one of the most damning accusations leveled against Johnson concerns her failure to start from the received faith of the Church in her theology. Yet we must ask: what theology of revelation is presupposed by the committee? Johnson herself has challenged this accusation, noting that her theology indeed draws on divine revelation but presupposes a different fundamental theology, one that does not equate revelation with doctrine but follows Vatican II in employing a more Trinitarian and personalist approach to revelation.[16] In *Dei Verbum* the council had reappropriated a theology with deep roots in an early Christian tradition that viewed revelation more as a divine pedagogy aimed at the transformation of humankind. By contrast, the committee's critique suggests a quasi-propositional understanding of divine revelation more at home in the theological world of neoscholasticism. Yet this was precisely what *Dei Verbum* sought to leave behind. In his commentary on the council's teaching a young Joseph Ratzinger writes:

> The Council's intention in this matter was a simple one. . . . The fathers were merely concerned with overcoming neo-scholastic intellectualism, for which revelation chiefly meant a store of mysterious supernatural teachings, which automatically reduces faith very much to an acceptance of these supernatural insights. As opposed to this, the Council desired to express again the character of revelation as a totality, in which word and event make up one whole, a true dialogue which touches man in his totality, not only challenging his

---

[15] Donald Cardinal Wuerl, "Bishops as Teachers," 5. Available on the USCCB web site: http://old.usccb.org/doctrine/BISHOPS-AS-TEACHERS-%20CARDINAL-WUERL-4-18-11.pdf. Pagination will be to the online version.

[16] Johnson, "To Speak Rightly of the Living God," 132–34.

reason, but, as dialogue, addressing him as a partner, indeed giving him his true nature for the first time.[17]

This neoscholastic theology is what Juan Luis Segundo had in mind when he wrote of a "digital" presentation of Church doctrine, one which purges doctrine of its imaginative and transformative character and renders it strictly informational and regulative.[18] The substance of the committee's complaint appears to be that Johnson does not privilege central dogmatic formulations in *Quest*. They admit in their "Response to Observations" that "the task of theological reflection is never accomplished by the mere repetition of formulas,"[19] but contend that the problem with Johnson's work is not that she fails to cite doctrinal formulas but rather that her theology simply does not adequately express the faith of the Church. This needs to be considered further.

Theology is, at its best, always a fragile enterprise. It moves forward tentatively, often exploring certain questions while leaving others behind. One finds in the committee's judgment little appreciation for the way in which theology contributes to the development of doctrine precisely through its exploration of "new frontiers." As Newman once noted, truth "is the daughter of time."[20] The current magisterial tendency to rush to doctrinal judgment with every new theological foray forgets Newman's important insight: divine truth emerges only slowly, patiently, and always with a certain tentativeness. The work of theology is akin to the ministrations of a midwife; it is the work of theology to assist patiently in the birthing of God's Word in our time. By contrast, the rush to doctrinal judgment is not unlike the frantic father wishing to hasten the birthing process even if it places mother and child at risk.

The principal justification for the committee's preemptive action was a familiar trope, the danger of confusing the faithful who were exposed

---

[17] Joseph Ratzinger, "Dogmatic Constitution on Divine Revelation, Origin and Background," in *Commentary on the Documents of Vatican II*, vol. 3, ed. H. Vorgrimler (New York: Herder, 1969), 155–98, at 172.

[18] Juan Luis Segundo, *The Liberation of Dogma: Faith, Revelation and Dogmatic Teaching Authority* (Maryknoll, NY: Orbis, 1992), 108.

[19] "Response to Observations by Sr. Elizabeth A. Johnson, C.S.J. Regarding the Committee on Doctrine's Statement About the Book *Quest for the Living God*," 10. The October committee statement is included in this volume but it can also be found on the USCCB web site at: http://www.usccb.org/about/doctrine/publications/upload/statement-quest-for-the-living-god-response-2011-10-11.pdf. Pagination will refer to the online version.

[20] Newman, *An Essay on the Development of Christian Doctrine*, 47.

to Johnson's ideas because her book was being used widely in college classrooms and parish study groups. This kind of argument has appeared with alarming frequency in contemporary exercises of the magisterium at both the local and universal levels and it has led to a dramatic expansion of the exercise of magisterial authority in the last few decades. The result has been an ecclesiastical impatience with the work of theology and an unwillingness to allow new theological developments to be both subject to academic critique from peers and tested by the *sensus fidelium.*

Now let us turn to consider the conservative nature of the exercise of episcopal teaching authority. The bishops are charged with the task of preserving the integrity of the faith by ensuring theology's congruence with our basic doctrinal commitments. This is not the same as the task of assessing the coherence and adequacy of new theological trajectories. The bishops must, on occasion, pronounce judgments on theology; but these judgments ought to be limited to an assessment of a theological project's congruence with Church doctrine (its doctrinal "soundness"). One would expect in such judgments clear and compelling evidence that a theologian has rejected or seriously distorted Church doctrine. Yet the committee believes it is legitimate to criticize not just the rejection or distortion of doctrine but also the failure to offer a clear and comprehensive defense of the faith. As Johnson insists in her final statement, it is certainly legitimate for the bishops to judge whether a theological work is in conformity with the basic creedal commitments of the Church, but it is not legitimate to criticize a theological work for not addressing every element of the Church's teaching as if it were a catechetical text.[21]

The genuinely conservative character of the bishops' teaching authority demands that the bishops honor the distinction between theology and doctrine. The committee consistently conflates the two. This happens at multiple levels. The committee skewers Johnson's book for its critique of "traditional Catholic teaching."[22] Yet it is apparent to any reader not preoccupied with a hermeneutic of denunciation[23] that the object of Johnson's theological critique was, more often than not, problematic *theological formulations and imaginative construals* of the Church's doctrinal

---

[21] See her brief public statement included in the dossier, 273–75 above.

[22] Committee on Doctrine, "Statement," 4–5.

[23] A practice of interpretation that begins with a set of a priori convictions regarding the presumed deficiencies of a text, and which is undertaken with a determination to build an argument in support of those prior convictions.

tradition and not the doctrine itself. Frequently she is content to summarize a range of theological perspectives.

Consider the issue of divine impassibility, where Johnson is accused of denying Church doctrine. A careful reading of her text reveals a summary of diverse theological perspectives on the topic (Jürgen Moltmann and Dorothee Sölle on one side and Johann Baptist Metz on the other) with the author noting the valuable contributions made by each side, without committing herself decisively to one position or another. In her response to the committee, she admits to struggling with the question herself (in the company, she adds, of such distinguished theologians as Cardinal Walter Kasper).[24] In its final statement the committee acknowledges her summary of the views of three theologians, but contends that only Metz's view is orthodox and then faults her for not siding with orthodox Catholic teaching (ignoring altogether Johnson's observation that Cardinal Kasper had raised similar theological questions!). Their judgment treats her work as a catechetical exposition of the entirety of the Church's faith rather than a tentative theological exploration.[25]

This brings us to the heart of the issue. To read the committee statements is to feel as if one has been drawn into a dispute between diverse theological commitments, not a dispassionate assessment of the doctrinal soundness of a theological work. This feeling is strengthened when one considers the profound resonance between the judgments of the committee and the theological corpus of one of the principal theological advisors to the committee and its executive director, the Capuchin theologian, Fr. Thomas Weinandy. An accomplished theologian in his own right, many would be in sympathy with the theological arguments he has advanced in his own work, some of which implicitly challenge Johnson's own theological commitments.[26] And therein lies the problem: to the extent that both the Committee on Doctrine's initial and concluding statements echo Weinandy's own work (and in several instances key formulations found in the statement are clearly drawn from his own work), they ought more properly to have been advanced in theological journals and at academic conferences rather than in the court of doctrinal judgment.

---

[24] Johnson, "To Speak Rightly of the Living God," 139–40.

[25] Committee on Doctrine, "Responses to Observations," 8.

[26] See Thomas G. Weinandy, *Does God Change?* (Still River, MA: St. Bede's Publications, 1985); *The Father's Spirit of Sonship* (Edinburgh: T & T Clark, 1995); *Does God Suffer?* (Notre Dame, IN: University of Notre Dame Press, 2000).

Finally, we must consider the extent to which the action of the Committee on Doctrine reflects the dialogical interdependence of the three authorities. "Bishops as Teachers" rightly affirms that "the bishop and the theologian have a special relationship that can and should be reciprocally enriching." Yet the failure of the committee to approach Johnson privately with an invitation to offer clarifications of her views seems to violate the demands of a genuinely reciprocal and dialogical relationship. This failure is all the more striking when one considers that procedures for mediating such disputes are already developed in the 1989 document, *Doctrinal Responsibilities*. The committee justified its decision to bypass these guidelines by noting that they were intended to mediate disputes between individual theologians and bishops.[27] Yet *Doctrinal Responsibilities* remains useful, not simply because of the specific procedures it offers for mediating disputes, but because it articulates ways in which a more general climate of mutual trust and respect can be cultivated. At the minimum, one would hope that the committee would heed the insistence in *Doctrinal Responsibilities* that the theologian's "right to a good reputation" be honored.[28]

One explanation for the committee's non-dialogical approach to its exercise of authority may be found in "Bishops as Teachers."[29] There we discover a generally disappointing account of the bishop-theologian relationship. The document envisions a healthy, reciprocal relationship between bishops and theologians as one in which theologians would submit "their personal theological ideas for the bishop's evaluation." The model for this "reciprocity," the document suggests, is the process of applying for an *imprimatur* for one's work. Yet any author who has sought an *imprimatur* can confirm that there is very little in this process that is truly dialogical. The absence of genuine reciprocity is evident in a predictable asymmetry: theologians are encouraged to submit their work to a bishop for his *doctrinal* evaluation, yet nowhere do we find the suggestion that bishops should submit their work to theologians for *scholarly* evaluation (a legitimate expectation, since the sacrament of orders does not confer scholarly expertise on the bishop).

---

[27] Committee on Doctrine, "Responses to Observations," 12.

[28] NCCB, *Doctrinal Responsibilities: Approaches to Promoting Cooperation and Resolving Misunderstandings between Bishops and Theologians* (Washington, DC: National Catholic Conference of Bishops, 1989), 8.

[29] Cardinal Wuerl, "Bishops as Teachers," 8.

In sum, it is difficult to avoid the conclusion that whereas Johnson appears to have properly exercised the teaching authority appropriate to theologians, the basic presuppositions and subsequent actions of the Committee on Doctrine were more problematic. Perhaps a final bit of light can be shed on the matter by considering an analogy offered by "Bishops as Teachers" to elucidate the bishop-theologian relationship, namely, the role of the referee/umpire in sports.

The Magisterium as Referee

We find the following passage in "Bishops as Teachers":

> It is essential for the health and progress of theology, then, that it take place within the context of a clearly articulated community of faith, that its creativity be channeled and maximized by boundaries delineated by the received revelation. Identifying these boundaries of the authentic faith constitutes the bishop's contribution to the flourishing of the theological sciences. Saint Paul often uses examples from the realm of sports, and perhaps one would serve us well here. In any sporting match, football, tennis, baseball, there are referees and umpires. The game can only proceed with the supervision of a referee. In a tennis match, it is not the player who calls the ball "out of bounds" but the referee. The player may object that it was not his or her intention to hit the ball out of bounds. He or she may even question whether the ball was out of bounds. But it is the referee who must make the call. Otherwise, there can be no coherent game, no enjoyment of the match, no sense of progress in learning the sport: in short, the "tennis game" would devolve into a fruitless exchange of individuals hitting the ball at will.[30]

This analogy has much to commend it.

First, it recognizes that the referee/umpire's role is clearly circumscribed. He does not actually play the game but rather preserves the conditions (by enforcing the rules of the game) that allow for maximum creativity and healthy competition on the field of play. Indeed, some theologians (e.g., Lindbeck, Dulles, Tilley) have made use of a cultural-linguistic interpretation of doctrine as establishing the rules that govern theological discourse (e.g., one must not discuss the person of Jesus in such a way as to deny his divinity). This aspect of the analogy is useful

---

[30] Ibid., 6–7.

with regard to our topic because it reinforces the distinction between doctrine (the rules of the game) and theology (the game itself). It is precisely this distinction that tends to be overlooked in many recent magisterial interventions. Consider the respective roles of umpires and players in the game of baseball. Imagine that a batter has decided to lay down a bunt at a crucial point in the game. An umpire can legitimately rule on whether, in the process of laying down the bunt, the batter prematurely stepped out of the batter's box (a violation of the rules) but he cannot challenge the batter's decision to bunt in that situation. The batter's decision can be legitimately challenged by his teammates, coaches, and even fans, but such criticism is *not* the prerogative of the umpire! In the Johnson case, I would argue that the theological debates regarding the adequacy of God-language and the meaning of divine impassibility are more akin to debates regarding the decision to lay down the bunt rather than a ruling on whether the bunt was legal.

Second, referees/umpires are fallible. They occasionally make mistakes and the best among them recognize that when they admit their mistakes their reputation is enhanced rather than diminished. Professional baseball fans will recall the poignant missed call in June of 2010 by the first base umpire, Jim Joyce, which deprived the Detroit Tiger pitcher, Armando Galarraga, of one of the most statistically rare accomplishments in baseball, the perfect game. Joyce, soon after the game, admitted that he blew the call and Galarraga graciously accepted his apology. Many baseball players and coaches voiced their appreciation of Joyce's admission of error and defended his sterling reputation as an umpire. In striking contrast, bishops (including popes) seldom if ever admit their mistakes in acts of doctrinal or pastoral judgment and, predictably, their reputation and credibility is often diminished in consequence.[31]

Third, in professional sports, there is usually an established system for evaluating referees/umpires. Only those who have passed rigorous evaluations are allowed to work at the highest levels of a sport. Although the system is far from perfect, theologians are held accountable in their profession through peer review of their scholarship. The complaint that the magisterium must intervene because theologians are not taking this element of their profession seriously enough does not hold up to scrutiny. Attendance at professional associations like the College Theology Society or the Catholic Theological Society of America would reveal lively

---

[31] This does not constitute a challenge to Catholic teaching on infallibility since the charism of infallibility is only rarely exercised in magisterial teaching.

and often quite critical exchanges among theologians. Unfortunately, no analogous form of accountability can be found that ensures that bishops have an adequate grasp of contemporary theological trajectories and are skilled in assessing the doctrinal integrity of a given theological project. The Catholic Church has no such system of accountability for bishops save the threat of Vatican intervention in the case of bishops who exhibit an openness to reconsider certain important doctrinal/theological issues.

Finally, the skills required for referees/umpires are not the same as the skills required for athletes. Yet refereeing, in almost any sport, *is a skill* with clear standards of excellence that demand much more than simply knowing the rules of the game. A baseball umpire can grasp the rule that establishes the dimensions of the strike zone, but that does not mean that he can accurately judge whether a 98 mph fastball is, in fact, a strike. Following the analogy, the bishops must not only know Church doctrine, they must also be well versed in the dynamics of advanced theological discourse without necessarily being scholars themselves. This last point merits further development.

It may seem odd to speak of "skills" with respect to the office of the bishop. After all, it is Catholic teaching that the bishops are aided by an assistance of the Holy Spirit in the exercise of their office. This divine assistance, however, must be interpreted in light of the Thomistic maxim that grace brings nature to its perfection. In that light we can legitimately speak of the need for a set of "natural" skills proper to the task of doctrinal judgment. Just as the theologian must first possess the proper intellectual aptitude and academic training necessary to fulfill her theological vocation, this too should apply, *mutatis mutandis*, to the office of the bishop. But where then does the assistance of the Holy Spirit come into play? The late John Boyle once noted the "absence in most theological discussions of church teaching authority of any extended consideration of the work of the Holy Spirit."[32] As Thomas O'Meara has observed, when we do encounter references to the assistance of the Holy Spirit, particularly in ecclesiastical documents, it often betrays Baroque theology's preoccupations with "actual graces." Consequently "a mechanics of grace has colored the sparse theology of the Spirit enabling the ordinary magisterium of bishops."[33] O'Meara calls for the recovery

---

[32] John Boyle, *Church Teaching Authority: Historical and Theological Studies* (Notre Dame, IN: University of Notre Dame Press, 1995), 167.

[33] Thomas F. O'Meara, "Divine Grace and Human Nature as Sources for the Universal Magisterium of Bishops," *Theological Studies* 64 (2003): 683–706, at 688–89.

of a theology of grace that is more attentive to St. Thomas' concern to preserve legitimate human freedom.

The late Jesuit moral theologian Richard McCormick remarked on the importance of avoiding two extremes in our consideration of the role of the Holy Spirit in the exercise of the magisterium's teaching responsibilities. First, we must avoid any explanations which overlook the important role of ordinary human processes for discovering truth, and second, we must avoid any approach which would reduce this assistance to the exercise of human processes by themselves.[34] If the assistance of the Holy Spirit bypassed human processes, we would have no alternative but to recognize in every hierarchical teaching act the charism of infallibility. If the official teachers of the Church had access to divine truth wholly apart from human processes, it would be difficult to imagine the possibility of error. On the other hand, the second extreme reduces the activity of the Spirit to the exercise of human investigation and can lead to a kind of rationalism.

In between these two extremes it is possible to imagine a real assistance of the Spirit as an immanent principle active within the exercise of human processes.[35] This full employment of the human processes was alluded to at the Second Vatican Council in *Lumen Gentium*: "The Roman pontiff and the bishops, in virtue of their office and the seriousness of the matter, work sedulously through appropriate means duly to investigate this revelation and give it suitable expression" (LG 25). The assumption is that the divine assistance promised the Church is only effective when conjoined with the proper cooperation of the Church's ministers.

But what are these "appropriate means"? McCormick divides the relevant human processes into two categories: evidence gathering and evidence assessing. *Evidence gathering* refers to the manifold ways in which the human person inquires after the truth through study, consultation, and investigation. With respect to the exercise of the teaching authority of the bishops, this would involve a study of the Church's tradition (giving primacy of place to the testimony of Scripture), a consultation of scholars and theologians (representing diverse schools of thought

[34] I will largely follow McCormick's reflections on this topic which can be found in his collection, "Notes in Moral Theology," which appeared in *Theological Studies* for so many years. See Richard A. McCormick, *Notes on Moral Theology: 1965 through 1980* (Lanham, MD: University Press of America, 1981), 261ff.

[35] Much of the work of Karl Rahner can be read as an attempt to develop a theology of grace in which grace functions precisely as this kind of immanent principle.

and theological/historical perspectives), a consideration of the insights of pertinent related fields (e.g., the contributions of the social sciences, genetics), and an attempt to discern the *sensus fidelium*, the sense of the faithful in and through whom the Spirit speaks. Insufficient attention to this evidence gathering can hamper the activity of the Spirit in bringing forth wisdom and insight.

Evidence assessing involves the proper consideration and assessment of the "evidence" gathered. Here again recourse to a diversity of theological scholarship will be important, but so will patient reflection and authentic conversation in contexts where the free exchange of views is clearly welcomed. The value of real conversation and deliberation as a prelude to authoritative teaching was demonstrated at Vatican II. The vast majority of the bishops who traveled to Rome in the fall of 1962 were content to participate in a relatively quick council which would, by and large, continue the *status quo*. That this *status quo* was not maintained can be attributed to the conversation and deliberation in which the council bishops were engaged and the freedom of inquiry and disagreement that was preserved against the coercive intentions of a few. New insight, a new penetration into divine truth, resulted from the council's free and extended interaction.

The emphases on evidence gathering and assessing should not be seen as preludes to the assistance of the Spirit, as if they were mere "natural" processes necessary before the work of the Spirit could "kick in." Rather, the claim here is that the Spirit is operative in and through these human processes. If the teaching ministry of the Church is to be an expression of the Church's essential nature as a communion, then the processes engaged in the teaching ministry must reflect this *communio*. An authentic theology of the assistance of the Spirit precludes seeing the authoritative teaching of the Church as isolated ecclesial acts engaged by autonomous authority figures. Consultative activities, dialogue, and deliberation are constitutive of *communio*. These are the means by which the Spirit brings the Church to truth. For this reason, when bishops engage in true consultation—with fellow bishops, theologians, and the faithful—they are not merely engaging in prudent gestures and they are certainly not, as some might suggest, compromising their own teaching authority. In the fulfillment of their teaching ministry they must make themselves available to that Word as it emerges within the whole Christian community. Consultation and conversation are integral to the teaching process, and must be acknowledged as one of the privileged instruments of the Spirit. In conclusion, the assistance of the Holy Spirit given to the bishops at sacramental ordination cannot become an excuse to avoid the demands of their teaching authority; they must cultivate the skills proper to their office.

We live in a time in which authority is almost habitually viewed with suspicion. Yet Catholics believe that there is a need for authentic teaching authority in the Church that can assist the pilgrim people of God on its earthly journey. That authority is pluriform in nature; all Christians are called to exercise the distinctive authority that derives from their baptism just as theologians and bishops must fulfill their own obligations to "teach with authority." Sadly, the Johnson case demonstrates what happens when the diverse forms of ecclesial teaching authority are not honored and exercised in a genuinely collaborative form. In this case, the reputation of a respected theologian has been tarnished and the credibility of the bishops' own authority has been undermined. The Church is the poorer for it.

Contributors

James Coriden is Professor of Canon Law and Dean Emeritus at the Washington Theological Union, Washington, DC.

Richard R. Gaillardetz is the Joseph McCarthy Professor of Catholic Systematic Theology at Boston College in Massachusetts.

Anthony Godzieba is Professor of Theology at Villanova University in Philadelphia, Pennsylvania.

Bradford Hinze is Professor of Theology at Fordham University, Bronx, New York.

Colleen Mallon, OP, is Professor of Theology at the Aquinas Institute of Theology, St. Louis, Missouri.

Gerard Mannion is Director of the Frances G. Harpst Center for Catholic Thought and Culture and Professor in the Department of Theology and Religious Studies at the University of San Diego in California.

Vincent Miller is the Gudorf Professor of Catholic Theology and Culture at the University of Dayton in Ohio.

Ormond Rush teaches theology at St. Paul's Theological College, Australian Catholic University, Brisbane, Australia.